D0414914

ONE WEEK LOAN

LOCKE

Edited by

VERE CHAPPELL

OXFORD UNIVERSITY PRESS
1998

Oxford University Press, Great Clarendon Street, Oxford OX2 6DP

Oxford New York

*Athens Auckland Bangkok Bogota Bombay Buenos Aires
Calcutta Cape Town Dar es Salaam Delhi Florence Hong Kong Istanbul
Karachi Kuala Lumpur Madras Madrid Melbourne Mexico City
Nairobi Paris Singapore Taipei Tokyo Toronto Warsaw*

*and associated companies in
Berlin Ibadan*

Oxford is a registered trade mark of Oxford University Press

*Published in the United States
by Oxford University Press Inc., New York*

*British Library Cataloguing in Publication Data
Data available*

*Library of Congress Cataloging in Publication Data
Data available*

*ISBN 0–19–875196–6
ISBN 0–19–875197–4 (Pbk.)*

1 3 5 7 9 10 8 6 4 2

*Typeset by Best-set Typesetter Ltd., Hong Kong
Printed in Great Britain
on acid-free paper by
Bookcraft (Bath) Ltd
Midsomer Norton, Someset*

CONTENTS

NOTE ON REFERENCES

References are made parenthetically within the text.

Most references to the works of Locke use an abbreviation for the title of the work or its source. The following editions and sources (with abbreviations in brackets) are cited:

C   *The Correspondence of John Locke*, ed. E. S. de Beer, 9 vols. (Oxford: Clarendon Press, 1976–).

D   *Drafts for the* Essay concerning Human Understanding, *and Other Philosophical Writings*, ed. Peter H. Nidditch and G. A. J. Rogers, 3 vols. (Oxford: Clarendon Press, 1990–).

E   *An Essay concerning Human Understanding*, ed. Peter H. Nidditch (Oxford: Clarendon Press, 1975).

EL *Essays on the Laws of Nature*, ed. W. von Leyden (Oxford: Clarendon Press, 1954).

W   *The Works of John Locke*, new edn., corrected, 10 vols. (London: Thomas Tegg et al., 1823); repr. (Aalen: Scientia, 1964).

In such references, the abbreviation is followed by an array of numerals designating internal divisions of the item referred to—volumes, books, parts, chapters, sections—and then a page number, preceded by a colon. Thus 'E II.xxi.47: 263' refers to Book II, chapter xxi, section 47, page 263 of the *Essay concerning Human Understanding*; and 'W VII: 140' refers to volume VII, page 140 of Locke's *Works*.

In a few cases, reference is made to works of Locke published as or included within particular editions. In these cases the author-date system is used, with 'Locke' as the name of the author. The following such editions are cited:

Locke 1700   Locke, John, *Essai philosophique concernant l'entendement humain*, tr. Pierre Coste (Amsterdam, 1700).

Locke 1936   Locke, John, *An Early Draft of Locke's Essay*, ed. R. I. Aaron and Jocelyn Gibb (Oxford: Clarendon Press, 1936).

Locke 1968   Locke, John, *Epistola de tolerantia* (Gouda, 1689); ed. Raymond Klibansky, tr. J. W. Gough (Oxford: Clarendon Press, 1968).

The author-date system is also used for most references to works by authors other than Locke. In such references the author's last name is followed by the publication date of the work or edition cited and a page number preceded by a colon. So 'Yolton 1956: 86' refers to page 86 of John Yolton's *John Locke and the Way of Ideas*, which was published in 1956.

This system is not used, however, for ancient and medieval authors such as Aristotle and Aquinas. Here the work cited is referred to by its title, followed by letters or numerals designating its internal divisions. Thus '*Metaphysics*, A.1' refers to the first chapter of the first book of the *Metaphysics* (of Aristotle).

References to works of Descartes are made to the English translations of Cottingham, Stoothoff, Murdoch, and Kenny (Descartes 1985 and Descartes 1991). In some cases, the edition of Adam and Tannery (Descartes 1964–74), abbreviated 'AT', is cited as well.

Full information about secondary works cited is provided in the list of References.

INTRODUCTION

VERE CHAPPELL

IT is now twenty years since Ian Tipton published his collection of articles on Locke—*Locke on Human Understanding*—in the Oxford Readings in Philosophy series. The series was well established by then, with more than twenty volumes in print; but Tipton's was the first volume devoted to the work of a single philosopher. It also was the first to deal with any subject in the history of philosophy, although this was, then as now, one of the main traditionally recognized subfields of philosophical study. But history was not a major interest of 'working' philosophers at that time, at least in the English-speaking world. Some of them openly disdained it, and steered their students into areas in which, by their lights, more exciting, and indeed more exacting, work was being done.

How things have changed in those twenty years! History is now one of the 'hot' areas for philosophical research. A large number of scholars are actively working in the field, and some of the most talented students are being drawn to it. New journals devoted to the history of philosophy in general, or to particular figures or periods within it, have been established; and a wealth of new books and articles on historical topics, superior in quality as well as number to their predecessors, have been published. The Oxford series itself has added three more single-philosopher volumes since 1977—one each on Leibniz, Kant, and Hegel—and the Press has now undertaken to launch a new subseries of Oxford Readers specifically devoted to the thought of individual thinkers. Volumes on Plato, Aristotle, Aquinas, Descartes, Hume, Kant, and Wittgenstein, along with the present volume on Locke, comprise the initial cohort projected for this new venture.

It is fitting that a volume on Locke should be included among the first members of this new Oxford subseries, even though a volume on Locke has already been published. Besides being one of the eight or so greatest philosophers in the whole Western canon, Locke is one of the two greatest to write in English—and, unlike Hume, was himself an Oxford man.

Furthermore, the study of Locke has flourished in the past twenty years—perhaps not more, but certainly not less than that of Descartes and Hume and Kant. Anglophone scholars have long felt a special affinity for Locke, and now seem to do so more than ever. But beyond that, the study of Locke has recently been stimulated by a special circumstance, the opening of the so-called Lovelace Collection of Locke's *Nachlass* to the public. The availability of this material, now held in the Bodleian Library at Oxford, has enabled Locke scholars to find out much more about their subject than was known before. It has also prompted Oxford University Press to undertake a whole new edition of Locke's works, the Clarendon Edition, in a projected thirty volumes.

The first volume in this new edition was the magnificent *Essay concerning Human Understanding* by Peter Nidditch, which itself has done much to renew scholars' interest in Locke, *inter alia*, by allowing them to see how Locke's thinking on crucial matters changed as he reviewed and modified successive new editions of the *Essay*, from the second, which appeared in 1694 (four years after the first), to the fifth, which came out in 1705, just after his death. A year after the Nidditch *Essay*, the first volume of Esmond de Beer's monumental eight-volume compilation of Locke's correspondence was published as part of the Clarendon Edition, and that work too, now completed save for its index, has had a large impact on Locke scholars, encouraging them to attend more to the intellectual and social context in which Locke's thinking developed. These new resources were already appearing at the time that Tipton's collection was being produced, but they were too late for his authors to have been much affected by them. In the last twenty years, several additional volumes in the Clarendon Edition have been published (see the Selected Bibliography at the end of this volume for a listing of them), and several more are imminent.

Another factor in the growth and vigour of current Locke scholarship has been the work of two dedicated scholars, John Yolton and Roland Hall. Both were already active at the time Tipton's collection appeared; but their efforts have continued and have had an even greater impact in the years since 1977. Yolton, besides chairing the Editorial Board of the Clarendon Edition, published several valuable books on Locke's thought and influence in the 1980s and 1990s, including a *Locke Dictionary* and, with his wife, Jean Yolton, a major bibliography of works by and about Locke. Hall has maintained and indeed expanded the *Locke Newsletter*, which he founded in 1970; and he has kept a comprehensive record of recent Locke scholarship, not only in the annual 'Recent Publications' section of the *Newsletter* but in a book, *80 Years of Locke Scholarship*, which, together with Roger Woolhouse, he published in 1983.

Whatever the reasons for the blossoming of Locke studies, the fact is indisputable: scholars have produced an astonishing amount of illuminating commentary on Locke's thought in the past twenty years. Many of the papers included in the Tipton collection stand as classics, not only good for their time but of permanent interest. But the work done since then has added new dimensions of knowledge and understanding to the study of Locke's philosophy. Familiar topics have been seen from new perspectives, new lines of interpretation opened up, and new solutions to old problems proposed. Furthermore, some hitherto neglected portions of Locke's thought have been attended to, notably his treatment of human freedom and his philosophies of language and of science. This does not mean that all of Locke's views are now being discussed, for there are sections of the *Essay* that still have not been adequately canvassed, either by recent scholars or by those of the pre-Tipton period. Examples are Locke's account of space, time, and number in chapters xiii–xix of Book ii, the general theory of relations he presents in chapters xxv–xxviii of the same Book, and his discussion of belief and probability in the second part of Book iv. Even so, the range of scholarly interest in Locke's philosophy is now much broader than it used to be.

Tipton called his volume *Locke on Human Understanding*, suggesting a concentration on the subject matter of the *Essay concerning Human Understanding*. This is also, very largely, the subject matter of the two philosophical subfields of metaphysics and epistemology, within which, together with the political philosophy contained in the *Two Treatises of Government*, Locke's most substantial and most enduring contributions to philosophy are to be found. The present volume is meant to have the same focus as that of the Tipton collection. It is true that the *Essay* has seemed to many readers to be a work primarily of epistemology and not of metaphysics. Locke himself says that his purpose in it is 'to enquire into the Original, Certainty, and Extent of humane Knowledge; together, with the Grounds and Degrees of Belief, Opinion, and Assent' (E i.i.2: 43). (It is also true that Locke sometimes speaks disparagingly of metaphysics in the *Essay*, as at E iv.viii.9: 615. But when he does so, it is a particular kind of metaphysical doctrine—the tired Aristotelianism of the Schools—that he has in mind, and not the field itself or its subject matter.) But that it is also a work of metaphysics is obvious from the specific topics that Locke discusses in it: substance, modes, and qualities; space, time, and number; bodies, minds, and persons; existence and identity; God, freedom, and immortality—the list could be extended. Locke himself makes no explicit division between these kinds of topics and those that would traditionally be counted as epistemological. Nor does he give any indication that he even views himself as working in two different subfields of philosophical enquiry. But that hardly means that he is not doing so.

The papers reprinted in this volume are arranged, as were those in Tipton's book, in the order in which their topics are treated in the *Essay*, except that Michael Ayers's paper is put first because it is 'a broad discussion of Locke's general philosophy' (although it also deals in some detail with the specific topic of substance). But Locke's order is different from the one (or the ones) traditionally followed by either metaphysicians or epistemologists. A reader might well wonder whether the sequence of topics in the *Essay* is controlled by any rational or systematic plan at all, so loose and rambling and uneven does Locke's discussion sometimes seem. Locke does have trouble staying on the paths he sets for himself; he is a frequent and voluminous digressor. He also is wont to go over the same ground several times: he himself apologizes for the 'repetitions' to be found in his text (E Epis: 8). But the *Essay* does have a controlling plan, one that, besides being coherent is quite highly structured. And Locke does follow this plan quite well. There are digressions, to be sure, but these are never totally irrelevant to the subject at hand: the plan, as it were, provides for them even if it does not require them. For example, Locke need not have said anything about human freedom (at E II.xxi) in the course of surveying the fundamental ideas that we have in our minds, the task to which his plan commits him. But what he does say is connected to the main line of his enquiry by the fact that freedom is one special kind of power, and the idea of power is one of the fundamental ideas that his survey must include. As for Locke's repetitions, they are not merely to be tolerated but welcomed. Locke never uses exactly the same words twice, and his different ways of putting things on different occasions often help the reader to get a better grasp of the intended message. Or, if the message is different on different occasions, then this fact raises questions about the consistency of Locke's thinking, or its growth or development, or what he really means—just the questions that keep the commentator in business!

In the rest of this Introduction I propose to lay out the plan of the *Essay*, and to describe the main topics of Locke's concern in the order in which he considers them, showing, as I do so, the ways in which these topics are connected with one another and the place each has in the overall scheme. Since these are—or many of them are—the topics addressed by the essays comprising this volume, I shall also, along the way, sketch the approach to or stand taken on each topic by the essay or essays pertaining thereto, and so provide a preview of each essay's contents.

At its most general level, the plan of Locke's *Essay* is dictated by his general conception of knowledge. Knowledge, he holds, is a complex achievement of the human mind, not something we simply find in ourselves but a product of the mind's activity. But the mind does not fashion knowledge out of nothing; it must use pre-existing materials. These materials are the various *ideas* it has within itself. How then do these ideas get into the mind? Locke has both a negative and a positive answer to this question. His negative answer is that ideas are not 'innate' in the mind, any more than knowledge is. That is, they are not in it from birth (which is to say, from the birth of the human individual to whom the mind belongs), as part of its natural endowment. This is Locke's anti-innatism. His positive answer is that all ideas come into the mind, after birth, from experience. This is his empiricism.

Locke undertakes to prove the truth of his anti-innatism; that is, he offers arguments by which, he maintains, its denial, innatism, is conclusively refuted. He makes no comparable claim to prove his empiricism. This positive doctrine is incompatible with innatism, but is not simply equivalent to its denial: other options are available to the anti-innatist. Hence the arguments designed to refute innatism do not themselves serve to establish empiricism. And in fact Locke offers no arguments directly in support of empiricism. What he does do is try to show that all the ideas we have, or at least all those that are required for the knowledge we have, can be accounted for on empiricist grounds, as having come into our minds from experience. Success at that venture will justify empiricism, not by proving it true or its denial false, but by demonstrating its explanatory adequacy. And that is all that Locke aspires to do in the *Essay*.

The central task, then, that Locke sets for himself is that of carrying out this empiricist programme, of showing that and how the ideas we have arise in our minds from experience. Or rather, this is the first part of his central task, for he has also to show how the mind, its materials given, proceeds to produce knowledge out of them. Locke devotes the second of the four Books of the *Essay*, entitled 'Of Ideas', to this first part of his task. The second part is then taken up in the fourth Book, 'Of Knowledge and Opinion', although it turns out that Locke says relatively little, there or anywhere, as to how knowledge is generated. What he does discuss in Book IV is the general nature of knowledge, its various characteristics, and its limitations, along with the nature and different degrees of its surrogate, probable opinion. Together these two Books, II and IV, contain the heart of the *Essay*.

What then of Books I and III? Book I, 'Of Innate Notions', is devoted to Locke's arguments against innatism. These arguments are meant to prepare for the constructive work of Book II—if nothing else, by opening readers' minds to the possibility that it might be successful—but are not themselves part of it. Book III, 'Of Words', is also not part of Locke's main line of enquiry, starting with ideas and proceeding to knowledge; it is, strictly, a digression from that. But because of the close 'connexion' between ideas and words, Locke says, 'it is impossible to speak clearly and distinctly of . . . Knowledge . . . without considering, first, the Nature, Use, and Signification of Language' (E II.xxxiii.19: 401). So the discussion of Book III is intended to improve the form of that of Book IV, without contributing to its content.

So far we have considered Locke's project in quite general terms. The authors of the essays that follow, however, focus on particular details of particular parts of it. All do, that is, except Michael Ayers who, at least in the first and third parts of his paper, takes a similarly general view of the *Essay*. (The second part, concerning the specific topic of substance, will be considered in due course below.) Ayers begins with a characterization of Locke's empiricism, comparing it with that of Hobbes and Gassendi and with the ancient empiricism of the Stoics and Epicureans, and contrasting it with the rationalism of Descartes and Arnauld. Along the way Ayers makes some useful observations about the impact of scepticism on Locke's thinking. He then introduces an important epistemological distinction, that between 'the abstraction from sense experience of concepts . . . and the acquisition of propositional knowledge', that had not been made by empiricists preceding Locke. Ayers shows how, although Locke too drew no such distinction in his earliest epistemological enquiries, he began to notice it in writing the early drafts of the *Essay*, and came to place considerable weight upon it in the *Essay* itself.

Ayers then turns to what he calls 'the chief theoretical problem facing Locke as an epistemologist', that of 'developing an account of the two sorts of science, moral and natural, which would explain . . . why the one is possible for us while the other is not'. He outlines Locke's conceptions of these two sorts of science in the course of pursuing this theme. In the short final part of his paper Ayers posits 'two related divisions' around which Locke's general philosophy is 'structured'. One distinguishes 'a priori, abstract science' from 'enquiry into the real world'; the other distinguishes 'coarse experiential or pretheoretical knowledge of natural things' from 'speculative hypothesis or theory about the ultimate nature of those things'. Both these divisions are under attack, Ayers points out, by contemporary 'relativistic conceptualists'; but he maintains that Locke's kind

of realism is capable of withstanding these attacks. For Locke is, he concludes, 'one of the great dead from whom . . . philosophers still have much
to learn'.

Let us move now to a more detailed survey of Locke's enquiry in the
Essay. First comes his attack on innatism in Book I. His initial target is the
doctrine of innate knowledge: that there are certain 'principles' which are,
as it were, inscribed on the mind at its inception, such that they can be
apprehended without effort and are incapable of being doubted. Locke
distinguishes between two versions of the doctrine, one applying to theoretical or 'speculative' principles, the other to action-oriented or 'practical'
ones, and brings several arguments against each of them. In the final
chapter of Book I he turns to the doctrine of innate ideas, which holds that
whether or not there is knowledge that is innate, some of the materials
of knowledge—that is, some ideas—are. He then marshals a new set of
arguments against this second form of innatism. His conclusion at the end
of the book, as he puts it at the beginning of Book II, is that the human
mind is 'white Paper' at birth, 'void of all Characters' (E II.i.2: 104). It is
thus, as he thinks, ready and waiting to be written upon by experience.

In her paper on Locke on innateness, Margaret Atherton raises two
sorts of questions. One has to do with the relation between Locke's attack
on innateness doctrines and the rest of his work in the *Essay*. The other
concerns the details of this attack, the nature and impact of the arguments
that Locke uses. Atherton criticizes what she calls the 'standard view'
taken by commentators, according to which Locke's 'rejection of innateness is a consequence of his empiricism'. The truth is just the opposite, she
argues: Locke's empiricism 'follows from his rejection of innate ideas', and
that, in turn, 'depends upon his theory of the nature of mentality' in
general. Atherton sketches some features of this theory in the course of
examining Locke's particular arguments, which she claims often have a
more limited target than Locke's critics have realized. Besides analysing
these arguments, Atherton undertakes to pinpoint the differences between
Locke's position and that of various innatists, both from his time (such as
Descartes) and from ours (such as Chomsky).

In Book II Locke takes up his main positive task, the first part of which
is to show how the ideas we possess all have their origins in experience. He
begins by distinguishing two forms of experience, sensation and reflection.
Sensation is sensory experience, involving the five external senses; reflection is the awareness of the processes occurring within our minds. Some of
our ideas, Locke says, arise from one of these sources, some from the
other, and some from both. He next introduces a distinction between
simple and complex ideas. Simple ideas come directly from experience and

the mind is purely passive in receiving them. Complex ideas are those which the mind has an active role in producing, constructing them out of simple ideas which it already possesses. Locke then puts the two distinctions together, thereby generating a scheme by which all the ideas we have can be classified. It turns out that most of the ideas that are divided according to origin, those from sensation, or from reflection, or both, are simple ideas. Simple ideas of sensation are then subdivided into those which come through a single one of the external senses, and those which come through more than one. As for complex ideas, they fall into three groups: modes, substances, and relations (or, as Locke sometimes says, ideas of modes, of substances, and of relations); and modes are further subdivided into simple and mixed modes. (Although Locke does not divide complex ideas in general according to origin, he does seem to apply this division to simple modes: the ideas of distance and of remembering are both (ideas of) simple modes, but the former is an idea of sensation, while the latter is an idea of reflection.) The whole scheme is shown in Figure 1, which also gives some examples of specific ideas that Locke places in the resulting categories.

This scheme largely determines the organization of Locke's presentation in Book II, though he does not always follow it perfectly. The book as a whole consists of thirty-three chapters. After an initial chapter, in which he sets up his enquiry and contrasts his conception of mind and thinking

Simple Ideas
   Of Sensation
      Of one sense

Of Sight	Colours (e.g. red)
Of Hearing	Sounds (e.g. that of a bell)
Of Taste	Tastes (e.g. that of wormwood)
Of Smell	Smells (e.g. that of a rose)
Of Touch	Heat, cold, solidity
Of more than one sense	Space, figure, motion
Of Reflection	Perception or thinking, volition or willing
Of both Sensation and Reflection	Pleasure, pain, existence, unity, power

Complex Ideas
   [Of] Modes

[Of] Simple Modes	Distances, durations, numbers
[Of] Mixed Modes	Obligation, drunkenness, a lie
[Of] Substances	Individual bodies, finite spirits, God
[Of] Relations	Causation, identity, moral rectitude

FIG. 1. Locke's Classification of Ideas in Book II of the *Essay*

with that of the Cartesians, four chapters deal with the various kinds of simple ideas of sensation; the next briefly introduces the two basic simple ideas of reflection; the next after that lists a few simple ideas conveyed into the mind 'by all the ways' of both sensation and reflection; chapter viii presents 'some farther considerations concerning our simple ideas'; and chapters ix–xi examine perception or thinking and a few of its specific modes, the ideas of which are ideas of reflection.

Locke then turns to complex ideas and, after a short introductory discussion in chapter xii, spends fourteen of the next sixteen chapters examining various sub-categories thereof: simple modes compounded of certain simple ideas of sensation (chapters xiii–xviii), simple modes of thinking (chapter xix), mixed modes (chapter xxii), (ideas of) substances (chapters xxiii–xxiv), and relations (chapters xxv–xxviii). In the remaining two of these chapters, he discusses (out of order) the ideas of pleasure and pain (chapter xx) and that of power (chapter xxi); these discussions are out of order because these three ideas are not only not simple modes, they are not even complex ideas: they are rather simple ideas of both sensation and reflection.

At the end of this survey of complex ideas, Locke devotes four chapters (xxix–xxxii) to various properties that may be attributed to ideas of all categories, simple or complex, of sensation or of reflection. These properties come in pairs, of which there are five: clarity–obscurity, distinctness–confusedness, reality–fantasticalness, adequacy–inadequacy, and truth–falsity. The final chapter of Book ii takes up the association of ideas; this chapter in fact was not included in the *Essay* until its fourth edition, so that in the first three editions Book ii ended with chapter xxxii.

Although Locke's stated purpose in Book ii is to explain how the ideas in each of the categories he distinguishes originate in our experience, he often stops to consider these ideas themselves, that is, their content as opposed to their genesis. Otherwise (though equivalently) put, he stops to examine the natures of the things or phenomena which these ideas are the ideas of. Thus in chapter viii he points out that the simple ideas of sensation that he has been presenting are ideas of the qualities of physical objects existing outside our minds—whereas ideas themselves are entities existing within our minds. He then launches into a discussion of qualities, in the course of which he draws and defends his famous distinction between primary and secondary qualities. In chapter ix Locke turns to ideas of reflection, beginning with that of perception or thinking. But instead of examining how we acquire this idea, he details the nature of perception itself, and what the mind does when it performs this operation. In the two following chapters he does the same for several other mental operations—

remembering, discerning, comparing, abstracting, and such—hardly noting that the ideas of these operations are ideas of reflection. And in later chapters of Book II this same pattern recurs. In chapter xxi Locke moves from a discussion of the idea of power to a searching analysis of one specific power, that of free action on the part of a human being; he even lays out a positive theory as to how such action is motivated. In chapter xxiii he starts with the idea of substance and proceeds to discuss the nature, first of an individual substance such as a horse or a stone, and second of a sort of component or ingredient that he claims every such substance must contain. The latter he also calls 'substance', though he sometimes calls it 'substratum' or 'pure substance in general' to distinguish it from substance in the first sense of the word. And in chapter xxvii, where the official subject is identity conceived as one specific (idea of) relation, Locke's main concern is to establish wherein identity through time consists for different kinds of entity, including especially persons.

It is in these accounts of the things that our ideas represent that much of Locke's metaphysical doctrine is contained. These are also the parts of the *Essay* that have most attracted the attention of commentators and critics: the secondary literature is dominated by discussions of Locke on qualities, Locke on substance, and Locke on personal identity (though not, oddly, of Locke on freedom). One or more essays on each of these topics (including freedom) is to be found in the present volume. But scholars have also been interested in certain general questions that are raised in Book II, questions pertaining to recurring themes or to assumptions underlying Locke's discussion as a whole. One such general question concerns ideas: what is an idea for Locke, what sort of thing does he take it to be? Another, closely related to this, has to do with Locke's conception of sense perception (what he calls 'sensation'), by which the earliest and the most numerous of the ideas we acquire are conveyed into our minds.

Both of these questions are addressed by John Mackie in 'Locke on Representative Perception'. Mackie is concerned not only to understand Locke but to discover a theory of sense perception that is defensible in its own right. The options Mackie considers are, first, some form of representative theory, according to which perception involves intermediary objects distinct from the things ordinarily said to be seen, heard, and so forth; and second, direct realism, which posits no such intermediaries. He then distinguishes representative theories in which the intermediaries are physically real images located in perceivers' brains from those in which they are merely intentional objects having none but a mental existence. The best sort of theory, Mackie maintains, is the intentional-object form of representationalism; and he next argues (somewhat tentatively, to be sure) that this is the sort of theory that Locke accepts too. Locke's ideas are thus best conceived as intentional objects, according to Mackie, rather than physical images. Mackie also rejects the view that ideas for Locke are not objects of any kind, intentional or physical, but are merely acts of perceiving. Such a view has recently been advocated by John Yolton and others, as part of a more general campaign to interpret Locke as a direct realist regarding perception: but Mackie claims that there is textual evidence against this interpretation. Mackie also works to undermine one of Yolton's principal reasons for wishing to read Locke as a realist: that he would otherwise be saddled with an insoluble 'veil-of-perception' problem (the phrase is Jonathan Bennett's: see Bennett 1971). Mackie maintains that though representationalists, of the sort he takes Locke to be, are committed to some form of perceptual veil, this need not constitute a problem, or at any rate an insoluble problem.

We may now turn to the essays that deal with the particular topics Locke discusses in Book II. First up is John Campbell's on qualities. Locke's distinctive contribution on this subject is, first, a general definition of qualities as powers to produce ideas in our minds, and second a distinction between two kinds of qualities, which he dubs 'primary' and 'secondary'. The primary qualities (of a body) are those which, as he says, 'are utterly inseparable from' it (E II.viii.9: 134); secondary qualities are those which 'are nothing in the objects themselves but powers to produce various sensations in us by their primary qualities' (E II.viii.10: 135). Critics from Berkeley on down have attacked Locke's position, especially the distinction he draws. Either there is no such distinction, they have argued, or, if there is, Locke has radically mischaracterized it. Campbell, by contrast, contends that Locke's distinction 'is both careful and coherent', though he grants that it needs to be spelled out a bit and qualified in certain places to meet objections. Campbell proceeds to formulate revised definitions of 'primary' and 'secondary quality', and of 'quality' itself, on Locke's behalf; and then subjects the resulting account to 'the crucial test of any interpretation' of Locke on this subject, which is 'its ability to cope with [Locke's] "resemblance" thesis'. This is the thesis that 'the ideas of primary qualities of bodies are resemblances of them [whereas] there is nothing like our ideas [of secondary qualities] existing in bodies themselves' (E II.viii.15: 137). Not only does his interpretation pass this test, Campbell argues, but it makes the thesis itself plausible.

Locke discusses human freedom, and the way in which free action is motivated, at considerable length in chapter xxi of Book II. My own essay is focused on a single theme of this discussion, what I call Locke's 'volitional determinism'. Locke takes it for granted that human beings have freedom with respect to their actions (or rather, with respect to some of them), and he explains what this freedom amounts to. But then he asks: do they also have freedom of the will? Although most thinkers have answered 'yes', Locke argues that the very question is absurd—at least as it is commonly construed. He grants, however, that there is another way of taking the question: not 'Is the human will free?' but 'Are human beings free to will to do this or that, as well as free to do this or that?' This is an intelligible question, Locke thinks; still, the answer to it is negative. That negative answer is volitional determinism: we have no freedom with respect to our volitions. I examine the arguments that Locke provides for this position, and find them wanting. I then note the changes that occurred in Locke's thinking after the publication of the *Essay*'s first edition. Locke's new account of 'what determines the will', appearing in the second edition, includes a 'doctrine of suspension', according to which an agent is often able to suspend her desires in the course of deliberating what to do and thereby keep her will from being determined to any action. The question I raise is whether this new doctrine is consistent with volitional determinism. I argue that there is both reason to think that it is and reason to think that it is not, and leave the issue unsettled. Locke, however, under pressure from his friend van Limborch, came to think that there is an inconsistency here, and said so in some passages he added to the fifth edition of the *Essay*, in which he repudiated volitional determinism. But Locke was not logically bound to have taken this step.

The next two essays, by Martha Bolton and Jonathan Bennett, concern Locke's treatment of substance, in the sense of 'substratum', in chapter xxiii; the second part of Michael Ayers's paper also is devoted to this topic. Locke's discussion here, perhaps more than any other in the *Essay*, has drawn the fire of critics; and he himself seems unusually uncertain in the course of it, appearing to speak now on one side, now on the other, of several issues. The basic problem for Locke is that, on the one hand, he is convinced that an individual body is more than the sum of its qualities, that there must be something else which unites these qualities and in which they inhere—the substance of the body in question; and yet, on the other hand, the idea he has of this substance seems utterly devoid of content— which ought not to be possible given his theory of ideas and his empiricist doctrine as to their origins.

Not only does Locke seem to be of two minds regarding substance, but his interpreters have held sharply different opinions of his treatment of it. In our own day, two distinguished Locke scholars, Bennett and Ayers, have kept up a lively debate on this matter for several years; and each of them spends some time in his essay here attacking the view of the other.

Briefly stated, Bennett holds that the idea of substance for Locke is that 'of a pure logical subject underlying all properties, known or unknown, and for that reason unknowable in principle' (Ayers's formulation). For Ayers, by contrast (in Bennett's words) 'Lockean substratum is inner constitution or real essence'; that is, the substratum of a body is the 'invisibly fine microstructure' on which its observable properties 'supervene' and which is 'therefore [only] in practice unknowable by us'. Bennett's paper here contains a detailed statement and defence of his interpretation of Locke's position, along with a criticism of Ayers's 'rival' reading. Ayers, however, attacks Bennett's view without really developing the positive interpretation with which he would replace it. For that readers must refer to other works by Ayers, chiefly Ayers 1977 and Ayers 1991.

In her paper Martha Bolton does not explicitly take sides in the Ayers–Bennett debate, although she criticizes Bennett for making substratum (in Bennett 1971) a 'property-less supporter of properties'; and she comes close to identifying the substratum of a thing with its 'constitution' which, although we have no idea of it, 'unites' and 'gives rise to' its sensible qualities—which is more or less the view of Ayers. But Bolton's concerns are broader that those of Bennett and Ayers (in their essays in this volume, that is; they are not so in general). Her chief purpose is to determine the basis for Locke's distinction between complex ideas of substances (where 'substance' means not 'substratum' but 'individual body or spirit') and those of mixed modes. The idea of substratum plays a crucial role in this, she argues, and it is that role she focuses on. Bolton also has an interest in Locke's philosophy of language: she wants to establish what the difference is between the way in which the meanings of general words for substances (which she identifies with 'natural-kind terms') are determined and that in which the meanings of general words for modes ('conventional-kind terms') are determined. We will consider this aspect of Bolton's paper later on, as we examine Locke's discussion of language in Book III of the *Essay*.

The last essay on a topic addressed in Book II is Kenneth Winkler's; the topic is personal identity, treated by Locke in chapter xxvii. This too has been a focus of particular interest on the part of Locke's readers, but in this case, unlike that of substance, the response has not been so uniformly negative. For many philosophers have borrowed from Locke's account in their own efforts to deal with the 'problem of personal identity', which 'problem' indeed was discovered by Locke, previous thinkers having taken little notice of it. Locke actually discusses four distinct issues in chapter xxvii: (1) the 'principle of individuation', whereby two simultaneously existing individuals are distinguished from one another; (2) the nature of identity through time for things of different kinds, that is, the conditions under which something is the same thing from one moment to another; (3) the nature of persons considered as a specific kind of thing; and (4) the identity conditions for persons. Winkler has something to say about each of these issues, but it is the last of them that he concentrates on. His aim is, as he says, 'to place Locke's discussion of personal identity in the setting Locke intended for it, and to consider some of the difficulties it presents once it is placed there'. The chief innovation in Winkler's account is the emphasis he places on what he calls 'the subjective constitution of the [Lockean] self'. For Locke holds that one's self comprises all and only that of which one is, or could become, immediately conscious, and this gives the self, as Winkler puts it, 'a certain authority over its own constitution'. The chief difficulty which this view presents is that it appears to be in conflict with the principle of justice whereby a person shall be punished for all and only the crimes she actually commits. This is a principle which Locke is sure will be upheld by God on Judgement Day if not by men in this life. But what if some person is conscious of having done some evil deed which she in fact did not perform, or is not conscious of one which she did? The question is a live one for Locke; he himself raises it as one that must be faced. His faith tells him that God will make the necessary 'adjustments' or 'rectifications' so that justice is served. But doesn't this simply contradict the subjective-constitution doctrine of personhood? Some commentators—Antony Flew for one (see Flew 1968)—have thought that it does. Winkler, however, is more cautious and, in the end, having explored some possible ways out for Locke, he leaves the question unresolved. 'At the very least', he says, 'the dominant themes in chapter xxvii—the subjective constitution of the self, and the possibility of objective criticism and adjustment—cannot easily be combined.'

So much, then, for the essays on Book II. It should be noted, however, that although there is no essay here that is wholly devoted to the last five chapters of this book, in which Locke considerably elaborates his account of ideas in general and their relation to the world they (are supposed to) represent, discussions of portions of this material are included in several essays that deal mainly with other matters. Martha Bolton, for example, in her paper on ideas of substances, has a good bit to say about the reality and the adequacy of ideas—topics Locke treats in chapters xxx and xxxi of Book II. And Jennifer Ashworth, John Campbell, and Ruth Mattern (in her essay on knowledge) all make several references to matters treated in chapters xxix–xxxii.

In Book III, Locke's general target is language. His treatment of it can be divided, roughly, into three parts. In the first, comprising chapters i and ii,

Locke presents a general theory of 'the signification of words'. In the second, consisting of the next six chapters, he considers different categories of words: 'general terms' in iii, 'names of simple ideas' in iv, 'names of mixed modes' in v, 'names of substances' in vi, 'particles' in vii, and 'abstract and concrete terms' in viii. And in the third part, which covers the three final chapters of Book iii, Locke examines various defects in language and its use. Some of these are natural 'imperfections of words'; these are described in chapter ix. Some are the product of 'wilful faults and neglects' on the part of language users; these 'abuses of words' are taken up in chapter x. Finally, in chapter xi, Locke suggests a number of 'remedies' of the imperfections and abuses lately catalogued.

The things in Book iii that have most attracted the attention of scholars are, first, Locke's theory of signification, and second, his discussion of general terms and essences, which occurs in chapters iii and vi. In this volume, Jennifer Ashworth's paper is devoted to the first of these things, Margaret Atherton's and Martha Bolton's (their second papers in each case) to the second.

Locke's theory of signification is encapsulated in two well-known formulas: first, that 'Words in their primary or immediate signification, stand for nothing, but the ideas in the mind of him that uses them' (E iii.ii.2: 405); and second, that though the words speakers use immediately signify their own ideas, 'yet they in their thoughts give them a secret reference to two other things', namely 'ideas in the minds also of other men, with whom they would communicate' and 'the reality of things' outside the mind (E iii.ii.4–5: 406–7). But it is far from obvious just how these formulas are to be understood, especially in view of other doctrines Locke professes, and there has been a good deal of controversy over the proper interpretation of them. Ashworth takes up the issues presented by both formulas and, besides spelling out her own accounts of Locke's meaning, defends these accounts against the views of other scholars. When Locke claims that ideas immediately signify ideas, Ashworth claims, he is not stating a theory about the meanings of words, in the sense that certain recent philosophers of language have charged him with doing. Rather, he is using the term 'signifies' for a semantic relation different from that meant by 'means' (in their use of it). This is the same relation that Scholastic philosophers were seeking to explicate in their theories of signification. Ashworth sketches the main features of these Scholastic theories, and provides evidence that Locke knew about them from his undergraduate studies at Oxford. Then in the later parts of her paper, she turns to Locke's other formula, regarding the 'secret reference to two other things'. What Locke is expressing by means of this formula, she contends, is a doctrine about the ideas that are signified by the words used by a speaker. This is the doctrine that such ideas have (or are intended to have) a 'double conformity', on the one hand to ideas belonging to other users of language, on the other to things in the world that the ideas of both speaker and hearer are supposed to represent. Ashworth explains how this doctrine is to be understood and provides evidence in support of the attribution of it to Locke. She concludes her paper with the overall judgement that when Locke's discussion of language is correctly understood, 'it can be viewed in a somewhat more sympathetic light than is usually the case'.

Scholars have been interested in chapters iii and vi of Book III, not only for their contributions to Locke's philosophy of language, but for the substantial discussions of epistemological and metaphysical issues they contain. In chapter iii, after noting that most of the words we actually use are general words, applying not to single individuals but to multitudes, or rather to kinds, of things, Locke asks how it is that 'general words come to be made'. This is a question for him because he takes it for granted, not only that 'all things that exist are only particulars', but that the first words a child learns are words standing for particulars. Locke's answer to the question is quite straightforward: 'words become general by being made the signs of general ideas', and the mind makes general ideas from particular ones 'by separating from them the circumstances of time, and place, and any other ideas that may determine them to this or that particular existence' (E III.iii.6: 410–11). This separating process Locke calls 'abstraction'; he has already described it in Book II as one of the operations by which the mind constructs complex ideas from simple ones.

The consequence of this account of the genesis both of our general words and of our general ideas, Locke points out, is that 'general and universal belong not to the real existence of things, but are the inventions and creatures of the understanding, made by it for its own use, and concern only signs, whether words or ideas' (E III.iii.11: 414). This is Locke's response to the traditional 'problem of universals'—a version of nominalism.

The next question to be raised, Locke then says, is 'what kind of signification . . . general words have'. It is in answering this question that he introduces his doctrine of nominal essences. In sum his answer is that what general words signify is 'a sort of things'—that is, a species or kind—and that they do that by signifying abstract ideas in the minds of the words' users. Since that which determines the extension of a sort, and which individuals belong to it, has traditionally been said to be the essence of (the things of) that sort, Locke thinks it appropriate to speak of the abstract ideas that are signified by general words as essences too (E III.iii.14: 416).

But then, noting that the word 'essence' has had other connotations for its traditional users, beyond that of determining sort membership, he proposes that his abstract ideas be called nominal essences, and that the contrary term 'real essence' be applied to something other than this. That to which it ought to be applied, he goes on to say, is 'the real internal . . . constitution of things, whereon their discoverable qualities depend'. For it is (probably) this, according to Locke's corpuscularian theory of (at least physical) reality, that most closely answers to the formula, 'the very being of any thing, whereby it is what it is', by which the term 'essence' has traditionally been defined (E III.iii.15: 417).

Having thus distinguished these two kinds of essence, real and nominal, Locke goes on to say quite a lot about both of them in the next three chapters of Book III. It could be misleading, however, to speak thus of two kinds of essence. For the terms 'nominal essence' and 'real essence' do not, as Locke uses them, stand for two coordinate species of a single genus. Nominal essences belong to one ontological category—they are ideas in people's minds—and real essences to another—they are physical objects somehow belonging to individual bodies. Still, there are philosophical problems whose resolution might reasonably be thought to involve either nominal or real essences or both; there are, that is, explanatory functions that real and nominal essences might equally be expected to fulfil. One such problem is that posed by Martha Bolton in her substances paper: the problem of determining the meanings of general terms, at least those that stand for sorts. The standard view of Locke's solution to this problem is that for him such meanings are determined solely by the general ideas we have—nominal essences, in other words. But Bolton claims that Locke assigns real essences an essential role in fixing the meanings of general names of substances. He gives them no such role in fixing the meanings of mixed-mode names, she thinks, but that is as it should be, given the difference he takes there to be between ideas of substances and ideas of mixed modes. The one difference is a consequence of the other.

Margaret Atherton, in her second essay, takes issue with this claim of Bolton's. Not only do real essences play no essential role in determining the meanings of sortal words for Locke, she argues, but nominal essences play no such role either. So Lockean essences of both kinds are 'inessential': they do no explanatory work in Locke's philosophy, nor is Locke an essentialist in any sense. Why then did he introduce the notion of essence in the first place, and expend so much effort distinguishing nominal from real essences? Atherton answers that he did so in order to 'downplay the notion of an essence and to show how little mileage could be gained from it'. She goes on to criticize the positions of recent commentators whose

interpretations of Locke's account of essences are different from hers,
among them J. L. Mackie, as well as Bolton. Against Mackie she maintains,
for example, that 'in the sense of real essence Locke approves of, . . . only
particular things have real essences', that modern scientists have not 'identified a lot of real essences', and that Locke does not 'give his approval to
a sense of real essence that implies there are immutable species or natural
kinds'.

Bolton does not respond to Atherton's argument in her second essay
here (although she has addressed some points of it in another paper; see
Bolton 1988). Her concern is rather with a different question, one that
pertains, indeed, only to nominal essences, for it is the doctrine of nominal
essence that carries the weight of Locke's opposition to the essentialist
philosophies of his day, Cartesian as well as Scholastic. The question
Bolton raises has to do with the basis of Locke's doctrine, and his reason
for rejecting the essentialism of his contemporaries. The consensus among
recent Locke scholars is that he did so on metaphysical grounds: because
he denied the existence of mind-independent general essences or natures.
Bolton does not reject this opinion; her point is that Locke has an additional basis or reason for opposing essentialism and advancing his doctrine
of nominal essences in its stead. This additional basis belongs to his theory
of ideas and not to his metaphysics. The crucial provision in this theory is
that, as Bolton expresses it, 'ideas involve objects of immediate perception
whose identity is specified entirely in terms of what they are perceived to
be'. In this, she claims, Locke's conception of ideas differed from that of
such essentialist philosophers as Descartes and Leibniz. She then undertakes to show how Locke, taking this point about ideas as a premises,
derives his doctrine of nominal essence, and thence his opposition to
essentialism.

As we have seen, Locke's discussion of language (and essences) in Book
III is a digression from the main line of enquiry in the *Essay*, from ideas to
knowledge—although his claims about essences connect at many points
with the metaphysical and epistemological doctrines stated in Book II. In
Book IV Locke returns to that main line and takes up the subject, first, of
knowledge, and second, of various surrogates of knowledge—judgement,
opinion, belief, and faith—and matters related thereto—reason, probability, and error.

Locke's discussion of knowledge extends through the first thirteen chapters of Book IV. The first four of these concern the nature of knowledge and
some of its properties. In the first chapter Locke states his famous definition of knowledge: 'the perception of the connexion and agreement, or
disagreement and repugnancy of any of our ideas' (E IV.i.2: 525). He then

distinguishes four 'sorts' of agreement or disagreement: 'identity or diversity', 'relation', 'co-existence or necessary connexion', and 'real existence'.
In chapter ii, he lists three 'degrees of our knowledge', which he labels
'intuition', 'demonstration', and 'sensitive knowledge of particular existence'. These labels are misleading, since what they connote are different
ways or means of achieving knowledge, not variations in the knowledge
achieved. Furthermore, that which admits of degrees, strictly speaking, is
not knowledge but the certainty or evidence which necessarily attaches to
it; for a perceptual or cognitive state of mind which lacks certainty, or at
least a high degree of it, is not knowledge at all, but opinion. In chapter iii,
on the 'extent of human knowledge', Locke considers the limitations on
our knowledge, stressing that, despite our pretensions, we know relatively
little. It is in this chapter that he makes his two startling pronouncements
about scientific knowledge: on the one hand, that 'morality is capable of
demonstration', so that a science of morals is possible for us (although no
one has yet achieved it); and that, on the other hand, physical science, a
science of bodies, is not possible for us. It is also here that Locke raises the
'scandalous' question of thinking matter. For all that we know, he says,
there is no reason why God should not, 'if he pleases, superadd to matter
a faculty of thinking' (E iv.iii.6: 541). Locke does not of course think that
God does or will do this; but merely suggesting the possibility of it was
enough to call forth charges of heresy and even of atheism against him. In
chapter iv Locke undertakes to show how it is that, even though 'all
knowledge lies only in the perception of the agreement or disagreement of
our own ideas', some knowledge is nonetheless 'real', that is, conversant
with real beings existing apart from our ideas.

   The next seven chapters of Book iv, v through xi, deal first with truth,
and then with several different kinds of propositions. The connection
between these topics and that of knowledge is as follows. Knowledge
entails truth, which is to say, one only knows that which is true. But truth,
Locke tells us in chapter v, is a property of propositions (as is its contrary,
falsity). Hence our knowledge is of propositions too; knowledge, as he puts
it at the end of Book ii, 'all consists in propositions'(E ii.xxxiii.19: 401). So
Locke must think that the agreement or disagreement of ideas that one
perceives when one has knowledge is not a relationship that holds between
just any ideas. It is only when ideas are joined in the particular way
required for them to form a single proposition that they stand in this
relationship. Exactly what this way is, however, and how the mind operates
to effect this joining, are questions that Locke does not consider in the
Essay.

   Having identified propositions as the bearers of truth and hence as the proper objects of knowledge, Locke next surveys the various kinds of propositions that are capable of being known. He begins with universal propositions, treating them generally in chapter vi and then examining two special types of them, 'maxims' and 'trifling propositions', in chapters vii and viii. He then takes up particular propositions in chapters ix–xi. These all turn out to be propositions which affirm or deny existence of particular things—universal propositions, he says, 'concern not existence' at all—and so the class of propositions he discusses is also that of existential propositions. There are only three things or kinds of things, Locke believes, whose existence we are able to know, and it happens that the knowledge we have has a different 'degree' in each case—that is, we arrive at it in a different way. Thus we have intuitive knowledge of the existence of our own selves, demonstrative knowledge of the existence of God, and sensitive knowledge of the existence of (some) bodies; Locke devotes a chapter to each of these. In chapter x, he states and defends an argument by which the existence of God, as he claims, can be demonstrated. The argument, however, is not an impressive one, and few commentators have paid much attention to it. In chapter xi Locke briefly considers the sceptical questions that philosophers have raised against the claim that we have knowledge of the existence of material objects, as opposed to merely probable opinion. But he does not take such questions seriously, and lightly dismisses them.

Rounding out Locke's treatment of knowledge in Book IV are two shorter chapters, xii on the 'improvement of our knowledge' and xiii on 'some farther considerations concerning' it. In the latter of these he considers the extent to which knowledge is under the control of our wills, concluding, characteristically, that 'it is neither wholly necessary, nor wholly voluntary' (E IV.xiii.1: 650).

There is a great deal of interesting material in Locke's discussion of knowledge, but scholars, predictably, have been quite selective in their study of it. One question that has been addressed is that to which Ruth Mattern's first paper is devoted: the proper interpretation of Locke's definition of knowledge, especially as it applies to the case of 'real existence'. The problem here is obvious: how can knowing that something really exists be a matter of perceiving a relationship between two or more ideas? Real existence is surely not itself an idea, nor is there any pair of ideas the perception of whose connection would count as the knowledge of real existence. Mattern details the nature of the problem and its seriousness for Locke, and criticizes some attempts by other scholars to resolve it. She then proposes her own resolution, relying heavily on Locke's stated, but perhaps insufficiently emphasized, doctrine that all knowledge is propositional in nature. She ends by trying to disarm various objections that are apt to be raised against her interpretation.

The other two essays in this volume pertaining to knowledge both concern the extent to which science is possible, physical science in the case of McCann's essay, moral science in that of Mattern's (her second, that is). The question McCann actually poses is that of Locke's mechanism: to what extent does Locke adopt the 'mechanical philosophy' of Boyle and Gassendi? This question was raised in an earlier paper by Margaret Wilson (Wilson 1979), who argued that Locke is committed to several doctrines that conflict with a thorough-going mechanism. If Wilson is right, then Locke would have another reason for denying the possibility of a science of bodies, beyond the reason he gives in chapter iii of Book iv: that we are ignorant both of the real essences of physical objects, and of how these essences give rise to such objects' observable qualities. For then the behaviour of bodies would not be fully governed by mechanical causes, but would be determined partly by the arbitrary—and hence for us radically unknowable—will of God. McCann argues, however, contra Wilson, that although Locke does hold the doctrines in question they are not inconsistent with mechanism, and that indeed Locke accepts the mechanical philosophy without qualification. McCann then spells out several implications of Locke's position, and connects it with his views about scientific explanation in physics.

Mattern's paper deals with moral science which, unlike physics, Locke believes can be achieved by human beings. In his earliest writings on ethics, Locke expressed confidence that we can derive moral truths from our knowledge of human beings, conceived as moral agents. But then, as he began writing the first draft of the *Essay*, he came to doubt that we could have such knowledge. At the same time he was working out a new understanding of mathematical science, one that stressed the conditional nature of our knowledge of mathematical truths. He realized that if we are to have an ethical science, our knowledge in this field must be conditional too. But that requires a different conception of moral agents from that with which he started, and so Locke took up the task of developing the requisite conception. The result of this effort, according to Mattern, is the concept of a person that he first presents in Book ii in the chapter on identity, a chapter that was not included in the *Essay* until the second edition. This is the same concept, Mattern claims, that provides the necessary basis for Locke's moral science. Besides making these points, and charting the development of Locke's thinking on the subject of moral knowledge, Mattern suggests some implications of Locke's views for some recent treatments of ethical issues.

Having finished with knowledge, Locke devotes the remaining eight chapters (xiv–xxi) of Book IV to cognitive states other than knowledge. He first considers judgement in chapter xiv. Judgement is a mental operation 'whereby the mind takes its ideas to agree . . . , without perceiving' that they do (E IV.xiv.3: 653). The products of judgement are beliefs or opinions, and these, like knowledge, 'consist in propositions'. Unlike knowledge, however, beliefs and opinions are characterized by probability rather than certainty. In chapter xv Locke discusses the nature of probability and how it is (or ought to be) determined, and in xvi he considers the different 'degrees of assent' that correspond to the different degrees of probability that we assign to our beliefs. Then in chapter xvii he turns to reason, which might seem surprising in view of the traditional tendency to associate reason exclusively with knowledge. Locke, however, is quite deliberately flouting tradition, here and throughout this part of the *Essay*. Reason is a faculty, he makes clear, that is capable of producing probable belief as well as certain knowledge. Locke does not quite explicitly draw the distinction between deductive and inductive reasoning that later philosophers were to do, but he does seem to be working towards it.

Next comes chapter xviii on 'faith and reason', where by 'faith' is meant 'religious faith'. This chapter is appropriate here because faith is a form of belief or assent, although it is different not only from knowledge but also from empirically justified opinion: its basis is revelation by God. The question of the proper relation between reason and faith was the subject of considerable discussion at the time Locke was writing the *Essay*. His position on it is that these two have 'distinct provinces', but that reason is the final authority in all cognitive matters, religious ones included. There may be truths of religion, he declares, which go 'beyond reason' and which it is legitimate for us to assent to 'on faith'. But there are no truths on any subject that go 'against reason'. The next chapter, on 'enthusiasm', was not part of the original *Essay*; Locke inserted it into the fourth edition. Its subject is a third supposed 'ground of assent' pertaining to matters religious, distinct both from reason and from (legitimate) faith. 'Enthusiasm', as the term was used in the seventeenth century, is a form of feeling or experience; and for the followers of certain religious sects this was the best or even the only proper means of discovering truths of religion. For Locke, however, enthusiasm really consists in 'the ungrounded fancies of a man's own brain' (E IV.xix.3: 698). Chapter xix is a vigorous attack on those who rely on it.

Book IV concludes, finally, with a substantial chapter (xx) on 'wrong assent or errour' and a short one (xxi) on 'the division of the sciences' (xxi); these were chapters xix and xx in the *Essay*'s first three editions.

Despite the variety and richness of this material, scholars generally have given scant attention to it, apart from a few studies on the topic of reason and faith. (The situation may now be changing, however: see Owen 1993 and especially Wolterstorff 1996.) In this volume only John Passmore's essay touches it, and the particular issue that Passmore addresses is somewhat tangential to the main thrust of Locke's discussion. This is the issue of the voluntariness of belief or assent: can one believe or disbelieve at will? This is a matter of the 'ethics of belief' because Locke sometimes speaks as if we have an obligation to believe or not believe certain things, or at least an obligation to apportion the probability we assign a proposition to the strength of the evidence we have for it. But if we have an obligation to believe (or even believe with a certain degree of conviction), then, given the principle that ought implies can (which there is no reason to suppose that Locke did not accept), it must be in our power not to believe, and so by our own will that we do believe. If on the other hand believing or not is not up to us, then we have no obligations regarding belief.

Passmore begins by formulating three specific questions about belief, will, and obligation, and then tries to determine how Locke would answer them. The task is complicated by the fact that the relevant texts provide grounds for answers that are inconsistent with one another. Passmore tries out several interpretations of these texts, seeking to render them consistent with one another. At one point he compares belief to knowledge, which Locke has said is partly necessary and partly voluntary. But these two are only somewhat alike: belief is voluntary in the way that knowledge is, but it also seems to be so in respects in which knowledge is not. Passmore also appeals to Locke's discussion of suspending desire in chapter xxi of Book ii, suggesting that belief too may be suspendable sometimes, and hence voluntary in that way. But in the end, Passmore concludes, there are tensions in Locke's thinking about belief, especially in conjunction with his faith in—or at least hopes for—human rationality, that cannot be fully resolved.

I

THE FOUNDATIONS OF KNOWLEDGE AND THE LOGIC OF SUBSTANCE: THE STRUCTURE OF LOCKE'S GENERAL PHILOSOPHY

MICHAEL R. AYERS

I. THE FOUNDATIONS OF KNOWLEDGE

GASSENDI, Hobbes, and Locke all categorically asserted the independent authority of the senses as knowledge-producing faculties. As Hobbes put it, '*Knowledge of Fact . . .* is nothing else but Sense and Memory, and is *Absolute Knowledge*' (Hobbes 1651: I.ix).[1] Locke announced the senses' immediate authority on questions of existence just as bluntly: they are 'the proper and sole Judges of this thing' (E IV.xi.2: 631).[2] On the other side, Platonistic or Augustinian philosophers such as Mersenne, Descartes, and Arnauld firmly subordinated the senses to the intellect. This division constitutes one of the great watersheds of early modern epistemology, and is well illustrated by Locke's response, as we may suppose it to be, to an argument in the Port Royal *Logic*. The *Logic* had argued, in effect, that the doctrine of transubstantiation does not contradict the senses, since even ordinarily the senses must be interpreted by reason. In the case of the Eucharist we simply have special reasons for taking the body of Christ to be behind a wafer-like appearance (Arnauld and Nicole 1965: IV.xii; cf. IV.i). Locke brought the independent authority of the senses in the Protestant cause. Because the Romanist is indoctrinated from childhood with the

From *Locke's Philosophy: Content and Context* (Oxford: Clarendon Press, 1994), 49–73.
This chapter was written in response to a request for a broad discussion of Locke's general philosophy, and necessarily overlaps material in my more recently published monograph (Ayers 1991). Nevertheless, since some of that material is here expanded (e.g. the discussion of Draft A and the Hellenistic parallels), and some compressed, while all has been taken from its various contexts and reordered, I hope that the present chapter will help to clarify (my view of) Locke's theory.

[1] 'Absolute' by contrast with the hypothetical sentences which constitute science.
[2] The phrase occurs in Draft A, in the original version of this passage (D I: 20–1).

principle that Church and Pope.are infallible, 'How is he prepared easily to swallow, not only against all probability, but even the clear evidence of his Senses, the Doctrine of Transubstantiation? This Principle has such an influence on his Mind, that he will take that to be Flesh, which he sees to be Bread' (E IV.xx.10: 713).[3]

It is well known that Gassendi's mature epistemology was built on Epicurean and Stoic sources. Locke's similar debt to ancient empiricism was less explicit and may or may not have been less direct, but it is no less certain. His treatment of 'sensitive knowledge of existence' is an example. He identified the 'evidence' of such knowledge with our immediate knowledge in sensation 'that something doth exist without us, which causes [an] *Idea* in us': accordingly 'I have by the Paper affecting my Eyes, that *Idea* produced in my Mind, which whatever Object causes, I call *White*; by which I know, that that Quality or Accident (*i.e.* whose appearance before my Eyes, always causes that *Idea*) doth really exist' (E IV.xi.2: 630–1). This direct causal realism has much the same general structure, and is expressed by means of the same example, as the theory attributed to the Stoic Chrysippus in a work present in Locke's library: 'An impression is an affection occurring in the soul, which reveals itself and its cause. Thus, when through sight we observe something white, the affection is what is engendered in the soul through vision; and it is this affection which enables us to say that there is a white object which activates us.'[4]

Even more convincing evidence of an ancient source is provided by Locke's argument that metaphysical mistrust of the senses is mistrust of a basic cognitive faculty, and is therefore self-destructive: 'For we cannot act any thing, but by our Faculties: nor talk of Knowledge it self, but by the help of those Faculties, which are fitted to apprehend even what Knowledge is' (E IV.xi.3: 631). The suggestion that the senses are the source of the sceptic's own capacity to conceive of knowledge itself echoes the Epicurean onslaught on the sceptic in *De Rerum Natura*: 'if he has never seen anything true in the world, from where does he get his knowledge of what knowing and not knowing are?' For Lucretius, the concept of (or acquaintance with) truth 'has its origin in the senses'. Since reason is the product of the senses, 'if the senses are not true, all reason becomes false as well'.[5]

---

[3] The thought was an early one: see D I: 71.

[4] Cited in Long and Sedley 1987: I. 237. The passage is from *De Placitis Philosophorum*, in Stephanus' edn. of Plutarch. As well as the similarity, there is a difference, in that Chrysippus' 'impression' not only gives notice of its cause, but reveals the intrinsic character of its cause.

[5] Lucretius, *De Rerum Natura*, Book IV, lines 474 ff.: 'at id ipsum/quaeram, cum in rebus veri nil viderit ante/unde sciat quid sit scire et nescire vicissim/notitiem veri neque sensus posse refelli/ . . . an ab sensu falso ratio orta velebit/dicere eos contra, quae tota ab sensibus orta est?/

A more pervasive debt, however, was to the doctrine of signs, notes, or marks through which we can have knowledge of things not evident in themselves. A distinction was widely drawn in ancient philosophy between reminiscent signs of such things as are only sometimes not evident and indicative signs of things which are by nature never evident. In the case of reminiscent or empirical signs constant experience sets up a connection between the sign and what it signifies. In the case of indicative signs, we reason to something which is such that, unless it existed, the sign would not exist: for example, sweating is an indicative sign of invisible pores in the skin, and certain motions of the body indicate the presence of the soul. The Sceptic Sextus Empiricus granted the cogency of reminiscent signs as a basis for opinion, but rejected indicative signs. Against Sextus, Gassendi argued on behalf of indicative signs that the proof of pores in the skin appeals only to principles founded on experience. Locke structured his treatment of probability around the same distinction between beliefs based on correlations falling *within* experience and inferences going *beyond* experience. With respect to the latter he agreed with Gassendi, arguing that hypotheses about what lies 'beyond the discovery of the senses' can properly be based on a 'wary reasoning from Analogy' (Gassendi 1658: I. 79–86; E IV.xvi.12: 666).

Trust in the senses and the doctrine of signs came together in the principle that sensory appearances are always true indicative signs. The Epicurean thought seems to have been that, even if the same thing presents different appearances in circumstances in which it has not itself changed, or appears different to different observers at the same time (as in the standard sceptical example of water appearing hot to one person and cold to another), the difference in appearance accurately reflects a difference in the conditions of perception and so is a true sign of the object in those conditions. If we wrongly place the difference in the object itself, it is that judgement which is false, not the appearance. One example, repeated by Gassendi, is the changing appearance of an object as it grows more distant: the appearance is not false, although a judgement that the object is itself growing smaller or changing shape would be false.[6] In the *Essay* this doctrine took the form of the principle that simple ideas are always 'true', 'real', and 'adequate': 'their Truth consists in nothing else,

---

qui nisi sunt veri, ratio quoque falsa fit omnis' (cited by Long and Seldey 1987: I. 78–9. The argument is recorded in Gassendi's *Syntagma Epicuri Philosophiae*, which was plagiarized in Thomas Stanley's *History of Philosophy* of 1655. Of these, Locke owned Lucretius and only a later (1687) edn. of Stanley.

[6] Lucretius, *De Rerum Natura*, Book IV, lines 499–500; Gassendi 1658: I. 79–86. Gassendi's source is Sextus Empiricus, *Against the Professors*, 7. 206–10, cited in Long and Sedley 1987: I. 81.

but in such Appearances, as are produced in us, and must be suitable to those Powers, [God] has placed in external Objects, or else they could not be produced in us' (E II.xxxii.14: 388). The final clause echoes the Stoic characterization of a 'cognitive' (or 'grasping') impression as 'of such a kind as could not arise from what is not', and there are other Stoic resonances in Locke's account of simple ideas.[7] Yet the general point here is the broadly Epicurean one that simple ideas are dependable 'distinguishing marks' which serve their purpose whatever unknown difference lies behind the sensible distinction. For that reason they can fulfil the role of 'signs' of another kind, signs in the natural language of thought which signify their unknown causes. The signs that naturally *indicate* qualities or powers naturally *stand for* them in thought. (cf. E IV.v.2–5: 574–6; E IV.xxi.4: 720–1). This neat conjunction of epistemology and theory of representation, encapsulated in the ambivalence of the terms 'sign' and 'signify' in Locke's usage, lies at the heart of his general philosophy.

The principle of the truth of simple ideas derives from ancient empiricism, but also responds to the very different Cartesian trust in innate 'simple notions' or 'simple natures', not to speak of the Scholastic doctrine, appealed to by Arnauld in his objections to the *Meditations*, that concepts or 'simple apprehensions' are all true.[8] It play an important part in Locke's explanation of both the certainty and the limitations of sensitive knowledge: the idea of white naturally signifies the power to cause that idea, i.e. the quality whiteness, however wrong we may be in our hypotheses about what constitutes whiteness in the object. Sensitive knowledge of existence, in other words, is theory-neutral or pre-theoretical, and that is why it is secure. Moreover, the principle was readily extensible to all *powers*: by means of the idea of power the sensible change in wax can be employed as a sign both of whatever in the sun melts wax and of whatever in wax causes it to be melted. Hence, with a murmured apology, Locke could treat ideas

---

[7] Locke's account of 'clear and distinct' simple ideas corresponds to the other main features of a Stoic cognitive impression, that it 'arises from what is and is stamped and impressed exactly in accordance with what is': as Locke puts it, 'our *simple Ideas* are *clear*, when they are such as the Objects themselves, from whence they were taken, did or might, in a well-ordered Sensation or Perception, present them' (E II.xxix.2: 363). The expression 'clear and distinct' is, of course, Cartesian, but it echoes equivalent Stoic expressions, as Descartes was doubtless well aware. Cf. Long and Sedley 1987: I. 241–53, II. 243–54.

[8] Cf. Descartes 1985: I. 44–7 [AT x: 419–23]; II. 145 [AT VII: 206]. In Draft A Locke accepts even with respect to complex ideas of substances the Scholastic argument that a false concept of *x* is impossible because it would not be a concept of *x* but of something else (D I: 18). In the *Essay* he affirms its traditional, more correctly Aristotelian rival, the principle that 'our ideas . . . cannot properly and simply in themselves be said to be true or false' (E II.xxxii.1: 384). In the sense in which ideas can loosely be said to be true in relation to reality, not all ideas are true, although all simple ideas are true.

of powers as simple ideas and knowledge of powers as effectively foundational (E ii.xxi.3: 234; E ii.xxiii.7–9: 299–301).

In one respect Locke's determination to keep the deliverances of the senses independent of reason and prior to all inference or 'judgement' led him into an even more extreme position than Gassendi's. Gassendi recognized that individual deliverances of the senses may by themselves prompt judgements which need to be corrected, falling back on the not implausible thought that the senses are here correcting themselves rather than being corrected by independent reason. His account of Epicurus accordingly placed the criterion of truth in the consensus or 'suffrage' of the senses (cf. Gassendi 1658: iii. 7). It is possible that Locke regarded any such move as too great a concession to reason, a denial of the immediate, unreasoned 'evidence' of sensitive knowledge. That would help to explain what might otherwise seem an amazing fact: the *Essay*, dedicated to the examination of the extent and limits of knowledge, contains no direct discussion of that most hackneyed of epistemological topics, sensory illusion. Locke did mention a standard sceptical example of something like illusion in the chapter on primary and secondary qualities, but his employment of the primary–secondary distinction to explain 'how the same Water, at the same time, may produce the *Idea* of Cold by one Hand, and of Heat by the other' was in effect a denial that *either* sensation is illusory. For *each* sensation, he suggested, is an appropriately differentiated sign of what gives rise to such sensations, namely 'the increase or diminution of the motion of the minute Parts of our Bodies, caused by the Corpuscles of' other bodies. Much the same point emerges from a discussion of the possibility of people with reversed sensations of colour (E ii.viii.21: 139; E ii.xxxii.15–16: 389–90).[9] Behind these arguments lies the ancient doctrine that appearances are always true.

There is, however, a much more significant difference between Locke's mature epistemology and that of Gassendi. Epicurean philosophy seems not to have distinguished sharply between the abstraction from sense experience of concepts giving meaning to our words, and the acquisition of propositional knowledge constituting the starting-points of reasoned enquiry. As Epicurus himself put his theory of generalized images or 'preconceptions', 'First . . . we must grasp the things which underlie words, so that we may have them as a reference point . . . and not have everything undiscriminated for ourselves as we attempt infinite chains of proofs, or have words which are empty.'[10] The preconception of *man* was identified

[9] For fuller discussion of both these topics, see Ayers 1991: i. 166–7, 207 ff.
[10] Cited by Long and Sedley 1987: i. 87 f. See the editors' note on these passages.

with the knowledge that 'Such and such a kind of thing is a man' and was treated, in effect, as at once an empirical summation of experience, a definition, and a foundational premiss of rational proof. Accordingly Gassendi, working within a logical tradition which laid great emphasis on the distinction between concept and judgement, term and proposition, held not only that all our concepts are acquired in experience, but also that all our knowledge derives from sensory knowledge. As he put it, 'all the evidence and certainty which attaches to a general proposition depends upon that which has been gained from an induction of particulars' (Gassendi 1981: 61).

Locke himself, whether or not in imitation of Gassendi, adopted broadly the same position in his earliest extant essay in epistemology, in what is now known as *Essays on the Law of Nature*. He there claimed that know-ledge of our duty to God and our fellows lies within reach of human reason employing concepts and *premisses* derived from sense experience. Like Epicurus, he supported the claim that we need empirical premisses by an appeal to the principle that all reasoning is *ex cognitis et concessis*. Like Gassendi, he extended the claim to mathematics. Not only are such math-ematical notions as those of a line, a plane, and a solid drawn from experience, but 'other common principles and axioms too' are given to reason by the senses (EL iv: 146). In ethics, the senses supply reason with two kinds of premiss: first, evidence of design in the world from which we can infer the existence of a Creator whose will it is our duty to obey; and, second, knowledge of various characteristics of human nature which reveal God's particular purposes in creating us, and so the content of his will for us, the law of nature. That might suggest that the law of nature is contin-gent, but Locke emphasized, in opposition to extreme voluntarism, that it is not arbitrarily mutable insofar as it is tied to human nature: it has a conditional necessity in that it stands or falls with human nature 'quae iam est', as it now is (EL iv: 150–8; EL vii: 190–202).

Locke apparently became dissatisfied with this account of knowledge and its foundations in the course of writing the so-called Draft A of the *Essay* in 1671. At first he was still able to say that the certainty of geometri-cal demonstration 'can be no greater then that of discerning by our eyes, which the very name "Demonstration" how highly magnified soever for its certainty doth signifye'; and that the axioms or maxims of geometry gain assent 'only by the testimony and assureance of our senses' (D I: 22–3). At the same time he asked whether axioms might not relate 'to the significa-tion of the words them selves they being relative words'. The model is essentially Epicurean: first, 'by constant observation of our senses espetialy our eys', we find certain proportions to hold without exception;

we then assume they hold universally, employing them in some unexplained way as 'standards' of measurement embodied in the meaning of our terms (D I: 22–3).[11] In effect, Locke was here offering a choice: axioms can be regarded either as straightforward empirical summaries, open to empirical refutation, or as quasi-definitions founded on experience, and so 'barely about the signification of words'. Throughout Draft A he continued to develop the thought, with particular reference to propositions about substances, that universal propositions are either, if 'instructive', uncertain or, if certain, mere assertions or denials of identity with respect to our ideas, and consequently 'only verbal . . . and not instructive'.[12] Yet very soon mathematical propositions came to be located unequivocally in the class of propositions about ideas employed as standards, so that demonstration was now explained as 'the beare shewing of things or proposeing them to our senses *or understandings* soe as to make us take notice of them' (the 'understanding' being here the imagination) (D I: 50).[13] At the same time Locke evidently had doubts about regarding them as merely verbal, more than once hinting that mathematics has a guaranteed relation to reality. This thought was expressed, for example, in an interpolated qualification of the instructive–verbal dichotomy: 'Mathematicall universal propositions are both true & instructive because as those Ideas are in our mindes soe are the things without us' (D I: 57).[14] The assumption appears to be that a condition of the instructive certainty of mathematics is the existence of its objects, and it is claimed that that condition is necessarily fulfilled just because of the simplicity of the ideas with which mathematics deals. Yet a final 'memorandum' draws a sharp contrast between particular knowledge of existence (which is dependent on the senses) and universal knowledge (which is hypothetical and 'only supposes existence'), seeming to record Locke's recognition that he had more work to do (D I: 82).[15]

So in the shifting course of Draft A Locke moved discernibly closer to

[11] Cf. Long and Sedley 1987: I. 87–8.

[12] Cf. D I: 55: 'Indeed all Universall propositions are either Certain and then they are only verball but are not instructive. Or else are Instructive & then are not Certain.'

[13] But the preference for this explanation of mathematical truths as 'truths of eternall verity' is fixed as early as pp. 26–7. For explicit reference to imagination, see p. 28: 'any mathematical figure imagind in our mindes'.

[14] On p. 26 the certainty of mathematics is attributed to 'the cleare knowledge of our owne Ideas, & the certainty that quantity and number existing have the same propertys and relations that their Ideas have one to another'. Cf. pp. 25 and 28.

[15] Cf. the disclaimer on p. 75 (strictly true, but as glossed false), 'That I never said that the truth of all propositions was to be made out to us by the senses for this was to leave noe roome for reason at all, which I think by a right traceing of those Ideas which it hath received from Sense or Sensation may come to knowledge of many propositions which our senses could never have discovered.' Locke *had* said that axioms, unless merely verbal, were known only through the senses.

the doctrine of the *Essay* itself, in particular towards a clear decision to restrict the essential role of the senses to the acquisition of simple ideas and (apart from questions of probability) to knowledge of particular existence and coexistence. Such less extreme empiricism, however, was entirely consistent with his original and continuing purposes. For his interest in epistemology seems to have been motivated by two early concerns: first, by his dissatisfaction with arbitrary appeals to conscience and divine inspiration (not to speak of their threat to civil order); and, second, by the study of medicine and corpuscularian science. In ethics his first considered epistemological reaction was to uphold the possibility of a reasonable morality based on the light of nature, empirically conceived. In natural philosophy, however, he adopted an opposite, if similarly 'empiricist' line: the senses give knowledge of no more than the sensible effects and powers of substances, while the intrinsic properties underlying these effects remain beyond the reach of our faculties. The 'corpuscularian' theory is simply our best inadequate speculation. The combination of epistemological optimism in ethics with pessimism regarding the possibility of a proper 'science' of nature was not, of course, in the least inconsistent. Together with his claim that careful observation and experiment can yield probabilities sufficient for the direction of action, it constituted his pious thesis that the 'candle, that is set up in us', for all its limitations, 'shines bright enough for all our purposes' (E i.i.5: 46; see e.g. E iv.xii.11: 646). Certainly it answered to his actual targets, on the one hand religious dogmatists and enthusiasts immune to what Locke saw as the reasonable argument of the natural law tradition, and on the other hand scientific dogmatists who trusted too much in reason's power to penetrate to the essences of things.

The chief theoretical problem facing Locke as an epistemologist was that of developing an account of the two sorts of science, moral and natural, which would explain very clearly why the one is possible for us while the other is not. From the first an analogy between ethics and the indubitably available science of mathematics was a promising line of approach. Yet his original quasi-Gassendist view of mathematics as a science with empirical axioms was a predictable loser, and the felt need for an explanation of the *necessity* of mathematics was surely Locke's motive for the experimental departures of Draft A.[16] In consequence the analogy between mathematics and ethics was actually weakened. If mathematics is a priori, what about ethics? In 1671 he was already attracted by the thought that moral notions, unlike ideas of substances, are constructed by us without reference to reality, and are therefore clearly knowable. Yet that left

---

[16] Cf. D i: 26: 'proportions of numbers & extensions ... are soe ex necessitate rei'.

or even exacerbated the problem of how we can know whether they correspond to natural law, in Locke's terms the real problem of the foundations of ethics. As he himself pointed out, that is not a question that the senses can answer. In Draft B the problem was noted and set aside (D ɪ: 41–2; D ɪ: 269–70).

It was eventually solved by a number of changes to the accounts both of mathematics and of ethics which restored the analogy between them to its full force. Mathematics was no longer taken to have existential import (cf. E ɪv.iv.8: 566), and its subject matter was accordingly reclassified as arbitrarily constructible *complex* ideas, ideas of simple modes, comparable to the mixed modes which comprise the subject matter of ethics (E ɪɪ.xiii–xvi: 166–209). Locke now dealt with the problem of its informativeness by developing a distinction between trifling knowledge of *identity* and informative knowledge of *relation*, the acknowledged ancestor of Kant's distinction between analytic and synthetic a priori judgement (E ɪv.i.5: 526; E ɪv.i.7: 527; E ɪv.viii.8: 614).[17] A corollary of these changes was a much sharper, but still firmly imagist, account of abstraction, owing something (as it seems) to Hobbes.

Already presaged in Draft A was an ordering of the degrees of certainty more like Mersenne's than Gassendi's. While maintaining the independent authority of the senses almost more rigorously than Gassendi himself, the *Essay* assigned to them no more than the third degree of knowledge, after intuition and demonstration (E ɪv.ii.14: 536–8).[18] Locke did not, however, adopt Mersenne's respect for maxims, and indeed, since axioms had lost their role as empirical premises even in Draft A, the principle that 'all Reasonings are *ex praecognitis, et praeconcessis*' was effectively abandoned (E ɪv.vii.8: 595). In fact the *Essay* deliberately seems to tread a careful path between Mersenne's and Gassendi's views about maxims and the relation between general and particular certainty. For Mersenne the proposition that the body is larger than a finger draws certainty from the prior certainty of the general maxim that the whole is greater than a part. For Gassendi, the latter is certain only insofar as supporting judgements like the former are certain. For Locke, both are equally self-evident, and his rider, that 'if one of these have need to be confirmed to him by the

---

[17] Cf. Kant 1783: sect. 3.

[18] Cf. D ɪ: 45: 'all such affirmations and negations [of universal identities] are made . . . as the clearest knowledge we can have which indeed is internal and mentall demonstration as certain and evident and perhaps more then the external' ('as . . . can have' interpolated). Contrast the earlier emphasis on the senses, p. 43: 'all a man can certainly know of things existing without him is only particular propositions, for which he hath demonstration by his senses the best ground of science he can have or expect and what soe comes to his understanding, he receives as certain knowledge and demonstration'.

other, the general has more need to be let into his Mind by the particular, than the particular by the general' (E iv.vii.11: 603),[19] is not Gassendi's inductivism, but the point that the immediate objects of universal intuition are particulars abstractly considered. We need to see the relation in the particular case before us (e.g. a geometrical diagram), in order to universalize the perception to all cases relevantly like that case.

Locke approximated his conception of morality to his reformed model of an a priori science chiefly by extending and elaborating a thought already hovering in the *Essays on the Law of Nature*: the moral law is necessarily binding on all rational creatures capable of pleasure and pain. What he added to this thought in the *Essay* was the clear statement that the law is independent of any other natural characteristics of human beings: 'were there a Monkey, or any other Creature to be found, that had the use of Reason . . . he would no doubt be subject to Law'. One advantage of this emphasis, whether or not it was a motive for it, was a stronger defence against the extreme voluntarism of revelationists than had been afforded by Locke's earlier model, according to which the law is rooted in nothing more secure than an empirically known, mutable human nature. The idea of 'the *moral Man*', Locke now said, is like the idea of a mode, an 'immoveable unchangeable *Idea*', a postulate of the hypothetical science which is independent of contingent facts (E iii.xi.16: 516–17). At the same time our own subjection to law, as satisfying this idea, is known intuitively with every thought we have, while the existence of the divine lawgiver is strictly demonstrable.

It should not be supposed that these changes related only to the a priori sciences of mathematics and ethics, since they constituted a clarification or development of Locke's conception of science in general. Since all universal knowledge is hypothetical (E iv.xi.14: 638), empirical premisses are unnecessary to *any* science with respect to its status as knowledge or *scientia*. Although he rejected the Cartesian understanding of geometry as explication of the essence of matter, the general model of the fully intelligible, demonstrative science suited both his mechanist sympathies and his scepticism about natural essences very well indeed. The ideal mechanics could be supposed to have a quasi-geometrical form with intuitively evident foundations, hooking on to reality through the medium of empirical existential propositions rather than by means of contingent premisses or axioms of the science itself. In other words, the propositions of natural science, if we could ever achieve such a thing, would be hypothetically

---

[19] The example of the body and a finger is discussed at E iv.xii.3: 640. Cf. Marin Mersenne 1652: 177 (cited in James 1987: 232); Gassendi 1981: 61. For the principle that 'the immediate Object of all our Reasoning and Knowledge, is nothing but particulars', cf. E iv.xvii.8: 680.

necessary in just the same way as those of ethics and mathematics.[20] Yet, whereas in the case of the latter hypothetical necessity is all that is aimed for by the science (and the two existential propositions necessary for the conclusion that ethics applies to *us* are known by intuition and demonstration), it would be useless to build a purported natural science unless we knew experientially that things exist with essences answering to our ideas (cf. E II.i.10: 108–9; E II.xxx.5: 374; E IV.xii.12: 647; etc.). Employing this model, Locke could argue, on the one hand, that our sensitive knowledge of existence is at too coarse a level for the purpose; and, on the other hand, that the corpuscularians' failure to achieve geometrical intelligibility in their speculative explanations is itself enough to show that their hypotheses have failed to capture the essences or natures of material things. It was thoughts like these which underlay his arguments about substance, to which it is now time to turn.

II. THE LOGIC OF SUBSTANCE

To understand Locke's claim that 'of Substance, we have no idea of what it is, but only a confused, obscure one of what it does', it is again useful to look at earlier empiricist argument. Gassendi offers an obvious precedent. In the Second Meditation Descartes had argued that it is by means of the intellect, not the senses or imagination, that we conceive of wax as 'something extended, flexible and mutable', underlying the variety of changing appearances which we perceive as it melts. Elsewhere he had claimed that further intellectual reflection allows us to identify extension as the principal attribute, or essence, of matter (Descartes 1985: II. 20–1 [AT VII: 30–2]; cf. II. 54 [AT VII: 78] and I. 227 [AT IXB: 46]). Gassendi's response was to agree with 'what everyone commonly asserts, *viz.* that the concept of the wax or of its substance can be abstracted from the concepts of its accidents', but to deny that this means 'that the substance or nature of the wax is itself distinctly conceived'. 'Admittedly', Gassendi remarked, 'you perceive that the wax or its substance must be something over and above such [sensible] forms; but what this something is you do not perceive. ... The alleged naked, or rather hidden, substance is something that we can neither ourselves conceive nor explain to others.' According to Gassendi's argument here the positive content of our ideas of material

---

[20] Cf. E IV.vi.11: 585: if we knew real essences, 'to know the Properties of *Gold*, it would be no more necessary that *Gold* should exist, and that we should make experiments upon it, than it is necessary for the knowing the Properties of a Triangle, that a Triangle should exist in any Matter, the *Idea* in our Minds would serve for the one as well the other'.

substances is wholly provided by the senses, and 'the mind is not . . . distinct from the imaginative faculty'. Hence essence always escapes us. Much the same goes for our idea of the mind or 'thinking thing': 'Who doubts that you are thinking?', he asked. 'What we are unclear about . . . is that inner substance of yours whose property is to think (Descartes 1985: II. 189–93 [AT VII: 271–7]). Consequently, Descartes 'can be compared to a blind man who, on feeling heat and being told that it comes from the sun, thinks that he has a clear and distinct idea of the sun in that, if anyone asks him what the sun is, he can reply: "It is a heating thing"' (Descartes 1985: II. 234–5 [AT VII: 337–9]).

It seems to me that whoever seriously reflects on Gassendi's meaning and motivation, and on the connections between his argument and Locke's, will be unlikely to adhere to that (to my mind) perverse interpretation of the latter, still ferociously defended in some quarters,[21] according to which the general idea of substance is for Locke the idea of a pure logical subject underlying all properties, known or unknown, and for that reason unknowable in principle.

One part of Locke's position, indeed, was common to all the 'New Philosophers', dogmatic or anti-dogmatic. That was the anti-Aristotelian point that the multiplicity of sensible qualities and powers through which we know any substantial thing is not a multiplicity in the thing itself, but a multiplicity of ways in which the thing affects the senses or sensibly interacts with other things. Hobbes called it 'a diversity of seeming', defining an 'accident' as 'concipiendi corporis modum', a way of conceiving of body (or a body). The model echoes Epicurus' account of attributes (Hobbes 1651: III.xxxiv; Hobbes 1655: II.viii.2),[22] and is present throughout Locke's *Essay*, even in passages which may seem to have little to do with substance. Here is a famous sentence: 'Though the Qualities that affect our Senses, are, in the things themselves, so united and blended, that there is no separation, no distance between them; yet 'tis plain, the *Ideas* they produce in the Mind, enter by the Senses simple and unmixed' (E II.ii.1: 119).

Such an explanation of the relation between the one substance and its many accidents was a common element in attacks on Scholastic 'real accidents', in particular on the debased account of the substance–accident

[21] Most recently, as far as I know, by Jonathan Bennett (Bennett 1987), an article which he elsewhere describes as showing that 'when Ayers gets down to details regarding Locke on "substratum", his main work is done for him not by special attention to the historical background, but by inattention to what Locke actually wrote' (Bennett 1988: 68).

[22] For Epicurus the attributes of body are individually picked out and spoken of in consequence of the way the mind perceives or focuses on the whole (*Letter to Herodotus*, 68–73, cited in Long and Sedley 1987: I. 34; II. 27).

relation involved in the doctrine of transubstantiation. Kenelm Digby attributed the Scholastic notion to a naive confusion:

what is but one entire thing in it self, seemeth to be many distinct things in my understanding: whereby . . . I shall be in danger . . . to give actuall Beings to the quantity, figure, colour, smell, tast, and other accidents of the apple, each of them distinct one from another, as also from the substance which they clothe; because I find the notions of them really distinguished (as if they were different Entities) in my mind. (Digby 1644: 3)

In one passage in the *Essay* Locke attacked the pretensions of the traditional doctrine of substance and accident in much the same terms as Digby, emphasizing the mistake of taking the one–many relationship to be a real relationship between really distinct beings: 'They who first ran into the Notion of *Accidents*, as a sort of real Beings, that needed something to inhere in, were forced to find out the word *Substance*, to support them' (E II.xiii.19: 175). But the chapter 'Of our Complex *Ideas* of Substances' opens with the obverse point. Because of the presumable unity of the thing, we fail to recognize the multiplicity in our idea of it: 'we are apt afterward to talk of and consider as one simple *Idea*, [that] which indeed is a complication of many *Ideas* together' (E II.xxiii.1: 295). The immediate target here is again Aristotelian, but this time it is the notion that we can achieve simple conceptions of substances correspondent to their real simplicity or unity. Those who think that their would-be scientific definitions capture unitary essences are misled. Just because in ordinary experience of coexisting sensible qualities we naturally (and, as Locke spelt out to Stillingfleet, reasonably and inescapably: cf. W IV: 18–19) take ourselves to be perceiving a unitary thing, we are liable to mistake our complex idea of it for a simple one. If the doctrine of real accidents mistakes ideal for real multiplicity, Aristotelian claims to know essences mistake real for ideal unity.

This first section of the chapter (E II.xxiii.1: 295) has been a main source of the more exotically inappropriate interpretations of Locke on substance. What seems not to have been adequately noticed is that Locke was describing an alleged process of the mind through four clearly distinct stages. First, there is sense perception of 'a great number' of sensible qualities; second, 'the mind takes notice also' that some coexisting qualities go 'constantly' together; third, the presumption that such recurrently grouped qualities belong to 'one thing', i.e. one and the same kind of thing, leads us to combine them, for convenience, in a single idea under a single name; fourth, 'by inadvertency we are apt afterward to talk of and consider' this complex idea 'as one simple idea'. We take this idea to correspond to the '*Substratum*, wherein [these simple *Ideas*] do exist, and from which they do result, which therefore we call *Substance*'.

The term 'we', it is clear, here includes the Aristotelians, as usual accused of merely formalizing the coarse or sloppy thinking of ordinary people. A footnote to the fifth edition, inspired by Locke if not actually written by him, warns us that this passage is not an account of the idea of substance in general, but an explanation of how the (general) names applied to 'Individuals of distinct Species of Substances' have been taken to be simple names standing for simple ideas.[23] The reference is to Aristotelian theory of definition. According to a commonplace distinction, a 'nominal' definition of man, such as 'featherless, two-footed, broad-nailed thing', picks out men by means of a set of mutually independent features, whereas the 'simple', 'real' definition, 'rational animal', unpacks a unitary essence.[24] Locke wanted to say that all candidate definitions of essences are in fact nominal, and of the first form. It should therefore be no surprise that the four stages of his explanation of the Aristotelian mistake correspond in close detail to the four stages which Aristotle himself had distinguished in the achievement of the principles of scientific knowledge.

Aristotle's four stages, as set out in a famous passage (*Posterior Analytics*, B. 19; cf. *Metaphysics*, A. 1), can be read as follows: first, the perception of any object (of whatever category); second, 'experience', or the memory of repeated perceptions of similar objects; third, the formation of a universal concept or thought; and, fourth, the understanding which comes with a scientific definition. In the case of substances, we first perceive, and then lay up the memory of, recurrent or repeated similarities between individuals. Third, we form a universal notion of the same species present on all these perceptual occasions. Finally, sustained observation and reflection enables us to pick out the genus and specific difference and so to arrive at a definition which will explain the concomitance of the 'properties' of the speacies, the cause of their union. Locke's commentary is to the effect that the concept formed at the third stage and associated with the specific name in fact remains complex and sensory, while the fourth stage is nothing but the process by which the existence of the single

---

[23] 'This section, which was intended only to shew how the Individuals of distinct Species of Substances came to be looked on as simple *Ideas* [i.e. presumably, simple objects of thought, objects of simple conceptions], and so to have simple Names, . . . hath been mistaken for an Account of the *Idea* of Substance in general' (E II.xxiii.1: 295 n.). Sect. 14, giving the example 'swan', repeats the message in terms also to be found in the drafts: 'These *Ideas* of Substances, though they are commonly called simple Apprehensions, and the Names of them simple Terms; yet in effect, are complex and compounded' (E II.xxiii.14: 305). The connection is not straightforward, but Locke seems to have been assimilating the most available Aristotelian notion of simplicity (which involves the contrast between 'simple' concepts or terms and 'complex' propositions) to the different (although arguably related) conception according to which scientific definitions of essences are 'simple' for other reasons.

[24] Cf. E III.x.17: 500: 'Thus . . . we say, that *Animal rationale* is, and *Animal implume bipes latis unguibus* is not a good definition of a Man.' 'We' again means Aristotelian orthodoxy.

name, together with the natural and proper assumption of a common, recurring substratum or explanatory nature behind the recurrent experience, creates the illusion that our complex idea is simple. Locke has rewritten the Aristotelian account of the apprehension of natural principles as the psychological explanation of a vain delusion.

The argument of the rest of Book II, chapter xxiii develops the claim that no idea formed on the basis of experience ever in any case captures the unity of the thing itself. The latter is never represented to the enquirer by anything more than a place-marker, the idea of substance in general, embodying 'only a Supposition of he knows not what support' of the sensible qualities 'commonly called Accidents'. The corpuscularian hypothesis that colour and weight inhere in 'the solid extended parts' leaves us with the problem of what solid extended substance is. For the unity of matter so defined remains mysterious to us. Here the question of the 'cause of the union'[25] of the qualities and powers of a body becomes entwined with the explanation of its physical or material unity: we do not know 'what the substance is of that solid thing . . . [i.e.] how the solid parts of Body are united, or cohere together to make Extension'. Corpuscularian explanations of cohesion by 'the external pressure of the Aether' fail to explain 'the cohesion of the parts of the Corpuscles of the Aether it self' (E II.xxiii.23: 30). It is evident that we lack a 'clear and distinct *Idea* of the *Substance* of Matter', and the same goes for 'the *Substance* of Spirit' (E II.xxiii.5: 298).[26]

I will not now try to map all the ramifications of Locke's theory of substance, but I would like to consider a late development of his argument which has been particularly associated with the view that for Locke 'substance' is a pure logical subject, unknowable in principle. After repeating that our ideas of the sorts of substances always include, together with ideas of qualities and powers, 'the confused *Idea* of *something* to which they belong, and in which they subsist', he commented:

and therefore when we speak of any sort of Substance, we say it is a *thing* having such or such Qualities, as body is a *thing* that is extended, figured, and capable of Motion; a Sprit a *thing* capable of thinking; and so Hardness, Friability, and Power to drawn Iron, we say, are Qualities to be found in a Loadstone. These, and the like fashions of speaking intimate, that the Substance is supposed always *something* besides the Extension, Figure, Solidity, Motion, Thinking, or other observable *Ideas*, though we know not what it is. (E II.xxiii.3: 297)

---

[25] Cf. E II.xxiii.6: 298: 'several Combinations of simple *Ideas*, co-existing in such, though unknown, Cause of their Union, as makes the whole subsist of itself.'

[26] While E II.xxiii concentrates on the point that the materialists are therefore no better off than immaterialists, the argument is consonant with the obverse point, notoriously made at E IV.iii.6.

Locke was here bringing his explanation of the substance–accident relationship to bear on language. To put the same point another way, he was
appealing to language in support of his explanation. The existence of the
distinction in language between things and their qualities, and in particular
the existence of primitive noun-predicates whose definitions reflect that
distinction, is taken to constitute an implicit confession of our ignorance of
what is really there behind the 'observable' qualities and powers: in other
words, ignorance of its real nature or essence.

I think that the difficulty that many commentators have had in reading
Locke in this way stems largely from the thought that he *must* have
realized that, even if (say) solidity had been the essence of matter, and we
knew it, 'matter' would still have been a noun-predicate definable as *thing
(or substance) which is solid*. If Locke is trying to explain primitive noun-
predicates and the logical primacy of the category of substance in terms of
our ignorance, it may be thought, he must surely have had in mind an
ignorance that is not merely contingent and remediable. Leibniz commented, 'If you distinguish two things in a substance—the attributes or
predicates, and their common subject—it is no wonder that you cannot
conceive anything special in this subject.' He accuses Locke of demanding
'a way of knowing which the object does not admit of' (Leibniz 1981: 218).
Does this, perhaps, say it all?[27]

Other passages in the *Essay*, however, make it clear that Locke proposed his epistemological explanation of the ontological category of substance with full acceptance of its implications: if we did know the true

---

[27] Bennett claims (in Bennett 1988: 68) that his 'interpretation of Locke's "substratum" texts
is exactly the same as Leibniz's', but Leibniz's remarks, unlike Bennett's, are consonant with his
understanding the disagreement to be over the question whether we have 'clear and distinct
notions' of body and spirit in a Cartesian sense: i.e. knowledge of their essences. To see this, just
suppose that the present interpretation of Locke's thesis is correct, and that Leibniz so understood Locke. To present his rival explanation of substance–attribute logic Leibniz would have
needed to claim that the subject–predicate form of definitions is merely formal, reflecting, not
ignorance of anything, but the possibility of abstracting the formal concept of substance from
our idea of any particular substance. This formal concept is not an obscure and confused thought
of something behind observable qualities, but is clear and distinct in that it can be employed in
abstract metaphysical demonstrations ('Yet this conception of substance, for all its apparent
thinness, is less empty and sterile than it is thought to be. Several consequences arise from
it . . . of greatest importance to philosophy'). To complain that 'we have no clear idea of
substance in general' is therefore to fail to recognize the nature of the substance–attribute
abstraction ('you have already set aside all the attributes through which details could be
conceived') and to 'demand a way of knowing which the [purely formal] object does not admit
of'. This is pretty much how Leibniz does argue. It is true that we do not get accurate
and sympathetic exposition of Locke's claims (any more than we do of, say, his accounts of
'reflection' and identity, or his rejection of innate principles), but that does not mean that
Leibniz really took Locke explicitly to hold the strange theory that beneath *essence* there lies a
further and unknowable unknown called substance. It just means that Leibniz was a polemical
writer.

essence of any substance, our account of it would *not* take subject–predicate form. Since essence and substance are one and the same, there would be no call for a noun-predicate distinct from the adjectival noun which names the essence. For example, if Cartesian analysis of our idea of body could reveal that its essence is extension, the two words would be interchangeable: 'we can never mistake in putting the Essence of any thing for the Thing it self. Let us then in Discourse, put *Extension* for *Body*. . . . He that should say, that one Extension, by impulse, moves another extension, would, by the bare Expression, sufficiently shew the absurdity of such a Notion.' On the other hand, 'to say, an extended solid thing moves, or impels another, is all one, and as intelligible, as to say, *Body* moves, or impels' (E iii.vi.21: 450). The whole argument implies that the reason why 'extension' can stand as neither subject nor object of 'impels' is not because it is an adjectival or abstract noun, but because it is the wrong adjectival noun. If *x*-ness were what extension is not, the essence of body, then to say that one *x*-ness impelled another *would* make sense. The same argument, Locke continued, can be brought against the doctrine that reason is the essential property of man: 'no one will say, That Rationality is capable of Conversation, because it makes not the whole Essence, to which we give the Name Man'.

To understand how Locke could advance such an argument, and to recognize its historic force, we need to appreciate how he was neatly turning Cartesian logic against Cartesian pretensions to science. Descartes had himself warned against distinguishing between a substance and its principal attribute in a prominent passage: 'Thought and extension can be regarded as constituting the natures of intelligent substance and corporeal substance; they must then be considered as nothing else but thinking substance itself and extended substance itself—that is, as mind and body' (Descartes 1985: i. 215 [AT viiiA: 30–1]). The distinction between thought or extension and the thinking or extended substance is, on Descartes's account, a merely conceptual distinction, a piece of abstraction.[28] To think

---

[28] Despite what Descartes says here, it has been suggested (e.g. by Nicholas Jolley in Jolley 1984: 78–9) that Descartes might at least sometimes have thought of the substance as something over and above even its essential attributes, as when he wrote, 'We do not have immediate knowledge of substances . . . We know them only by perceiving certain forms or attributes which must inhere in something if they are to exist; and we call the thing in which they inhere a "substance"' (Descartes 1985: ii. 156 [AT vii: 222]; cf. ii. 114 [AT vii: 161]; ii. 124 [AT vii: 176]; Descartes 1976: xxv). But what Descartes seems to have in mind in these passages is something like the view advanced by Epicurus and Hobbes, that attributes in the general sense (i.e. attributes and modes in the technical Cartesian sense) are not things but, as it were, aspects of things, ways of conceiving of them. The substance cannot be known 'directly', if that means its being known otherwise than via an attribute, a way of conceiving of it. The substance is what can be conceived or known in all these ways: it cannot be reduced to them, but is not something

of the substance as something other or more than its nature is to make a confused division of the substance from itself. Yet this claim left an open-ing for those who rejected Descartes's dogmatic premiss to put his argu-ment in reverse. Since we *can* intelligibly make just those distinctions he condemned, between extension and the thing which is extended, thought and the thing which thinks, doesn't that show that they are not, after all, cases of dividing a substance from itself? On the contrary, it was the Cartesian tendency to employ 'extension' and 'matter' interchangeably which appeared to Locke to fall into nonsense. Malebranche, for example, argued that extension is a substance or 'being', since it is not a mode of anything as roundness is a mode of extension (Malebranche 1980: iii.ii.8). Locke remarked sniffily, very likely with Malebranche in mind as well as Descartes's argument against a vacuum, 'That *Body* and *Extension*, in common use, stand for two distinct *Ideas*, is plain to any one that will but reflect a little. For were their Signification precisely the same, it would be as proper, and as intelligible to say, *the Body of an Extension*, as *the Extension of a Body*; and yet there are those who find it necessary to confound their signification' (E iii.x.6: 493).[29]

Malebranche's argument appealed to the standard Cartesian claim, re-peated in their own terms by other corpuscularians such as Hobbes, that the ontological relationship between substance and accident, unintelligible on the Aristotelian account, becomes perspicuous when it is identified as the relation between determinable attribute and determinate mode. There is no mystery about the relation between extension and a particular shape, as there would be between the shape and the colour of a thing if we took colour to be irreducible to geometrical accidents (cf. Descartes 1985: i. 213–14 [AT viiiA: 29–30]).[30] In other words, substance and accidents form an intelligible unity on the corpuscularian account of matter. That is just what Locke was denying.

Malebranche stated that the crucial question is 'whether matter does not have still other attributes, different from extension', so that 'extension itself might not be essential to matter, and might presuppose something

---

beyond them. Its unity is grasped by grasping the unity of its attributes (i.e. the necessary connections between Cartesian attributes, and the attribute–mode relation), not by abstracting it from those attributes as if they were distinct from it (cf. Descartes 1976: xxii; Descartes 1985: i. 44–6 [AT x: 418–21]; i. 296–9 [AT viiiB: 347–51]; ii. 277 [AT ixA: 216]).

[29] In Draft A Locke chided Descartes for arbitrarily using the names 'extension', 'body', and 'space' for the same idea, but the significance of the grammatical difference between them was not there an issue. Cf. D i: 45–6.

[30] For the possibility of clearly conceiving how modes of quantity exist in objects, and the impossibility of so conceiving of colours, see Descartes 1985: i. 218 [AT viiiA: 34–5]; cf. Hobbes 1655: ii.viii.3).

else what would be its subject and principle'. He argued that the distinction between extension and its subject is a merely conceptual distinction employing the general idea of being:

And what is said of [something else's] being the *subject* and *principle* of extension is said gratuitously and without a clear conception of what is being said, i.e. without there being any idea of it other than a general idea from logic, like principle and subject. As a result a new *subject* and a new *principle* of this subject of extension could in turn be imagined, and so on to infinity, because the mind represents general ideas of subject and principle to itself as it pleases. (Malebranche 1980: III.ii.8)

The immediate context of this criticism was an attack on Aristotelian matter. Because Aristotelian matter is conceived of as *subject* to extension, it is thought of as a being which is distinct from extension. Yet nothing clear can be said about this merely 'logical entity' just because it is abstracted from any attributes through which it might be conceived. It was polemical misrepresentation on Malebranche's part to suggest that the Aristotelians envisaged matter's having definite attributes underlying extension, but the immediately relevant point is simply this: Malebranche's claim that the concept of a subject of extension is a 'disordered abstraction', an abuse of 'the vague idea of being in general', represented the subject–predicate sentence 'Matter is extended' as misleading, if not ill formed, as if the tautology ought rather to be expressed in the form of an identity, 'Matter is extension'. It is therefore easy to see why Locke, who *did* want to postulate an unknown essence underlying extension, should have insisted that 'Body is extended' is evidently *not* a gratuitous solecism, but the way we all have to talk, determined by the distinct ideas we have. It would appear, at any rate, to have been after his reading of Malebranche in the early 1680s that he introduced elements into his argument not present in the drafts of 1671: not only the direct appeals to language under discussion, but the term 'idea of substance in general', later explained to Stillingfleet as 'the general idea of something, or being' (W IV: 19).[31]

Another Cartesian argument concerned with the alleged mistake of dividing a substance from itself had been advanced in the Port Royal *Logic*. In their explanation of predication and nominalization, its authors distinguished three kinds of objects of thought: things, modified things, and modes of things. The full theory need not concern us, but a part of it was that primitive noun-predicates directly signify things, adjectives directly signify modified things (or things as modified), while adjectival or 'ab-

---

[31] The notion of substance was linked with the ideas (or idea) of 'Entity Being Something Existing' in Draft A (D I: 19–20), but that argument, dropped in Draft B, had quite a different form, turning on the claim that an idea of being cannot be separated from the ideas of particular sensible qualities and powers.

stract' nouns directly signify modes. They then denounced the practice of employing 'abstract' forms of primitive noun-predicates, *humanitas* from *homo*, *animalitas* from *animal*, and so forth. It arises, they argued, because we generally know and name things through their modifications, as modified things, so that we become accustomed to dividing our ideas of them into subject and mode (as we might distinguish, in our idea of a ball, the idea of a body from the idea of its roundness). The habit once acquired, *homo* comes often to be 'considered as the subject of humanity, *habens humanitatem*, and so to be a modified thing'. This mistake treats 'the essential attribute, which is the thing itself', as a mode, and as 'in a subject'. Hence the Scholastic solecisms 'humanitas', 'corporeitas', and 'ratio'. 'Reason' may seem an odd member of this list, but is clear enough why a Cartesian should include it, and that 'extension' would have the same right to be there (Arnauld and Nicole 1965: i.ii).

The Port Royal argument differs from Malebranche's in an interesting way. Although both deplore the division of a substance from its essence, i.e. from itself, Malebranche seems to have regretted the misleading character of primitive noun-predicates, and to have favoured the abstract noun 'extension' over 'matter', whereas Arnauld and Nicole took the reverse view. For them, the proper role of primitive noun-predicates is to name substantial things, and of abstract nouns to name modes. Locke's response to the issue is also interesting. On the one hand, he held not just that some, but that all, substantial things are known *qua* 'modified things', so that the division of our ideas of them into subject and mode (in Arnauld's sense of 'mode') is always legitimate. In effect he was suggesting that it would never occur to us to divide a substance from its true essence, if ever we had knowledge of such a thing. The terms 'extension' and 'reason' are on his view, of course, entirely legitimate, and their legitimacy demonstrates that they are not true essences. On the other hand, he followed Arnauld in recognizing the illegitimacy of such abstract terms as are created by attempting to renominalize a primitive noun-predicate. His explanation of that illegitimacy, however, given in the fascinating, neglected chapter 'Of Abstract and Concrete Terms', is quite the opposite of Arnauld's and hinges on the bold claim that the proper function of abstract terms is to name known essences. Just because we know the mind-dependent real essences of non-substances, ordinary language abounds with such words as 'whiteness', 'justice', and 'equality'. On the other hand, our not ordinarily employing such terms as 'animalness' or 'manness' constitutes 'the confession of all Mankind, that they have no *Ideas* of the real Essences of Substances . . . And indeed, it was only the Doctrine of *substantial Forms*, and the confidence of mistaken Pretenders to a knowledge that they had not, which first coined, and then introduced *Animalitas*, and *Humanitas*, and the like' (E III.viii.2: 475).

Locke's logico-linguistic arguments, then, arose naturally and plausibly enough in the context of Aristotelian and Cartesian logic as an ingenious way of advancing his kind of scepticism about essences. Leibniz's criticisms raised no new issues. Nor was the Lockean doctrine a passing aberration. It made a deep impression on much eighteenth-century logic and permanently influenced the course of philosophy.[32] Kant himself drew on it, arguing *both* (with Locke) that the possibility of dividing subject from attribute indicates that the latter does not constitute the ultimate nature of the former, *and* (with Malebranche and Leibniz) that we can in principle continue dividing subject from attribute indefinitely.

Pure reason demands that for every predicate of a thing we should look for its appropriate subject, and for this, which is necessarily in turn only a predicate, its subject and so on to infinity (or as far as we can reach). But it follows from this that nothing which we can reach ought to be taken as a final subject, and that the substantial itself could never be thought by our understanding, however deeply it penetrated, and even if the whole of nature were disclosed to it. (Kant 1783: sect. 46)

By means of the premiss that we could always legitimately generate the concept of an underlying subject, *however much we knew*, Kant turned Locke's idea of substance in general into something he never intended, the pure concept of a logical subject which exists in us solely as an intimation of a 'thing in itself' which is in principle unknowable. For later idealists, it became an intimation of the Absolute, the ultimate subject of all predication.

III. CONCLUSION

To stress Locke's influence on later philosophy—even on Kant—is not quite the same as to establish his excellence. The standard English estimation of the greatest English philosopher is perhaps illustrated by the comment, made in a public discussion of his philosophy in which I recently took part, that no other philosopher 'has had a greater influence in proportion to his merits'. Such faint praise, I feel, is entirely inappropriate. That examination of Locke's arguments in relation to their context which reveals their meaning and point also reveals the theoretical ingenuity, quality of judgement, and pertinacity in the search for consistency and compre-

---

[32] A notable example of a Lockean treatment of substance in logical theory was in William Duncan's popular *Elements of Logic* (Duncan 1748).

hensiveness which is characteristic of the very greatest philosophers—all of whom have used and responded to the tradition within which they have worked. The question no doubt arises whether Locke's contributions to seventeenth-century debates, despite their high quality, are irremediably dated. Speaking as an unregenerate realist, I would suggest that philosophical thought is now in dire need of the rich context of recognized explicanda and suggestive (if, just as they stand, untenable) explanations supplied by the *Essay*.

The present imperfect sketch of the skeleton of Locke's general philosophy has left out a number of important bones, if not whole limbs. I hope, nevertheless, that it will be seen how its two halves, one centred on the mind of the knower, the other on the objects of knowledge, fit together and presuppose each other. Both are structured round two related divisions. The first division is between, on the one hand, a priori, abstract science concerned with ideal, constructed objects and, on the other hand, enquiry into the real world of naturally unitary, given objects, enquiry which cannot for us achieve the status of 'science'. The second division is a division of levels between, on the one hand, the level of coarse experiential or pre-theoretical knowledge of natural things and, on the other hand, the level of speculative hypothesis or theory about the ultimate nature of those things. This second division is presupposed in Locke's conception of the authority and limitations of sensitive knowledge. It also corresponds to his distinction between the nominal and the real essences of substances, the former constituting the objects of natural history, the latter, the unattainable objects of natural science.

It is easy to assume that this epistemology is utterly outdated, partly because the barriers Locke perceived to lie in the way of natural science seem to have been bypassed, partly because his perception of them was in any case based on a misguided geometrical ideal of what a science should be, and partly just because we hear so much didactic rhetoric from relativistic conceptualists against both divisions, between the a priori and the empirical and between experience and theory (not to speak of foundations of knowledge), that it is easy to assume that there must be something wrong with them. How could so many, so voluble, so confident writers be completely wrong?

Now I do not suppose that Locke's conception of 'sensitive knowledge', neatly hingeing as it does on a purely causal understanding of the relation between sign and significatum, satisfactorily defines the scope of perceptual knowledge. It leaves us, implausibly and incoherently, with no more than perceptual knowledge of a world of powers. Nor do I find tenable the conception of infallible knowledge-delivering faculties which Locke took over, in common with other philosophers of his time, from the ancient debates over the existence of criteria of truth. But I do suppose that, unless the senses naturally and normally presented the world to us at a conscious level, and we naturally and normally accepted their deliverances, we would have no knowledge at all; and I am no more impressed than most opticians by the curious modern thought that what we see or otherwise perceive by the senses is a direct function of our theories, scientific or 'folk'. Moreover, we need to recognize that the unfashionable notion of 'evidence', purged of its implications of infallibility, still has valuable work to do in characterizing that central and primary kind of knowledge, typified by ordinary perceptual knowledge, which we possess when belief is engendered in circumstances of full awareness of its source and basis. In the context of perception we normally not only acquire beliefs, but do so in such a way that there is no mystery to us how and why we have come to have just those beliefs. We believe what the senses make evident to us. Without an understanding of 'evidence' in this sense, we shall never achieve a satisfactory philosophical account of what knowledge is. Fortunately it looks as if philosophers will be nudged in this direction by psychology, which has begun to take a fresh interest in the role of consciousness in cognition.

Furthermore, while I do not suppose that Locke's distinction between constructed modes and natural substances satisfactorily captures and explains the undoubted difference between geometry or political theory on the one hand and chemistry or biology on the other, his assumption does seem right that a horse is a naturally unified thing as a gallop or a procession is not, and that this is connected with the role of primitive noun-predicates in our language. For such predicates give names to natural, material individuals whose individuality is prior to their individuation by us or by 'our concepts'. I do not accept Locke's claim that the role of such noun-predicates serves as a confession of our ignorance of natural essences, but at least one feature of that claim strikes me as extremely suggestive. The New Philosophy tore traditional ontology and logic apart just because it proposed that science requires knowledge, not of the essences of those material objects which natural language treats as the fundamental objects of predication, horses, oak trees, and the like, but of the essence of such an abstract or hypothetical entity as corpuscularian matter. Most philosophers felt the need to adapt the notion of substance to fit the new physics. Consequently the theory of substance tended to lose its direct connection with the logic of natural language, while the metaphysics or ontology of science remained to an extent trammelled with inappropriate logical baggage. Locke, on the other hand, kept his explanation of the category of substance to the level which is relevant to an understanding of natural language: not the level at which reality might become fully intelligible to us, but the level at which it actually impinges on us in experience.

I could go on, but my point is simply that Locke is one of the great dead from whom, for all the differences, philosophers still have much to learn. He knew where he was going and he argued and theorized in an informed, intelligent, ingenious and powerful way about issues which have long been unfashionable, and to which we should return.

II

LOCKE AND THE ISSUE OVER INNATENESS

MARGARET ATHERTON

EMPIRICISM is a position often linked with the rejection of innate ideas. Indeed, not believing in the possibility of innate ideas is sometimes taken to be a defining characteristic of an empiricist: an empiricist is one who believes that all knowledge comes from experience and, hence, rejects innate ideas. John Locke is a key figure in the development of empiricism because he believed that the mind is a blank tablet on which experience writes, and, for that reason, argued against the possibility of innate ideas and principles. Although this account of Locke's role in the development of empiricism is a familiar one,[1] it has disguised rather than uncovered the impulses that led to Locke's empiricism. It is true that lately the nature of Locke's empiricism has been recognized to be such a clouded issue that it is sometimes thought better not to call him an empiricist at all. But this heroic step will not be necessary if we can be a little clearer about the actual nature of Locke's arguments. For the standard view gets the order of Locke's argument wrong in suggesting that his rejection of innateness is a consequence of his empiricism. In fact, Locke's demonstration of where our ideas come from depends upon his rejection of the possibility of innateness, which, in turn, stems from a picture of what mentality is like and what mental states consist in.

The interpretation of Locke that I am calling the *standard view*, the view that takes Locke's rejection of innateness to follow from his adoption of

From *How Many Questions? Essays in Honor of Sidney Morgenbesser* (Indianapolis: Hackett, 1983), 223–42.

[1] What I am trying to present here is a kind of 'common knowledge' picture of Locke and his relationship to empiricism. This is the version of Locke that has entered the psychological literature, for example, and the version that has informed the view of empiricism in the contemporary debate on innateness in the work of Noam Chomsky and Jerrold J. Katz and others; see e.g. Chomsky 1965; Chomsky 1966; Chomsky 1968; Chomsky 1975; Katz 1966; Chomsky and Katz 1975. An excellent bibliography of contemporary work about innateness can be found in Stich 1975.

empiricism, supposes his empiricism to be constituted by a set of basic commitments about the origin of ideas. On this sort of account, empiricists are held to be committed to a highly economical theory of the structure of the mind. They are thought to believe that a mind is endowed only with simple combinatorial networks, and so to reject explanations of mental phenomena that would suggest that it possesses any richer kinds of mental structure. On this version of Locke's programme, the most important feature of his empiricism is his claim that the furniture of the mind consists in a stock of simple ideas from which the rest, the complex ideas, are constructed by means of a few principles of association. His line of reasoning with respect to innateness is thought to be that, since he has shown that all our ideas are either simple or built out of simples and since this construction can be accomplished without any appeal to innate ideas, there will be no reason to suppose that there are any. So conceived, Locke's attack on innateness is thought to be open to several counterarguments. Defenders of innateness claim that Locke's rejection of innate ideas and principles depends upon the success of his own constructive programme, but that his programme does not in and of itself provide sufficient reason to reject innateness. For, even if Locke's programme were successful, it too must depend upon innate principles, inasmuch as the combinatorial rules by means of which complex ideas are put together from simple ideas amount to innate principles. The success of such a programme would not show that all our knowledge can be acquired without innateness. Empiricists like Locke are not really opposed to innateness at all, it is said; they just have a prejudice in favour of simpler as opposed to richer mental processes. And, the argument continues, Locke's programme is not actually successful. He could claim to have succeeded only if he had really shown that any complex idea has been constructed in the appropriate manner. But since Locke has not actually considered all ideas, it is possible that someone could produce an example of an idea we have, but could not have acquired as a construction out of simple ideas. That is, this sort of argument places the burden of proof on Locke. Locke is thought to be putting forward a rival theory to one that includes innateness, which he takes to be preferable because it is simpler and just as powerful. But this approach to Locke's views on innateness presupposes that a theory with innateness will be justified so long as there is no successful rival. If an 'empiricist' theory, one that constructs ideas from simples by associative principles, can't do the job, then there must be innate ideas or principles.

All these arguments against Locke, however, rely on an approach to what divides empiricists from rationalists which is not particularly helpful in understanding Locke. In the end the arguments encouraged by such an approach get the relationships among Locke's claims quite wrong. It is not in the least necessary for Locke to develop a successful or a complete programme of constructing complex ideas, for his arguments against innate ideas or principles to hold. His arguments against innateness are not only independent of his own or any other constructive programme; they in no sense reflect a predilection for the metaphysical economy of associative networks. Instead, Locke was worried about quite different issues, issues which more readily reflect difficulties in the theories appealing to innateness he would have been familiar with, such as Descartes's.

Locke did not, after all, begin his *Essay* by laying out his views on simple and complex ideas. Instead, he began with an extended attack on innate ideas and principles. But these arguments in Book I against innateness have frequently received short shrift. Locke is often accused of attacking a straw man and of failing to do justice to any interesting version of innateness.[2] Such charges, however, are based on a misunderstanding of the nature and scope of Locke's arguments. Locke talks a great deal about what is said to be a very naïve version of the innateness claim, namely, that innate knowledge is knowledge we are born with, in the sense that we are born consciously apprehending and assenting to such knowledge. And since theories of innateness, typically, are not intended to make this naïve and indeed absurd claim, it is supposed that Locke's arguments fail to touch on any interesting version of innateness (see e.g. Adams 1975; Edgley 1970). Theories of innateness generally are committed to a much weaker claim: that innate ideas or principles are present tacitly, or as dispositions or capacities. Even when it is recognized that Locke does seem inclined to reject this dispositional version of innateness as well, his rejection is not taken seriously, because Locke himself makes claims about capacities and faculties. To put the Book I arguments in proper perspective, however, requires that Locke's enterprise there be understood as a demonstration that theories of innateness are either unintelligible or, if intelligible, obviously false or trivially true.[3] He produces the 'naïve' version as an example of an innateness claim that succeeds in being intelligible, but is clearly false, while those theories making reference to capacities which he finds intelligible are, he argues, trivial as theories of innateness.

The argument Locke proposes to discuss is one that he says is 'commonly taken for granted'. It claims that there are certain practical and speculative principles to which all persons give assent, and says that this

---

[2] Many of these arguments occur in the literature cited above. The contemporary complaints about Locke, in some cases, echo earlier ones. Thomas Webb, writing in the middle of the 19th cent., reports that Cousin regarded Locke's polemic as a 'mere chimera', Coleridge said he was attacking a 'man of straw', and Hamilton considered Locke to have been led astray by an 'ignis fatuus' (Webb 1857).

[3] Nelson Goodman calls attention to this reading of Locke's arguments in Goodman 1967.

universal assent would be too great a coincidence except on the assumption that the principles are innate (E I.ii.2: 49). Locke points out that this argument is unconvincing in and of itself because universal assent would not imply innateness unless there were no other means by which such assent could be gained. But the real flaw in the argument, as Locke sees it, is that there are no principles to which everyone gives assent. This is a serious flaw, not just because the absence of universal assent constitutes a lack of evidence for innateness. Locke's argument is that someone who claims there are principles that everyone is born knowing is in fact committed to claiming there is universal assent to these principles. For to call these principles *innate* is precisely to say they are part of the equipment we are born with. And to call these principles innate *knowledge* is to say the principles we are born with are known to us. If they are known to us, we are aware of them, and in being aware of them, will have perceived their truth and have assented to them. Locke says: 'If therefore these two Propositions, *Whatsoever is, is*; and *It is impossible for the same Thing to be, and not to be*, are by Nature imprinted, Children cannot be ignorant of them: Infants, and all that have Souls must necessarily have them in their Understandings, know the Truth of them, and assent' (E I.ii.5: 51). What Locke is saying is that the claim that people, by virtue of their native endowment, from birth all assent to innate principles is a false claim which nativists (possibly unbeknownst to themselves) are committed to making.

So stated, Locke's argument escapes the charge that he is attacking a straw man, but rests instead on a premiss that has been considered highly implausible. For this argument of Locke's now requires the claim that if we were born with innate knowledge, we would be born conscious of this knowledge. It seems to insist that if we want to say that someone knows something, we must be willing to say that that person is in a state of consciously knowing that something. His reason for making such a claim is that it seems nonsensical 'to say, that there are Truths imprinted on the Soul, which it perceives or understands not; imprinting, if it signify any thing, being nothing else, but the making certain Truths to be perceived. For to imprint any thing on the Mind without the Mind's perceiving it, seems to me hardly intelligible' (E I.ii.5: 49–50). So Locke's reason for rejecting innate ideas rests on a conviction that having ideas requires that we be conscious of them.

That Locke's attitudes with respect to innateness depend so heavily on his perception of a strong connection between 'being in the mind' and 'being in consciousness' has sometimes been overlooked, in part perhaps because such a view seems to be quite unnaturally restrictive. Jonathan Barnes, for example, wants to save Locke from the consequences of saying that the only ideas or propositions people can be said to have in their minds are those they are conscious of by suggesting that Locke never intended to make such a claim. 'Locke's language is careless,' he says, 'but all he requires, and all he means to maintain is that being "in the mind" consists in, or at least entails, being believed: innate principles are innately *believed*' (Barnes 1972: 200). But Locke's language is not careless, if he would not have accepted any account of believing that did not tie it closely to conscious episodes of entertaining and consenting. Locke would certainly reject an account of believing that says that we believe a proposition if we are disposed to act as if it were true, whether or not we had ever consciously considered such a proposition. His argument, for example, which occurs in several places (e.g. E i.ii.23: 61) that young children know 'that sweet is not bitter' before they know 'that it is impossible for the same thing to be and not to be' depends upon the assumption that we know or believe only ideas we find in our minds and would be nonsense if Locke had any inclination to allow that we can be said to believe a proposition if we merely act as if it were true. Nor does it seem that Locke would be willing to attribute to people as beliefs propositions they *would* assent to, when such propositions were presented to them. His discussion of the possible innateness of self-evident propositions makes clear that he considers it quite empty to claim that a person has implicit knowledge of a self-evident proposition before that proposition has been consciously considered. He says: 'This cannot be deny'd, that Men grow first acquainted with many of these self-evident Truths, upon their being proposed: But it is clear, that whosoever does so, finds in himself, that he then begins to know a Proposition which he knew not before; and which from thenceforth he never questions: not because it was innate; but, because the consideration of the Nature of the things contained in those Words, would not suffer him to think otherwise, now, or whensoever he is brought to reflect on them' (E i.ii.21: 59). It seems reasonable to conclude from this that Locke would not want to say that a person has actually come to believe a proposition, whether self-evident or very easy to reason to, until such time as it has been consciously considered.

Locke, however, does not need to be saved from what many consider to be the most serious consequence of linking what is in the mind with what is being consciously entertained, for he is not committed to the claim that only those beliefs can be attributed to people that they happen to be consciously considering at a particular moment. In discussing what he calls 'habitual knowledge', Locke specifically rules this out (E iv.i.8: 528). What he does do is develop an account of habitual knowledge which maintains the connection between being in mind and being in consciousness. He makes clear that habitual knowledge of propositions we have once come to believe and hence assent to upon presentation, is a species of memory. The only sort of beliefs, moreover, Locke is willing to say a person has when not conscious of them are memories, beliefs that have at one time been consciously considered. He lays strict constraints on what it means to continue to attribute these propositions to a person when they are not thought of. He says:

But our *Ideas* being nothing, but actual Perceptions in the Mind, which cease to be anything, when there is no perception of them, this *laying up* of our Ideas in the Repository of the Memory, signifies no more but this, that the Mind has a Power, in many cases, to revive Perceptions, which it once had with the additional Perception annexed to them, that it has had them before. And in this Sense it is, that our *Ideas* are said to be in our Memories, when indeed, they are actually no where, but only there is an ability in the Mind, when it will, to revive them again. (E II.x.2: 150)

A memory is literally 'in the mind' just when we are conscious of it; otherwise, we have only an ability to think of it again. On the basis of this ability we continue to attribute a belief in a proposition to a person who is not thinking of it, but it is a confusion to suppose that this means that the memory is stored somewhere, in propositional form.

Locke's treatment of memory, therefore, is consistent with an identification of being in the mind and being consciously in the mind. The only sorts of thing that can literally be in the *mind* are things we think of as mental, ideas or propositions, and they must be in the mind through our being conscious of them. Something of which we are not conscious, like a memory we are not remembering, is in the mind only in a derivative sense. Since Locke is opposed to the suggestion that there could be anything ideational or propositional in the mind unless it is being consciously thought, memories are mental only in the sense that they can be linked with episodes of conscious thought. What is unconscious is not something mental at all, but only an ability or power.

Locke insists, therefore, that an innate idea could only be an idea we are conscious of from birth, because be thinks it makes no sense to suppose someone could have an idea but have it unconsciously. As his discussion of memory makes clear, Locke thinks that something with the characteristics of an idea gets into a mind only by being perceived, that is, when we are sensible or aware of it. He says: '*To ask at what time a Man has first any* Ideas is to ask, when he begins to perceive; having Ideas and Perception being one and the same thing' (E II.i.9: 108). An idea, for Locke, just is a way of perceiving; so to have an idea is to perceive in some manner or other. Ideas, that is, have a specific content. Having an idea of water is different from having one of H_2O or having one of a colourless liquid or having one of something to drink. These ideas differ one from another because each is a different kind of awareness. The idea that a person has is the one that person is aware of, and if we want to know what kinds of ideas a mind can have, the answer will be in terms of the kinds of things it can be aware of. For something with the particular content characteristic of ideas comes about through awareness of that content. So it is nonsensical to attribute ideas to minds unless those minds are sensible of them. Locke says: 'Our being sensible of it is not necessary to anything but to our thoughts; and to them it is, and to them it will always be necessary, till we can think without being conscious of it' (E II.i.10: 109). The claim that there are ideas we are born with can be made intelligible as a claim that there are ideas we are conscious of from birth, but, in this form, is clearly false. Locke's argument with respect to innateness lays the burden of proof on the proponent of innate ideas to show in what sense such ideas can belong to minds who are not having—that is, being aware of—them.

Locke's discussion of memory also shows, however, that he is willing to talk of a capacity or faculty of memory, in addition to episodes of remembering. Advocates of innateness have argued that innate ideas are to be thought of as no more than tendencies or dispositions, in the way diseases run in families, or as veins in a block of marble, predisposing the shape of the statue to come.[4] And since Locke is prepared to talk about any number of mental capacities, in addition to memory, it is argued that his theory does not really differ from that of nativists (Bracken 1967).[5] This claim, however, overlooks an important aspect of Locke's approach. His argument is addressed to the claim that mental capacities can be *explained* in terms of innate ideas or principles. Explanations of capacities are to be distinguished, he points out, from the considerably less interesting claim that the mind has capacities or tendencies. If, by calling a principle innate, all we mean is that we are capable of recognizing that it is true, then this will fail to distinguish innate principles from any principle whose truth we have recognized, since we are clearly capable of recognizing all such principles as true. He says: 'So that if the Capacity of knowing be the natural Impression contended for, all the Truths a Man ever comes to know, will, by this Account, be, every one of them, innate; and this great Point will amount to no more, but only to a very improper way of speaking; which whilst it pretends to assert the contrary, says nothing different from those,

---

[4] This approach is to be found among supporters of innate ideas in Locke's own era, such as Descartes (Descartes 1985: I. 294–311) and Leibniz (Leibniz 1981), as well as in Chomsky 1968.

[5] It is also common in contemporary claims about innateness to suppose there is no real issue about innateness, since both nativists and empiricists admit the existence of dispositions and tendencies. See Searle 1973.

who deny innate Principles' (E I.ii.5: 50). To say that we have a capacity and to say that we have an innate capacity is to say one and the same thing, in the sense that we are and have been from birth capable of doing whatever we end up doing. Since no one could possibly want to deny this, it cannot be that, simply by talking about capacities, Locke has ended up committing himself to innateness.

Someone who says that innate ideas are present as dispositions is typically intending to say more than that humans have the capacity to perform in one way or another. To identify someone as having abilities or psychological dispositions is, according to a recent claim of Chomsky's 'merely a promissory note' (Chomsky 1980: 48). Talking about innate knowledge is a way of cashing in on the promissory note. Capacities are to be explained by referring to ideas or propositions, the innate knowledge of which is supposed to account for the capacity. It is this move, which assumes that a capacity can be explained by talk of the possession of unconscious knowledge, to which Locke takes exception. In the same way that he objected to explaining a capacity to remember in terms of the possession of the proposition that is to be remembered, Locke wants to reject, for example, attempts to explain a capacity to assent to self-evident propositions by attributing a knowledge of some such proposition as 'whatever is, is'. Since having an idea is an act of awareness, ideas are not available to explain capacities unless they are ideas we are aware of. Locke is not objecting to claims that humans are predisposed toward some states or behaviours and not others. He says he sees nothing wrong with saying that humans have a natural tendency to seek happiness and avoid misery, so long as these tendencies are not understood to be represented in the form of ideas:

I deny not, [he says] that there are natural tendencies imprinted on the Minds of Men; and that, from the very first instances of Sense and Perception there are some things, that are grateful, and others unwelcome to them; some things that they incline to, and others that they fly: But this makes nothing for innate Characters on the Mind, which are to be the Principles of Knowledge, regulating our Practice. (E I.iii.3: 67)

Locke's arguments are addressed only to theories that try to account for our predispositions and tendencies in mentalistic terms, that is, in terms of ideas and principles present to the mind, but unconsciously. Locke is objecting to attempts, on the level of explanation, to use words like 'idea', which make sense, he thinks, only on the conscious level.

Locke's discussion of the reality of simple ideas (E II.xxx: 372–4) makes it especially clear that his objection is to attempts to explain capacities in terms of knowledge of ideas and principles, and not to the claim that our mental states are highly determined by an inborn constitution. What he says there suggests that he believes we are 'wired up' by nature to have simple ideas in the way that we do. He argues that we are entitled to take simple ideas as reflective of real qualities in nature just because such ideas are nothing more than the effects of the powers of bodies to work changes in us of which we can be sensible.

> But though Whiteness and Coldness are no more in Snow, than Pain is; yet those *Ideas* of Whiteness, and Coldness, Pain, etc., being in us the Effects of Powers in Things, without us, ordained by our Maker, to produce in us such Sensations; they are real *Ideas* in us, whereby we distinguish the Qualities, that are really in things themselves. (E II.xxx.2: 372)

But in arguing that our simple ideas are effects in us whose nature is in part due to the way our inner constitution is ordained by God, Locke is not committing himself to the sort of innateness claim he has argued against. This would be the case only if he had wanted to argue that our ability to, for example, receive colour ideas ought to be explained in terms of an innate knowledge of colour categories. But Locke's actual position is that we are ignorant of the nature of the mechanism by means of which outside events result in sensations in us.[6]

Locke therefore has no objection to talk of capacities dependent upon an inborn constitution. But he would certainly deny that in either case he is making a concession that commits him to the use of innate ideas or principles. For he will not accept any account of capacities or any description of an inborn constitution that says that what we are born with is 'in our minds' or has ideational content. This does not mean that Locke thinks that capacities or dispositions don't require further explanation. But the conclusion he wants to draw about these capacities has to do with limitations on the kinds of explanations available to us. Here, as in many other places, Locke's attitude is one of agnosticism. He thinks that we simply do not always know what accounts for our mental capacities. His quarrel with the nativist stems from the fact that the nativist gives an explanation in terms of innate ideas on occasions when Locke thinks it is appropriate to

---

[6] Locke, therefore, would not be inclined to accept a way Hume proposes of understanding the innateness controversy. Hume says that since we show ideas are not innate by showing they are derived from impressions and since impressions are natural and copied from nothing else, then we can say that all impressions are innate and no ideas are innate (Hume 1739–40: I.i.2; Hume 1748: II). Hume's way of talking about the issue presupposes that the way to go about showing whether or not an idea is innate is just to find out whether it can be learned. That Hume talks in this way has been cited by Jerry Fodor (Fodor 1981: 276) as a reason for saying that nativists differ from empiricists only in the kind of ideas they take to be innate. But to Locke, no one has any simple idea until he is conscious of it, so that which ideas are in our minds is a matter of our histories. That we are born with the capacity to become conscious of simple ideas does not single them out from any other idea we end up with.

give none, preferring to talk of 'something or other' underlying or accounting for some capacity.

It is true that if Locke indeed believed that our mental capacities amounted to a series of simple combinatorial principles, then there might be some justice to the charge that he, too, is committed to some kind of nativism. But Locke does not have any interest in showing that all complex ideas can be accounted for on the basis of a few principles of association. Although he introduced the phrase, 'association of ideas', into the literature, it was as a pejorative term, so that he could warn against associations made by custom as a source of prejudice. Locke's theory of the relation between simple and complex ideas is difficult to understand, but it does seem, at the very least, that he thinks complex ideas can be the result of several mental operations, which include combining, but also discerning and abstracting. What is clear, however, is that he is not rejecting innateness because he is committed to a simpler rival. Rather, having ruled out theories that appeal to innateness on grounds of unintelligibility, he is calling our attention to the explanatory power of mental operations of whose presence within us we can be aware. But though Locke thinks we can understand a good deal about our mental capacities by paying attention to the mental operations we find within ourselves, there is no reason to suppose that he would think that, by pursuing such a method, we ought to be able to offer an explanation for everything a nativist claims to be able to explain.

It is in fact the emphasis Locke places on the possibility of uncovering limitations on our knowledge that creates an important area of difference between his approach and that of someone like Descartes, who is committed to the use of innate ideas. Descartes thought there could be no knowledge at all unless we could know some things with certainty. Descartes also thought that whatever we learn from experience is probable only, and, therefore, that anything we know with certainty is unlearned and due to our faculty of knowing. On these sorts of grounds, Descartes supported claims about innateness. Locke, on the other hand, thought it must remain a question pending investigation whether or to what extent we can know anything with certainty (E i.i.5: 46). He is opposed to an approach that first claims there is some kind of knowledge we must have and then constructs hypotheses about what the faculties that deliver this knowledge must be like. Rather, Locke thinks the correct order of investigation is first to establish what our cognitive faculties are like and only then to go on to find out what we can and can't be said to know, using these faculties. Locke's demonstration that it is unintelligible to suppose that our faculties are endowed with innate knowledge constitutes one such investigation of the nature of our cognitive faculties. His further investigations into what we can or cannot know will make use of this demonstration to rule out the possibility of our having knowledge that could only have been acquired with the help of innate ideas or principles. Locke cannot be seen as putting forward his constructive programme as an independent piece of evidence against nativism or as a way of showing that he can do everything the nativist thinks needs doing. Rather, Locke is able to undertake his positive exploration of what our faculties can do on the assumption that one thing they can't do is have innate knowledge, and he is willing to accept as a consequence that there are some ideas we can't have. The arguments against innateness in Book I constitute a necessary first step in the development of Locke's theory.

It is a mistake, therefore, to see Locke as arguing for the non-existence of innate ideas from the success of his own constructive programme. For Locke has no commitment at all to showing that his account of how we construct our ideas describes a system that is just as powerful as that of the nativist, and he feels no need to say that he can explain whatever the nativist seeks to explain. His position is that explanations in terms of innate ideas or principles can be rejected out of hand on grounds of incoherence. This is because he believes there is no way to have such mental states as ideas or principles except through being aware of them, so that the mark of the mental is that mental states are conscious states. Thus, it is quite inappropriate to talk about anything having ideational content as existing in an unconscious form. If a capacity is to be explained by talking about such underlying ideas or principles, then, at the very least, we are owed an account of some alternative way, other than being aware of them, of 'having' these ideas or principles. Such an account, however, Locke thinks cannot be forthcoming.

Whether or not Locke intended his arguments to be directed against Descartes or against some other target, in fact they raise a serious problem for Descartes. Descartes is, of course, the *locus classicus* for the doctrine that mental states can be distinguished from physical states because mental states are transparent to their possessor. Consciousness for Descartes, as for Locke, is the distinguishing characteristic of thought. But, as Margaret Wilson points out (Wilson 1978: 164), in grounding knowledge in innate ideas, Descartes is acknowledging a 'hidden structure' to thought, a structure of ideas we have but are not aware of. Descartes is apparently driven to this inconsistency because he wants to hold both that the distinguishing feature of mentality is consciousness and that whatever is responsible for thought will itself be a kind of thought, rather than, for example, something physical. Locke avoids this inconsistency by rejecting the possibility of thoughts we have but are not aware of and adopts an agnostic rather than an explicitly dualistic attitude toward the nature of what it is that is responsible for thought.

Thus Locke's reasons for rejecting innateness cannot be understood as following in some direct manner from assumptions about an empiricist programme. They are independent of any account of how complex ideas are to be constructed out of simple ones. Nor are they focused on issues of metaphysical simplicity or economy. It might be appropriate to look at, say, the issue dividing Hume from Kant in that light, and to argue that what distinguishes Hume's associative principles from Kant's categories is the simplicity of the former. There is no reason, however, to identify Hume's position with Locke's. Locke's quarrel with an innateness theory such as Descartes's is over a different issue, although one that is central to any innateness claim: the issue of whether it is justifiable to give a description of the hidden structure underlying thought which identifies this structure as itself something mental, something that can be thought of as knowledge of ideas or principles. It is Locke's negative decision with respect to this issue that motivates the story he wants to tell about how ideas are constructed. Thus, Locke's empiricism, his account of how the ideas we have derive from experience, follows from his rejection of innate ideas, which, in turn, depends upon his theory of the nature of mentality.[7]

[7] I learned a lot about the issues with which this paper is concerned in a seminar Robert Schwartz and I taught with Sidney Morgenbesser on problems concerning the analysis of mental states. I would also like to thank David Rosenthal and Stephen Nathanson for their help with earlier versions.

III

LOCKE AND REPRESENTATIVE PERCEPTION

J. L. MACKIE

A NATURAL way to approach this topic would be first to enquire what view Locke held about perception, to go on to consider whether it counts as a representative theory, and finally whether it is defensible or not. But I prefer—and I believe it will be more economical—to reverse this order, and first outline what I think is a defensible theory of perception, then ask in what sense this is a representative theory, and only at the end discuss whether such a view can be plausibly ascribed to Locke.

In *Problems from Locke* (Mackie 1976) I distinguished two variants of the picture-original theory, one which made the pictures physically real objects somewhere inside the perceiver's head, the other which made them merely intentional objects, existing as the contents of states of awareness, and therefore literally mind-dependent. I also made, but perhaps did not sufficiently stress, a further distinction within the first alternative. One view would be that the alleged physically real pictures are contemplated and made the objects of an initial class of perceptual judgements, and that judgements about the material or external world are inferred from these by some explicit process of reasoning. The other would be that though physically real intermediates occur and play some important role in perception, they are not themselves normally taken as objects of perception, let alone as pictures representing some originals distinct from them, from which the existence and characters of the originals are to be inferred; that on the contrary ordinary perception is judgementally direct, that we make claims and form beliefs non-inferentially about how things outside our heads are. Of these two possible views involving physically real pictures, the first is so evidently false that we need pay no further attention to it, while the second is almost uncontroversially true. In my book I devoted some space to this second view, mainly in order to get clearer what might be meant by the claim that we see ordinary outside things directly; but I

From *Logic and Knowledge: Selected Papers*, i (Oxford: Clarendon Press, 1985), 214–24.

said there, and I would still maintain, that the important sort of representationalist or picture-original view is that which takes the pictures (perhaps Locke's 'ideas') to be intentional objects. It is this account that I am concerned to defend.

In this defence, the first and vital step is to show that there are such intentional objects. But this is surely undeniable. At the moment a large number of birds are twittering outside my window. There is a perfectly sensible question, 'How does it sound to me?' Of course, I can't answer this question adequately in words, but simply in hearing the birds I am aware of the answer: *that* is how it sounds to me. And this answer could hold unchanged even if there were in fact no birds, and I were hearing a tape-recording or having an hallucination. Or I put a bit of salt on my tongue: *that* is how it tastes to me. But the crucial case is that of visual perception; can I say equally lucidly, '*That* is how it looks to me'? One complication is that a more satisfactory verbal answer is now available: 'It looks to me as if there is a level floor covered with a grey carpet, several wooden chairs standing on it, and behind them bookshelves containing books of various shapes, sizes, colours, and so on.' This is, indeed, only a rough and far from adequate description: how it looks has far more detail in it than any verbal description can capture. Still, the important thing is that how it looks to me includes the recognition of persisting solid objects in a three-dimensional space. On the other hand, I can, with an effort, pick out 'how it looks to me' in another sense: I can concentrate on a purely visual presentation—a combination of variously coloured areas in a two-dimensional visual field. That is, I can distinguish an uninterpreted how-it-looks from an interpreted how-it-looks. But it is the interpreted how-it-looks that is really how it looks to me in all normal adult visual perception. Yet that it looks thus-and-so, even in the interpreted way, is one thing, that it is thus-and-so would be another. The intentional object is not an external object or state of affairs.

The second step in this defence is to insist that it is by virtue of my having these intentional objects that I perceive the outside world. But this, too, seems undeniable. Moreover, it is on the whole body of such perceptions that all my ordinary knowledge or belief about the material world rests, directly or indirectly.

This much, as I say, seems undeniable. But does it constitute or commit us to a representative theory in any interesting sense, to anything that direct realists have denied or would want to deny?

Does it entail that we do not see tables and chairs but only our ideas of tables and chairs? This unnatural way of speaking would be forced on us only if we assumed, quite unnecessarily, that to see *x* is to have a form of

awareness that informs us infallibly and completely about *x*. Or does it
entail that all we perceive directly or immediately is ideas or percepts or
sense-data, and that we perceive tables and chairs only mediately or indirectly? I cannot answer this question, because I find both this claim and its
opposite unclear: I am not sure what issues are being raised. We can and
must still say that even when we allow for these intentional objects perception is ordinarily judgmentally direct though causally mediated.

For this is in a way a causal theory. Its looking as it does to me now is a
causal product of how things are: outside objects act upon my sense organs
and so upon my brain; the antecedent condition of these is also causally
relevant; how it looks (or sounds, or tastes, etc.) to me is a result of this
interaction. To what extent causation enters into a correct analysis of our
concept of perception, or into the meaning of perception statements, is
more doubtful. It is plausible to take '*He* sees a chair' as implying that
there is a chair which is giving rise to his visual perception. But if I simply
say, while seeing it and because I see it, 'There is a chair over there', I may
well not be making any causal claim, even an implicit one. And 'I see a
chair' can be used as practically equivalent to this.

What is more important is that this account leaves room for the suggestion that our ideas, in the sense of these intentional objects, may either
resemble or fail to resemble the outside things. It looks to me as if there is
a level floor, chairs, shelves, books, that is to say, solid objects of certain
three-dimensional shapes and sizes arranged at various distances from me
in a three-dimensional and at least roughly Euclidean space. And perhaps
there are things with pretty much these positions and sizes and shapes. But
it also looks to me as if all these things had colours as intrinsic features of
their surfaces. And perhaps they do not. I don't mean that I may be getting
the colours a little bit wrong, as I may well be making small mistakes about
the shapes and sizes: I mean that the things may have no colours as I see
colours at all. No doubt, if one book looks red to me while another looks
blue, under standard illumination and in good conditions for seeing, this
will be because there is *some* intrinsic difference between their surfaces,
and we could use the adjective 'red' (or 'blue') to mean 'such as to look red
(or blue) to a standard observer in good conditions'. (Locke himself suggests something like this in E II.xxxii.14–16: 388–90.) But something which
is red or blue in this sense may well not have, intrinsically, any colour-as-
I-see-it. Thus the intentional object view leaves room for the question
whether our ideas are or are not resemblances of objective qualities, and
for Locke's distinction on this ground between primary and secondary
qualities, his claim that our ideas of primary qualities resemble those
qualities, while our ideas of secondary qualities do not resemble anything

intrinsic to the objects. My account is enough of a representative theory to leave room for Locke's way of drawing the primary/secondary quality distinction, whereas direct realism would either exclude the distinction or allow it to be drawn only in some other way.

(Admittedly it is controversial whether, as Locke thinks, we ordinarily take our ideas of secondary qualities to be such resemblances. On the one hand I find in myself a strong tendency to ascribe colours-as-I-see-them to the surfaces of things. On the other hand it is hard not to realize that colours-as-I-see-them depend somehow on illumination. Again, just where do we naïvely locate sounds-as-we-hear-them? And do I, even in my most naïve moments, really want to ascribe saltiness-as-I-taste-it to that white powder, the salt? That is to say, we might consider offering the Lockean distinction between primary and secondary qualities as an analysis of the conceptual scheme of not very sophisticated people, rather than as a correction of it. But this is a minor matter.)

A still more important question is whether this is a representative theory in the sense of being one which leaves room for scepticism about the external world as a whole, one which has what Jonathan Bennett calls a veil-of-perception problem built into it. Prima facie it is. For once we have distinguished its looking, sounding, tasting, etc. thus-and-so from its being thus-and-so, we have made it at least logically and conceptually possible that there is nothing which is, in any respect at all, as things look and sound and taste. Summing up all these elements that consist in how it looks, how it sounds, and so on as the contents of my experience, I can ask coherently whether there is anything at all which these contents resemble or even represent. In fact, several options are open here.[1] There is the common-sense realist view which draws no distinction between primary and secondary qualities, allowing not only shapes but also colours-as-we-see-them and the like to be resemblances of intrinsic qualities of things. There is the Lockean view which allows this for shapes, etc., but denies it for colours and the like. Again, there is a view which Bertrand Russell held at one time, in effect that such spatial qualities as shape are secondary qualities, that physical space is quite distinct from perceptual space; there is something which gives rise to our percepts, but it corresponds to them only structurally, not qualitatively in any respect. But also, it seems, there is the sceptical possibility: perhaps there is just my experience with its contents, its intentional objects, and nothing else at all.

It may be argued that this last suggestion is incoherent. 'Where is there

---

[1] In a marginal note at this point Mackie suggests adding a reference to 'the very naïve view which makes no distinction between content of experience and reality'.—Edd.

nothing else?' 'Outside us.' But 'outside' has meaning only if we accept the very thing we are supposed to be doubting. Or if we say, 'Perhaps there is just my experience with its contents' we are using a set of concepts which involves the identification and reidentification of myself as a subject of experience, and this makes sense only along with the concepts of a spatio-temporal world of persisting things which I can observe with some success, which again is the very thing we are supposed to be doubting. However, I do not find this argument cogent. From whatever source I have derived them or however I have constructed them, I have these concepts now. It is part of the contents of my experience that things seem to be, objectively, thus-and-so. Once I have also introduced the notion of the contents of my experience, of its looking thus-and-so, I can raise the question whether things are like this in a sense which is not automatically answered in the affirmative merely because they look like this. It is true that I cannot report the contents of my experience with any approach to adequacy except in terms which relate to a supposed material world. But it does not follow that I have to presuppose the objective existence of a material world in order to ask whether these contents really represent any such world, and so undermine this question itself.

The account of perception which I am defending has, therefore, some of the main characteristics of representative theories, including the one often thought to be fatal to them, that they leave room for sceptical doubts and a veil-of-perception problem, that they compel one to raise what is thought to be, once raised, the unanswerable question, 'How do we know that there is anything which our percepts resemble or represent?', or 'If all that we are directly acquainted with are ideas (or percepts, or contents of experience, or intentional objects), how can we ever break out of this circle so as to have even beliefs, let alone knowledge, of a real world?'

However, this supposedly unanswerable question can be answered. But in order to answer it we must split it into its two components, a problem of meaning and a problem of justification. The first problem is, 'How can we make meaningful claims about a reality other than our ideas, percepts, etc.?' The second is, 'Given that we can make such claims, how can we support them?'

Now it is clear that for anyone who adopts a verificationist theory of meaning these questions are not separable: what justified any claim would be what gave it its meaning, and, what is more serious, would wholly determine and restrict the meaning given. Since the ultimate verification of any claims I make about the material world must consist in how things look or feel or sound or taste or smell to me, the real meaning of those claims would also be that I should have just such-and-such contents of experience.

But this is only a further reason for not adopting a verificationist theory of meaning, which in any case has little initial plausibility. A plausible empiricist doctrine of meaning would say rather that the meanings of any claims we make must be built up somehow out of elements which figure within the contents of our experience, and this does not entail that what we meaningfully say must be wholly about actual or possible experiences.

It is obvious that if we think of the content of our experiences on the model of what I called an interpreted how-it-looks there is no real problem in the meaning part of the supposed veil of perception. If it looks to me as if there is a level floor, chairs, books, and so on, then this how-it-looks already includes the standard meanings of the material object language in which we make claims about the external world. But what if we attend rather to items of the form of an uninterpreted how-it-looks? This is important, because if we deny, as Locke denied, that we have innate ideas of space and time and substance and causation, we must suppose that at an early stage in our lives we started with experiences whose contents were only of the uninterpreted sort, and somehow developed the interpreted sort out of these. The plausible empiricist doctrine must be applicable also to these, though even if we deny innate ideas we need not deny that we have several innate perceptual propensities, tendencies to seek and pick out and concentrate on certain kinds of feature within the content of our experience. It would require detailed work in conceptual analysis to show how we might have built up the interpreted from the uninterpreted content, and it would require detailed work in genetic psychology to find how we have actually done so. But the main point, and the only one I can make here, is that there is no barrier in principle to this development. Even an uninterpreted how-it-looks is a cluster of features seen simply as being there. These features are not given *as* appearances, *as* mind-dependent, so there is no danger that claims given meaning in terms of them will be limited to what is purely phenomenal. The meaning part of the veil-of-perception problem is therefore soluble in principle, and there is no reason to doubt that by detailed work it can be solved in full.

The disposal of the problem of meaning brings the problem of justification into focus. If we can meaningfully claim that there is an objective material world which the contents of our experience represent, we can also meaningfully frame the suggestion that there may be no such world. Of course, this problem arises only in retrospect. We did not raise it in infancy and then construct a rational argument for the material spatio-temporal world. We just came automatically to have our ordinary view of the world by processes in which what we can roughly call imagination and innate propensities played a large part: no question of justification arose at that

time. But when it does arise, in retrospect, we can surely give and defend
the well-known answer that the broad outline hypothesis of the existence
of material things is well confirmed, by the success with which it explains
our having experiences with just such contents as our experiences do have.
Though we can find coherent formulations of, for example, Descartes's
suggestion that it may all be a dream, or of Berkeley's thesis that a more
powerful mind, rather than a material world, is responsible for those of our
experiences that we mark off as perceptions of real things, no such rival
hypotheses yield nearly so good an explanation of all the details of our
experience. An important part of these details is the way in which we can
develop, within our outline hypothesis, causal accounts of our perceptual
processes themselves.

If there is a defensible view of this sort, and it is in some interesting ways
a representative theory, we can turn to the question whether Locke held
any such view—in particular whether we can identify his 'ideas', in contexts where he is writing about perception, with intentional objects. I
would concede that this question does not admit of a conclusive answer.
Locke is too careless in his terminology and, perhaps surprisingly, too little
concerned to describe exactly what goes on when we perceive something,
to have committed himself firmly to any one view. Yet there are several
things that at least favour the proposed identification.

There was repeated controversy, in the century or so after Descartes, on
the question whether ideas should be taken as internal real objects of
perception and judgement or whether having ideas should be taken merely
as a synonym for perceiving. A key figure in this controversy is Arnauld.
Malebranche had argued that 'in order to the mind's perceiving any object,
it is absolutely necessary that the idea of that object be actually present to
it'; 'the immediate object of the mind, when it sees the sun, for example, is
not the sun, but something which is intimately united to the soul'. And
then, rejecting various other possible ways in which ideas can be actually
present to our minds, he concludes that it must be God's ideas that achieve
this. That is why 'we see all things in God'. But Arnauld criticizes this
whole approach, saying that ideas are not objects whose existence is distinct from their being perceived. They are rather modifications of our
minds, namely acts of perception: 'I take the *idea* of an object, and the
perception of an object, to be the same thing'.

Now John Yolton has pointed out, in a paper which he read recently in
Oxford (Yolton 1970b), that Locke not only had Arnauld's criticism of
Malebranche in his library, but marked his copy of it extensively and
apparently with approval. Locke seems both to have known Arnauld's
arguments and to have been inclined to agree with them. (Yolton mentions

this also in his introduction to the Everyman abridged edition of Locke's *Essay*: Yolton 1961: xxi–xxii.) And there are quite a number of passages in the *Essay* which seem to endorse Arnauld's view, especially if we read them in the light of this controversy. For example:

Whatever *Idea* is in the mind, is either an actual perception, or else, having been an actual perception, is so in the mind, that by the memory it can be made an actual perception again. (E I.iv.20: 97)
External Objects furnish the Mind with the Ideas *of sensible qualities*, which are all those different perceptions they produce in us. (E II.i.5: 106)
To ask, *at what time a Man has first any Ideas*, is to ask, when he begins to perceive; having *Ideas*, and Perception being the same thing. (E II.i.9: 108)
I conceive that *Ideas* in the Understanding, are coeval with *Sensation*; which is such an Impression or Motion, made in some part of the Body, as produces some Perception in the Understanding. (E II.i.23: 117)
If then external Objects be not united to our Minds, when they produce *Ideas* in it; and yet we perceive *these original Qualities* in such of them as singly fall under our Senses, 'tis evident, that some motion must be there continued by our Nerves, or animal Spirits, by some parts of our Bodies, to our Brains or the seat of Sensation, there to *produce in our Minds the particular* Ideas *we have of them*. (E II.viii.12: 136)

That is, Locke assumes that in sensory perception there will be some bodily modification, but the function of this is to produce a perception in the understanding (and this is the idea), not to be itself inspected or contemplated.

But our *Ideas* being nothing, but actual Perceptions in the Mind, which cease to be any thing, when there is no perception of them, this *laying up* of our *Ideas* in Repository of the Memory, signifies no more but this, that the Mind has a Power, in many cases, to revive Perceptions, which it has once had, with this additional Perception annexed to them, that it has had them before. (E II.x.2: 150)

This insistence that ideas do not actually exist as ideas in our memories except when they are being consciously recalled comes closer than any other passage I know of to committing Locke to denying that his ideas are physically real intermediates, say images, and hence to identifying them either with acts of perceiving or with the intentional objects of such acts.

... our *Ideas*, being nothing but bare Appearances or Perceptions in our Minds ... (E II.xxxii.1: 384)

It is true that these considerations might be taken to point in a different direction from that which I want. They might make us identify having an idea of a table, as this occurs when we are actually seeing a table, simply with perceiving the table, while the latter is itself construed in a direct realist way, with no representative factor present at all. But this is surely ruled out by all of Locke's talk about ideas sometimes resembling and sometimes failing to resemble something in the objects. The intentional object interpretation is the one which best accommodates both this way of speaking and the denial that ideas have any existence distinct from that of the act or process of perceiving.

There is at least one passage in which Locke tries explicitly to deal with the contrast between what I have called the interpreted how-it-looks and the uninterpreted how-it-looks. This is E II.ix.8–10: 145–7, where he discusses Molyneux's problem. The way he puts it is that '... *the Ideas we receive by sensation, are often* in grown People *alter'd by the Judgment*, without our taking notice of it'. When we have before us a globe of uniform colour, he says ' 'tis certain, that the *Idea* thereby imprinted in our Mind, is of a flat Circle variously shadow'd', but 'the Judgment presently'—that is, immediately—'alters the Appearances into their Causes' and 'frames to it self the perception of a convex Figure and an uniform Colour'. This remark seems to equate 'idea' with the uninterpreted how-it-looks, or perhaps even with some physical intermediate which is literally received, and to contrast this with the 'perception' produced by the judgement. But a page later Locke reverses this terminology, saying of the same sort of example that 'we take that for the Perception of our Sensation which is an *Idea* formed by our Judgment'. And a litttle later again he says ' 'tis not so strange, that our Mind should often change the *Idea* of its Sensation, into that of its Judgment, and make one serve only to excite the other, without our taking notice of it'.

This passage illustrates what is in any case abundantly shown elsewhere, that Locke has no precise terminology, and that it is therefore pointless to ask exactly what he means by, say, 'idea'. But what is more important is that it shows also that he was well aware of the threefold contrast between what is there, how it looks in the uninterpreted sense, and how it looks in the interpreted sense. Moreover, he knew that in ordinary sophisticated adult perception we are often not consciously aware of the second at all. We have the third not by explicit and time-taking inference from the second, but by unconscious automatic and immediate interpretation. Yet this interpretation, he holds, results from past experience of, for example, 'what kind of appearance convex Bodies are wont to make in us; what alterations are made in the reflections of Light, by the difference of the sensible Figures of Bodies' (E II.ix.8: 145). Also, these matters can be deliberately taken into account, and are so used by painters.

I would, therefore, defend the intentional object variant of the representative theory of perception, both in itself and as the account which can best do justice to the various points on which Locke insisted, and was right to insist.

IV

LOCKE ON QUALITIES

JOHN CAMPBELL

LOCKE'S division between primary and secondary qualities in chapter viii of Book II of the *Essay* is a hardy philosophical perennial which has weathered centuries of misrepresentation. Gradually, however, a new dawn in Locke scholarship is breaking, in the light of which it transpires that the importance and interest of the dichotomy belongs not to classical philosophy of perception but to philosophy of science. The excellence of current Locke exegesis, however, should not blind us to the fact that recent readings are in urgent need of supplementation: and one aim of this paper is to show how this might be achieved.

I shall have little to say on the contemporary relevance of Locke's account. I think, however, that we may appreciate the force of his discussion rather better if we see him as grappling with a curious conceptual tension which is still with us. For in our uncritical moments, we yet tend to think of qualities of objects (e.g. colour) as somehow pasted onto them, and, with the coming of a theory of microstructures, we think of microstructures as what the qualities are pasted onto—hence the currently fashionable contrast between *superficial* properties vs. *internal* essences. Yet when spelt out, this picture is obviously untenable (what happens when we slice an object in two?). Locke, I submit, provides an alternative.

Section I is devoted to the definitions which, I shall argue, constitute the framework of II. viii of the *Essay*.

I

My first contention is that Locke's development of a distinction between types of quality is both careful and coherent. This contention is uncommon; for example, offhand dismissal is the currently popular treatment of

From *Canadian Journal of Philosophy*, 10: 4 (1980), 567–85.

the first, and often of the second, of Locke's three preliminary definitions, viz.:

(1) A quality of x is a power of x to produce any idea in our mind (E ii.viii.8: 134).
(2) Primary qualities of body are those which are utterly inseparable from it; are such as sense finds constantly in every perceptible particle of matter, and the mind finds inseparable from every particle (E ii.viii.9: 134–5).
(3) Secondary qualities are nothing in objects themselves but powers to produce various sensations in us by their primary qualities (E ii.viii.10: 135).

In justice to the current treatment, it must be admitted that there is considerable initial tension between these three. Locke clearly considers the primary/secondary distinction exclusive; yet *prima facie* there is no reason to suppose that no quality satisfies both (2) and (3), and no explicit argument for this supposition is provided. Why then should the distinction not be drawn as one between those qualities satisfying (e.g.) (3) and the rest? More serious problems arise from (1): Locke argues that *all* sensations are *only* produced in us by the primary qualities of bodies; therefore, apparently, everything satisfying (1) satisfies (3); therefore (given exclusiveness) there are no primary qualities, and *a fortiori* no primary qualities of bodies which produce our sensations, and thus no secondary qualities either. These surface tensions may, then, appear to constitute a *reductio* of Locke's entire discussion.

Some commentators (e.g. Bennett in Bennett 1971: 103–4; Alexander in Alexander 1974: 54) evade the problem by tactfully rejecting (1); Mackie is more explicit, however, arguing that Locke's 'usage is partly inconsistent with this proposal [(1)] for what he identifies as *primary qualities* are "solidity, figure motion or rest, and number" and these are not powers: rather they are intrinsic properties of things which may be the grounds or bases of powers' (Mackie 1976: 12)—only partly inconsistent, Mackie thinks, for he holds that secondary qualities *do* satisfy (1). From this view, that only satisfiers of (3) satisfy (1), the above *reductio* immediately follows. Mackie holds this view on the grounds that it is just obvious that (e.g.) solidity is not a power. Earlier in the *Essay*, however, we find Locke tentatively identifying solidity with the power of impenetrability (E ii.iv.1: 123); thus the appeal to intuition here seems unlikely to be finally satisfactory.

Moreover, one of the first arguments Locke develops in E ii.viii depends on a corollary of (1):

(1a) (ϕ is a quality) $\Rightarrow$ (ϕ is a power to produce ideas in us).[1]

The argument runs:

(A) The only way we can conceive bodies to operate in is by impulse.[2] So since bodies are not united to our minds when they produce ideas in it, some singly imperceptible particles must come from them to the eyes, and thereby convey to the brain some motion which produces those ideas we have of them in us.

(B) Therefore all ideas of quality are produced by the primary qualities of insensible particles.

(C) Therefore primary qualities really exist in the objects themselves, whereas secondary qualities are nothing in the objects themselves *but* powers to produce various sensations in us (E II.viii.11–15: 135–7).

Now for the moment the point to note is this: the premisses of the argument refer only to the explanation of the powers of bodies to produce ideas in us; the conclusion is a thesis dealing generally with *all* qualities. Thus, given the form of the argument alone, it seems that either it is seriously incomplete, or that it relies on (1a), which states that all qualities are powers of bodies to produce ideas in us. Charity then appears to dictate that we attribute (1a) to Locke—but does not this threaten to reinstate the *reductio*? Surely, however, there are other ways of escaping the *reductio* than by denial of (1a), and consequently of (1): we might, for example, look to Locke for a distinction between those qualities which are, *inter alia*, powers to produce ideas in us, and those which are (nothing but) powers to produce ideas in us. That is, we might read (1), not as a strict identity, but as a biconditional; the conjunction of (1a) and its converse.

Let us turn to the role of (2) in Locke's argument. It is usually supposed that the distinction between qualities conceptually inseparable from body and qualities not so inseparable is but one of many distinctions Locke is simultaneously drawing in E II.viii, but that it is unrelated to those others— perhaps doubts about maintaining the exclusiveness of the primary/ secondary split on any other interpretation partly account for this. Bennett (Bennett 1971: 105) and Alexander (Alexander 1974: 57) exemplify this line. Now both writers agree that for Locke, the primary qualities may be picked out by reference to thesis (B); the primary qualities are all and only those used in explaining our ideas of qualities. How are some qualities to

---

[1] I defer consideration of the question of how 'insensible parts' may be said to possess qualities. (But cf. E IV.xvi.12: 665–7 here.)

[2] The same point, incidentally, is made at E IV.ii.11: 535–6.

be selected as explanatory? Is it a matter of trial and error, requiring massive experimentation? Alexander writes that the strategy is just to try to divide all qualities 'into two groups, one as small as possible, the other as large as possible, such that the smaller group can plausibly be made the basis for explanation of, *inter alia*, our ideas of the larger' (Alexander 1974: 57). According to Bennett, certain qualities are singled out as explanatory in 'the *de facto* absence of any other suitable candidate' and notes with pleasure that Locke concedes that our perceptions *may* not depend upon the primary qualities of insensible particles, but 'upon something yet more remote from our comprehensions' (E iv.iii.11: 544) (Bennett 1971: 105). Now it seems to me that both authors miss the largely a priori character of Locke's reasoning in E ii.viii.11–14. Note that the only expressly empirical premiss in Locke's argument (A) for the necessity of the appeal to insensible particles in explaining perception is the statement that external objects are not united to our minds when we perceive them; consider then what qualities may be possessed by insensible particles. Clearly, they *must* possess all those qualities conceptually inseparable from body—else they would not be bodies. Could they possess any qualities which were nothing but powers to produce ideas in us? Clearly not, else they would not be insensible. Thus we see, not only that definition (2) is a functional part of Locke's argument for thesis (B), but that the primary/secondary split generated by (2) and (3) is indeed exclusive. If this is accepted, then, I submit, the passage cited by Bennett should *not* be read as saying that we might appeal to some other qualities of insensible particles than those conceptually inseparable from body; rather, it must be read as saying that since the existence of insensible particles is but hypothesis, it might be false, though we cannot at present even conceive of any alternative explanations of perception.

This account of Locke's argument is, I think, obviously preferable to that of Bennett or Alexander, according to whom Locke has stated his definition (2) carefully and at length only to ignore it for the remainder of his discussion. Mackie, however, reads E ii.viii.9 not as a definition, but as an argument for supposing that the particular qualities Locke calls 'primary' are indeed fundamental in explanation. But, Mackie replies to Locke's 'argument': 'If the mind discriminates thus [i.e. singling out as primary certain qualities] it will be because it has already adopted the distinction: this cannot be the evidence on which the distinction itself is based' (Mackie 1976: 20–1). The reply here is that Mackie has failed to notice that *two* related distinctions are involved here: we can only understand his criticism on the supposition that he takes Locke to be contending that it is self-evident that some qualities, viz., those listed as primary, are all we need to invoke in explaining the facts of perception. If indeed Locke held this rationalist view, however, it is a little difficult to see why, on Mackie's account, he should have thought the remainder of his discussion necessary or useful.

There is then at least a prima facie case for taking seriously Locke's lengthily expounded definitions; but let us note two difficulties in maintaining all three. The power to produce an idea of green if examined before t, or the idea of blue if not so examined, is clearly a power to produce ideas in us; but can it plausibly be held to be a quality? Secondly, if all qualities are powers to produce ideas in us, how can insensible particles, which have no such powers, have *any* qualities?

I shall now state in contemporary terms what I take to be Locke's main thesis, show how he argues for it, and display how it copes with these points.

II

The possession of any power by any body can be explained in terms of the fine structure, the microphysical constitution, of the body. Some powers are such that all objects possessing them do so in virtue of one and the same fine structure; some are not. My contention is that Locke's 'primary' qualities are, *inter alia*, powers (to produce ideas in us) of the first kind; the 'secondary' qualities are powers (to produce ideas in us) of the second. Now if all and only objects with a certain fine structure have a power ϕ, then it is reasonable to suppose that an object's possession of that fine structure, and consequently of ϕ, will reveal itself not just through manifestations of ϕ, but in many and various of the object's interactions with others. That is, all objects possessing a primary quality may be expected to have many more powers in common than the power to produce an idea in us. (To see this, remember that the only justification we have for supposing that a certain class of objects has a common fine structure is that, roughly, we are thereby enabled to subsume a large number of macroscopic regularities under a small number of microscopic regularities.) If we now identify the primary quality with the sum of those powers, we arrive at what we sought earlier: a clear reading of the claim that primary qualities are, *inter alia*, powers to produce ideas in us.

It might be protested: if this distinction is Locke's, why did he not make it explicit? Consider, however, that in our time we have a well-established atomic theory: consequently, notions such as 'microphysical constitution' are now readily intelligible to the layman. What analogous notions were available to Locke? The notion of 'texture' was a technical term of Boyle's; a lengthy exposition of it would have seemed inappropriate to one who apologizes for being overly 'engaged in physical enquiries' already in E II.viii.22: 140. All that remains is that battleground for conflicting schools, the notion of 'real essence', use of which would have obscured rather than clarified Locke's point. It is then hardly surprising that Locke provides no clear and succinct statement of the dichotomy intended; there were none available.

The major objection to the line I shall canvass, however, is this: there are, apparently, a host of qualities such that all objects possessing them do so in virtue of one and the same structure—the qualities, e.g. of being gold, of being acid, of being magnetic. And none of these are listed as primary by Locke. Yet, given his sophistication concerning 'real essences', is it not incredible that Locke should not have done were he using the notion of 'primary' I have defined?

In reply, we first note that throughout 'Further Considerations Concerning Simple Ideas' the distinction between simple and complex ideas is never once invoked. If those considerations do specifically concern simple ideas, therefore, we are surely intended to read 'simple idea' for 'idea' throughout. In particular, we must rewrite (1) as:

(1b) ϕ is a quality $\Leftrightarrow$ ϕ is a power to produce a simple idea in us.

(The singular article is motivated by the need to eliminate the claim of 'grueness' to qualityhood, and plainly achieves this end.) The reply to the objection is now immediate: goldness does not qualify as primary on our definition. For a primary quality is a sum of powers such that all objects possessing one of them, a power to produce a simple idea in us, do so in virtue of a common fine structure, possession of which structure by an object also results in its having the rest of that sum of powers. That is, the sum is effectively determined by one of its constituents which is a power to produce a simple idea in us. Now if goldness is primary, then which such power determines the sum with which it is to be identified? The power to produce the idea of yellow in us? The power to produce the idea of malleability in us? Clearly none of these will do: and the conclusion is, then, not just that goldness is not primary, but that it is not a quality at all, for it is not (even, in the sense defined, *inter alia*) a power to produce a simple idea in us. As for acidity and magnetism, they are not powers to produce ideas in us at all, but powers to interact with other bodies in certain ways. Our interpretation thus rings true; given Locke's adherence to (1b), it seems that we must draw some distinction between the qualities that are nothing but powers, and those that are, *inter alia*, powers to produce simple ideas in us. And there is, so far, no objection to the definition of '*inter alia*' I have given; shortly, I will adduce evidence to show that it is Locke's. Two points first, however.

1. On the assumption that this interpretation is correct, we may reply to a criticism of, *inter alia*, Locke raised by J. J. MacIntosh in the course of his useful review of the primary/secondary literature:

> We are, to put it shortly, owed a doctrine of qualities as a prerequisite to a doctrine of primary and secondary qualities, for the intelligibility of the one presupposes the intelligibility of the other. But I know of no such doctrine. (MacIntosh 1976: 102)

The problem MacIntosh then propounds is that, in the absence of such a doctrine, all predicate-expressions may be taken to be quality-ascribing; but, e.g., 'is the only even prime', 'is a manufactured article', 'marks a turning point in the course of the campaign', 'don't seem to fit at all happily in the primary/secondary boxes' (MacIntosh 1976: 102). On our reading of Locke, this is no surprise, however, for those expressions are clearly not counted as *quality*-ascribing.

2. There is running through ii.viii of the *Essay* a tendency in Locke to hold that the secondary qualities are not qualities at all. Since the popular view rejects (1b), Locke's only attempt to say what a quality *is*, as a slip of the mind, the popular view is understandably in some difficulty when it encounters such claims. Consider, however, the following passage:

> ... *Manna* by the Bulk, Figure, Texture, and Motion of its Parts, has a Power to produce the Sensations of Sickness, and sometimes of acute Pains, or Gripings in us. That these *Ideas* of *Sickness and Pain are not in the* Manna, but Effects of its Operations on us, and are no where when we feel them not: This also every one readily agrees to. And yet Men are hardly to be brought to think, that *Sweetness and Whiteness are not really in Manna* ... (E ii.viii.18: 138)

Manna has a power to produce the simple idea of pain in us (that power is (in the sense defined) 'nothing but' a power)—nevertheless it is surely not a quality of the manna. The example makes trouble for Locke's definition (1b); but, Locke thinks, it is only by preserving (1b) that we can preserve the common way of speaking, under which colours, tastes, etc. are qualities. So the options here are two: we can preserve (1b) at the cost of accounting the power of manna to produce pain a quality; or we can reject (1b) as worthless, along with the claim that (e.g.) colours are qualities.[3]

---

[3] A subsidiary attack on the 'common notion' of qualities is developed in E ii.viii.10: 135: if all powers to produce simple ideas *in us* are accounted qualities, so too should all powers *simpliciter*. Yet the 'common notion' does not make this move; retaining an unscientific emphasis on the importance of man in the universe.
Locke nevertheless seems to have been unhappy with the dichotomy between accounting only

Locke clearly thinks we should take the latter route, and so presumably
has a preferred definition of 'quality' which, interestingly, he does not
explicitly state—because, I submit, it would lead him too far into physical
enquiry to expound it. Let us now see Locke's use of our definition in
action.

In the absence of direct access to the fine structures of objects, how may
we determine whether a quality is primary or secondary? As an immediate
consequence of our reading of 'primary' we have it that one way is to ask
the following question: how does any object's possession of that quality
reveal itself? In a wide variety of ways, or only through producing some
simple idea in us? So consider, then, Locke on establishing that the 'light,
heat, whiteness or coldness' of fire or snow are secondary:

Take away the Sensation of them; let not the Eyes see Light, or Colours, nor the
Ears hear Sounds; let the Palate not Taste, nor the Nose Smell, and all Colours,
Tastes, Odors, and Sounds, as they are such particular *Ideas*, vanish and cease, and
are reduced to their Causes, i.e. Bulk, Figure, and Motion of Parts. (E II.viii.17: 138)

In the absence of sensory organs, there are no longer any ideas of those
qualities; all 'as they are *ideas*, vanish and cease'. In this absence, how, if at
all, does an object's possession of them reveal itself? It is true, as Locke
points out, that for each constituent particle, each of its qualities of bulk,
figure and motion still reveals itself. But that is all: no powers which are
constant concomitants of an object's possession of the quality are thereby
revealed. Therefore we may conclude that none of those qualities are such
that all objects possessing them do so in virtue of one and the same fine
structure.

Locke backs this up with an argument in which he clearly uses his
preferred definition of 'quality' (which, I urge again, is none other than our
definition of 'primary'):

Let us consider the red and white colours in *Porphyre*: Hinder light but from striking
on it, and its Colours Vanish; it no longer produces any such *Ideas* in us: Upon the
return of Light, it produces these appearances on us again. Can any one think any
real alterations are made in the *Porphyre*, by the presence or absence of Light; and
that those *Ideas* of whiteness and redness, are really in *Porphyre* in the light, when
'tis plain *it has no colour in the dark*? It has, indeed, such a Configuration of

primary qualities as qualities and retaining the 'common notion' which seems to allow the
powers to produce pleasure and pain the status of 'quality'. So in E III.iv.16: 428 he tries again,
defining 'quality' as 'power to produce a simple idea which comes into the mind by only one
sense': excluding the powers to produce pleasure and pain, but also, as Locke notes, all the
primary qualities from qualityhood. So this revision is swiftly abandoned; in E III.vi.29: 456–7
'shape' is referred to as a quality and in E III.vi.30–2: 457–60 simple ideas and qualities are
identified outright. Seeking the intentions behind these latter formulations, it seems only fair to
suppose that we are by Book IV back with the original definition of E II.viii.8.

Particles, both Night and Day, as are apt by the Rays of Light rebounding from some parts of that hard Stone, to produce in us the *Idea* of redness, and from others the *Idea* of whiteness: But whiteness or redness are not in it at any time, but such a texture, that hath the power to produce such a sensation in us. (E II.viii.19: 139)

There is an echo of the 'manna' argument in the appeal to the 'obvious' fact that porphyry has no colour in the dark, and the silent use of the preferred definition (as opposed to (1b)) when maintaining that whiteness and redness are *not* in it: but I take it that the main point is the following. The absence of light brings about no changes in the fine structure of porphyry—no 'real alterations'—and therefore no changes in its powers to produce ideas in us. So its redness, i.e. the power it has to produce ideas of red in us, is a *limited* power; limited in a way unlike the qualities cited as primary, which are accessible under *almost* all circumstances to the sense of touch. All powers have their conditions of course: but the point here, I take it, is that even when we restrict ourselves to the production of ideas in us, the regularities governing secondary qualities are much more limited than those governing primary qualities. And this point, I submit, could only be used to show that colour qualities are not, in the sense I have defined, primary.

Furthermore, having grasped the nature of Locke's distinction, and that felt temperature is secondary while shape is primary,

> . . . we may understand, how it is possible, that the same Water may at the same time produce the Sensation of Heat in one Hand, and Cold in the other; which yet Figure never does, that never producing the *Idea* of a square by one Hand, which has produced the *Idea* of Globe by another. (E II.viii.21: 139)

And this, clearly, is nothing but the point of E II.viii.19 over again.

Yet, as we saw earlier, Locke's definition (2) of 'primary' is initially used to derive, in E II.viii.13, the claim that all our ideas of qualities are to be explained by reference to the primary qualities of insensible parts. From this it is inferred in E II.viii.14 that all *powers* to produce ideas of secondary—and equally, presumably, of primary—qualities are to be thus explained. Therefore, from our reading of (1b), the possession of any quality by an object may be explained by reference to the primary qualities of insensible parts. What is the connection between this notion of 'primary' and the one I have defined?

I have maintained that Locke in effect argues from cases to the coextensiveness of the two. Even if he is correct, however, why should this coextensiveness be thought to be of any importance? To approach the point, let us consider the query noted earlier: how can Locke talk of ascribing *any* qualities to insensible particles, given his adherence to (1b)? The rationale should I hope be obvious by now: if, as I have suggested, a primary quality is the sum of a very large number of powers, then the justification for attributing such a quality to an insensible particle is simply that the particle possesses all, save one, of the relevant powers. Indeed, what other rationale might there be for attributing one and the same quality to both a macroscopic and a microscopic object? Now suppose that the two notions are not coextensive; that, for example, some of the qualities which it is necessary to ascribe to insensible particles in providing scientific explanations are not primary in the sense I have defined—let φ be one such quality. Then the corpuscular programme, of providing detailed explanations of phenomena in terms of the qualities of insensible particles, will simply be impossible of achievement. For ascription of φ to some insensible parts is *ex hypothesi* necessary for completion of the programme; yet since φ is not primary in the sense I have defined, there can be no justification ever for attributing it to an insensible particle. Thus it is not surprising to find Locke, as an underlabourer for the corpuscularians, not only advancing the considerations already described in favour of coextensiveness, but attempting to make it further plausible to the layman that even in explaining colours and tastes, it is not necessary to appeal to qualities which are not obviously primary in the sense I have defined:

Pound an Almond, and the clear white *Colour* will be altered into a dirty one, and the sweet *Taste* into an oily one. What real Alteration can the beating of the Pestle make in any Body, but an Alteration of the *Texture* of it? (E ii.viii.20: 139)

It has been recognized (Alexander 1974: 63) that Locke is here issuing a challenge: show me how the change in colour and taste can be causally explained otherwise than as a result of changes in the aggregate shape and size, and the motion or rest, of insensible parts. But the point of this challenge has not often been understood. Incidentally, it does not seem to matter whether some qualities primary in the sense I have defined turn out not to be conceptually necessary to body; there just seem to be none such. The important point is that all qualities 'conceptually necessary', and therefore fundamental in explanation, be primary; and that there be no other qualities fundamental in explanation which are not, in the sense defined, primary.

There is then a strong *prima facie* case for the interpretation we have canvassed; let us briefly consider some alternatives. One current view is that the only distinction Locke is seriously concerned to draw is the *causal* one; between qualities fundamental in explanation and qualities not so fundamental—this is the view for example of Alexander and Mackie (Alexander 1974: *passim*; Mackie 1976: ch. 1). One problem for this account is that the passages E ii.viii.17; ii.viii.19; and ii.viii.21 already cited cannot possibly be construed as *arguments* for the causal distinction, though it is mentioned in all of them. One is therefore reduced, like Alexander (Alexander 1974: 61), to contending that these passages *en bloc* are to be read as lengthy expositions (and hopelessly obscure expositions at that) of the causal distinction. If, like Alexander, one compounds the error by failing to spot the 'a priori' argument for the primacy in explanation of those qualities conceptually inseparable from body, it appears that Locke is transmitting, with a minimum of argument (and no source-references) a distinction of Boyle's which is to be taken on trust by the reader. We ought to be careful that we do not count deficiencies of interpretation as sins of the interpreted: and we have seen already that we can make somewhat better sense of the passages E II.viii.17; II.viii.19; and II.viii.21.

Bennett and Mackie, however, make kindred points which might be thought to tell against our interpretation. Bennett argues that it is a fundamental assumption of Western science that not all qualities are powers, and that therefore Locke cannot have held the contrary; Mackie (Mackie 1976: 14–15) that the truth of the assumption is obvious, and must have been known to Locke. More explicitly, the 'assumption' is that, if x has the power to be H under conditions F, then 'there is some non-dispositional ϕ such that: x is ϕ, and it is a causal law that if anything is both ϕ and F then it is H' (Bennett 1971: 104). The argument is already undermined by Locke's explicit statement and use of (1b), however: furthermore, the underlying intuition is surely accommodated by Locke's view that powers of macroscopic objects are to be explained by reference to *powers* of microscopic objects. And these latter powers may or may not be themselves explainable in turn. Incidentally, it is particularly surprising that Bennett is party to the prejudice against (1b). For surely his discussion of size vs. colour blindness suggests the importance of powers in Locke's argument (Bennett 1971: 100). Yet, failing to invoke the underpinning notion of 'fine structure', that discussion yields, uselessly, at best a distinction between qualities which do, and qualities which do not, manifest their instantiation in many and various ways: a distinction, that is, of degree.

III

It seems to me that the crucial test of any interpretation of Locke's primary/secondary split is its ability to cope with the 'resemblance' thesis of E II.viii.15. Now this passage presents a peculiar and not generally recognized problem. For initially at least it appears to be in some tension with Locke's insistence that *all* simple ideas *conform to their archetypes* (E iv.iv.4: 563–4); are *real* (E ii.xxx.2: 372); *adequate* (E ii.xxxi.2: 375); or *true* (E ii.xxxii.14: 388). The terminological variations between these four theses reflect no substantive divergence; they are important only when the theses are stated for the case of e.g. our complex ideas of substances (cf. E ii.xxxii.18: 390–1). Locke supplies the same argument in support of each. Yet how, we may ask, can Locke maintain that *all* simple ideas 'conform to their archetypes' while holding that where our simple ideas of secondary qualities are concerned, 'There is nothing like our *Ideas* existing in the Bodies themselves' (E ii.viii.15: 137)?

I shall focus on the 'conformance' claim, as being both more readily comprehensible than the 'resemblance' thesis and supported by the clearest statement of Locke's quadruplicated argument.

Knowledge, Locke writes in E iv.iv, is *real* only insofar as the ideas it concerns 'conform to their archetypes'; only, that is, insofar as they fulfil their intended functions. Thus ideas of mixed modes, being their own archetypes, are bound to conform to them; those ideas being compounded from simples without any intention that they reflect features of the world (E iv.iv.5: 564). Ideas of substances, however, are referred to real essences underlying nominal essences—it is in this that they are distinguished from ideas of mixed modes. They thus 'conform to their archetypes' only if there are real essences of the required kinds (E iv.iv.11–12: 568–9).

Simple ideas fall between those of mixed modes and those of substances. They are like ideas of mixed modes in invariably conforming to their archetypes, and like ideas of substances in that they are referred to something external: for each is intended to conform to some quality of objects.

The conformance is guaranteed by the fact that the mind cannot produce new simple ideas of itself: so the production of a simple idea in one's mind must be the manifestation of the power of some external object to produce that idea.

Thus the 'conformance' claimed appears to consist in there answering to (being the power to produce) each simple idea just one, actually instantiated quality which uniquely answers to that idea. Further, that idea will be the very one whose production in perception generally reveals the presence of the associated quality.

Locke states the point as follows:

... simple Ideas, which since the Mind, as has been shewed, can by no means make to it self, must necessarily be the product of Things operating on the Mind in a natural way, and producing therein those Perceptions which by the Wisdom and Will of our Maker they are ordained and adapted to. From whence it follows, that *simple* Ideas *are not fictions* of our Fancies, but the natural and regular productions of Things without us, really operating upon us; and so carry with them all the conformity which is intended; or which our state requires: For they represent to us Things under those appearances which they are fitted to produce in us: whereby we are enabled to distinguish the sorts of particular Substances, to discern the states they are in, and so to take them for our Necessities, and apply them to our Uses. Thus the *Idea* of Whiteness, or Bitterness, as it is in the Mind, exactly answering that Power which is in any Body to produce it there, has all the real conformity it can, or ought to have, with Things without us. (E iv.iv.4: 563–4)

Incidentally, the use of 'simple ideas' here plainly diverges from that in which Locke holds that there are 'simple ideas' of reflection; for, just as with complex ideas, the mind alone is operative in producing ideas of reflection (cf. E ii.vi.1: 127).

Locke exegesis, rather than Locke criticism, is my object here; but the following points may be found suggestive:

(1) Hume's 'missing shade of blue' (Hume 1739–40: i.i.1) may be held by the sceptic with respect to conformance to show that even if it is plausible to suppose that there is a class of ideas not all of which can be produced by the mind alone, any one of them can be: so that we cannot tell *which* of our simple ideas actually owe their first entrance to the mind to an external cause.

(2) Locke's cavalier and generally innocuous disregard of the fact that all powers have their conditions seems to lead him here to claim a result stronger than he is entitled to: for the qualities to which our simple ideas are held to conform are presumably powers to produce, *under normal circumstances*, those ideas in us. Thus the presence of a simple idea in the mind seems to yield no more than a rational presumption (given the prima facie reasonableness of supposing that normal circumstances obtain) that the appropriate quality is indeed instantiated.

IV

But now another question arises. We saw that for Locke an idea of substance conforms to its archetype only if there is a real essence of the required type; for ideas of substances are referred to real essences. Now throughout the *Essay* (cf. e.g. E ii.xxiii.1–6: 295–9; E ii.xxxi.6–10: 378–82; E iii.iii.17: 418; E iv.iv.13–17: 569–73) Locke criticizes various ways in which our ideas of substances might be thought to be so referred. His own view of how this 'referral' occurs emerges most clearly at E iii.iii.17: 417–18:

Concerning the real Essences of corporeal Substances, (to mention those only,) there are, if I mistake not, two Opinions. The one is of those, who using the Word *Essence*, for they know not what, suppose a certain number of those Essences, according to which, all natural things are made, and wherein they do exactly every one of them partake, and so become of this or that *Species*. The other, and more rational Opinion, is of those, who look on all natural Things to have a real, but unknown Constitution of their insensible Parts, from which flow those sensible Qualities, which serve us to distinguish them one from another, according as we have Occasion to rank them into sorts, under common Denominations.

It appears, then, that an idea of substance conforms to its archetype only if all objects answering to the idea do so in virtue of one and the same fine structure. (On careful reading, Locke, even in the 'zahab' example of E III.vi.46: 468, reveals no appreciation of the importance of Kripkean 'paradigms' here.) Thus, in the sections on the conformance to their archetypes of our ideas of substance, Locke maintains that given the current lack of knowledge of microphysics, the only way to ensure that there is *at least* one fine structure in virtue of which an object may answer to some idea of substance is to ensure that there is at least one object with the appropriate qualities (E IV.iv.11–12: 568–9; cf. E II.xxx.5: 374).

We have seen that the question of whether a simple idea conforms to its archetype is not settled on such grounds. Yet having raised the issue of whether certain complex ideas are such that all objects answering to them do so in virtue of one and the same fine structure, a similar query concerning simple ideas arises naturally. For if each simple idea is such that all objects answering to it do so in virtue of the same fine structure, then, clearly, all complex ideas (to which some object actually answers) will be so too. Hence, I suggest, the importance of the primary/secondary division for Locke's discussion of ideas of substances—it raises the difficulty alluded to in E II.xxix.7: 365: that an idea of substance may fail to determine *at most* one real essence, being made up of '*too small a number of simple Ideas*'.

Now in considering this issue for the case of simple ideas we are asking whether the relation between simple ideas and their archetypes (qualities) is *closer* than mere *conformance*. Locke has contended that to each simple idea there corresponds one quality: we are now asking whether to each simple idea there corresponds one fine structure, underlying the appropriate quality. A natural way of expressing this relationship, closer than conformance is, I suggest, in terms of *resemblance*. So we should not be surprised to find Locke insisting that:

... the *Ideas of primary Qualities* of Bodies, are *Resemblances* of them, and their Patterns do really exist in the Bodies themselves; but the *Ideas*, *produced* in us *by* these *Secondary Qualities*, *have no resemblance* of them at all. (E II.viii.15: 137)

Thus our interpretation adequately, and easily, copes with Locke's 're-semblance' thesis. The possibility of achieving the corpuscular programme we have noted, appears to imply that our idea of a quality 'resembles' that quality just in case it is a quality fundamental in causal explanation. So, having argued for the corpuscular hypothesis and the 'causal' dichotomy in E II.viii.11–14 Locke draws the 'resemblance' thesis as a consequence in E II.viii.15. And we have see how in his discussion of the ways in which various qualities reveal their instantiation, Locke continued to attack the question of which qualities are (in the 'resemblance' sense) primary, supporting his earlier claims.

V

Yet for those who hold that the primary/secondary split is nothing over and above the 'causal' division, the 'resemblance' thesis poses a sticky and, I think, insurmountable problem—viz., to find a natural reading of E II.viii.15 under which the thesis actually has some connection with the primary/secondary distinction. *Pace* Bennett, the thesis is surely not a simple *restatement* of the 'causal' division; yet if the 'causal' story is the whole truth, resort to Bennett's method of interpretation-by-transformation seems to be the only way to secure the required connection.[4] Thus the difficulties already noted in the interpretation of Locke I am criticizing come to a head here, with its simple inability to deal with the 'resemblance' thesis.

But let us see how Mackie and Alexander handle the problem. Mackie writes that for Locke:

To say that an objective quality resembles the idea of that quality is simply to say that in this respect things are just as they look in a strictly sensory sense of 'look' (with the proviso that we may still say that ideas resemble qualities if how things look is a bit distorted from how they are, but within the same category or

---

[4] Here is Bennett on E II.viii.15:

Since ideas cannot resemble either bodies or qualities of bodies, this must be either discarded or transformed. The only plausible transformation is into something like the following: in causally explaining ideas of primary qualities, one uses the same words in describing the causes as in describing the effects (shape-ideas etc. are caused by shapes etc.); whereas in causally explaining ideas of secondary qualities one must describe the causes in one vocabulary and the effects in another (colour-ideas etc. are caused by shapes etc.) If this is not what Locke's 'resemblance' formulations of the primary/secondary contrast mean, then I can find no meaning in them. (Bennett 1971: 106)

I have little to add to this. The need to resort to the method of interpretation-by-transformation is in my view strong prima-facie evidence of misreading of Locke.

determinable); to say that there is nothing in the things like an idea of a certain class is to say things are not at all as they sensorily appear in this respect. (Mackie 1976: 49–50)

Alexander proposes essentially the same interpretation, with an infusion of semantic ascent (note that, as the final sentence makes clear, he uses 'describing the qualities' as elliptical for 'describing the objects having the qualities'):

We describe an idea by saying that it is an idea of red or of an extension of one foot . . . Now [according to the 'resemblance' thesis] primary qualities are such that the words we use in describing our ideas of them are also the appropriate words for describing the qualities; secondary qualities are such that the words we use in describing our ideas of them will not do for describing the qualities. The description of an idea of a primary quality is of the form 'of x' and the description of the object having the quality is 'has x' or 'is x'; the resemblance is in the description. (Alexander 1974: 66)

The lemon *looks* yellow; but in fact it's not the way it looks (the word 'yellow' doesn't apply). And it's not even as if the lemon is actually green or red; it's not coloured at all. There are two strong objections to this interpretation, which jointly render it quite untenable. Firstly, Locke repeatedly and emphatically rejected scepticism *in toto* (cf. e.g. E IV.xi: 630–9 *passim*). I have already suggested that Locke rejected scepticism with respect to *all* simple ideas of sensation; and he can be found explicitly rejecting scepticism with respect to various of our ideas of secondary qualities at, e.g. E IV.ii.14: 536–8; E IV.xi.5–7: 632–4; and E IV.xi.11: 636–7. Yet if the Mackie/Alexander reading of E II.viii.15 is correct, Locke is there espousing the view that sceptical doubts with respect to *all* our ideas of secondary qualities are in fact fully justified; that the only role of those ideas in perception is to invariably mislead us about the nature of the external world. Secondly, it is quite unclear how adherence to the 'causal' distinction could lead to commitment to this mitigated but quite radical form of scepticism. Why should the view that some qualities are not fundamental in causal explanation result in the belief that, in perception, our ideas of those qualities are radically misleading? Certainly Locke (like his commentators) provides no account of how one might with an appearance of plausibility pass from one view to the other. Uniting those two points, we see that if this reading of E II.viii.15 is correct the appearance of the 'resemblance' thesis must be accounted a grossly inconsistent thunderbolt from a clear sky. I have shown, however, that we can do rather better than this: and this concludes my case against the 'causal' reading of Locke's distinction between types of quality, and for its supplementation along the lines I have indicated.

Recapitulating briefly, we may say that Locke's discussion of qualities splits into two sections, pivoting around the 'resemblance' thesis. The major concern of the second, as we have seen, is to defend the view that the qualities conceptually inseparable from body, and hence fundamental in explanation, are just those which are such that all objects possessing them do so in virtue of one and the same fine structure. The first section introduces the definitions (1)–(3) used by Locke in arguing (E II.viii.11–14) for the corpuscular hypothesis and the identification of the qualities fundamental in explanation with those conceptually inseparable from body. The qualities fundamental in explanation are just those ascribable to microscopic particles: so they cannot be 'nothing but' powers to produce simple ideas in us, and the conclusion is, apparently that these qualities are *sums* of powers, each sum being fixed as the sum of those powers which are found constantly conjoined with some particular power to produce a simple idea in us (with that power). The connecting link between the two sections, I have argued, is the identification of those sums of powers with the qualities which are such that all objects possessing them do so in virtue of one and the same fine structure.

Our discussion shows clearly, I think, the importance of Locke's definition of 'quality' and the dichotomy between simple and complex ideas, for the division he draws between primary and secondary qualities. In the light of the considerations I have advanced, agreement as to the *nature* of that division may now, I hope, prove possible. If, finally, my remarks have seemed unduly polemical at times, I can only plead my belief that the principle of charity in Locke exegesis continues to be undervalued: that too often we are ready to see obscurity and self-contradiction where what we have found is rather prima facie evidence of misinterpretation.[5]

[5] I am indebted to J. J. MacIntosh for criticism of earlier drafts.

V

LOCKE ON THE FREEDOM OF THE WILL

VERE CHAPPELL

LOCKE believes in human freedom. To be sure, his conception of freedom is different from that of many libertarian philosophers. Some such philosophers maintain that an agent is free only if her action is uncaused; whereas Locke thinks that all actions have causes, including the free ones. Some libertarians hold that no action is free unless it proceeds from a volition that is itself free; whereas Locke argued that free volition, as opposed to free action, is an impossibility. On the other hand, Locke agrees with the typical libertarian that free actions depend on volitions— or, as he often puts it, that an agent is free only with respect to the actions she wills, to those that are voluntary. And he also refuses to make voluntariness sufficient for freedom, whereby a free action is merely one that is willed. The free agent, Locke insists, must also be able or have been able to do something other than she does or did. Thus both Locke and the libertarian require indifference as well as spontaneity for freedom. But Locke's freedom is not contra-causal; and he denies that it extends to volition.

In this paper I want to focus on just this last component of Locke's view of freedom: that freedom in willing, far from being required for free agency, is not even possible. I call this the thesis of volitional determinism. Locke presents an argument for this thesis in the *Essay*, but scholars have never paid much attention to it: I want to examine it. But I also have a further concern. It is well known that Locke's views on freedom and motivation changed considerably after he first presented them in the chapter 'Of Power' in the first edition of the *Essay*. This chapter was extensively rewritten for the second edition of 1694, and Locke made significant

From *Locke's Philosophy: Content and Context* (Oxford: Clarendon Press, 1994), 101–21.
A version of this chapter was presented at the Clarendon Locke Conference in Oxford in Sept. 1990. More-distant ancestors of it were read at Dartmouth College and to the Seventeenth-Century Study Group at the Institute for Advanced Study. I am grateful to my auditors on those occasions, and especially to Martha Bolton, Willis Doney, Robert Sleigh, and James Tully, for helpful questions and suggestions.

further additions to it both for the fourth edition, published in 1700, and for the fifth, which came out after his death in 1706. These subjects are also discussed in his correspondence with his Arminian friend Philippus van Limborch in 1701 and 1702. One of the most striking features of Locke's 'second thoughts' on freedom appears in the middle of the revised version of Book II, chapter xxi that was included in the *Essay*'s second edition. This is the observation that an agent may, while deliberating what to do, '*suspend* the execution and satisfaction of any of [his] desires' (E **2–5** II.xxi.47: 263),[1] and so keep his will from being determined to any action. This doctrine of suspension at least appears to conflict with the volitional determinism that Locke affirms and argues for earlier in the chapter, in its revised no less than in its original version. But not only did Locke at first fail to see that there might be a conflict between the two doctrines; he refused to acknowledge the problem of reconciling them when van Limborch pointed it out to him. Eventually, it appears that Locke did see the problem, and he altered his views and made some adjustments in the text of the *Essay* accordingly. Even so, he did not make all the adjustments that a full change of view would have called for. Hence doubts remain, both as to the actual bearing of these doctrines on one another and as to Locke's understanding of their relationship. My further purpose, therefore, is to consider Locke's volitional determinism in relation to his doctrine of suspension, and to ascertain his final position concerning it.

I begin with a more exact statement of Locke's view of freedom. The idea of freedom (or liberty) is introduced early in chapter xxi of Book II, the official subject of which is power. Power in general, Locke says, is an attribute of an individual substance, by which it is able to do or suffer something. The power is active when it enables the substance possessing it to perform an action of some kind; it is passive when it makes the substance liable to be affected in some way. Will is an active power belonging to rational agents; volition or willing is the exercise of this power, i.e. the action that having a will enables an agent to perform. Volitions are actions in their own right, but every volition is ordered or directed to some further action of the same agent—what might be called the *target* of the volition. A volition, more specifically, is either a volition to do or a volition not to do something—to forbear doing it.

When an agent wills to do something, and does it, and does it because she has willed it, she is said to have acted in accord with her will, and her action (i.e. the target action) is voluntary. When an agent doesn't do

---

[1] Numerals in boldface refer to specific editions of the *Essay*. When no such numerals appear, the passage quoted or cited occurs in all five of the editions that Locke himself published or revised.

something she wills to do, or does something else instead of that, then her forbearance or alternative action is involuntary, and she is said to have forborne or acted against her will. Also involuntary are actions performed merely without being willed, though these are not done against the will of the agent. Only the actions of rational agents are voluntary, since only such agents are capable of willing. But involuntary actions are performed by non-rational as well as by rational agents. Indeed, all of the actions of beings without reason or thought are involuntary.

Locke first defines freedom as the property of a rational agent whereby he has the power to act or not to act 'according to the preference or direction of his own mind' (E II.xxi.8: 237), i.e. in accord with his will. It might appear from this that Locke identifies free with voluntary agency—that being free for him just consists in doing or being able to do what one wills. And so a number of commentators have taken him to do (see e.g. Law 1781: 186 n.42; Yolton 1970a: 144; D. Locke 1975: 96; O'Higgins 1976: 119). But in fact his position is that voluntariness is merely a necessary condition of freedom. This is the point of his famous example of the man locked in a room with someone he longs to be with. The man 'stays willingly' in the room, i.e. his doing so is voluntary. But his staying is not free because, being locked in, 'he is not at liberty not to stay, he has not freedom to be gone' (E II.xxi.10: 238). Hence 'where-ever any performance or forbearance are not equally in a Man's power; where-ever doing or not doing, will not equally follow upon the preference of his mind directing it, there he is not *Free*, though perhaps the Action may be voluntary' (E II.xxi.8: 237). And again, 'where-ever . . . compulsion takes away that Indifferency of Ability on either side to act, or to forbear acting, there *liberty* . . . presently ceases' (E II.xxi.10: 238). Locke's freedom, therefore, includes this liberty of indifference as well as the liberty of spontaneity: freedom means having a choice in addition to choosing. To be free an agent must not only do something because she has willed it, and thus be able to do what she wills; she must also be able, by willing, to do something other than that—her action must be avoidable, she must have an alternative to it.

Things that lack freedom, for Locke, are necessary; the word 'necessary', at least in the chapter on power, just means 'not free'. Necessity, like freedom, is properly an attribute of agents; but Locke sometimes calls actions with respect to which an agent is 'under necessity' 'necessary actions'.[2] An action may be necessary because it is done by an inanimate or

---

[2] Though he never, I think, makes the parallel move from 'free agent' to 'free action'. But since there is no reason for him to avoid the latter expression, I shall myself use it in expounding Locke's position.

otherwise non-rational agent; or because its (rational) agent either is com-
pelled by some irresistible internal or external force to do it against his will,
or else merely fails to exercise his will with respect to it. Thus all involuntary actions are necessary for Locke. But likewise necessary are those
voluntary actions which an agent cannot avoid doing because of internal or
external constraints which prevent him from performing any alternative
action, including that of merely forbearing the action he does.

It is important to note that no action is necessary for Locke simply by
being the effect of antecedent causes. Locke's use of 'necessary' thus
differs from that of certain 'compatibilist' philosophers with whose views
on freedom his is often associated—Hobbes and Hume, for example. For
the latter, 'necessary' means 'causally determined'; and in this sense, they
maintain, an action can be necessary *and* free: this is what makes them
compatibilists. For Locke, on the contrary, since 'necessary' means 'not
free', the same action cannot be both free and necessary. Is Locke then an
incompatibilist? In one way he is; but in another not. For his disagreement
with Hobbes and Hume is only verbal. He believes, as they do, that
all human actions are causally determined, and hence that all free actions
are. So Locke accepts the substance of the compatibilists' view: his
incompatibilism concerns 'necessity' only in *his* sense of the word.

Locke claims that it follows from his view of freedom that the 'long
agitated' question, 'Whether Man's Will be free, or no', is 'unintelligible'.
It makes no more sense to say that the will is, or is not, free than to say that
one's sleep is swift or one's virtue square. This is so because '*Liberty*, which
is but a power, belongs only to Agents, and cannot be an attribute or
modification of the *Will*, which is also but a Power' (E II.xxi.14: 240).

Later on, however, Locke concedes that those who dispute 'Whether the
will be free' may have a different question in mind. What they may mean
to ask is not whether the will itself has the property of freedom, but
whether an agent having a will is free to exercise it upon occasion:
'Whether a man be free to will' (E II.xxi.22: 245). This question, Locke
allows, is perfectly intelligible, and he proceeds to provide his own answer
to it. It is in the course of doing this that he puts forward his doctrine of
volitional determinism.

In fact Locke construes the question here in two different ways. What he
actually considers, therefore, are two distinct questions. In the one case,
the question is whether a man is free 'in respect of willing any Action in his
power once proposed to his Thoughts'. In the other, the question is
whether 'a Man be at liberty to will either Motion, or Rest; Speaking, or
Silence; which he pleases'. Locke takes up the first of these questions in
section 23, the second in section 25.

His answer to the first question is negative. Once a man considers an action, or starts deliberating about it, he 'cannot be free' in respect of willing it, since it is 'unavoidably necessary' that he will either to do it or not to do it. Locke argues for this position as follows:

Willing, or Choosing being an Action, and Freedom consisting in a power of acting, or not acting, [1] *a Man in respect of willing any Action in his power once proposed to his Thoughts, cannot be free*. The reason whereof is very manifest: For [2] it being unavoidable that the Action depending on his *Will*; should exist, or not exist; and its existence, or not existence, following perfectly the determination, and preference of his Will, [3] he cannot avoid willing the existence, or not existence, of that Action; it is absolutely necessary that he *will* the one, or the other, *i.e. prefer* the one to the other: since one of them must necessarily follow; and [4] that which does follow, follows by the choice and determination of his Mind, that is, by his *willing* it: for [5] if he did not *will* it, it would not be. So that [1] in respect of the act of *willing*, a Man is not free: Liberty consisting in a power to act, or not to act, which, in regard of Volition, a Man has not: it being necessary, and unavoidable (any Action in his power being once thought on) to prefer either its doing, or forbearance, upon which preference, the Action, or its forbearance certainly follows, and is truly voluntary. (E **1–3** II.xxi.23: 245; bracketed numerals added)

Locke's reasoning here has the form of a constructive dilemma. A more perspicuous statement of it, with suppressed premisses and lemmas filled in, is the following (numbers in square brackets refer to the text just quoted):

       (1) [2] Every action a man considers doing must either exist or not exist.

       (2) [5] If the man considering such an action did not will it to exist, it would not exist.

So (3) [4] If such an action exists, the man wills it to exist.

       (4)   If the man considering such an action did not will it not to exist, it would not exist.

So (5)   If such an action does not exist, the man wills it not to exist.

So (6) [3] Every such action must either be willed to exist or be willed not to exist by the man considering it.

       (7)   If a man wills an action to exist, he wills.

       (8)   If a man will an action not to exist, he wills.

So (9)   A man considering an action must will.

     (10)   If a man considering an action must will, then he is not free in respect of the act of willing: he cannot avoid willing.

So (11) [1] A man considering an action is not free in respect of the act of willing: he cannot avoid willing.

This argument, clearly, is valid. But equally clearly, it has a false premiss. The obvious offender was spotted by Leibniz. Here is Theophile's response to Philalethe's summary of section 23 in the *Nouveaux essais*:

I would have thought that one can suspend one's choice, and that this happens quite often, especially when other thoughts interrupt one's deliberation. Thus, although it is necessary that the action about which one is deliberating must exist or not exist, it doesn't follow at all that one necessarily has to decide on its existence or non-existence. For its non-existence could well come about in the absence of any decision. (Leibniz 1981: 181)

Leibniz's point is directed against premiss (4) of Locke's argument. This premiss is not stated explicitly, but clauses 3–5 in the text quoted above plainly imply it; and in any case the argument requires it. So if Leibniz is right—as surely he is—then Locke's reasoning fails to establish its conclusion.

But if Locke is thus guilty of accepting an evident falsehood, that is not the whole of his fault in this matter. For he also expressly acknowledges the very ability to 'suspend one's choice' that Leibniz uses to refute his argument in section 23. That agents have such an ability is precisely the point of his doctrine of suspension, stated in section 47 of the same chapter of the *Essay*. Thus, not only is premiss (4) of Locke's argument false, it is directly contradicted by something he himself affirms. Indeed, the doctrine of suspension contradicts the argument's conclusion also. It is true that these inconsistencies are not to be found in the first edition of Locke's work. For though the argument of section 23 was present from the outset, the doctrine of suspension did not appear until the second edition. But the inconsistencies did exist then, and they continued to do so thereafter. For Locke made no changes in the doctrine of suspension in subsequent editions of the *Essay*, nor did he excise or amend the (false) premiss of his argument in section 23—although he did finally, in his revisions for the fifth edition, qualify the argument's conclusion.

There is more to be said about Locke's position here; but to say it would take me away from my central concern in this paper. For the thesis that a man who thinks about doing something is unavoidably bound to will one way or the other regarding it—call this the unavoidability thesis—is not volitional determinism; nor is there any logical relation between this thesis and that. Volitional determinism applies to concrete acts of willing, and it ascribes necessity *de re* to all of them. It says of every volition that it is a necessary action on the part of its agent. The unavoidability thesis, by contrast, ascribes necessity *de dicto* to a proposition about agents, agents operating, furthermore, under a special condition. It says that if an agent thinks about doing something *x* then it is necessary that either he will to do *x* or else he will not to do *x*.[3] Not only does this thesis attribute necessity to no individual volition, but it is less than universal in scope, since not all of the actions that agents perform, or even their voluntary actions, are 'proposed to their thoughts' before being done. We often do things, and will to do things, quite spontaneously, without first thinking about them.

To discover Locke's volitional determinism, then, we must look to the second of the two questions he considers in sections 23–5. This second question is whether a man is free to will what he does will—free to will to move, for example, as opposed to willing to stand still, or willing not to move, or not willing to move, or even not willing at all. Locke's immediate response is that

This Question carries the absurdity of it so manifestly in it self, that one might thereby sufficiently be convinced, that Liberty concerns not the Will in any case. For to ask, whether a Man be at Liberty to will either Motion or Rest; Speaking, or Silence; which he pleases, is to ask, whether a Man can *will*, what he *wills*; or be pleased with what he is pleased with. A Question, which, I think, needs no answer; and they, who can make a Question of it, must suppose one Will to determine the Acts of another, and another to determinate that; and so on *in infinitum*. (E ii.xxi.25: 247)

What is Locke's position here? The question, he says, has an 'absurdity' in it. But he does not say that it is an 'insignificant' or an 'unintelligible' question. Furthermore, he pronounces the absurdity 'manifest'; but then, as if not trusting us to see it, takes steps to locate it. He suggests that the absurdity lies not in the question itself, but in an affirmative answer to it; that it consists in some sort of viciously infinite succession of wills; and that it arises somehow from the idea of iterated willing, of willing to will. It seems plain that Locke is urging a substantive, albeit negative answer to the question at issue, and that he is basing it on an argument of the *reductio ad absurdum* form. This negative answer is in fact the thesis of volitional determinism.

But what exactly is the reasoning by which Locke seeks to establish this thesis? His argument is barely adumbrated in the text I have quoted from section 25; and in the fifth edition of the *Essay* the section ends with the words '*in infinitum*'. But in the first four editions these words are immediately followed by a reference to an earlier statement of the same argument: 'an absurdity before taken notice of'. This earlier statement occurs in section 23—or did in the first four editions, after which it too was dropped,

---

[3] This is one possible way of construing Locke's unavoidability thesis, as a conditional necessity. Another is to take it as a necessary conditional: it is necessary that if an agent thinks about doing *x* then either he wills to do *x* or he wills not to do *x*.

along with the reference to it. This section originally contained two distinct arguments, both ostensibly in support of the unavoidability thesis. The second of these is indeed the *reductio* argument of section 25, more fully and more explicitly set forth. (The fact that the unavoidability thesis is logically distinct from the thesis of volitional determinism may explain why, assuming he realized it, Locke cut this passage out of the fifth edition.) Here is the earlier statement:

Besides, to make a Man free after this manner [sc. free with respect to the act of volition], by making the Action of *willing* to depend on his *Will*, there must be another antecedent *Will*, to determine the Acts of this *Will*, and another to determine that, and so *in infinitum*: For where-ever one stops, the Actions of the last *Will* cannot be free . . . (E **4** II.xxi.23: 245)

This statement enables us to identify three of Locke's premises:

(1) An agent's action of willing must, to be free, 'depend on his Will': i.e. it must be voluntary. This is just the general requirement that free actions be voluntary applied to the special case of actions of willing.

(2) To say that an action 'depends on a will' is to say that the will 'determines' that action. When the action determined is a volition, then there is a will to which that action belongs: a volition just is the act of a will. It might be supposed that the will by which a voluntary volition is determined is the same as that to which the volition belongs, or at least that it could be the same. On this supposition, a will would be capable of determining itself, i.e. of determining its own acts of willing. Locke, however, is clearly denying such self-determination on the part of the will. His position is, in fact, that a voluntary action of willing can only be determined by 'another antecedent will'—a will distinct from the will to which it belongs. (That the will can determine itself is what I shall call the 'autonomy principle'; its denial is then the 'heteronomy principle'.)

(3) Given that a voluntary volition requires a second will, distinct from the one it belongs to, why should any third will be required, let alone the infinite series of wills invoked by Locke's argument? Locke holds that when a will determines an action, it does so by acting, i.e. by performing one or more volitions. Let us say that the volition by which a will determines an action 'produces' the action, to distinguish the relation the volition bears to the action from the relation the will bears to it. If a volition, belonging to a will, is voluntary, then there is another volition, belonging to a second will, which produces it. But there is so far no need for this second volition to be voluntary also: that is, the fact that the first volition is *voluntary* does not require this. What does require it, according to Locke, is the fact that the first volition is *free*, besides being voluntary. For in this

passage he embraces what I shall call the 'inheritance principle' of free action. This is the principle that a free action must 'inherit' its freedom from the volition which produces it. More precisely, it is the principle that an action is free only if the volition which produces it is free; or, contrapositively, that if a volition is necessary then any action produced by it also is necessary. By this principle, a free volition requires a second volition that is free, and not merely voluntary; and this in turn requires a third free volition; and so on without end. 'For where-ever one stops, the Actions of the last Will cannot be free.'

It appears, then that the argument of section 25—and of section 23 in editions 1–4 of the *Essay*—can be represented as follows.

(1) Acts of willing are acts.
(2) Every act with respect to which an agent is free is voluntary.
(3) An act is voluntary if there is an act of willing which produces it.
(4) An act of willing is voluntary if there is a will which determines it.
(5) Every act of willing belongs to a will.
(6) The act of willing which produces a voluntary act of willing belongs to the will which determines that act.
(7) No will determines itself, i.e. determines the acts of willing which belong to it. (Heteronomy principle)
(8) An agent is free with respect to an act, only if he also is free with respect to the act of willing which produces that act. (Inheritance principle)
(9) If an act of willing is such that (*a*) there is an act of willing which produces it, and (*b*) there is a will which determines it, and (*c*) the act of willing which produces it belongs to the will which determines it, and (*d*) no will determines its own acts of willing, and (*e*) an agent is free with respect to an act only if he also is free with respect to the act of willing which produces that act; then there is an infinite series of wills running back from the will to which the first act of willing belongs.
(10) An infinite series of wills running back from the will to which a specified act of willing belongs is an absurdity.
(11) There are no absurdities.
So (12) No agent is free with respect to an act of willing.

Locke's argument, as I have rendered it, is valid. The task of evaluating it is therefore reduced to that of assessing its premises. We need not reach the question of the truth of these premises, however. For one of them turns out to be such that it cannot have been held to be true by the argument's own author, i.e. by Locke himself, which means that he cannot consistently have used the argument against its intended victims. The premiss in question is (8), the inheritance principle, which specifies a necessary condition for an action's being free: the action is free only if the volition that makes it a voluntary action itself is free. That such a condition holds is a fundamental doctrine of the very philosophers who were Locke's opponents on this issue. It is these philosophers who pronounce that 'Man's will is free', although what they must mean is that 'Men are free to will'. And it is at them that Locke's sarcastic jab in section 22 is directed: 'It passes for a good Plea', he remarks, 'that a Man is not free at all, if he be not as free to will, as he is to act, what he wills' (E ii.xxi.22: 245). This remark by itself might convince us that Locke would not have accepted premiss (8). But beyond that, there is a passage farther on in chapter xxi in which he explicitly rejects it. A prisoner, Locke writes,

> that has his Chains knocked off, and the Prison doors set open to him, is perfectly at *liberty*, because he may either go or stay, as he best likes; though his preference be determined to stay, by the darkness of the Night, or illness of the Weather, or want of other Lodging. He ceases not to be free; though the desire of some convenience to be had there, absolutely determines his preference, and makes him stay in his Prison. (E ii.xxi.50: 266)

In any case, the conjunction of premiss (8) with Locke's own belief in freedom directly contradicts the conclusion of his *reductio* argument. Locke begins his discussion of freedom in chapter xxi with the declaration that 'every one finds in himself' the power of acting freely. But if the volitions by which free actions are produced also have to be free, it would follow that some volitions are free, which is just the position that Locke's argument is directed against.

There is, to be sure, another way of using a *reductio* argument against an opponent.[4] Instead of reaching an absurdity via premises that he himself would accept, the author of a *reductio* may reason *ad hominem*, seeking to show that the absurdity follows from the opponent's own premises. The conclusion then drawn is that some part of the opponent's position is faulty, no matter whether it be the proposition originally tagged for 'reduction' or some other premiss, since in any case the position is damaged. It might then be suggested that Locke's *reductio* argument was meant to be used in this *ad hominem* way, with libertarians such as Bramhall and the Arminians the intended targets. There is no doubt that premiss (8) of the

---

[4] This point was suggested to me by Martha Bolton, who heard an earlier version of this paper.

argument had a crucial place in the credo of these thinkers (see e.g. Bramhall 1655: 13–16; van Limborch 1982: 368). Most of the other premisses, as well, would have been acceptable to the philosophers that Locke was attacking.

But the *ad hominem* use of a *reductio* argument can succeed only if *all* of its premisses would be accepted by the *homine* against whom it is directed. For otherwise the intended target can disarm the argument simply by rejecting any premiss that fails to accord with his overall position. And there is one premiss of Locke's argument which most of his opponents indeed would have rejected, namely (7), the heteronomy principle, that no will is self-determining. These thinkers subscribed, on the contrary, to the autonomy principle: for them, the power of self-determination is the central feature of the will. It is also the key to the will's freedom, and thence the basis of all human freedom, freedom with respect to acts other than volitions as well as volitions themselves. William King, for example, in a direct comment on section 23 of (the first edition of) the *Essay*, says of the claim 'that there must be an antecedent will to determine this will and so in infinitum', that 'this were true if the will were a passive power'. But in fact, King maintains, the will 'is an active power [that] determines it self in its choice and is not determined by another', adding that 'he that doth not understand this understands nothing of liberty'.[5] 'And Bishop Bramhall, in his *Castigations of Mr. Hobbes*, declares that it 'is a truth not to be doubted of' that 'the will doth determine itself' (Bramhall 1842: IV. 221). It is extremely unlikely, therefore, that Locke's *reductio* was intended to show the absurdity of his opponents' position upon their own premisses. But even if it had been so intended it would not have succeeded.

But if Locke's argument fails, it does not follow that its conclusion, the thesis of volitional determinism, is false. We have not shown even that any of its premisses are false—we have not raised any question as to their truth—only that their relation to other positions held by Locke and by his opponents is such that effective use of the argument is barred. Perhaps, after all, the thesis is true; and perhaps there is some other argument that Locke could have used to establish it.

Perhaps indeed. But the fact is, as I have noted, that Locke's view of freedom and motivation changed considerably after he published it in the *Essay*'s first edition. One significant new element in the position set forth in the second edition is the doctrine of suspension. This doctrine, far from providing support for volitional determinism, seems rather to undermine it: and Locke himself seems, near the end of his life, to have given it up.

[5] King's comment is made in a letter to William Molyneux, who conveyed it to Locke with his own letter of 15 Oct. 1692 (C IV: 540).

I turn now to consider this doctrine. It is stated in section 47 of the revised version of chapter xxi that Locke wrote for the second edition. At this point in the chapter Locke is presenting his new view of 'what determines the will'. His exposition here is subtle and intricate, and to do justice to it I should have to lay out at length not only what the new view amounts to, but how it differs from the old one, what led Locke to give up the one and develop the other, and what it is to 'determine the will' in the first place. In this paper, however, a rough sketch is all that is needed, to indicate the context in which the doctrine of suspension is introduced.

According, then, to Locke's second thoughts on the subject, what determines the will of an agent who is set to do something 'is not, as is generally supposed', and as he himself used to think, 'the greater good in view: But some . . . *uneasiness* [the agent] is at present under' (E 2–5 II.xxi.31: 250–1). This uneasiness is the troublesome feeling that constitutes, or at least is a part of, desire. Since 'desire' is defined as 'an uneasiness of the Mind for want of some absent good' (E 2–5 II.xxi.31: 251), we cannot say that 'uneasiness' has simply, in Locke's later view, been substituted for 'the greater good in view' as the one factor that makes agents will as they do. Originally, the mere perception of something as good was deemed sufficient to determine the will to an action, an action designed to attain the good so perceived; and desire and volition were hardly distinguished. In Locke's revised view, 'desiring and willing are two distinct Acts of the mind' (E 2–5 II.xxi.30: 250), related as cause and effect. The will, moreover, is not actually affected, we are not 'set on work', unless our desire for the good we perceive 'makes us uneasy in the want of it' (E 2–5 II.xxi.35: 253). For ' 'tis uneasiness alone [that] operates on the will' (E 2–5 II.xxi.36: 254); only uneasiness 'immediately determines' its choice (E 2–5 II.xxi.33: 252). Still, 'Good and Evil, present and absent', do 'work upon the mind' (E 2–5 II.xxi.33: 252), even if they do not do so directly. Indeed, they are always involved in the motivational process.

A simple example may help to convey Locke's position. Suppose a man to be hungry. Hunger is a form of desire, a desire either for food or for the relief that eating will bring. Relief is pleasant, and food produces pleasure; but the hunger itself is painful, an uneasy state. Depending on his situation and his beliefs, our hungry man wills to go to the fridge or a restaurant, or to pick a strawberry, or to perform some other action which is apt to satisfy his desire, bring relief from his pain, remove his uneasiness. Now the object of our agent's desire, food or relief, being pleasant or productive of pleasure, is good, at least in his eyes. The target of his volition is the action he opts for, e.g. to go to the fridge. And his desire determines his will, meaning that his desire causes his will to settle upon the action chosen, in the sense both of eliciting an actual volition and of specifying it as a volition to perform precisely that action.

The agent in our example has only one desire, hunger. In real life, however, Locke observes, we are 'beset with sundry *uneasinesses*, distracted with different *desires*' (E **2–5** II.xxi.40: 257), all clamouring for attention, the will being incapable of being determined to more than one action at once (E **2–5** II.xxi.36: 254). Locke then asks himself which of these competing desires 'has the precedency in determining the *will* to the next action' (E **2–5** II.xxi.40: 257). It is in addressing this question that he introduces the doctrine of suspension.

> There being in us a great many *uneasinesses* always solliciting, and ready to determine the *will*, it is natural . . . that the greatest, and most pressing should determine the *will* to the next action; and so it does for the most part, but not always. For the mind having in most cases, as is evident in Experience, a power to *suspend* the execution and satisfaction of any of its desires, and so all, one after another, is at liberty to consider the objects of them; examine them on all sides, and weigh them with others. . . . we have a power to *suspend* the prosecution of this or that desire, as every one daily may Experiment in himself. . . . [And] during this *suspension* of any desire, before the *will* be determined to action, and the action (which follows that determination) done, we have opportunity to examine, view, and judge, of the good or evil of what we are going to do . . . (E **2–5** II.xxi.47: 263)

Two features of Locke's position are worth noting. The first is that the doctrine of suspension is not a logical consequence of any element of his (revised) view of motivation. He presents it rather as an empirical datum. Second, the point of suspending one's desires, for an agent, is to effect some change in their content or relative strength. The doctrine of suspension does not presuppose, but it nicely supports, Locke's conviction that an agent may, through diligent effort and (especially) rational consideration, control his desires. Thus 'due, and repeated Contemplation' is capable of bringing some absent good, which we have recognized as such but have not judged to be essential to our present happiness, 'nearer to the Mind', of giving 'some relish' to it, and raising 'in us some desire; which then beginning to make a part of our present *uneasiness* . . . comes in its turn to determine the *will*' (E **2–5** II.xxi.45: 262). In this way, Locke continues, 'by a due consideration and examining any good proposed, it is in our power, to raise our desires . . . whereby [that good] may come to work upon the *will*, and be pursued' (E **2–5** II.xxi.46: 262). It follows, he later notes, that it is within 'a Man's power to change the pleasantness, and unpleasantness' of things (E **2–5** II.xxi.69: 280). This is not the position Locke had taken in his original version of chapter xxi. Indeed, he had explicitly maintained the contrary, saying that it is not 'in [anyone's] choice, whether he will, or will not be better pleased with one thing than another' (E **1** II.xxi.28: 248).

Locke's doctrine of suspension, I said earlier, appears to conflict with his volitional determinism. I said 'appears to conflict' because I believe that although there is some reason to think that the two positions do contradict each other, there is also some reason to think that they do not.

Volitional determinism is the thesis that no volition is free. This thesis is inconsistent with the doctrine of suspension if the latter entails that some volitions are free. According to Locke's view of freedom, a volition is free for an agent if two requirements are met: first, the volition is voluntary—the agent wills to perform it—and second, it is avoidable—the agent can forbear from performing it by willing not to do so.

The case for holding that Locke's two positions are in conflict is this. If one is able to suspend all of one's desires then the second requirement is met: that one can avoid performing some volition. For suppose that agent m has several desires, the most pressing of which is about to determine her will to action s. Thus m is about to perform the volition of willing s. Now suppose that m suspends these desires, and thereby keeps her will from being determined to s. It is plain that m has avoided willing s; but has she done so by willing not to will s? That depends on whether suspension is a voluntary action on the part of its agent, whether suspending one's desires is something one does in consequence of willing to do it. But Locke surely did hold that suspension is voluntary, although he never says so explicitly.[6] And if so, then m suspends her desires by willing to do so. And thus it is by willing also that she forbears from willing s. Hence there is a volition that m is able to avoid by willing.

As for the first requirement, that some volitions are voluntary, the doctrine of suspension entails that it too is met, provided we make a small and plausible addition to Locke's actual statement of the doctrine. Locke says that an agent can suspend all of her desires during deliberation and so avoid performing the volition that the desires would otherwise have caused. It is plausible to add to this that an agent also has the power of lifting or rescinding a suspension once imposed, thus reinstating the suspended desires and allowing them, or the most pressing among them, to proceed to determine her will. But if any suspension is voluntary, so too must its rescission, or the desuspension, if I may so call it, of the suspended desires, be voluntary. It is true that most volitions that are or could have been avoided because of a suspension would not have been or were not the result of a rescission of a previous suspension by their agent, or of any other voluntary action on her part. But those that do follow (voluntary)

---

[6] It is worth noting, however, that two professed followers of Locke, Anthony Collins and Jonathan Edwards, do explicitly say that suspension is a voluntary act on the part of its agent: see Collins 1717: 73–4; Edwards 1957: 210.

rescissions are themselves voluntary: their performance is consequent upon the will. Since all such volitions follow suspensions as well, they are also such as could have been avoided. Hence both requirements for free volitions are met in their case. So there are free volitions if agents have the power of suspending (and subsequently desuspending) their desires.

So goes the case for holding that the doctrine of suspension is in conflict with volitional determinism. The case for the contrary proposition runs as follows. It is true that an agent who suspends her desires, or desuspends desires previously suspended, exercises control over her will; and that, since suspending and desuspending are voluntary actions on her part, she does so by willing: she wills or forbears from willing at will. But her (first-order) willing or not willing is not the direct or immediate target of her (second-order) willing in such cases. (I use Harry Frankfurt's terminology to distinguish the two willings here involved; see Frankfurt 1971.) The precise and immediate target of someone who wills to suspend her desires is the action of suspending such and such desires. The forbearance from willing that then ensues is only the consequence or result of that action, a distinct event that is brought about by it. This is so even if the agent wills the suspension for the purpose of preventing the first-order volition; even if suspension is the means employed by the agent in order to bring about the end of keeping her will from being determined. But Locke's view of freedom limits free actions to those than an agent wills, and whose forbearance she could will, directly, i.e. to those whose performance and forbearance are themselves targets of the agent's willing. Volitions which an agent manages to accomplish or prevent by willing something else which in turn brings about their existence or non-existence do not meet this condition, and hence are not free actions. The doctrine of suspension, therefore, poses no challenge to volitional determinism: the two positions are perfectly compatible.

In my view, neither one of the two lines of reasoning just sketched is conclusive. The issues whereover they differ have been discussed by philosophers for centuries, without ever, to my mind, having been definitely settled. There surely is a difference between direct and (what we might call) instrumental willing—between the things we simply will to do and those we can only accomplish by willing to do other things that cause the former to occur. But just where and how is the line dividing these two to be drawn? Clear cases exist on both sides: on the one hand, I move my right arm; on the other, I turn on the light by flipping the switch. But suppose I scratch my left elbow (by moving my right arm), or (Descartes's example) enlarge my pupils by looking at a far-distant object? These cases seem to fall between the first two, but is it still clear that the one is, whereas the other is not, an instance of direct willing? And even if it is clear with these actions, are there not others which fall between them, and whose position with respect to the direct-instrumental divide is not clear? Furthermore, even in the clear cases of direct willing, as when I move my right arm, can we not treat the action here as a kind of result brought about by other things I do—more 'basic' things such as intending or trying to move my arm, or moving various muscles? And in the clear cases of instrumental willing, such as turning on the light by flipping the switch, is there not a sense in which the one action just *is* the other differently described, so that there is really only one action being performed? Or if there really are two, is not their relation such—that of the means to an end—that willing carries over from the one to the other? Some philosophers at least would agree with St Thomas that 'when you will the means to an end you thereby also [*eodem actu*] will the end' (*Summa theologiae*, I–II.viii.3 ad 2).

In the absence of definitive answers to these questions, there is, I believe, no certain basis for pronouncing that Locke's doctrine of suspension either does or does not entail the denial of his volitional determinism. That is, there is no basis for any pronouncement concerning the relationship of these two positions considered in and of themselves. It is of course a different question what Locke thought about that relationship. And as to that, there is no evidence in the text of the second, third, or fourth editions of the *Essay* that he had any thought about it at all. To be sure, since he explicitly affirms both volitional determinism and the doctrine of suspension in all three editions, we might ascribe to him the implicit view that the two positions are consistent. But it is probably more accurate to say that he simply had no view whatsoever about their relationship, not having perceived it to be a matter one needs to have a view about.

Some time after the publication of the fourth edition in 1700, however, Locke's perception changed. Not only did he come to see a conflict between the doctrine of suspension and volitional determinism, but he repudiated the latter because of this conflict, thus opting for the one position at the expense of the other. The result is set forth in a passage Locke wrote to be added to the *Essay*'s fifth edition, which was actually published, as it turns out, after his death.

Liberty 'tis plain consists in a Power to do, or not to do; to do, or forbear doing as we *will*. This cannot be deny'd. But this seeming to comprehend only the actions of a Man consecutive to volition, it is farther enquired, whether he be at Liberty to *will*, or no? and to this it has been answered, that in most cases a Man is not at Liberty to forbear the act of volition; he must exert an act of his *will*, whereby the action proposed, is made to exist, or not to exist. But yet there is a case wherein a Man is at Liberty in respect of *willing*, and that is the chusing of a remote Good as an end to be pursued. Here a Man may suspend the act of his choice from

being determined for or against the thing proposed, till he has examined, whether
it be really of a nature in it self and consequences to make him happy, or no.
(E **5** ii.xxi.56: 270)

Locke indicates here that he takes the doctrine of suspension to conflict
with his unavoidability thesis, defended in section 23 of chapter xxi, as well
as with the volitional determinism of section 25. But he plainly abandons
the latter as well as the former of these two positions: the admission of 'a
case wherein a Man is at Liberty in respect of *willing*' is all that is needed
to refute the proposition that 'Liberty concerns not the will in any case' (E
1–4 ii.xxi.25: 247).

What accounts for this change in Locke's outlook? The answer lies in
several letters that passed between Locke and Philippus van Limborch in
1701 and 1702. Van Limborch found much to dispute in Locke's account of
liberty, not only as presented in the *Essay*, but especially as Locke restated
and elaborated it in response to his friend's criticisms. One major point of
difference is just Locke's refusal to admit free volitions—his thesis of
volitional determinism. In one of his letters Locke insists that liberty
'consists solely in the power to act or not to act consequent on . . . the
determination of the will' (C vii: 329). To this van Limborch replies,
'altogether to the contrary, that liberty consists solely in a power by which
a man can determine, or not determine, an action of willing' (C vii: 368).
He goes on to claim that this power of determining the will is manifested
in a man's ability to 'suspend his action' of willing on occasion, and declares that he 'thought that [Locke's] opinion was the same' on this, citing
section 47 of the chapter on power (C vii: 370). He also says that though he
agrees with several of the things set forth in section 47, he 'cannot reconcile
them with' certain other features of Locke's position, including, presumably, his denial of free willing (C vii: 370).

At first, Locke either failed or refused to grasp the significance of van
Limborch's point here—more likely the latter, in view of the blustery
manner of his initial reply (C vii: 402–14). But van Limborch pressed the
matter in his next letter; and in responding to that Locke did acknowledge
the problem at issue, albeit not directly. For in lieu of a direct answer to
several of van Limborch's criticisms, Locke sent along with his letter a set
of 'explications' to be inserted at various places in chapter xxi of the *Essay*.
Among them was the passage I quoted a moment ago, in which Locke
affirms the incompatibility of the doctrine of suspension with volitional
determinism. It is past doubt that this passage was written because of van
Limborch's efforts. But as further confirmation of van Limborch's role I
would note that Locke did at last, in a letter written a year later, inform his
friend directly of his change of mind. 'Generally', Locke writes,

in my opinion a man is free in every action, as well of willing as of understanding, if he was able to have abstained from that action of willing or understanding; if not, not.

More particularly, as regards the will: there are some cases in which a man is unable not to will, and in all those acts of willing a man is not free because he is unable not to act. In the rest, where he was able to will or not to will, he is free. (C VII: 680)

Locke's final position, therefore, is that the doctrine of suspension is incompatible with the thesis of volitional determinism, and that, since the former is true, the latter is false: there are free volitions, cases in which a man is indeed free with respect to his willing this or that. The last question I wish to discuss concerns the consequences of this about-face on Locke's part for his overall view of human free action. It seems clear that he himself did not go very far in working out these consequences: for example, he made no change in the text of that portion of section 25 in which volitional determinism and the argument supporting it are stated (although he did, as I noted earlier, drop another statement of the same argument from section 23). Furthermore, whereas some of Locke's readers have judged his doctrine of suspension, along with the free volitions he took it to entail, to be inconsistent with the main thrust of his theory of freedom, others have made the contrary claim.[7]

The central core of Locke's theory of freedom comprises the following propositions:

(1) Freedom is a property only of rational agents.
(2) Human beings are free agents; i.e. they are free with respect to some of their actions.
(3) The human will is not an agent; hence the will is not a free agent.
(4) A free action is an action whose agent is free with respect to it.
(5) Every action is the effect of antecedent causes.
(6) Every free action is voluntary; i.e. its causes include a volition on the part of its agent.
(7) Every free action is avoidable; i.e. its non-occurrence can be effected by a volition on the part of its agent.
(8) The volition that causes a free action need not itself be a free action.

Now it is obvious that it doesn't follow from any of these propositions, or from all together, that no volition is a free action. Hence volitional

---

[7] One reader who has taken the former position is Edmund Law; see Law 1781: 214–16 n. 48. On the other side, both Collins and Edwards maintain that there is no conflict between the doctrine of suspension and the rest of the Lockean theory of freedom, which is also the theory (more or less) that each of them wishes to defend. See Collins 1717: 73–4; and Edwards 1957: 209–11.

determinism is not a logical consequence of them. Hence the denial of volitional determinism is perfectly consistent with the essential core of Locke's theory of freedom. Locke's admission, therefore, late in his life, that there are free volitions neither conflicts with the main thrust of his original thoughts on the subject, nor produces an incoherent new body of thought.

In particular, Locke is not, by allowing free volitions, joining forces with libertarians of the Bramhallian or the Arminian stripe. To give up on volitional determinism is not to give in to the inheritance principle. Nor does the admission of some free volitions commit one to holding that all volitions are free. Surely the right view, on empirical grounds, is both that most of the volitions that agents perform are not free, and that very few of their free actions are brought about by free volitions. And this is the view, one presumes, that Locke in the end held as well.

On the other hand, if there are free volitions, then Locke's *reductio* in section 25 of chapter xxi is unsound. But the loss of this argument does no damage to his overall theory. Indeed, as I hope to have shown, it could not have fulfilled the purpose he intended it for in any case.

As for the doctrine of suspension, I have not myself endorsed Locke's final view that it entails the admission of free volitions. But nor have I rejected it. In my judgement, the correctness of that view is an open question, pending further investigation. But it is clear that the doctrine of suspension itself is perfectly compatible with the central core of Locke's theory—although it is not, as I remarked earlier, entailed by it. And I agree with Locke, again on empirical grounds, that the doctrine is true.

If there are free volitions, then there are second-order volitions, i.e. willings whose targets are other willings, these being volitions of the first order. There may even be volitions of the third and fourth orders. Some philosophers, Hobbes and Leibniz for two, have objected to the very idea of such iterated willing (Hobbes 1840: 240; Leibniz 1981: 182). But no solid argument has ever been offered, to my knowledge, in support of these objections. To be sure, the capacity of human consciousness is limited, in such wise that we can be sure that seventeenth-order volitions, say, never occur, and that even third-order willing is exceedingly rare. But the warrant for our assurance here is empirical; and not only is the idea of willing to will coherent, but it can be used to provide valuable light in moral psychology, as recent work by Frankfurt and others has shown (see Frankfurt 1988; Wolf 1981; Stump 1988).

Nothing that I have said in this chapter, however, should be taken to imply that I accept, or even that I understand, the general theory of will and volition that underlies Locke's view of freedom. I have tried to work around this theory, taking Locke more or less at his word with regard to it, and leaving his meaning, for the most part, unexplored. But I am well aware that a full account of Locke's thought would have to include a detailed examination and critical assessment of this theory also.

VI

SUBSTANCES, SUBSTRATA, AND NAMES OF SUBSTANCES IN LOCKE'S *ESSAY*

MARTHA BRANDT BOLTON

I

THE distinction between ideas of substances and ideas of mixed modes is an integral part of the theory of ideas in Locke's *Essay*. Roughly speaking, it differentiates natural kinds of things from conventional kinds, and this is central to Locke's theory of knowledge, his division of the sciences, and his semantic theory.[1] The distinction is unfortunately difficult to understand. It is very obscure what features distinguish ideas of the one sort from those of the other sort. In the account of substances, it is the notion of substratum which predominates; in contrast to ideas of all other sorts, ideas of substances always include the idea of an 'unknown support in which qualities are supposed to inhere'. This doctrine of substratum is itself obscure and it has often been said to be misguided. As a result, the difference between ideas of substances and modes, so important to the theory developed in the *Essay*, is usually discussed with little or no mention of substratum (see e.g. Perry 1967; Aaron 1971: 154–79). This distorts Locke's view; whatever the doctrine of substratum involves, Locke took the inclusion of the idea of substratum to embody the most outstanding characteristic of ideas of substances. In this paper, I develop an account of the distinction between ideas of substances and of mixed modes, and an account of substratum and its function in differentiating those two kinds of ideas.

The difference in the form of ideas of substances and those of mixed modes determines a difference in Locke's account of the semantics of

From *Philosophical Review*, 85: 4 (1976), 488–513. Copyright 1976 Cornell University. Reprinted by permission of the publisher and the author.

[1] There is not universal agreement that this correctly describes the distinction, although I will argue that it does. For an alternative account, see Bennett 1971: sects. 11, 15; cf. Ryle 1933. Recently the distinction has been discussed in several articles in the *Journal of the History of Philosophy*: Perry 1967; Aronson and Lewis 1970; Woolhouse 1972.

names of substances and names of modes. So I shall also discuss Locke's theory of the meaning of names for substances, or natural kind terms, and the names for mixed modes, or terms for some non-natural kinds. I shall argue that the notion of substratum has an essential role in Locke's account of the meanings of natural kind terms.

Ideas of substances and modes are both complex ideas,[2] supposed to be combinations of simple ideas received from sensation or reflection. The term 'ideas of modes' is introduced with the explanation that it means 'complex *ideas*, which however compounded, contain not in them the supposition of subsisting by themselves, but are considered as dependences on, or affections of substances; such are the *ideas* signified by the words *triangle, gratitude, murder, etc.*' (E II.xii.4: 165).[3] On the other hand, ideas of substances are said to be 'such combinations of simple *ideas*, as are taken to represent distinct particular things subsisting by themselves; in which the supposed, or confused *idea* of substance . . . is always the first and chief'; Locke gives as examples the ideas of lead, a man and a sheep (E II.xii.6: 165).[4] On the basis of these passages, one can say that there are three differences between ideas of these two kinds: (i) ideas of substances portray things which subsist by themselves, but ideas of modes portray things thought to depend on a substance; (ii) ideas of substances represent distinct particular things, but ideas of modes do not; (iii) ideas of substances include the confused idea of substratum, but ideas of modes do not.

However these three points do not go far toward explicating the difference between the two sorts of ideas. The phrase 'subsists by itself' is open to a wide variety of interpretations, each compatible with Locke's examples of substances and modes.[5] Although the expression 'distinct particular

---

[2] Locke divides ideas of modes into ideas of simple modes and those of mixed modes. Simple modes include infinity, number, space and time; in general, simple modes require a treatment much different from that Locke gives to mixed modes. In this paper, I will be mainly concerned with mixed modes.

[3] Locke exhibits here a tendency, often noted, to speak of modes as if they were a sort of idea, rather than a sort of thing of which we have ideas. I will use the word 'mode' to refer to things of certain sorts and the words 'idea of a mode' to refer to the ideas of such things.

[4] Locke uses the word 'substance' in two ways: (i) to mean an entity of a certain kind (contrasted with modes), such as a man, a sheep, or gold; and (ii) to mean substratum, or the 'unknown support of qualities' of things belonging to the kind referred to in (i). I will follow recent practice and use the word 'substance' only as in (i) and the word 'substratum' as in (ii).

[5] Woolhouse (in Woolhouse 1971) offers a complicated interpretation of the phrase 'subsists by itself' which fits Locke's examples of substances; he claims that Locke mistakenly thinks the doctrine of substratum is required to explain how substances 'subsist by themselves', as he interprets that phrase. He also claims that the doctrine of substance Locke offers in other parts of the *Essay* (especially II.xxiii and III.vi) is different, and indeed closer to the account of substances I am proposing here. It seems to me, however, that it should be assumed that Locke has a unified view of substances until that assumption is shown to be untenable. The initial sections of II.xxiii seem to indicate that substratum is central to the view of substances developed

things' might naturally be taken to mean Aristotelian individuals, or count-
able things, that interpretation is ruled out at once by the appearance of
lead, a sort of matter, as an example of a substance. Finally, it is most
obscure what the idea of substratum is supposed to be.

Indeed it seems to me that these passages in which Locke gives explicit
accounts of ideas of substances and modes are sufficiently ambiguous and
obscure that there is little hope of understanding the classification of ideas
by scrutinizing them alone. There are other contexts in which Locke claims
that there are significant differences between ideas of substances and those
of modes. I propose to investigate what is implied in those contexts about
the two sorts of ideas and the notion of substratum.

In the next section, I argue that the familiar accounts of Locke's view
about substratum are not supported by what he says about it. In sections III
through VI, I develop another account of substratum by analysing passages
in which ideas of substances and modes are treated differently; section VI is
an examination of the role of substratum in Locke's semantic theory for
kind terms. In section VII, I make use of my analysis to sketch a way of
understanding Locke's explicit accounts of ideas of substances and modes,
such as the one just quoted, and his explicit remarks about substratum.

II

Locke remarks that the idea of substratum is obscure and his own discussion appears to confirm it. He maintains that when we find several sensible
qualities 'occur frequently together', we cannot imagine how they can
'subsist by themselves'; we are thus led to suppose that they are 'united and
supported by something' and having no idea what it is, call it a 'substratum'
(E II.xxiii.1–3: 295–7; *et passim*). The argument explicit in this account is far
from convincing—why can't qualities subsist by themselves? How does
substratum solve the problem?

It has often been thought that Locke is motivated by concern for the
dependent ontological status of *properties* in general. The concern arises
from the supposition that a property cannot exist on its own; to exist it
must be the property of some *thing*. Locke's category of substances is
thought to be the category of things which *have* properties and thereby
support their existence. As such, the category must include things of all

in that chapter. Moreover, the earlier claim that substances 'subsist by themselves', and Locke's
explicit remarks about substratum, are open to *many* interpretations. I will propose an interpretation which I think not only fits these passages, but also shows that they are part of a unified
account of substances found throughout the *Essay*.

sorts: not just water, gold, and a man but also a table, laundry soap, and a postage stamp. Substratum is supposed to have entered his thinking when Locke reflected that such things—a man, a table, soap—can be analysed in terms of their properties; that is, a table is what has the properties of being flat, elevated from the ground, used in a certain way, and so forth. Thinking that no property can be attributed unless something which supports it is presupposed, Locke falls into the mistake of thinking that a table must be nothing other than a thing which supports properties. This property-less supporter of properties is said to be Locke's substratum.

Various philosophers have supposed that something like this mistaken reasoning accounts for Locke's doctrine concerning substratum. Jonathan Bennett (Bennett 1971: 59–63), for example, suggests that substratum is introduced in a misguided attempt to give a general account of property instantiation, according to which the existence of *any* property requires a thing which has it; ultimately, the 'thing' cannot be characterized by any property—hence, a substratum. R. I. Aaron (Aaron 1971: 172–9) suggests that Locke is concerned to explain the difference between a case in which any set of properties belongs to one thing and a case in which the same properties belong to various things; substrata provide the ontological glue for properties belonging to any one thing. According to E. M. Curley (Curley 1969: 4–11), Locke holds that we perceive only properties, and subscribing to the thesis that properties in general cannot exist without a thing which has them, he posits an imperceivable substratum to be the anchor of properties. (See also Leibniz 1981: 218; O'Connor 1967.)

This sort of account of Locke's doctrine, as concerned with the existence of properties in general, is thought to be supported by passages such as this one:

The *idea* then we have, to which we give the general name substance [substratum], being nothing, but the supposed, but unknown support of those qualities, we find existing, which we imagine cannot subsist, *sine re substante*, without something to support them, we call that support *substantia*; which . . . is in plain *English*, *standing under*, or *upholding*. (E II.xxiii.2: 296)

And also this one:

when we speak of any sort of substance, we say it is a *thing* having such or such qualities, as body is a *thing* that is extended, figured, and capable of motion; . . . These, and the like fashions of speaking, intimate that the substance is supposed always *something* besides the extension, figure, solidity, motion, thinking, or otherwise observable *ideas*, though we know not what it is. (E II.xxiii.3: 297)

In fact, however, these passages do *not* support the traditional interpretation of the doctrine of substratum. Careful reading of them shows that Locke argues only that certain properties of certain things (namely, qualities of substances) are supported by substrata. He does not *say* that every property inheres in a substratum, and as I will show, the account of substrata cannot plausibly be extended to provide a general account of property instantiation.

In the first place, substrata cannot provide a general account of the *things* required to instantiate properties, because it is *only* substances which have substrata. Properties clearly belong to things other than substances. A mode, such as murder, bristles with properties; properties themselves have properties. Each of them belongs to something, but does not subsist in a substratum; each is one of several properties belonging to the same thing with no substratum to glue them together. Locke does not *say* that all things with properties have substrata; moreover, he could have *thought* that they do only if he thought that things such as modes do not have properties, and there is no reason to think he held that unlikely view.

One might still think that substrata are supposed to account for the instantiation of properties in general, but argue that some properties are instantiated only indirectly by substrata. The argument would be that according to Locke, some properties can be instantiated without belonging directly to a substance; they can belong to other properties. But any series of such properties cannot continue indefinitely. The series exists only if it ends in a property which belongs to some *thing*. So, substrata are the *things*, as opposed to properties, by which all properties are instantiated. However, even on this account, substrata are not the *only things* which instantiate properties. Modes are the *things* to which modal properties belong; on the view that the instantiation of a property requires a thing *as opposed to a property*, modes are clearly able to instantiate properties.

To be sure, Locke holds that modes are *somehow* dependent on substances, but there is no reason to think that he holds that substances *instantiate* modes or modal properties. The properties of a mode do not belong to the substance on which the mode depends. Macbeth's murder of Duncan has the property of being a crime of ambition, but clearly Macbeth does not have that property. Neither Macbeth nor his substratum provides a *thing to which* that modal property belongs; although Macbeth, and his substratum, may be required in some way for the existence of that modal property, it is absurd to suggest that either of them instantiates it.[6] So, although Locke holds that substrata provide some sort of support for

---

[6] It was suggested to me that the properties of Duncan's murder might be thought to be reducible to properties of Duncan and Macbeth, and perhaps this is plausible for *some* properties of the murder. However Locke would not have thought it true of all the murder's properties. For example, the murder has the property of *being a mode* and that does not reduce to a property inhering in Macbeth or Duncan. If it did, they would *be modes*.

modes, it is not that they provide a *thing to which* modal properties belong. Substrata are basic in some way, but they cannot be construed as the basic things which instantiate properties.

In the second place, only *some* properties of even a substance are said by Locke to subsist in its substratum. *Qualities* of substances are said to require substrata[7] and it is clear that Locke does not use the word 'quality' to refer to the full range of properties of substances. Locke's well-known classification of qualities into primary, secondary and a third sort of causal power is exhaustive (see E II.xxiii.9: 300–1; E II.viii.9–10 and 23: 134–5 and 140–1). Material substances have no further *qualities* although they clearly have additional *properties*. Locke explains what he understands a quality to be: '. . . the power to produce any *idea* in our mind, I call *quality* of the subject wherein that power is' (E II.viii.8: 134).[8] In Locke's terminology, the qualities of a substance are its causal powers.[9] The qualities of gold include its being yellow, fusible, and malleable, but not its properties of being valuable, being used as a monetary standard, or being the metal of which Locke's ring was made. It is only the causal powers of a thing, not its properties in general, which are supposed to be supported by a substratum. This is a further reason why the doctrine of substratum cannot be understood as a general account of property instantiation.

Finally, it seems that Locke would not count as substances the wide variety of kinds of things required by the familiar accounts. Once one understands that substrata support qualities, rather than properties in general, it appears that the doctrine of substratum is concerned solely with kinds of things characterizable in terms of qualities alone. This does not

---

[7] There are a few places where Locke says it is simple ideas, or 'observable ideas', that inhere in substrata; see e.g. E II.xii.6: 165; E II.xxiii.1 and 6: 295 and 298–9. A simple *idea* cannot literally be a property of a substance such as gold. So these passages must be read in the light of Locke's admission that he sometimes speaks of ideas as if they were 'in the things themselves', when he means the powers things have to produce ideas in us; see E II.viii.8: 134.

[8] It was objected to me that this explanation cannot be taken as definitive of Locke's use of the word 'quality', on the grounds that *insensible* particles do not have the power to produce ideas and Locke clearly holds that they have primary qualities. This point has recently been maintained by Robert Cummins (1975). The fact that a particle is insensible, however, does not show that it has *no* powers to produce ideas; for example, it would produce ideas if sufficiently magnified. Moreover, Locke holds that it is by means of the primary qualities of insensible particles that our ideas of colours, odours, etc. *are* produced (see e.g. E II.viii.10: 135). Finally, it is because of the primary qualities of insensible particles that a body has its 'tertiary' powers, or powers to cause changes in other bodies, thereby altering the ideas they produce (see E II.viii.23: 140–1). Thus, the primary qualities of insensible particles *are*, in part, powers to produce ideas.

[9] There is some indication that qualities are not limited to powers to produce ideas, but include *all* the causal powers of a body. A body's 'tertiary' qualities are powers to produce ideas only indirectly, by affecting the idea-producing powers of another body. Further, in one passage, Locke describes secondary and 'tertiary' qualities without mentioning ideas, simply as '. . . powers to act differently upon other things' (E II.viii.23: 141).

include tables or postage stamps, for the properties typical of those kinds of things involve their uses or histories, not just their powers to produce ideas.[10] So the familiar accounts of Locke's doctrine of substratum are mistaken and do not help to explicate the difference between substances and modes.

III

In order to develop an account of the difference between ideas of substances and those of modes, I am now going to examine several contexts in which Locke treats the sorts of ideas differently. One such context is that in which Locke distinguishes between 'real' and 'fantastical' ideas:

> By *real ideas*, I mean such as have a foundation in nature; such as have a conformity with the real being, and existence of things, or with their archetypes. *Fantastical* or *chimerical*, I call such as have no foundation in nature, nor have any conformity with that reality of being, to which they are tacitly referr'd, as to their archetypes. (E II.xxx.1: 372)

In other words, an idea is real if it represents some real thing which it is supposed to represent and fantastical if it does not.

Locke continues:

> *Mixed modes and relations*, having no other *reality*, but what they have in the minds of men, there is nothing more required to those kind of *ideas*, to make them *real*, but that they be so framed, that there be a possibility of existing conformable to them. . . . Our *complex* ideas of *substances*, being made all of them in reference to things existing without us, and intended to be representations of substances, as they really are, are no farther *real*, than as they are such combinations of simple *ideas*, as are really united, and coexist in things without us. On the contrary, those are *fantastical*, which are made up of such collections of simple *ideas*, as were really never united, never were found together in any substance; *v.g.* a rational creature, consisting of a horse's head, joined to a body of humane shape, or such as the *centaurs* are described: . . . (E II.xxx.4–5: 373–4)

There are different requirements for the reality of ideas of the one sort than for those of the other. An idea of a mode, if merely consistent, cannot fail to be real; an idea of a substance, even if consistent, is not real unless

---

[10] About some kinds of things it is difficult to decide whether they are characterizable by qualities, or causal powers, alone. An artefact such as a clock can be considered as a certain sort of mechanism which can be characterized in terms of causal powers and qualifies to be a substance. On the other hand, it may be that such a mechanism is not a *clock* unless it is used to tell the time. Locke reflects this uncertainty about how to classify clocks and other artefacts with mechanisms. See esp. E III.vi.39–41: 463–5; although this is a chapter on substances in which clocks are mentioned, Locke refrains from saying definitely that clocks are substances; but also see the brief suggestion in E II.xxiv.2: 318 that a ship is a substance.

there is some actual thing which conforms to it. Why does the idea of a horse require the existence of horses, if the idea of gratitude does not require the existence of gratitude? It is, Locke says, because ideas of substances are 'tacitly referred' to actual things and are 'intended to be representations' of those actual things, whereas ideas of modes are not intended to represent anything in particular. What does this imply about the difference between ideas of modes and those of substances?

At first glance, it may seem most natural to suppose that the different intentions as to whether an idea represents an actual thing are contingently, extrinsically attached to the idea.[11] That is, a given complex idea such as that of gold might or might not be formulated with the intention of representing actual stuff; it is a fact about its history that it was formed with that intention and that fact is in no way reflected in the collection of simple ideas which makes it up. On this account, it is a contingent fact that each substantial idea was formed with this intention, and that each modal idea was not. Whether a given idea was intended to copy things, or not, is to be discovered by tracing the history of the idea.

There are several respects in which this account of the intentions which characterize ideas of substances and modes does not conform to Locke's doctrine. In the first place, it does not allow Locke to say absolutely whether an idea-type *has* the intention supposed to characterize substantial ideas, in contrast to modal ideas. For, different people might form tokens of the same idea-type with different intentions, so an *idea-type* could be classified only *relatively* to certain people. Moreover, the characterization based on people's intentions concerning an idea would be liable to change, so that the *idea* might change from substantial to modal. But Locke nowhere suggests that the classification of an idea as substantial or modal is relative, or that it is liable to change. Also according to this account, Locke should have provided historical evidence for his claims as to which ideas are substantial and which are modal. Locke does not support his classifications with historical evidence about ideas, however; instead he seems to think that it is clear from acquaintance with an idea whether it is substantial or modal.

In fact, there is textual evidence that it is *not* Locke's view that it is a contingent fact that each idea of a mode was not taken from actual things, whereas each idea of a substance was. He allows that sometimes an idea of a *mode* is formed by observing something; there are three ways in which we are said to get ideas of mixed modes, the first of them is '. . . by experience and *observation* of things themselves. Thus by seeing two men

---

[11] This appears to be Perry's view (Perry 1967: 222-3).

wrestle, or fence, we get the *idea* of wrestling or fencing' (E II.xxii.9: 291–2; see also E II.xxii.2: 288–9; E III.v.6–7: 430–2; E II.xi.15: 162).[12] But if in some cases the idea of a mode is taken from actual occurrences, then the difference between ideas of modes and those of substances cannot be simply that *as a contingent fact* ideas of substances are intended to be copies of actual things and ideas of modes are not. It seems that the difference must be that ideas of substances are *necessarily* intended to copy things.[13]

One way in which ideas of substances and modes differ is, then, that an idea of a substance *must* be intended to copy certain actual things, but an idea of a mode need not be. Now it is difficult to see how it could be necessary that an idea be supposed to represent some actual things unless this intention were somehow reflected in the combination of ideas which make it up. An idea that did not have the intention built into it, as part of its content, could be regarded without that intention. That is, Locke gives no indication that ideas, considered merely as mental entities and without regard for their content, carry restrictions on the intentions, or other attitudes, one may have toward them. So the intention of representing something actual is neither contingently nor extrinsically attached to each idea of a substance. Of course, the only component common to all and only ideas of substances is the idea of substratum. So the argument shows that at least part of what is involved in the idea of substratum is the supposition that certain actual things are represented by the complex idea in which it is found.[14] In sum, any idea of a substance includes, as part of its content,

[12] Perry (Perry 1967: 224–5) claims that Locke is inconsistent in saying (i) that there are real things that conform to our ideas of modes and (ii) that 'mixed modes . . . [have] no other *reality*, but what they have in the minds of men' (E II.xxx.4: 373). But there is no inconsistency. A mixed mode, e.g. a murder, is a *thing* in that it belongs to a certain *kind*. Locke's view is that *kinds* do not exist independently of minds (see E III.v.9: 434; E III.v.4–6: 429–31; E IV.iv.6 and 17: 565 and 573). A kind, he seems to reason, is not delineated by every set of properties, but only by those sets of properties used by human beings to identify or classify things. Independently of our forming the idea of a murder, the properties combined in it might occur (in the appropriate relation to substances), but they would not constitute *a murder*. Only because we classify things as murders is the occurrence of that set of properties an instance of the kind murder. By the same token, it is only because we have the idea of murder that that occurrence is *one event*, namely *a* murder. Cf. Aronson and Lewis 1970: 195–6.

[13] Aronson and Lewis (Aronson and Lewis 1970) suggest an alternative account. According to it, what makes an idea the idea of a substance is that it succeeds in copying something; an idea of a mode is one which fails to copy anything actual. However this is not Locke's doctrine, for he holds that some ideas of substances, such as the idea of a centaur, *fail* to copy an actual thing. Since some ideas of substances are fantastical, it must be the *intention* of copying something actual, rather than success in doing so, that distinguishes ideas of substances.

[14] There is direct support for this claim that *substratum* involves existence in a letter from Locke to Stillingfleet: '. . . the general idea of substance [substratum] . . . is a complex idea, made up of the general idea of something, or being, with the relation of a support to accidents' (W IV: 19). For Locke's use of the word 'being' to mean 'existing thing' see e.g. E IV.x.2: 619–20; E IV.vii.4: 592–3; E III.iii.9: 412.

that it represents certain actual things; and an idea of a mode has a content which does not include that there are any actual things which conform to it.

So far, however, it is unclear how the stipulation that the idea represents actual things is built into the idea of a substance. Locke says that with *ideas of modes*, '. . . things are no otherwise regarded but as they are conformable to them' (E IV.iv.5: 564); and ideas of modes differ in this respect from ideas of *substances*. Whereas the idea of a mode is designed to represent whichever things happen to conform to it, the idea of a substance is designed differently. So it seems that the idea of a substance is not just a list of properties representing whatever has those properties, but rather it is 'made . . . in reference to things existing without us' and intended to represent those particular things.[15] The idea must then include a reference to certain actual things, as well as a description of their properties. The idea of a man might be described as the idea of *those actual things* which are rational animals. In contrast, the idea of a mode is to be described without reference to any particular things; for example, the idea of a triangle might be described as the idea of *anything* which is a three-sided plane figure. Described in this way, ideas of substances clearly presuppose the existence of what they represent in a way in which ideas of modes do not.[16] This account of the content of ideas will be confirmed by further evidence, but it will also need to be refined.

IV

Further indication of the difference between ideas of modes and substances is found in Locke's discussion of adequate and inadequate ideas. The distinction applies only to *real* ideas, or ones which succeed in representing what they are supposed to represent. Adequate ideas 'perfectly

---

[15] Further direct support for the view that ideas of substances carry a reference to actual things includes this passage: '[the ideas of modes] are made . . . without patterns, or reference to any real existence. Wherein they differ from those of substances, which carry with them the supposition of some real being, from which they are taken, and to which they are conformable' (E II.xxxi.6: 378–80). Also see E II.xxxi.6: 378–80; E III.v.12: 435–6; E III.x.32: 506–7; E III.xi.24: 520–1; E IV.vi.15: 589–90.

[16] In the case of a centaur, the idea involves a presupposition which is false. Locke clearly wants to consider such fantastical ideas as ideas of substances even though he knows that what they presuppose is false. The situation is in some ways analogous to that of a statement in which a referring expression is used which does not in fact refer to anything. Just as one can use and understand the statement knowing that the reference fails, one can have the idea of a centaur knowing that it presupposes what is false. Presumably, one could also form the idea in a way that presupposed that certain things had the head of a man and body of a horse knowing that in fact they did not. The situation would be similar for the idea of a substance which does not exist, but is predicted on the basis of scientific theory.

represent' the archetypes they are supposed to, whereas inadequate ideas are 'but a partial, or incomplete representation' of their archetypes. Locke continues:

> our *complex* ideas *of modes*, being voluntary collections of simple *ideas*, which the mind puts together, without reference to any real archetypes, or standing patterns, existing anywhere, *are*, and cannot but be *adequate ideas*. . . . But in our *ideas* of *substances*, it is otherwise. For there desiring to copy things, as they really do exist; and to represent to our selves that constitution, on which all their properties depend, we perceive our *ideas* attain not that perfection we intend: . . . and so all are *inadequate*. (E II.xxxi.1–3: 375–7)

Ideas of modes are formed 'without reference to standing patterns', but ideas of substances are representations of certain actual things. For ideas of substances, the internal constitutions of certain things, and the collections of properties dependent on them, are said to serve as patterns. However it is not clear exactly how this contrast between the two sorts of ideas yields Locke's claim about the difference in their adequacy.

One explanation of the inadequacy of ideas of substances which may seem natural is offered by Aronson and Lewis.

> A complex idea is adequate if it is isomorphic with that combination of properties of which it is an idea, that is, for every property there is an idea which is the idea of that property. Complex ideas of substances are inadequate for there is no guarantee that a complex idea of a substance contains as a constituent an idea of every property of that substance. (Aronson and Lewis 1970: 196)

On the other hand, ideas of modes are adequate, Aronson and Lewis urge, because they must contain an idea of each property of the modes they represent. Locke however does not hold this thesis supposed to explain the adequacy of ideas. According to him, it is no more the case with modes than it is with substances that their ideas always include all of their properties. After observing that the properties of a substance extend far beyond those collected in our idea of it, Locke continues: This 'will not appear so much a paradox to any one, who will but consider, how far men are yet from knowing all the properties of that one, no very compound figure, a *triangle*. . . .' (E II.xxxi.10: 382; see also E IV.iii.18–20 and 30: 548–52 and 560–1).

Ideas of substances are inadequate, not because they omit some properties of the things they represent; it is because the properties they omit are *determined* by something other than those ideas. The properties of a substance, not included in our idea of it, are determined by its constitution. That constitution, and the combination of properties united by it, is the *pattern* for the idea. As long as we are ignorant of that constitution, we lack a complete account of the principle which determines the properties of the things represented by the idea. Provided that the idea successfully represents actual things, we can identify the principle, but we cannot say precisely what its content is. In this sense, there are 'external patterns' inadequately represented by (real) ideas of substances. On the other hand, with a mode, nothing determines its properties but the idea that defines it; we may not have an exhaustive list of its properties, nevertheless we can fully state the principle which determines them. It involves reference to no standard external to the idea.

I have already argued that the fact that there *are* actual patterns which they are supposed to represent is part of the *content* of ideas of substances, represented by the idea of substratum. It is now clear what those patterns are; they are the internal constitutions of actual things and the combinations of sensible qualities dependent on them. So the idea of substratum not only carries a reference to certain actual things, but also represents their constitutions.

In the light of this, the account of the content of ideas can be further developed in this way: the idea of a substance has, as part of its content, that it represents certain actual things whose constitutions combine certain properties; and it is not part of the content of the idea of a mode that it represents things whose properties are determined by anything external to that idea. The idea of a substance can be at least partially described as the idea of *those actual things* whose constitutions give rise to such-and-such properties, whereas the idea of a mode is described as the idea of *anything* which has such-and-such properties. This account of the content of ideas, however, requires still further refinement.

Before proceeding, I want to consider a certain objection which might be raised to this account of ideas of substances. The objection is that the account is inconsistent with Locke's theory of the origin of ideas and the limits that theory places on the content of complex ideas. Locke's theory is that all simple ideas are received by sensation or reflection and all complex ideas are made by combining simple ones (see esp. E II.xii.1: 163–4). Accordingly, complex ideas of substances, as those of modes, *should* include nothing but simple ideas of sensible qualities. On the proposed account, ideas of substances include, in addition, the idea of certain constitutions which unite sensible qualities. But we have *no idea* of those constitutions, nor how they give rise to qualities.[17] So, the proposed account of

---

[17] Locke believes that these constitutions are collections of insensible particles with certain primary qualities, and he sometimes allows that we might someday *have* ideas of them. If we did, however, we might then suppose that there is an internal constitution of the *particles* which gives rise to their primary qualities; at any rate, we would not be sure when to stop seeking a constitution in terms of which a collection of qualities is to be understood. So, the proposal that substrata involve constitutions which give rise to qualities is supported by Locke's famous

ideas of substances does not conform to this theoretical restriction on the content of complex ideas. One might think that this shows that Locke did not hold the proposed account.

In fact, however, the incompatibility of the proposed account of substratum and Locke's theory of the origin of ideas is *not* reason to think he did not subscribe to that account of substratum. For he himself acknowledges that his doctrine of substratum conflicts with his theory of the origin of ideas.[18] Unfortunately, Locke does not indicate how he would resolve the inconsistency in his doctrines. Perhaps it is because Locke did not know how to resolve the problem that he does not emphasize or develop the view that ideas of substances carry a reference to actual things whose constitutions combine qualities; often in describing the ideas, he mentions only the ideas of qualities, omitting altogether the idea of a substratum. In any case, the point I want to emphasize is that Locke was not willing to give up the idea of substratum even though he acknowledged that the idea is not derived from sensation or reflection. So, the inconsistency is not an *objection* to the account of ideas of substances which I am proposing.

V

Another context in which ideas of substances are treated differently than ideas of modes is that in which Locke discusses real and nominal essences. The essences in question here are essences of *kinds*. The nominal essence of a kind is a complex idea which sets the criterion we use to identify members of the kind, determines everything which is essential to the kind, and is the 'immediate signification' of the name of the kind (E III.iii.15: 417; E III.vi.2: 439). Locke often indicates that a thing belongs to a given kind if and only if it conforms to the complex idea which is the nominal essence of that kind. On the other hand, the real essence is 'the very being of any thing, whereby it is, what it is' (E III.iii.15: 417). The properties of a thing of a given kind are said to 'flow from', 'depend upon', and be 'inseparably annexed to' the real essence of the kind. In classifying or naming things, we appeal to their conformity to a nominal essence, but it is the real essence that 'makes' a thing have the properties typical of its kind.

comparison of our reasoning about substrata to that of the Indian philosopher; see E II.xiii.19: 175 and esp. E II.xxiii.2: 295–6. In the latter passage, Locke explicitly says that colour and weight inhere in particles with primary qualities, and suggests that we do not know what *those* primary qualities inhere in.

[18] See E I.iv.18: 95 and Locke's correspondence with Stillingfleet on this point: W IV: 21. For a more detailed account of the inconsistency between the doctrine of substratum and Locke's theory of the origin of ideas, see Mabbott 1973: ch. 3.

Locke's doctrine is that the real and nominal essences of a substantial kind are always different, whereas the real and nominal essence of a modal kind are always the same. In explanation of this doctrine, Locke writes:

Thus a figure including a space between three lines, is the real, as well as nominal *essence* of a triangle; it being not only the abstract *idea* to which the general name is annexed, but the very *essentia*, or being, of the thing it self, that foundation from which all its properties flow, and to which they are all inseparably annexed. But it is far otherwise concerning that parcel of matter, which makes the ring on my finger, wherein these two *essences* are apparently different. For it is the real constitution of its insensible parts, on which depend all those properties of colour, weight, fusibility, fixedness, *etc*. . . . which makes it to be *gold*, or gives it a right to that name, which is therefore its nominal *essence*. (E III.iii.18: 418–19)[19]

It is fairly clear how to understand the doctrine that the constitution of a material substance is the real essence of that kind of substance. Suppose that the nominal essence of gold includes ideas of yellowness, malleability, and solubility in aqua regia. These qualities 'depend upon' the constitution of gold in a familiar sense. There are laws of nature in which certain features of the constitution of gold are causally connected with its observable properties. By reference to this constitution, we can explain why a particular thing, which happens to be gold, is yellow, malleable, and soluble. Moreover, gold has a number of qualities in addition to those listed in its nominal essence, such as a certain specific gravity and melting point. These qualities too are connected by laws of nature to the constitution of gold. That constitution is the real essence of gold, because it, together with the laws of nature, *accounts for* the species-typical properties of gold.

The doctrine of *modal* real essence however is more difficult to understand. The physical constitution of triangular things does not, in general, afford an explanation of why those things have the properties of triangles. In fact, there *is* no general, non-trivial way to explain why a particular thing has the properties in the nominal essence of a triangle, or of murder. In every case, there may be an explanation of the occurrence of a triangle or

---

[19] There is an inconsistency in the passage: a nominal essence is said to be (i) the idea of certain properties, but described as (ii) those properties themselves. Much of Locke's doctrine requires that nominal essences be *ideas*; for example, his semantic theory is that all words signify *ideas* and general words signify *nominal essences* (see E III.ii–iii: 404–20); again, he says that nominal essences are imperishable *because* they are ideas (E III.iii.19: 419–20). So it is out of carelessness that Locke sometimes suggests that a nominal essence is a set of properties. In the quoted passage, when he says that the *nominal essence* is the 'very being' of a mode and the 'foundation of its properties', I think he should say that *conformity to* the nominal essence is the being of a mode and foundation of its properties. Compare Woolhouse 1972: 418–19.

murder, but there is not one general law which explains why things of either sort occur.[20]

Nevertheless modal kinds may still be said to have real essences. Their real essences are supposed to *be* their nominal essences; this means, I think, that the real essence of a modal kind, or what makes a thing have the properties of that kind, is just that the thing *conforms* to the nominal essence of the kind. Now the nominal essence gives the definition of the name of the kind; so it is because a thing conforms to the definition of a modal kind that it has the properties typical of that kind, and *conformity to the definition* is the real essence of the kind. Modal real essences have some explanatory functions analogous to those of substantial real essences. In the case of both modes and substances, we may be unaware of certain species-typical properties, but those properties can be derived from an account of the real essence of the species. In both cases, appeal to the real essence of a kind is (part of) an explanation of why things of that kind share certain properties.[21] Explanations in the two cases differ, however; the species-typical properties of substances are explained by reference to their real constitutions and the laws of nature, while the species-typical properties of modes are explained in terms of a man-made definition and what follows from it.[22]

This doctrine of real essence allows one to see more clearly the way in which substantial kinds differ from modal ones. I have argued that the idea of a substance represents the constitution which unites the sensible qualities of certain actual things. It now appears that this constitution unites certain qualities *because* of the causal connections it is determined to have by the laws of nature. So the sensible properties which depend upon the constitution of a substance involve causal connections among substances; furthermore, substantial kinds are ones to which reference might be made in a statement of the laws of nature. There is no reason to expect that the case will be the same for modal kinds. A modal kind has its species-typical properties, not because of the laws of nature, but rather because of a

---

[20] These considerations lead some to deny that the notion of real essence has any legitimate application to modes. See Woolhouse 1971: Sect. 23; O'Connor 1952: 146; and Bennett 1971: 122–3.

[21] It is not Locke's view that the real essence of a triangle (or gold) gives rise to all the properties of any particular instance of a triangle (or gold); but only to those properties shared non-accidentally by *all* things of that kind.

[22] The example of a triangle is not difficult to see in these terms, but other examples must be regarded as limiting cases. Murder may not share any properties in addition to those specified in its nominal essence, so that nothing 'depends upon' the real essence murder is supposed to have. Locke's point is however that whatever properties are shared by all things of a given modal kind, even if there are none, depend on the definition of that kind.

definition and its consequences. So the species-typical properties of modes do not generally involve causal relations. Modal real essences do not in general define kinds about which there are laws of nature.

The description of the content of ideas of substances and modes can now be further refined. The idea of a substance is the idea of *the actual things* whose constitutions are connected by the laws of nature to certain sensible qualities. In contrast, the idea of a mode is the idea of *anything* which conforms to a certain definition in which there is no reference to actual things. Once again, it is the idea of substratum which carries the distinctive content of ideas of substances.

VI

Ideas of both substances and modes are nominal essences of kinds, and as such they play a central part in Locke's semantic theory for kind terms. The nominal essence of a kind not only sets the criterion for membership in the kind (E III.vi.2: 439), but also furnishes the *meaning* of the general word for the kind. Locke says, for example, that the nominal essence is the 'immediate signification' of the name of the kind, that it is the idea to which the name is 'annexed' and for which the name stands.[23] Locke does not elaborate his semantic theory as much as one might desire. He clearly indicates, however, that a general word *has a meaning* only if it signifies an idea; also, the word applies to a thing if and only if that thing conforms to the criterion set by the idea signified by the word (see E III.iii.2 and 5: 409 and 410; E III.iii.6–7, 12–13, and 16: 410–11, 414–16, and 417). So the criterion for membership set by the nominal essence of a kind is a logically necessary and sufficient condition for membership in the kind; that is, it is necessarily true that something belongs to the kind if and only if it conforms to that criterion.

For modal kinds, the nominal essence is an idea of anything which meets a certain description, and meeting that description is the criterion for belonging to those kinds. For substantial kinds, however, the nominal essence is not as simple. It specifies a description, but it also refers to certain actual things which meet that description. One would expect Locke somehow to make *use* of those actual things in formulating the membership criteria for substantial kinds.

---

[23] For uses of these expressions, see respectively: E III.ii.2, 4, and 6–8: 405, 406, and 407–8; E III.iii.9, 13, and 20: 412, 415, and 420 and E III.v.1: 428; E III.ii.1, 3, 5, and 7: 405, 406, 407, and 408 and E III.iv.17: 428.

In fact, Locke does think that there is a problem in specifying the meanings of names for substantial kinds which is not involved in the meanings of names for modal kinds:

> There is ... a multiplicity of simple *ideas* to be put together, which makes the doubtfulness in the names of mixed modes; [and] a supposed, but an unknown, real essence, with properties depending thereon, the precise number whereof are also unknown, which makes the difficulty in the names of substances. (E III.iv.15: 427; see also E III.iv.17: 428)

The difficulty with the names for substantial kinds is that we do not know all the properties which characterize members of them, and we do not know how to describe the principles which determine those properties. In short, our ideas of substances are always *inadequate*. They somehow manage to represent things of a certain kind, but we are unable to describe things of that kind in a way that distinguishes them from members of every other possible kind. The *difficulty* is that Locke's semantic theory requires that the nominal essence specify a condition which *is* sufficient to distinguish members of one kind from those of all other possible kinds. For meeting the condition specified by the nominal essence of a kind is necessarily sufficient for belonging to the kind.

The semantic doctrine does not raise the same difficulty in the case of modal kinds, for all of the properties typical of a member of a modal kind are derivable from our idea of the kind. Anything which conforms to the idea *cannot fail* to have all properties typical of the kind or to belong to the kind represented by the idea. The difficulty is acute, however, in the case of substantial kinds. In those cases, it is *possible* for the available description of the kind to apply to something which *does not* belong to the kind. For example, the idea of gold represents things of a kind with many species-typical properties in addition to those by which we describe gold. So it is possible for something to conform to our description of gold, but lack some of the properties typical of gold, and so fail to *be* gold. This is possible because the idea of gold *represents* a kind which it *inadequately describes*.

The idea of a substance, however, does not just describe things, it also carries a reference to actual things which meet that description. It appears that Locke can use the reference to complete the specification of a logically sufficient condition for belonging to a kind. After all, it is the actual things which conform to our inadequate description which our idea of a substantial kind represents. Those things, or their constitutions, are the patterns which determine the full range of properties typical of a kind. The species-typical properties *are* just all the shared properties to which the constitution(s) of those actual things give rise, according to the laws of nature.[24] The *actual* things described in our idea have an appropriate constitution and are subject to the laws of nature, so they are assured of having all species-typical properties, including those of which we are ignorant. In short, being among the actual things whose constitution combines the properties listed in the inadequate nominal essence is a logically sufficient condition for belonging to a substantial kind; nothing which is among those things can lack any species-typical properties or fail to belong to the kind.

So being among the actual things with certain properties is logically sufficient for membership in a substantial kind; but Locke seems not to think that it is also a necessary condition. On that view, it would be impossible that there should have been more members of a substantial kind than there actually are. Instead Locke seems to think that it would have been possible, for example, for there to be suns other than ours (see e.g. E III.vi.1: 439).[25] To be a sun, a thing would need to have all the properties to which the constitution of the actual sun gives rise, according to the laws of nature.

If this is a correct analysis of the conditions Locke holds to be logically necessary and sufficient for belonging to substantial kinds, then the account of the content of ideas of substances must be refined once more. Let me refer to any property a thing has because it is a law of nature that anything with its constitution has that property as a 'property based on the constitution' of that thing. The idea of a substance is the idea of anything with *all* the shared properties based on the constitution(s) of those actual things whose constitutionally based properties include $P_1, \ldots, P_n$.

Now Locke repeatedly attacks certain views about unknown real essences of substances, and it is important to notice that although unknown constitutions of substances are mentioned in the proposed account, they are *not* mentioned in a way which Locke rejects. According to the view which Locke rejects, real essences are 'a certain number of forms or molds, wherein all natural things, that exist, are cast' and these forms distinguish things into various species (E III.iii.17: 418). The view is that our names for substantial kinds stand for these real essences, so that having the

---

[24] In case all things which conform to the nominal essence share the same constitution, the species-typical properties are just all those to which that constitution lawfully gives rise. Locke usually assumes that there is only one such constitution (see e.g. E III.vi.36: 462), but he sometimes allows that there may be different constitutions belonging to instances of the same sort of substance (see e.g. E III.vi.8: 443). In that case, the species-typical properties are all those to which *every* constitution lawfully gives rise, or all the *shared* lawfully based properties; reference to the actual constitutions is still required, because we do not know what all the *shared* properties are.

[25] It was commonly believed in the 17th cent. that there is but one sun.

appropriate essence is the criterion for a thing's belonging to a substantial kind. Locke has mainly two related objections to this view:[26] one is that it is impossible for a word immediately to signify anything but an idea, and in particular, impossible for it immediately to signify an unknown real essence;[27] the other objection is that the criterion we use in applying the name of a substantial kind cannot be possession of an unknown real essence, for the criterion must be known to those who understand the word (see e.g. E III.iii.15: 417; E III.vi: *passim* and esp. 9–20, 24–5, 27, and 49–50: 444–9, 452–3, 454–5, and 469–70; E IV.vi. 4–5: 580–2).

It should be clear that the account of ideas of substances proposed here does not involve the objectionable view of real essences, or unknown constitutions. For, the account does not suggest that names of substances immediately signify real constitutions, rather than ideas. Moreover, according to the proposed account, we can classify substances without knowing the nature of their internal constitutions. To be sure, classification requires that we know what it is for certain qualities to depend upon an unknown constitution, but that is just to say that we must know what it is for qualities to be supported by a substratum; and that is a view to which Locke is firmly committed.

Locke holds that the definition of a general word is the description of the idea it signifies (see E III.iii.10: 412–13; E III.iv.6 and 12: 422 and 425–6). If the ideas of substances have a form different from those of modes, as I have been arguing, then the definitions of names for substances differ in form from those of names for modes. In general, the definition of a substantial kind term involves reference to actual things, and it implies that those things exist. On the other hand, the definition of a modal kind term refers to nothing in particular and has no existential implication. For example, the definition of 'man' might have this form: a man is anything with all the shared properties based on the constitution(s) of those actual things whose constitutionally based properties include being a rational

[26] There are other minor objections; see E III.vi.8, 15–18, and 32: 443, 448–9, and 459–60; E IV.iv.13: 569.

[27] For the general argument, see E III.ii.1–5: 404–7; for the particular argument concerning unknown real essences, see E III.vi.49–50: 469–70; E III.x.17–21: 499–503. When Locke denies, for instance, that 'those names [of substances] stand for a thing having a real essence, on which [its] properties depend' (E III.x.18: 500), it is important to see how he is using the expression 'stand for'. For there is *a* way of understanding it according to which Locke's denial is clearly inconsistent with what he says elsewhere; that is, there is a sense in which a word such as 'gold' *stands for gold*, and Locke often says that *gold* has a real essence on which its properties depend. What he means to deny is not this, but rather that the name 'gold' *immediately* stands for a thing *rather than* an idea. It is the main contention of Locke's semantic theory that this is impossible (see E III.ii: 404–8). It is not, however, any part of that theory that the idea immediately signified by a word may not itself represent things of a kind supposed to have an unknown real essence. See Kretzmann 1968.

animal. The name of a mode, such as 'triangle', is defined more simply: a triangle is anything which is a figure enclosed by three lines.

Locke's semantic theory, at least for natural kind terms, is less easily shown to be mistaken than it is often thought to be (see also Kretzmann 1968). Locke is usually thought to share with many other empiricists the view that the meaning of a general word is a mental entity formed 'in' one's mind without regard for the existence of anything 'outside' the mind. In fact, Locke's theory is not vulnerable to arguments against that view of language in general or the meaning of natural kind terms in particular. It has also been thought that Locke's view is defective, because he defines the names of kinds simply by listing properties, offering no account of the sort of thing to which the properties must belong; such a list clearly does not define words such as 'gold'.[28] In fact, Locke defines the names for substantial kinds in terms of properties which belong to a certain sort of thing, namely a thing whose constitution gives rise to a *lawfully explicable combination* of properties; it is not obvious that this is not the *sort* of thing, involved in the meanings of natural kind terms. One reason why Locke's semantic theory is misrepresented is that discussions of his views about language usually emphasize his theory of concept acquisition, and as I have already suggested, *that* theory is inconsistent with his account of the meanings of names for substances.

VII

I began by suggesting that Locke's explicit attempts to explain the difference between ideas of substances and those of modes are too vague and obscure to be understood in isolation. By studying various ways in which Locke treats ideas of the two sorts, I suggested, we might be better able to understand the difference and to interpret Locke's explicit account of it. I want now to examine the account in the light of the doctrine of ideas developed in earlier sections of this paper.

In the difficult passage in which the distinction between ideas of substances and modes is introduced (see e.g. E II.xxiii.2–3: 295–7), we found three ways in which they are contrasted. I have argued at length for an account of the third contrast: (iii) ideas of substances always include the idea of substratum, but ideas of modes never do. The idea of substratum, when included in a complex idea, signifies in part that the idea represents

---

[28] I am indebted to Bernard Harrison for drawing my attention to this objection to Locke's *semantic* theory.

certain actual things; lacking this, ideas of modes carry no reference to actual things. This leads to a natural account of the second contrast: (ii) ideas of substances represent distinct particular things, but ideas of modes do not. There are certain things which the idea of a substance is designed to represent; the idea delineates the kind to which those *particular* things belong and it is patterned after them. Ideas of modes, on the other hand, do not purport to represent any thing in particular, but rather *whichever* things may have certain properties.

The first of the contrasts remains to be considered. It is: (i) ideas of substances portray things which subsist by themselves, but ideas of modes portray things thought to depend on substances. If my account is correct, substances belong to kinds about which there are laws of nature, but modes do not. That is, gold and a horse are mentioned in the statement of general laws, but murder or a table are not. The doctrine that substances 'subsist by themselves' then seems to mean this: the existence of a substance requires nothing but what is dictated by laws of nature. For example, it is a *law of nature* that a man requires all those things, such as oxygen, water and amino acids, on which his existence depends. It is similar for natural kinds such as plastics, which may not be found 'in nature': everything required for their existence is determined by the laws of nature about them. Substances 'subsist by themselves', because they do not require modes or entities of another category in order to exist (although the laws of nature make them dependent on other substances). In contrast, modes do require substances, and their dependence on substances is not of the type dictated by laws of nature. There is no *law of nature* which states what is generally required for a table, a triangle, or a murder. A table is *subject* to laws of nature; it is subject because it has mass, is made of metal, and so forth, *not* because it is a *table*. Again, although there may be a cause of each murder, there is no general law about the cause of murders. Modes 'depend upon substances', because a mode can exist only if some substance does, and the dependence is not dictated by the laws of nature. Murder, for example, could not exist if there were no men to commit it, and tables and triangles could not exist if there were no substances such as wood or plastic out of which they could be made; but it is not a law of *nature* that murders require men, or that tables must be made out of some stuff or other.

In his account of substances, Locke breaks markedly from the usual version of an Aristotelian ontology. For Locke, it is not individuals that are fundamental, but rather things of a *natural kind*. Individuals made from a natural kind of stuff, if not themselves of natural kinds, depend upon the stuff; so, for example, lead pipes depend upon lead, whereas the stuff lead (or atoms of it) does not depend upon artificial things made of it. An individual of a natural kind is a substance, but it is not the fact that it is an individual which is important, but rather the fact that there are laws of nature about that kind of thing. In short, what is basic in Locke's ontology is all things of kinds which are proper objects of investigation *for natural science*.

We can now understand better other puzzling passages in Locke's treatment of ideas of substances. He argues, for example, that the qualities we observe cannot subsist by themselves and introduces a supposed substratum 'wherein they do subsist, and from which they do result'. His reasoning is clear enough in the light of the foregoing account of substratum. When we find certain *qualities* occurring, we suppose that there must be some constitution causally responsible for their occurrence. We do not perceive the constitution, so we have no idea of its nature and we only infer that it exists. However the inference must be correct if, as Locke says, qualities *are* powers to produce ideas. If there is a power to produce certain ideas, then it *does follow* that it 'subsists in' some enduring object constituted so as to cause those ideas.[29] Moreover, the constitution which causes the ideas remains 'something, I know not what'. It is now clear why qualities require substrata in a way in which other properties do not. A quality, or a power to produce ideas, requires a constitution capable of producing those ideas; other properties, which are *not* causal powers, do not depend in the same way on a constitution with specific law governed capabilities.

Locke also says about substances that we always suppose that they are *something* in addition to certain qualities (E II.xxiii.3: 297). There now seems a natural point to his saying this. It is that the logical structure of ideas of substances implies that they are ideas of *actual things*. Discourse about substances has existential import; it implies that something, having certain qualities, actually exists. One can talk about triangles, on Locke's account, without implying that there are any triangles, but talk about gold presupposes that there *is something* which is gold.

To have a substratum is to be an actual thing with an internal constitution (or real essence) which lawfully gives rise to certain properties. Locke often observes that we do not know what substratum, or 'substance in general', is. When one understands what that would involve, it is clear why he says so. An account of substratum *in general* would be an account of the

---

[29] In his correspondence with Stillingfleet, Locke says that qualities have a 'necessary connexion' to something which supports them, and that their existence is 'inconsistent' with there being no support; see W IV: 21.

ultimate nature of the constitution(s) on which the law governed properties of all bodies and spirits are based. Locke is properly scornful of his
contemporaries who pretend to say something useful about the *nature* of
substratum in general.[30]

[30] I am indebted to Robert Bolton and R. S. Woolhouse for useful discussion of the material
in this paper, to William P. Alston and Ruth Mattern for their comments, and to the editors of
this journal for their suggestions concerning the paper.

VII

SUBSTRATUM

JONATHAN BENNETT

I. INTRODUCTION

LOCKE has a theory about the idea of substance considered as a 'substratum' or 'support' of qualities.[1] It is a strange theory, according to which one part of our conceptual apparatus is both important and disreputable. Nothing else in the writings of any philosopher matches the doubleness of attitude of the passages about substratum in Locke's *Essay*. This duplicity has been noted by students of Locke, but not explained. I once suggested that Locke believed the hostile side of the theory and intended the favourable side sarcastically, but now I can do better.

My new answer—like my old wrong one—presupposes what I shall call the 'Leibnizian interpretation' of the substratum texts. This view about what the substratum theory is, though accepted by most Locke students from Leibniz onwards, has lately been attacked. I shall defend it against the most vigorous of those attacks, the one by M. R. Ayers.

II. LOCKE'S SUBSTRATUM THEORY

Locke thinks that in our experience of the world, the raw materials of what we experience are properties: we become aware of being in the presence of an orange by becoming aware of orangeness, sphericalness, and so on. When this happens, we think we are in the presence of something that has the properties, and this thought of 'the thing that is orange, spherical etc.' is what introduces the idea of substance in general.

The mind being . . . furnished with a great number of simple ideas, conveyed in by the senses as they are found in exterior things or by reflection on its own operations,

From *History of Philosophy Quarterly*, 4: 2 (1987), 197–215.

[1] The main texts are: E I.iv.18: 95; E II.xiii.17–20: 174–5; E II.xxiii.1–6, 15, 37: 295–9, 305, 316–17; E III.vi.21: 449–50; E IV.vi.7: 582.

takes notice also that a certain number of these simple ideas go constantly together; which being presumed to belong to one thing . . . are called so united in one subject by one name; which by inadvertency we are apt afterward to talk of and consider as one simple idea, which indeed is a complication of many ideas together; Because, as I have said, not imagining how these simple ideas can subsist by themselves, we accustom ourselves to suppose some *substratum* wherein they do subsist and from which they do result, which therefore we call *substance*. (E II.xxiii.1: 295)

Here, as often, Locke speaks of how substratum relates to 'simple *ideas*', but his topic is how it relates to qualities or properties. There is controversy about why Locke writes about qualities in the language of ideas, but not about the fact that he does. Here, for instance:

Our complex ideas of substances, besides all these simple ideas they are made up of, have always the confused idea of *something* to which they belong, and in which they subsist: and therefore when we speak of any sort of substance we say it is a *thing* having such or such qualities, as body is a *thing* that is extended, figured, and capable of motion. . . . These and the like fashions of speaking intimate that the substance is supposed always *something* besides the extension, figure, solidity, motion, thinking, or other observable ideas, though we know not what it is. (E II.xxiii.3: 297)

That is another of the substratum texts. Quite generally, when Locke writes about 'substance in general' and 'substratum', his topic is the instantiation of qualities; he is theorizing about the notion of a thing which. . . .

Jose Benardete has remarked to me that if Locke wanted his notion of substratum to help with property instantiation as such, then he ought to have applied it not only to his chosen sorts of examples but also to *The number three is odd*, *The problem of squaring the circle is difficult*, *My idea of man is abstract*, and so on; or else to have explained why it doesn't apply to these predications. He might have treated some of them reductively, e.g. claiming that 'The problem of squaring the circle is difficult' really means 'Some people would like to square the circle and nobody can easily do it', but he would not have been comfortable with a reductive programme for predications on *ideas*. So there is something here that he should have faced: granted that minds are enduring while ideas are evanescent, why don't we need a conceptual theory about attributing properties to evanescent particulars? As those remarks indicate, I take Benardete's observation as pointing to a gap in Locke's thought, not as showing that the Leibnizian interpretation of it is wrong.

III. WHAT IS WRONG WITH THE SUBSTRATUM THEORY?

Many philosophers have said that this notion of pure substance in general, or 'Lockean substratum' as it is often called, is impossible or intolerable.

They are right, but why? We can only smile at the idea that unless some-thing lies under the qualities and props them up they will . . . what? Fall flat? Scatter? Disintegrate? But if that were the whole source of the trouble, we could quietly walk away from it as a mere muddled metaphor in which substratum is like a shelf. Setting aside the metaphor, we are left with the notion of a thing that has various properties, e.g. a thing that is orange and spherical and sweet and middlingly heavy. What could be more innocent than this? Where's the problem?

The answer concerns conceptual emptiness: it is thought that because a substratum has to be the bearer of all the qualities it must therefore be, in itself, bare or unqualitied in some problematic way. Elizabeth Anscombe understands this in a way that makes it 'so idiotic as to be almost incred-ible' (Anscombe 1981: 38), but here, as so often, her victims are not such fools as she likes to think.[2] The substratum idea does involve a trouble that *could* be put in terms of the upholder of properties not itself having properties, yet it is not idiotic or absurd.

When someone thinks about the thing that is orange and spherical and F and G and H . . . and so on through all the qualities of the orange, and rightly takes that thought to involve the notion of a thing, a concrete particular, a substance, he may reasonably wonder 'What kind of item is that?' If he gives the answer 'The kind *substance*' or 'The kind *property haver*' he is safe. But he may not be satisfied: there is a temptation to want to know what an item must be like in order to qualify as a haver of properties, what monadic state or condition of it equips it for the property-bearing role. That desire could not be satisfied, however. It presupposes that something might fail the test because it was of such a kind, or in such a state, that it could not bear properties; but a thing's kind or state is determined how else?—by what properties it bears.

Alston has criticized the Lockean notion of substratum from a stand-point that is closely related to mine.[3] He argues that the notion of an *instantiation relation* that has substances and properties as relata is a source of troubles, of which the following is one. If we can think of an instantiating relation between a substance and one of its properties, we must be able to direct our thought at the substance—it must be available as an 'it' to which we can mentally refer—independently of its having this relation to any property. To have such a thought of the putative bearer of properties, of the bottom relatum (so to speak) of the relation, we must direct our thought onto a particular without help from any properties that we believe

---

[2] For a temperate treatment of the mistake that Anscombe derides as 'idiotic', see Alston 1954–5: 257.

[3] Personal communication, and Alston 1954–5.

it to have; and that seems to be impossible. Here, as implicitly in my own criticism, the substratum theorist is accused of requiring content in something that has been deprived of all content.

IV. LOCKE'S ATTITUDE TO THE SUBSTRATUM DOCTRINE

These criticisms are of a sort that would appeal to Locke himself. Though less doctrinaire about it than Hume, he was apt to be harsh with any general term that he saw as empty, not cashable in terms of actual or possible experience, etc. Should we then reject the Leibnizian account of what Locke means by 'substratum'? M. R. Ayers thinks so:

It is improbable to the point of impossibility that Locke, who is an anti-Aristotelian corpuscularian of the school of Boyle, should himself, using the very term *substratum*, advance a view so analogous to what Berkeley described as 'that antiquated and so much ridiculed notion of *materia prima* to be met with in Aristotle and his followers'.... Whatever Locke's *substratum* is, if he wrote *compos mentis*, it cannot be an entity that is undifferentiated, or 'other than' its properties. ... (Ayers 1977: 78–9)

Locke's substratum notion, according to the Leibnizian interpretation, is indeed like that of *materia prima*, and the latter is treated by scorn not only by Berkeley but by Locke himself (see E iii.x.15: 499). But Locke is also critical of whatever it is that he associates with 'substratum': as well as saying that we have and need the notion of substratum, he is scathing about its deficiencies, implying that it is confused and perhaps even non-existent:

The ideas of substances are such combinations of simple ideas as are taken to represent distinct particular things subsisting by themselves; in which the supposed or confused idea of substance, such as it is, is always the first and chief. (E ii.xii.6: 165)

That is typical of Locke's double-faced treatments of this matter, and one must wonder what he is up to. Here is my answer.

Locke's theory of meaning is permeated by his view that each meaningful general word *W* is linked to an idea-type, which serves as a pattern or criterion to help us to sort particulars into those to which *W* applies and those to which it doesn't. (In deploying this doctrine, we can take 'idea' in either of Locke's ways. One way, the idea-type is a kind of mental state or occurrence, my having which is evidence that I am perceiving a thing to which *W* applies; the other way, it is a property or quality, a thing's having which is proof that *W* applies to it.) But, for the sorts of reasons I have been presenting and of which Locke was aware, the word 'substance'—meaning 'pure substance in general'—cannot possibly have a meaning of that kind, or of either of those kinds; and Locke cannot see what other kind of meaning it could have.

So we have a semantic theorist in an *impasse*. On the one hand, we talk about things that *have* various qualities; we make sense of such expressions as 'the thing or substance that has all the qualities of the orange', and this seems to be an indispensable part of our conceptual stock-in-trade. On the other hand, Locke cannot see how the supposed idea of 'thing which . . .' or 'substance in general' could be made respectable, and he realized that he can't validate it along the lines he offers for most general terms.

Locke behaves like someone in a jam. Failing to find any account of how there could be a Lockean idea of substance in general, he had to conclude that we really have no idea corresponding to this way of talking; but then he backed off from that, seeing what an important way of talking it is. His ways of backing off vary. Early in the *Essay* he says that men don't have an idea of substance but it would be useful if they did because they generally talk 'as if they had it' (E i.iv.18: 95). But later he straddles the fence, speaking of 'the supposed or confused idea of substance, such as it is' as always the 'first and chief' conceptual ingredient in our thoughts of particular things (E ii.xii.6: 165). And there are other formulations: Locke writes that 'of substance we have no idea of what it is but only a confused obscure one of what it does' (E ii.xiii.19: 175), refers to our 'obscure and relative idea of substance in general' (E ii.xxiii.3: 296), says that 'we have no positive idea' of substance (E ii.xxiii.15: 305), remarks that 'Our idea of substance . . . is but a supposed I know not what, to support those ideas we call accidents' (E ii.xxiii.15: 305), and so on.

It is a strange performance, but an understandable one: Locke was caught between the fact that we do and perhaps must have the concept of a 'thing which . . .' and the inhospitable treatment of this concept by his theory of meaning. Where Ayers cannot believe that Locke would flout 'the familiar party line' (Ayers's phrase), I see him as more thoughtful and more honest than that. He finds the notion of an upholder of qualities *embarrassing*, but he grapples with it, the party line notwithstanding. It's no wonder that the substratum texts are two-faced: in them we see a genius in a bind.

V. HOW LOCKE COULD HAVE ESCAPED FROM THE IMPASSE

Locke needed a theory of meaning that gave him more elbow-room, allowing him to understand the concept of generalized 'thing which . . .'

not in terms of a defining 'idea' but rather as an operator on other concepts. Then instead of condemning it because it doesn't signify a corresponding idea-type, he could welcome it as a sign that ideas are being mentally operated on in a certain manner—which is the account he *does* give of the meanings of 'particles' such as 'if' and 'but' (E III.vii: 471–3).

Applied to the notion of substance in general, that approach would yield something like this:

When I say 'This is an orange' I mean that there are here instances of certain properties such as orangeness, sphericalness etc., and I indicate that I am operating on my ideas of those instances in a certain combining manner.

This, though not great, is less obviously doomed from the outset than what we get from the heartland of Locke's semantic theory, namely the view that if we are fully entitled to speak of 'the thing that has all the properties of the orange' we must associate some idea-type with the word 'thing'.

Objection: 'Locke would never accept that account of the concept of *thing* or *substance*, because it implies that although it is an objective fact that I am in the presence of an instance of *F*ness it is up to me whether I am in the presence of a thing that is *F*. Locke would never tolerate making statements about what substances there are *subjective*.' Indeed he wouldn't, but my suggested account of substance doesn't imply that. According to it, how my mind operates on its ideas determines what proposition a given sentence expresses, but has nothing to do with whether the proposition is true.

Anyway, it did not occur to Locke to handle 'thing' or 'substance in general' as he handles particles; so he went on butting his head against the fact that there could not be a Lockean idea of a 'thing which. . . .'

Leibniz saw what the trouble was. Commenting on this part of Locke's work, he says that 'we conceive several predicates in a single subject, and that is all there is to these metaphorical words "support" and "substratum",' and also:

If you distinguish two things in a substance—the attributes or predicates, and their common subject—it is no wonder that you cannot conceive anything special in this subject. That is inevitable, because you have already set aside all the attributes through which details could be conceived. Thus, to require of this 'pure subject in general' anything beyond what is needed for the conception of 'the same thing'— e.g. it is the same thing which understands and wills, which imagines and reasons— is to demand the impossible; and it also contravenes the assumption that was made in performing the abstraction and separating the subject from all its qualities or accidents. (Leibniz 1981: 217–18)[4]

---

[4] The phrase 'in a substance' is *dans la Substance*, which could be 'in substance'.

This is good, but Locke need not take it lying down. Leibniz rightly connects the concept of substance with that of identity; Locke holds that a viable concept of identity must be associated with ways of telling whether the F thing is the G thing; and he would say that the empty concept of pure substance in general cannot support any concept of identity that meets that minimal demand. That rejoinder would lead into a problem area where, in my opinion, neither Locke nor Leibniz would be comfortable; it is an area that still troubles us today.

VI. A RIVAL INTERPRETATION

Locke has an important theory which says that the properties we observe things to have supervene on an invisibly fine microstructure, a 'real internal constitution', and that the 'real essences' of things or kinds of things involve such internal constitutions and are therefore in practice unknowable by us.[5] It has been maintained, by Ayers and others, that *this* theory is what Locke is expressing when he writes about 'substratum' etc. In brief: Lockean substratum is inner constitution or real essence.

If that is right, Locke has not paraded the fact. The passages where the 'substratum' terminology is dominant have little overlap with the ones in which 'primary quality' and 'real essence' and 'internal constitution' predominate, and Locke does not even hint that these textually segregated clusters of terminology are explorations of the very same issues. Of the five sections of the *Essay* that contain both terminologies, three set them side by side in a manner that puts us under no pressure to think they are about the same issue, while in each of the others the two terminologies are made to collaborate as separate parts of a complex line of thought, thus positively signalling that they are different.[6]

There are, it is true, certain parallels or isomorphisms between things Locke says on one topic and things he says on the other, and this has led some of his successors—though probably not Locke himself—to run the two together in their minds. Berkeley radically failed to distinguish Locke's views about substratum from his views about primary-quality real essences; others have introduced the two doctrines as distinct but then proceeded to confuse them with one another.[7]

---

[5] The main texts are E II.viii.9–26: 134–43; E II.xxiii.11–13: 301–4; E II.xxxi.6: 378; E III.iii.17:417–18; E III.vi.2–3, 6, 19: 439–40, 442, 449; and E IV.iii.11–13, 25–6: 544–5, 555–7.

[6] The three: E II.xxiii.3, E II.xxiii.37, and E III.vi.21. The other two: E II.xxiii.2 and E II.xxxi.13.

[7] For details, see Bennett 1971: ch. 4; the evidence regarding whether Locke himself made the conflation is discussed in section 25 ('The conflation's sources in Locke').

More recently, however, some students of Locke have maintained that there was nothing to conflate: that when Locke uses the language of 'substratum' etc. he really is, always, only, talking about primary-quality internal constitutions and real essences. Locke's topic when he speaks of 'substratum' is not even approximately what the rest of us, from Leibniz on downwards, have thought it to be. The most vigorous proponent of this new position is M. R. Ayers, whose defence of it I shall now discuss (Ayers 1977).

VII. THE DOUBLENESS OF ATTITUDE

One enormous objection to the new interpretation is that it takes Locke's 'substratum' notion to be something that he is comfortable with. Unlike the Leibnizian interpretation, which attributes to him something that is not properly tenable by him, it cannot explain Locke's strained, awkward, two-faced way of writing about 'substratum' or 'substance in general'. It is time to look in more detail at the facts about that.

(1) With one exception that is right out of line with the rest,[8] the notion of substratum is presented as implicit in our ordinary ways of thinking and talking:

There is another idea which would be of general use for mankind to have, as it is of general talk as if they had it; and that is the idea of substance (E i.iv.18: 95)
[In] ideas of substances [the idea of substratum] is always the first and chief (E ii.xii.6: 165)
. . . not imagining how these ideas can subsist by themselves, we accustom ourselves to suppose some substratum . . . (E ii.xxiii.1: 295)
These and the like fashions of speaking intimate that the substance is supposed always *something* besides . . . (etc.) (E ii.xxiii.3: 297)
All our ideas of the several sorts of substances are nothing but collections of simple ideas, with a supposition of something to which they belong and in which they subsist (E ii.xxiii.37: 316)
. . . collections of such qualities as have been observed to co-exist in an unknown substratum (E iv.vi.7: 582)

(2) Yet the notion of substratum is also presented as highly criticizable:

we . . . signify nothing by the word *substance* but only an uncertain supposition of we know not what . . . which we take to be the substratum (E i.iv.18: 95)
. . . the supposed or confused idea of substance, such as it is (E ii.xii.6: 165)

---

[8] 'They who first ran into the notion of accidents, as a sort of real beings that needed something to inhere in, were forced to find out the word *substance* to support them' (E ii.xiii.19: 175). This is no help to Ayers either, for Locke could not have written those words as a comment on philosophers who believed that substances have real internal constitutions.

... the promiscuous use of so doubtful a term ... in ordinary use it has scarce one
clear distinct signification (E II.xiii.18: 174)
... of substance we have no idea of what it is, but only a confused obscure one of
what it does (E II.xiii.19: 175)
Our idea of [substratum] substance is equally obscure, or none at all (E II.xxiii.15: 305)
... the confused [idea] of substance, or of an unknown support (E III.vi.21: 450)

But if Locke means 'substratum' to refer to the real essences of kinds
of substance, it gives him no reason to say that the (1) 'first and chief'
ingredient in a common thought is a (2) 'supposed or confused' idea.

(1) He does not take the notion of real essence or internal constitution
to be implied in our untutored ways of thinking. Quite to the contrary:
when he argues that such real essences could not be our bases for classifying substances, Locke implies that we should leave thoughts about internal
constitutions out of our everyday thinking about the world, since they can
do no work for us. That is in striking contrast to the notion of 'substratum'
which, Locke says, is implied in the very notion of a *thing that is F*.[9]

(2) The worst that Locke finds to say about the idea of real essence or
internal constitution is that it is useless because we don't know what the
constitution is of any (kind of) things or stuff. Except in one isolated,
extraordinary sentence (E III.vi.43: 465), he never criticizes the idea of
internal constitution as 'supposed or confused', 'obscure', 'unclear', or the
like.

In brief, if the substratum texts concern real essences, neither side of
Locke's dilemma exists; so he is not in a bind; so how do we explain the
extraordinary contrast presented by the two sets of quoted fragments?

VIII. 'BESIDES ...'

The 'substratum' and 'real essence' terminologies are sharply separated in
the pages of the *Essay*. That supports the Leibnizian reading. The only two
passages where both are combined support it further. Here is one:

If we ... had in our complex idea an exact collection of all the secondary qualities
or powers of any substance, we should not yet thereby have an idea of the essence
of that thing. For since the powers or qualities that are observable by us are not the
real essence of that substance, but depend on it and flow from it, any collection

---

[9] Ayers says both that Lockean substratum is the 'underlying structure' that explains the
observable properties (Ayers 1977: 85), *and* that 'Locke believes that the idea of substance is
one that we ... cannot in reason avoid' (Ayers 1977: 87). This implies that Locke thought that
we cannot in reason avoid the idea of underlying structure; and I can find no textual evidence
for this.

whatsoever of these qualities cannot be the real essence of that thing. Whereby it is plain that our ideas of substances are not adequate; are not what the mind intends them to be. Besides, a man has no idea of substance in general, nor knows what substance is in itself. (E. ɪɪ.xxxi.13: 383)

On the face of it, this says that we lack knowledge or thoughts *both* of the real essence *and* of the substance, which implies that there are two concepts here, not one. Ayers argues for a different reading:

The word 'besides' is appropriate, not because knowledge of substance would be *additional* to knowledge of real essence, but because the former is, in a sense, a *lesser* knowledge, comprised within the latter, as knowledge that something is a plane figure is comprised within knowledge that it is a triangle. The whole sentence therefore means, 'What is more, human beings do not even know the *general* nature of substance, as it is in itself'. (Ayers 1977: 94)

I cannot tune my ear to the proposed use of 'besides'. Ayers would have us say things like this: 'She doesn't realize that the city block she lives on is square. Besides, she doesn't realize that it is rectangular.' This is not proper English.

IX. THE TWO-STEP PASSAGE

The other passage is even more telling. In it the notion of primary-quality real essences serves as a stepping stone to the notion of substratum, implying that the two are distinct: after we have put behind us the thought of secondary qualities as rooted in primary ones, we then face the thought of qualities as having bearers. Locke writes:

If anyone will examine himself concerning his notion of pure substance in general, he will find he has no other idea of it at all, but only a supposition of he knows not what support of such qualities, which are capable of producing simple ideas in us.... If anyone should be asked what is the subject wherein colour or weight inheres, he would have nothing to say, but the solid extended parts. And if he were demanded what is it that solidity and extension inhere in, he would [have to say it was] something, he knew not what. .... The idea then we have, to which we give the general name substance, being nothing but the supposed, but unknown support of those qualities we find existing, which we imagine cannot subsist ... without something to support them, we call that support *substantia*, which according to the true import of the word is in plain English *standing under* or *upholding*. (E ɪɪ.xxiii.2: 295–6)

Ayers sees the problem, and offers to solve it:

The answer to this difficulty [is] that the 'solidity and extension' here are *observable* solidity and extension. On this interpretation the 'solid extended parts' are the parts we can perceive, not the 'minute parts'. For the discussion explicitly concerns the unknown support of that which is known by observation, i.e. of 'such qualities which are capable of producing simple ideas in us; which qualities are commonly called accidents'. (Ayers 1977: 89)

Ayers and I agree that the passage goes in two stages. I think it goes from a thought about how secondary qualities are rooted in primary ones, to a thought about the primary ones as having a bearer. Ayers holds that it goes from a thought about secondary qualities as rooted in the primary qualities of big parts to a thought about the latter as rooted in the primary qualities of tiny parts, i.e. in those real essences that Ayers thinks are Locke's topic when he writes of 'substance in general'.

In defence of his reading, Ayers implies that Locke assigned double references to the terms 'solidity' and 'extension', taking them to denote either observable qualities or unobservable qualities. This supposed double use of quality words is supposed to help explain a phrase in Locke's next section, namely '. . . the extension, figure, solidity, motion, thinking, or other observable ideas'. Here, of course, 'ideas' are qualities; all the ones listed are indeed observable, in the sense that some things can be observed to have them; but Locke does not explicitly say, or even weakly imply, that the qualities he is discussing are possessed only by observable things and that invisibly small things have *other* qualities that go by the same names. If that were Locke's position, it would be a muddled mistake. But E ii.iv.1: 123 shows that he is not guilty.

This prop of Ayers's interpretation would have stood up better if Locke had spoken not of 'solidity and extension' but rather of 'size and shape'. It does make sense to say 'The big parts have different sizes and shapes from the small parts,' unlike the nonsense you get if in that you replace 'sizes and shapes' by 'solidity and extension' or its plural.

Even if the passage had obliged Ayers to that extent, however, its second prop is a broken reed. I refer to this:

> The 'solid extended parts' are the parts we can perceive, not the 'minute parts'. For the discussion explicitly concerns the unknown support of that which is known by observation. . . .

We are invited to believe that when Locke wrote 'solid extended parts' he meant 'big solid extended parts', because his topic is the unknown support (= cause) of what is known by observation. But when Locke discusses the cause of what is known by observation, he says—over and over again—that our ideas, both of primary and of secondary qualities, are produced 'by the operation of *insensible* particles on our senses' (E ii.viii.13: 136; emphasis added). Ayers's interpretation—'parts *we can perceive*'—stands Locke on his head.

So Ayers has no independent backing for his radical rewrite of the disputed passage, in which 'solidity and extension' becomes 'the shape, size etc. of parts that are big enough to observe', and 'solid extended parts' becomes 'solid extended parts that are big enough to observe'. There is no case for this busy rewriting, and there is good reason to take the two-step passage on its most natural, conservative reading: first, secondary qualities supervene on primary ones; second, basic primary qualities are underpinned by what has or instantiates or upholds them.

X. HOW DOES SUBSTRATUM RELATE TO INTERNAL CONSTITUTIONS?

I have been asked: If these are two distinct themes in Locke's thought, how does he interrelate them? He does not discuss this, but I am willing to answer on his behalf. There is a double answer, depending on whether he is thinking of 'substance', and thus 'substratum', strictly or generously.

He sometimes uses the term 'substance' quite strictly, confining it to *basic* thing-like items, which are not thought of as aggregates of items that are yet more basic. This, on the physical side, is Locke in his atomist frame of mind. When he is in it he presumably thinks of substratum as that which has the properties of an atom (on the physical side), and of whatever kind of item is to be taken as basic on the mental side. It would be in character for him then to think of a large physical thing as an aggregate of tiny things (at this point the doctrine of real essences comes into play), and to think of each of the latter as irreducibly a thing which . . . (and here the doctrine of substratum is invoked). This is closely related to the two-step passage discussed above.

More often, however, Locke uses the term 'substance' generously, to stand for thing-like items of any kind, including aggregates. In that frame of mind he thinks of substratum as that which has the properties of any thing-like item, and doesn't mind speaking of the substratum that has the properties of an orange, or of your body, or of a pebble. And then the substratum doctrine has no significant relation with the doctrine of real essences; essences are among the properties that are supported by substrata, and that's all there is to say.

Although I cannot find them actually making a difference to how 'substratum' is handled (except perhaps in the two-step passage), the two uses of 'substance' are visibly present in the *Essay*. Locke is using the term generously when he offers *man* and *horse* as prime examples of substances (E II.xxiii.3: 296 and E II.xxiii.4: 297); and he is using it more strictly when, in his famous chapter on identity, he says 'Animal identity is preserved in identity of life, and not of substance' (E ii.xxvii.12: 337), citing *man* and *horse* as examples (see Alston and Bennett 1988).

XI. WHAT KIND OF PHILOSOPHER WAS LOCKE?

Ayers connects the differing interpretations of Locke's treatment of 'substratum' with 'different opinions . . . as to the *kind* of philosopher Locke is', including different views about 'whether he is driven by an interest in "logical" questions as well as in philosophy of science' (Ayers 1977: 78). Ayers does not quite say that Locke was not driven by an interest in logical issues, but if that is not his opinion then I cannot see why he raised the question. If it is his opinion, I am still puzzled. I don't see how anyone could read the *Essay* without sensing, in Book iii and elsewhere, Locke's profound interest in problems about our conceptual structures, their expression in language, and their basis in our minds.

Ayers may be continuing that theme of what kind of philosopher Locke was when he characterizes the Leibnizian interpretation as 'brutal linguistic positivism', says that it 'is virtually a product of currently orthodox conceptions of philosophy', and hints that those who are given to it are insufficiently historical and ignore 'the intellectual background of Locke's thought'. I shan't discuss this.

XII. SUBSTANCES AND KINDS OF SUBSTANCE

According to Ayers, the substratum texts are concerned with the real essences of kinds of substances, not with particular substances. 'Locke's point is explicitly and always and necessarily made with reference to the definitions and ideas of *sorts* of substances' (Ayers 1977: 102). This is offered as going against the Leibnizian interpretation.

'Explicitly and always' is exaggerated, but it doesn't matter. Granting that when Locke speaks of ideas or names of substances he often means sorts of substances, it does not follow that in these discussions 'substratum' is playing the role of the primary–quality essence of a sort. Consider this passage, for example:

The ideas of substances are such combinations of simple ideas as are taken to represent distinct particular things subsisting by themselves, in which the supposed or confused idea of substance, such as it is, is always the first and chief. Thus if to substance be joined the simple idea of a certain dull whitish colour, with certain degrees of weight, hardness, ductility, and fusibility, we have the idea of lead. (E ii.xii.6: 165)

Suppose Ayers is right when he says that the example of lead makes it clear that the word 'thing' in this passage 'means "*sort of thing*" (embracing *stuff*)' (Ayers 1977: 104). That creates no embarrassment for the view that 'the supposed or confused idea of substance' refers to substratum as Leibniz and the rest of us understand it, namely as that which has the qualities of any particular. Look at the ingredients that Locke says make up the idea of lead: substance considered as substratum, off-whiteness, weight, hardness, ductility, fusibility. Each of those is possessed not by the sort, *lead*, but by individual portions of lead; and so the passage as a whole had better be about such individual portions. If it is coherent, the passage means that the general complex idea of lead collects such individual parcels of matter as are off-white, heavy, hard, ductile, fusible, *and substantial*. This last item, the one involving substratum, is thus connected with this or that individual portion of lead. How? Why, as the bearer of its qualities.[10]

XIII. 'NATURE OF SUBSTANCE'

Certain elements in the substratum texts don't fit the Leibnizian interpretation. Even if I could not explain them away, I would not conclude that the texts always concern primary-quality real essences, for the obstacles to that are even greater. But the untenability of Ayers's interpretation does not prove that the other is right; so the difficulties should be confronted.

I agree with Ayers that on the Leibnizian account of what substratum is Locke should see clearly that substratum cannot possibly have a 'nature' all of its own. Yet in a couple of substratum contexts he uses the phrase 'nature of substance'—once combatively and once sceptically, but not saying anything like 'Of course this is a nonsense phrase; nothing could possibly correspond to it.'

Perhaps there is nothing to be said about this. If I am right about substratum, Locke did fail to think through a certain aspect of his doctrines, and the 'nature of substance' passages might merely show that the failure was even worse than we thought. But I shall try to improve on that.

In one of the two 'nature of substance' passages, Locke suggests that if God, spirits and bodies are all substances it may follow that they, 'agreeing in the same common nature of substance, differ not any otherwise than in

---

[10] It was Alston who showed me that Ayers is right that when Locke discusses names and ideas of 'substances' his topic is usually *sorts of substances*, and that this makes no trouble for the Leibnizian interpretation.

a bare different modification of that substance' (E II.xiii.18: 174). The location of this is significant: it immediately precedes a section (quoted from in note 8 above) whose treatment of substratum does not square with the Leibnizian interpretation, or with Ayers's rival interpretation, or with the rest of the *Essay*. Here alone Locke treats substratum not as an embarrassing bit of public property but rather as a gratuitous, dispensable, and wholly criticizable invention of certain philosophers; and so we find him in the preceding section giving a rough handling to the question of whether God and finite spirits and bodies are all substances in the same sense.

(What mistake was made by those philosophers? Locke says that they were driven to look for a 'support' because they 'ran into the notion of *accidents*, as a sort of real beings' (E II.xiii.19: 175). This is intelligible as a handful of verbal gravel flung in the general direction of the scholastics, but if we interrogate it closely it is odd. Its best chance of saying something clear and true is to accuse the philosophers of believing that there are individual accidents, property-instances, abstract particulars, items such as *the rectangularity of this page*, as distinct from *rectangularity, which is possessed by (among other things) this page*. The substratum line of thought does perhaps flow more smoothly when it is conducted in terms of individual accidents or property instances; so Locke might be onto something here. But he does not follow it through, and his own work silently tolerates abstract particulars in several guises.)

These two sections where Locke rebuffs substratum as an intruder stand in marked contrast to his usual treatment of it as an embarrassing member of the family. Whatever is going on here, it can have little to do with the main thrust of the substratum passages throughout the *Essay*.

The other 'nature of substance' passage has a location that may also be significant. It is a sentence beginning 'Whatever therefore be the secret and abstract nature of substance in general . . .' (E II.xxiii.6: 298), and it follows one of the four sections in the *Essay* where Locke speaks of the substance *of* body and *of* spirit, and more specifically the substance of one's mind and of one's body. This peculiar 'substance of' locution occurs in E II.xxiii.5, 16, 23, 30: 297–8, 306, 308, 313 and nowhere else in the *Essay* that I know of. It can be reconciled with the Leibnizian interpretation, for 'the substance of body' could mean 'that which upholds the properties of any body'; but still the 'substance of' locution is anomalous, and one wonders if something special is afoot in those sections. Perhaps they are left over from a stage in the growth of Locke's thought when 'substance' and related terms were used for another purpose (though much of the chapter does involve substance as the support of qualities).

What could the other purpose be? If it were to express thoughts about primary–quality constitutions, that would explain why Locke here writes of substance as having a nature. It would also imply that Ayers is right about a few tiny pockets of E II.xxiii—leftovers from earlier drafts, expressing earlier thoughts. I wish I could believe it, but it isn't credible, because 'the substance of body' is too general to fit this reading, and 'the substance of spirit' is nonsense if 'substance' refers to a primary–quality inner constitution. The latter point deserves emphasis: Ayers ties substratum to primary-quality real essences, and does not mention the fact that Locke clearly thinks that the idea of substratum is as relevant to immaterial substances as to material ones.

There are two other main textual difficulties, which I shall discuss in turn.

XIV. SUBSTRATUM AS CAUSE

Locke often presents a thing's real essence or internal constitution as a *source* or *cause* of its being the way it observably is or of our observations of how it is. Here is a sample:

the peculiar constitution of bodies and the configuration of parts whereby they have the power to produce in us the ideas of their sensible qualities (E II.xxi.73: 287)

supposed to flow from the particular internal constitution or unknown essence of that substance (E II.xxiii.3: 296)

the real constitution on which their sensible qualities depend (E II.xxiii.11: 301)

those properties which flow from its real essence and constitution (E II.xxxii.24: 392)

the . . . unknown constitution of things whereon their discoverable qualities depend (E III.iii.15: 417)

a real but unknown constitution of their insensible parts, from which flow those sensible qualities (E III.iii.17: 418)

that real constitution of any thing which is the foundation of all those properties (E III.vi.6: 442)

these being all but properties, depending on its real constitution (E III.ix.17: 486)

In stark contrast, the substratum texts hardly ever bring in causal relations. All we can say about substratum is how it relates to ideas or qualities, Locke says, and the relations he usually invokes are not causation but possession, containment and support:

the substratum or support of those ideas we do know (E I.iv.18: 95)

were forced to find out the word *substance* to support them (E II.xiii.19: 175)

the supposed but unknown support of those qualities we find existing (E II.xxiii.2: 296)

the confused idea of something to which they belong and in which they subsist (E
    II.xxiii.3: 297)
we suppose them existing in and supported by some common subject (E II.xxiii.4:
    297)
which he supposes to rest in, and be as it were adherent to, that unknown common
    subject (E II.xxiii.6: 298)
a supposed I know not what, to support those ideas we call accidents (E II.xxiii.15:
    305)
a supposition of something to which they belong and in which they subsist (E
    II.xxiii.37: 316)
all united together in an unknown substratum (E II.xxiii.37: 317)
such qualities as have been observed to co-exist in an unknown substratum (E
    IV.vi.7: 582)

There is just one break in this pattern. In a passage already quoted, Locke
writes of 'some substratum wherein they do subsist *and from which they do
result*' (E II.xxiii.1: 295; my emphasis). The suggestion of substratum as
cause does not sit well with the Leibnizian reading, which seems to have
nothing causal about it.

A Leibnizian should try to explain this clause. But then Ayers should try
to explain why there is only one such expression in the *Essay*. Why is the
causal element that appears in about a hundred remarks in the terminology of 'real essence' and 'internal constitution' present in only one
clause—six words—in the context of the 'substratum' terminology?[11] No
one has tried to answer this question. I shall have a shot at the other.

XV. CAUSE OF UNITY

Actually there may be something causal about substratum even on the
Leibnizian view about what it is. Because there cannot be a thing with only
one property, each instance of substratum must uphold not just one idea/
quality but a lot of them:

. . . are called so united in one subject by one name (E II.xxiii.1: 295)
. . . we suppose them existing in . . . some common subject (E II.xxiii.4: 297)
. . . all united together in an unknown substratum (E II.xxiii.37: 317)
. . . such qualities as . . . coexist in an unknown substratum (E IV.vi.7: 582)

From this it is a short step to the idea that substratum doesn't just hold the
qualities up, so to speak, but *holds them together*, with this being understood causally. In one place Locke says as much:

[11] And why are the relations of possession, support and containment that are regularly said to
hold between 'substratum' and qualities *never* said to hold between 'essences' or 'real internal
constitutions' and sensible qualities?

Besides the several distinct simple ideas that make [up our ideas of substances], the confused one of substance, or of an unknown support and cause of their union, is always a part. (E iii.vi.21: 450)

This is not embarrassing to the Leibnizian interpretation. The latter can hardly avoid saying that substratum is a holder-together, a unifier of ideas or qualities, and that seems to imply that it *causes* their unity.

One might suspect, then, that when Locke wrote 'and from which they do result' he really meant 'and from which their unity results'. But I doubt it, because in a bit that was added in the fifth edition Locke again refers to 'the supposed simple substratum or substance which was looked upon as the thing itself in which inhere, and from which resulted, that complication of ideas by which it was represented to us' (E ii.xxiii.1: 295 n.). It is not likely that his pen slipped twice. I cannot explain Locke's use of 'result' in these two passages, unless it comes from his momentarily allowing his thought about substratum to become infected with isomorphic thoughts about some other topic.

XVI. POSSIBLE CONFLATIONS

The other topic *might* be real essences etc., but the two seem too disparate to be conflatable. How could Locke have spoken of 'the supposed *simple* substratum or substance' if he meant to be talking about internal constitutions? (Ayers, who badly needs an answer to this question, does not mention it. The nearest he gets to discussing substratum and simplicity is when he explains Locke's saying that 'the idea of substance is everywhere the same'. This is said, Ayers writes, 'not because Locke thinks that there is a mysterious undifferentiated substrate, the same in everything, but because the idea is equally lacking in positive content whenever it occurs; the idea of "something" is everywhere the same' (Ayers 1977: 91). This, of course, could not explain Locke's phrase 'the supposed simple substratum'.)

Here is a better guess. Locke sometimes uses 'idea' to stand neither for qualities nor for intellectual thoughts or concepts but rather for sensory states, sense-data, or the like; so perhaps he is here letting his substratum line of thought get mixed up with an issue about the outer-world counterparts or causes of our sensory states, i.e. the problem of what if anything lies behind the veil of perception. He has often been seen as running those two together, mostly by commentators who are doing the same thing themselves.[12]

---

[12] They seem to have been led into this conflation by Berkeley; but I was probably wrong to

There is an isomorphism that could encourage this conflation: with 'ideas' taken as mental particulars, they can be thought to result from 'some exterior cause, and the brisk acting of some objects without me' (E IV.xi.5: 632); with 'ideas' taken as qualities, they can be thought to be upheld by an underlying substance. Many philosophers have failed to distinguish these two thoughts, and Locke may sometimes have failed too.

XVII. 'A CERTAIN NUMBER . . . GO CONSTANTLY TOGETHER'

The remaining difficulty comes from the same passage as 'from which they do result'. Locke says that we suppose a substratum when the mind 'takes notice . . . that a certain number of these simple ideas go constantly together'. If the Leibnizian interpretation is right, the 'ideas' in question should be qualities or properties—*universals* of some kind—and in that case the notion of some of them constantly going together seems to be out of place. We can see why Locke should connect the supposition of a substratum with 'a number of [qualities]', since there couldn't be a thing that has only one quality; but the 'go constantly together' bit is awkward.

Ayers is comfortable with it because he holds that the role of substratum is to be the primary–quality essence of a *kind* of substance, and any notion of a specific kind of substance is associated with 'experienced constant concomitance of properties' (Ayers 1977: 86 n.). I could take over that reading of the phrase, suggesting that Locke has *temporarily* drifted into allowing the primary/secondary relation to get into the act when his proper topic is something else. But that would not be plausible, and I don't believe it; so I need some other explanation of 'going constantly together'.

The one I offered in my book invokes again the fact that Locke's term 'ideas' refers to, among other things, sensory states or sense-data. Throughout most of the section we are considering, I think the notion of 'ideas' as qualities is uppermost, and Locke's topic is the supposition of something like *materia prima* as a support for them; but when he wrote 'go constantly together' the notion of 'ideas' as sense-data may have come to the fore, in which case Locke is saying that the thought of a particular thing or substance—the thought that there is *an orange* here in my hand, for instance—arises from an awareness of a certain kind of sensory constancy: as I move my hand, different spherical portions of my visual field come to be qualitatively marked off from the rest, the qualitative difference always involves a certain colour sensation, the more of the field it occupies the

allege in Bennett 1971 that Berkeley himself was guilty of it. I owe this change of mind to writings, published and unpublished, by Ayers, Mackie, and Alston.

more strongly I have a certain olfactory sensation, and so on; and I explain these comcomitances—the fact that these 'ideas' of mine 'go constantly together' in *this* sense—by supposing that the 'ideas' in question are all perceptual intakes from *an orange*.

Ayers, commenting on my earlier presentation of this suggestion, says that it accused Locke of having 'flitted crazily from topic to topic even in mid-sentence'. That, however, is based on his view that Locke's use of 'idea' is simply ambiguous: sometimes he means one thing by it and sometimes another. But that doesn't survive examination in the light of the text of the *Essay* if the latter is read as carefully as Locke wrote it. My view is that, rather than Locke's using 'idea' ambiguously, he was guilty of a substantive conflation of properties and mental particulars, that his double use of 'idea' reflects this conflation, and that in the 'going constantly together' section *each* use of 'idea' is at least somewhat tinged with the property thought and the mental particular thought. I shall develop this matter in a separate paper.

Perhaps I am wrong about 'go constantly together'. It may have to be added to the tiny list of passages that are not properly reconcilable with the Leibnizian interpretation and that create no discomfort for Ayers's view. Those passages don't weigh much in the balance, however, against the dozens and hundreds that go the other way.[13]

[13] The help that William P. Alston has given me with this paper goes far beyond the specific mentions of him in the text and notes. I am also indebted to Ian Tipton and John Yolton for useful comments.

VIII

LOCKE ON PERSONAL IDENTITY

KENNETH P. WINKLER

THIS paper is an attempt to place Locke's discussion of personal identity in the setting Locke intended for it, and to consider some of the difficulties it presents once it is placed there. I begin by identifying a neglected feature of that discussion: its concern with what I shall call the subjective constitution of the self. This concern presents Locke with an intense case of a difficulty he faces elsewhere, that of reconciling or coordinating his chosen vocabulary—a vocabulary of persons and ideas—with the vocabulary of the philosophical tradition. I hope that a discussion of Locke's apparent response to the difficulty will provide a clearer picture of his overall project in the *Essay*.

Before turning to the text itself it might be helpful to summarize Locke's conclusions as they are usually understood. A person, Locke believes, is 'a thinking intelligent Being, that has reason and reflection, and can consider it self as it self, the same thinking thing in different times and places' (E. II.xxvii.9: 335). Personal *identity* extends as far as consciousness: a later person is the same as an earlier one just because the later person is conscious of some thought or action of the earlier. Locke's account of personal identity is the ancestor of all those that dispense with sameness of substance (whether soul or body) or stuff (whether mental or physical) and concentrate instead on psychological continuity. According to these accounts I am the same as any person with whom I am psychologically continuous, and although the recollection of past thoughts or actions is the only source of continuity recognized by Locke himself, it is certainly within the spirit of his account as it is usually interpreted to understand memory more broadly, so that it encompasses not just the conscious recollection of episodes but (for example) the retention of character, or the enduring habits of movement and speech. Leibniz, who was in many ways sympathetic to Locke's account, held a view of continuity broad

From *Journal of the History of Philosophy*, 29: 2 (Apr. 1991), 201–26.

enough to transform Locke's account (as it is usually understood) into something very close to twentieth-century accounts: 'for I believe that each of a man's thoughts has some effect, if only a confused one, or leaves some trace which mingles with the thoughts which follow it' (Leibniz 1981: 114).

Locke's chapter on identity and diversity, which was added to the second (1694) edition of the *Essay* on the advice of Molyneux, is one of a series of chapters on relations, beginning with the introductory 'Of Relation' (chapter xxv), continuing with 'Of Cause and Effect, and Other Relations' (chapter xxvi), and ending with 'Of Other Relations' (chapter xxviii), which is mainly devoted to moral relations. 'Of Identity and Diversity' (chapter xxvii) can be divided into two broad parts. In the first part, which occupies §§ 1–8, Locke is primarily concerned with the principle of individuation, which is, he says, 'Existence it self, which determines a Being of any sort to a particular time and place incommunicable to [that is, incapable of being shared by] two Beings of the same kind' (E II.xxvii.3: 330). Although he gives some account of the individuation of modes (§ 2), he devotes far more space to substances, which fall into three sorts: God, finite intelligences, and bodies. Because God is 'without beginning, eternal, unalterable, and every where', it follows that 'concerning his Identity, there can be no doubt' (E II.xxvii.2: 329). And because finite spirits always have a 'determinate time and place of beginning to exist', he explains that 'the relation to that time and place will always determine to each of them its Identity as long as it exists' (ibid.). Only the case of bodies calls for any real sophistication, and even here some cases are completely straightforward. Single particles of matter, 'to which no Addition or Substraction' has been made, can be handled in the same way as finite intelligences (ibid.). A mass of matter, which is 'only the Cohesion of Particles of Matter any how united' (E II.xxvii.4: 330), remains the same as long as its constituent parts are the same. The difficult case is that of an organized body, where particles are disposed in such a way that they constitute a watch, an oak, a horse, or a man. An oak, for example, continues to be the same plant 'as long as it partakes of the same Life, though that Life be communicated to new Particles of Matter vitally united to the living Plant, in a like continued Organization, conformable to that sort of Plants' (E II.xxvii.4: 331). The identity of man consists 'in nothing but a participation of the same continued Life, by constantly fleeting Particles of Matter, in succession vitally united to the same organized Body' (E II.xxvii.6: 331–2). In § 7 Locke reaches a conclusion already hinted at in § 3, and announces his intention to deal with personal identity:

'Tis not therefore Unity of Substance that comprehends all sorts of *Identity*, or will determine it in every Case: But to conceive, and judge of it aright, we must consider what *Idea* the Word it is applied to stands for: It being one thing to be the same *Substance*, another the same *Man*, and a third the same *Person*, if *Person*, *Man*, and *Substance*, are three Names standing for three different *Ideas*; for such as is the *Idea* belonging to that Name, such must be the *Identity*: Which if it had been a little more carefully attended to, would probably have prevented a great deal of that Confusion, which often occurs about this Matter, with no small seeming Difficulties; especially concerning *Personal Identity*, which therefore we shall in the next place a little consider. (E II.xxvii.7: 332)

Note that this passage does not commit Locke to the view that x can be the same plant as y without being the same substance.[1] Locke is clearly committed to saying that x can be the same plant as y without being made up of the same *particles*, but he avoids using expressions that pick out both plants and masses of matter. He uses expressions such as 'this oak' and 'that oak' to pick out *plants*, and he therefore has no way of saying both 'this oak is the same as that oak' and 'this oak is not the same mass of matter as that oak'. He can say only the first. Locke does write that it is 'one thing to be the same *Substance*, another the same *Man*, and a third the same *Person*', but this just means that the conditions two things have to satisfy in order to be the same man, for example, differ from the conditions two things have to satisfy in order to be the same person. It does not mean that one and the same pair of things might satisfy the conditions for being the same man and at the same time satisfy the conditions for being distinct masses of matter. Locke never identifies a plant or animal with the particles that compose it (or with the mass of matter to which it is at any moment 'annexed'), and the opening sentence of § 4 pretty clearly implies that they are always distinct.

Part 1 of chapter xxvii concludes with the observation that ''tis not the *Idea* of a thinking or rational Being alone, that makes the *Idea* of a *Man* in most Peoples Sense; but of a Body so and so shaped joined to it; and if that be the *Idea* of a *Man*, the same successive Body not shifted all at once, must as well as the same immaterial Spirit go to the making of the same *Man*' (E II.xxvii.8: 335).

The second part of chapter xxvii, §§ 9–29, is entirely concerned with personal identity. After defining a person as 'a thinking intelligent Being, that has reason and reflection, and can consider it self as it self, the same thinking thing in different times and places' (E II.xxvii.9: 335), Locke gives the following account of personal identity: 'Since consciousness always

---

[1] My discussion develops a point made in defence of Locke in Mackie 1976: 161.

accompanies thinking, and 'tis that, that makes every one to be, what he calls *self*; and thereby distinguishes himself from all other thinking things, in this alone consists *personal Identity*, *i.e.* the sameness of a rational Being: And as far as this consciousness can be extended backwards to any past Action or Thought, so far reaches the Identity of that *Person*; it is the same *self* now as it was then; and 'tis by the same *self* with this present one that now reflects on it, that Action was done' (ibid.). In § 10 he suggests that substances can be united into one person if they partake in the same consciousness, and in the following section he supports this by observing that a person survives even if he or she loses a limb. Our limbs, Locke insists, are parts of ourselves. But the real question, as he acknowledges in § 12, is 'whether if the same Substance, which thinks, be changed, it can be the same Person, or remaining the same, it can be different Persons' (E II.xxvii.12: 337).

He first replies to the question on behalf of those who think that the subject of thought is material. ''Tis plain they conceive personal Identity preserved in something else than Identity of Substance; as animal Identity is preserved in Identity of Life, and not of Substance', which suggests that the materialist's answer to at least the first half of the question must be yes (ibid.). In §§ 13–15 he operates on the assumption (which he takes to be more probable) that the subject of thought cannot be matter, and he considers the question one part at a time. The first part, he says, cannot be resolved until we know 'whether the consciousness of past Actions can be transferr'd from one thinking Substance to another' (E II.xxvii.13: 338). The consciousness of an action, Locke explains, is merely a present representation of a past act, rather than an individual action whose identity is rooted in the subject to which it is attached; as a result there is nothing internal to a consciousness which prevents another thinking substance from partaking in it. Until we learn more about the nature of thinking substance, he concludes, our assurance that such a transfer does not occur is 'best resolv'd into the Goodness of God' (ibid.). The answer to the second part of the question again depends on whether a thinking substance can be stripped of its consciousness of the past. If it can (as those who believe in pre-existing souls suppose), then the answer to the second part is yes, because personhood extends only as far as consciousness (E II.xxvii.14: 338–9). The answer to the first part of the question allows us to conceive how a resurrected body, 'not exactly in make or parts' the same as the body that housed the person on earth, might nonetheless house the person in heaven, 'the same consciousness going along with the Soul that inhabits it' (E II.xxvii.15: 340). The resurrected person would not be the same *man*, however, a point Locke illustrates with his famous story of the prince and the cobbler, souls who awaken in one another's bodies (ibid.).

It is in §§ 16–20 where the concern with the subjective constitution of the self is most prominent. In these sections Locke often takes the perspective of the first-person self, rather than the third-person point of view he takes with the prince and the cobbler. In § 16, for example, third parties are not asked whether a given person is the same as Noah; instead the 'I' is at centre stage: 'Had I the same consciousness, that I saw the Ark and *Noah*'s Flood, as that I saw an overflowing of the *Thames* last Winter, or as that I write now, I could no more doubt that I, that write this now, that saw the *Thames* overflow'd last Winter, and that view'd the Flood at the general Deluge, was the same *self*, place that *self* in what Substance you please, than that I that write this am the same *my self* now whilst I write (whether I consist of all the same Substance, material or immaterial, or no) that I was Yesterday' (E ii.xxvii.16: 340–1). He supports this conclusion by observing that I am as 'concern'd' for an action done a thousand years ago as I am for one done a moment ago, provided the ancient action has been 'appropriated to me now by this self-consciousness' (E ii.xxvii.16: 341). The focus on the first person and the interest in personal appropriation and concern are also present in §§ 17, 18, and 19, and they come out dramatically in § 20, where Locke replies to the objection that if I lose the memory of some parts of my life beyond all chance of recall, am I not (despite that) the same person who lived through them? Perhaps the *man* is the same, Locke replies, but the *person* is not (E ii.xxvii.20: 342). This reply makes perfect sense if we suppose Locke is interested in what we *take* the self to include, or in the self that comes about as a result of such takings. If I cannot remember certain past thoughts or actions, then they are not part of my *self*. They are not part of that consciousness whereby I am, in the language of § 24, 'my *self* to my *self*'. I am not concerned about them. I have not appropriated them. Were the self somehow constituted independently of my self-consciousness, these facts would not be very interesting. But because my self is constituted by what I take to be included in it, the actions and thoughts that I cannot remember are in no way part of me. The amnesia objection simply falls away.[2]

I am proposing that Locke is interested in a sense of the word *self* according to which what the self includes depends on what it appropriates.

[2] Mackie is one commentator who recognizes Locke's interest in appropriation, but he attacks Locke for offering what is properly a theory of appropriation as a theory of personal identity. See Mackie 1976: 183. Commentators with a more sympathetic view of the bond between consciousness and appropriation or concern include David P. Behan (Behan 1979: esp. 63–6) and Udo Thiel (Thiel 1983: 116–17 and 128–36).

I think we can all imagine finding a place for such a notion. 'Perhaps so-and-so did commit the crime, but if he is not aware of having done it, then there is a sense in which the action is not his own.' Insofar as Locke's thinking is dominated by this notion, Joseph Butler's famous criticism is irrelevant: 'One should really think it self-evident, that consciousness of personal identity presupposes, and therefore cannot constitute, personal identity, any more than knowledge, in any other case, can constitute truth, which it presupposes' (Butler 1813: I. 376–7). Butler fails to realize that for Locke, consciousness of a past act is merely a representation of it as one's own; it is not knowledge of the pre-existing fact that the act was one's own. If it were, Butler would be right to reply that consciousness cannot constitute identity. It might seem that Locke is no better off if consciousness is merely a representation of a past act, because circularity is then avoided only at the price of insufficiency: merely *representing* a past act as mine cannot make it mine. But it is enough on the notion of the self I have identified. So Locke avoids both circularity and insufficiency.

Perhaps the most powerful evidence for what I am proposing comes in § 26. Here we are told that '*Person*, as I take it, is the name for this *self*. Where-ever a Man finds, what he calls *himself*, there I think another may say is the same *Person*'. Personality extends itself beyond the present 'only by consciousness, whereby it becomes concerned and accountable, owns and imputes to it *self* past Actions, just upon the same ground, and for the same reason, that it does the present'. All this, Locke says, 'is founded in a concern for Happiness' (E II.xxvii.26: 346).

As § 26 makes clear, the self has a certain authority over its own constitution. It is important to realize that this authority is not consciously exerted. I do not wilfully disown one act and appropriate another; instead I accept what my consciousness reveals to me. There is also a severe limit on that authority, imposed by the transitivity of identity. The limit is established in an objection to Locke's account first made by Berkeley and later put in a more memorable form by Reid.[3] Reid's version of the objection, in iii.6 of the *Essays on the Intellectual Powers of Man*, runs as follows:

Suppose a brave officer to have been flogged when a boy at school, for robbing an orchard, to have taken a standard from the enemy in his first campaign, and to have been made a general in advanced life: Suppose also, which must be admitted to be possible, that, when he took the standard, he was conscious of his having been flogged at school, and that when made a general he was conscious of his taking the standard, but had absolutely lost the consciousness of his flogging.

These things being supposed, it follows, from Mr. Locke's doctrine, that he who

[3] Berkeley's version of the objection appears in *Alciphron* 7 (Berkeley 1948–57: III. 299).

was flogged at school is the same person who took the standard, and that he who took the standard is the same person who was made a general. Whence it follows . . . that the general is the same person with him who was flogged at school. But the general's consciousness does not reach so far as his flogging—therefore, according to Mr. Locke's doctrine, he is not the person who was flogged. Therefore, the general is, and at the same time is not the same person with him who was flogged at school. (Reid 1872: i. 351)

The general is the same as the young officer, who is in turn the same as the boy who was flogged at school. This makes the general the same person as the boy, despite the fact that none of the boy's thoughts or actions is recalled by the general. The general has apparently lost his authority over his own constitution.

Note that we cannot escape the objection merely by insisting on the self's authority. It might be said that the thoughts and actions of the schoolboy do not belong to the general. They are not part of the general *as he is conceived by his own self*, even though some of them are part of the young officer as he is conceived by his own self, and the officer and the general are one and the same. The problem with this is that it ignores what it is for the general to appropriate an earlier thought or action. When the general appropriates an earlier thought or action, he regards himself as its author, and he must therefore believe he is identical with the person who performed it. The general must therefore take himself to be identical with the young officer. But the young officer is identical with the schoolboy. The logic of identity then leaves us with no choice but to say that the general is identical with the boy; he cannot be the young officer unless he is.

I think it can be shown, however, that despite the objection our *personal* authority over our own identity remains intact. In the general's case a person's authority (the authority of a person at a time) is limited by *his own past*. The general and the young officer are the same, and it is therefore true of the general that he at one time recalled some of the thoughts or actions of the schoolboy. At the moment the general is unaware of those thoughts or actions; he does not include them in what he takes to be his self. But they are nonetheless parts of his self because they were appropriated by the young officer, whose acts of appropriation the general cannot disown without calling his identity with the officer into question. Because identity is undeniably transitive, and because a claim of identity is undeniably being made when we appropriate the thoughts or actions of a past self, Reid is right to say that the general and the schoolboy are the same person. But this does not show that consciousness does not constitute the self, or even that the self does not have the privilege of determining its own constitution. It shows only that a momentary or instantaneous consciousness does not constitute the self. Instead the constitution of the self takes place over time, and the self accumulates even when consciousness does not.

Locke occasionally suggests that the self is determined by what it *can* remember. What the self can remember might include what the self *has* remembered, *will* remember, or *would* remember if it survived beyond a certain point. But it is likely that Locke has something more modest in mind: perhaps being able to remember is simply to be disposed to remember if one is prodded, reminded, or asked to concentrate. Certainly this slight modification would pose no real threat to the self's authority. But the same is true of the more significant modification I have imposed under pressure from Berkeley and Reid. A person is responsible for his or her constitution, though constitution is not a feat of the moment: what the self includes at any moment depends on the past. Note the route we have taken to this conception of subjective constitution. We began with the idea that what I take (at a given moment) to be my self *is* my self, my *whole* self, an idea that was forced to yield to the logic of identity. But I think Locke can yield quite cheerfully. The self retains its authority, though the authoritative self is now a continuing rather than a momentary one. It is a self limited only by the logic of identity, and this limitation—because it is a purely logical limitation—is not really a limitation at all. I have suggested that Locke, rather than being embarrassed by the transitivity of identity, should take advantage of it. The limitation I have imposed has the effect of replacing the co-consciousness or remembering relation with the *ancestral* of that relation. The usual response to the transitivity objection (by commentators sympathetic to Locke) is simply to carry out the replacement. I have tried to show that it arises naturally from Locke's emphasis on subjective constitution, or that it can naturally be joined to such an emphasis.

Why is the constitution of the self I have described *subjective?* It is subjective because it cannot be criticized from a viewpoint wholly external to the self. Any legitimate criticism must be based on the self's own appropriations. It cannot be said that some act or thought should have been appropriated if it never was. I am not saying that the constitution of the self is subjective because other selves cannot know what I am conscious of. My point stands even if we assume that they can. Nor am I saying quite what Thomas Nagel says when he writes that 'from the point of view of the person himself, the question of his identity or nonidentity with someone undergoing some experience in the future appears to have a content that cannot be exhausted by any account in terms of memory, similarity of character, or physical continuity' (Nagel 1979: 200). One can acknowledge subjective constitution as I understand it here and at the same time accept an account of personal identity in terms of memory or consciousness. It has sometimes been suggested that objectivity consists in (or at least makes possible) a certain kind of criticism; my point is that according to Locke's emphasis on subjective constitution, criticism depends on what the self appropriates. The subjective authority to which I am calling attention resembles the authority one would have over one's own biography if the only evidence for one's thoughts or actions were one's own letters and diaries. Criticism would be possible, but it would be rooted in one's own actions; the evasive autobiographer could only be convicted by his or her own testimony.

I said earlier that Locke's concern with subjective constitution was only one of the concerns that structure his discussion of personal identity. The other dominant concern is more thoroughly objective, because it essentially involves third-person criticism and adjustment. And it may seem that this criticism and adjustment cannot take place without threatening the authority of the self.

The concern with the possibility of objective criticism and adjustment is a concern with divine retribution. The concern first emerges in § 13, where Locke speaks of our assurance that God will not permit transfer of the consciousness 'which draws Reward or Punishment with it' (E II.xxvii.13: 338); and it is clearly on Locke's mind in § 15, where he points out that the difference between personal identity and bodily identity allows us to understand how we might be resurrected in bodies other than our present ones (E II.xxvii.15: 340). But the concern is most explicit in §§ 22 and 26:

Humane Laws punish . . . with a Justice suitable to their way of Knowledge: Because in these cases, they cannot distinguish certainly what is real, what counterfeit; and so the ignorance in Drunkenness or Sleep is not admitted as a plea. For though punishment be annexed to personality, and personality to consciousness, and the Drunkard perhaps be not conscious of what he did; yet Humane Judicatures justly punish him; because the Fact is proved against him, but want of consciousness cannot be proved for him. But in the great Day, wherein the Secrets of all Hearts shall be laid open, it may be reasonable to think, no one shall be made to answer for what he knows nothing of; but shall receive his Doom, his Conscience accusing or excusing him. (E II.xxvii.22: 343–4)

For supposing a Man punish'd now, for what he had done in another Life, whereof he could be made to have no consciousness at all, what difference is there between that Punishment, and being created miserable? And therefore conformable to this, the Apostle tells us, that at the Great Day, when every one shall *receive according to his doings, the secrets of all Hearts shall be laid open*. The Sentence shall be justified by the consciousness all Persons shall have, that they *themselves* in what Bodies soever they appear, or what Substances soever that consciousness adheres to, are the *same*, that committed those Actions, and deserve that Punishment for them. (E II.xxvii.26: 347)

If we turn to works other than the *Essay* we can see that making sense of resurrection was highly important to Locke. In *The Reasonableness of Christianity*, a work that attempts to understand the Christian religion by 'the sole reading of the Scriptures', Locke explains that 'Adam being ... turned out of paradise, and all his posterity born out of it, the consequence of it was, that all men should die, and remain under death for ever, and so be utterly lost.' 'From this estate of death,' he continues, 'Jesus Christ restores all mankind to life.' 'The life, which Jesus Christ restores to all men, is that life, which they receive again at the resurrection. Then they recover from death, which otherwise all mankind should have continued under, lost for ever' (W VII: 3, 9).[4] Once resurrected, each of us will be judged according to his or her merits:

If any of the posterity of Adam were just, they shall not lose the reward of it, eternal life and bliss, by being his mortal issue: Christ will bring them all to life again; and then they shall be put every one upon his own trial, and receive judgment, as he is found to be righteous or not. And the righteous, as our Saviour says, Matt. xxv. 46, shall go into eternal life. Nor shall any one miss it, who has done what our Saviour directed the lawyer, who asked, Luke x. 25, What he should do to inherit eternal life? 'Do this', *i.e.* what is required by the law, 'and thou shalt live'. (W VII: 9–10)

No unrighteous person, no one that is guilty of any breach of the law, should be in paradise (W VII: 10).

It turns out, however, that all of us fall short of the law demanding perfect obedience. And so 'the benefit of life, restored by Christ at the resurrection, would have been no great advantage' had God not established, in addition to the inflexible law of works, a 'law of faith', by which 'faith is allowed to supply the defect of full obedience' (W VII: 11, 14). Only those

---

[4] For Locke's views on the fate of the wicked, see his manuscript on 'Resurrectio et Quae Sequuntur', published by Lord King (King 1830: II. 139–56). There Locke writes that it is 'plainly declared in Scripture' that the wicked 'shall not live for ever'. In Scripture it is 'everywhere inculcated' that 'the wages of sin is death, and the reward of the righteous is everlasting life' (King 1830: II. 144, 145). Locke asks 'whether the wicked shall not rise with such bodies of flesh and blood as they had before'. He replies that he does not recall 'any change of the bodies where the resurrection of the wicked can be supposed to be comprehended' (King 1830: II. 150). The wicked will apparently rise in bodies of flesh and blood, to be judged and then condemned to death. D. P. Walker (Walker 1964: 93–5) uses the 'Resurrectio' as evidence that Locke denied eternal torment, a point contested by W. M. Spellman (Spellman 1988: 109). Spellman does not discuss the 'Resurrectio', and the manuscript passage he quotes says only that God has the power to prolong pleasure and pain for 'as long as he pleases'. But the passage Spellman cites from the *Letter concerning Toleration*, according to which 'every man has an immortal soul, capable of eternal happiness or misery' (W VI: 41), does weigh against Walker's view—supposing, that is, that the passage is sincere, and meant to bear its most obvious interpretation. This topic clearly calls for further study. A good starting point is Wainwright 1987: I. 51–5.

who satisfy the law of faith can expect to receive the heavenly bodies which, according to Locke's paraphrase of 1 Corinthians 15: 44, will be 'powerful, glorious, and incorruptible' (W viii: 174). Locke's description of these 'spiritual bodies' in a note to the paraphrase very strongly suggests that they are not the same 'animal bodies' that the faithful inhabited on earth. This is, of course, no objection to the possibility of resurrection as Locke understands it, since in his opinion it requires only the survival of the person. As he writes to Stillingfleet, 'the resurrection of the dead I acknowledge to be an article of the Christian faith: but that the resurrection of the same body, in your lordship's sense of the same body, is an article of the Christian faith, is what, I confess, I do not yet know' (W iv: 303).[5] Locke tells Stillingfleet that he believes in the resurrection not on the basis of argument but because it is revealed in Scripture, yet the subsequent discussion (W iv: 303–4) shows how important it is to Locke that what he arrives at by reason or argument be consistent with what Scripture reveals. His account of personal identity is consistent with the possibility of resurrection whether or not our bodies on Judgement Day are the same as our bodies here on earth; it is equally consistent with the possibility that we are thinking matter, systems of particles 'fitly disposed' to acquire the attribute of thought (E iv.iii.6: 540), which will dissolve on our death and never be reassembled.[6]

Although satisfaction of the law of faith—belief that Jesus is the Messiah—is necessary for eternal life it is not sufficient. Repentance and a good life (though not, of course, a perfect one) are also necessary,[7] which means that the existence of the law of faith does not render superfluous Locke's concern that God reward or punish the resurrected according to

---

[5] The topics of resurrection and identity were closely associated in a large number of books and pamphlets published before and after the *Essay*. See the useful bibliography compiled by William Rounseville Alger (Alger 1864: 804–6), as well as Thiel's invaluable discussion in Thiel 1983: 161–6 (on the 17th cent.) and 176–80 (on the 18th cent.). Thiel considers Locke's views on resurrection on 166–71 and 173. Also useful is Fox 1988: esp. 22–3, 37, 52, 70, and 108.

[6] Locke judges it more probable that 'consciousness is annexed to, and the Affection of one individual immaterial Substance' (E ii.xxvii.25: 345). It is often said that Locke has no reason for this, but a crude case can in fact be constructed out of Lockean materials. We know by demonstration that God is a single immaterial substance (E iv.x: 619–30; E iv.iii.6: 541; E ii.xxvii.2: 329), and Locke believes that conjectures are more or less probable 'as they hold proportion to other parts of our Knowledge and Observation' (E iv.xvi.12: 665). In fact, 'we draw *all* our grounds of Probability' from likeness or analogy (ibid.; emphasis mine). Hence if God, being cogitative, is immaterial, it is likely that we are as well. This argument (which may lie behind W iv: 33) is no more far-fetched than one Locke himself develops for the probable existence of untold orders of higher spirits (E iii.vi.12: 446–7; cf. E iv.xi.12: 637). In view of Locke's assumption that these spirits are 'separate' or disembodied (E ii.x.9: 154; E ii.xxiii.13: 304; E ii.xxiii.36: 316), that argument actually strengthens the induction I have constructed here.

[7] See *The Reasonableness of Christianity*, W vii: 103–5, where Locke stresses the importance of repentance, and W vii: 111–14, where he stresses the importance of obedience.

their acts. It is essential—if God is to be just—that we are held responsible for all and only the acts we have performed. We cannot be justly punished for an act unless we are conscious of it, and thus our memories of forgotten misdeeds must be restored. God will also have to erase any consciousness that has (by some 'fatal Errour') been 'transferr'd'. But when he makes these adjustments to what will he appeal? Will he have to resort to the kind of objective criticism that is apparently ruled out by Locke's account of personal identity?

Before attempting to settle these questions I want to take up a related question which is, perhaps, more tractable. It has to do with finding a place in Locke's ontology for persons. Locke seems to believe both

(1) persons are not substances (see Shoemaker 1963: 45–8);

and

(2) persons are somehow less fundamental than substances.

But if the conjunction of (1) and (2) entitles us to say that Lockean persons supervene on substances, or that they are somehow constructed out of them, it is far from clear what the supervenience or the process of construction amounts to. I would like to propose an understanding of this which, I am aware, goes beyond anything Locke says. Locke worries hardly at all about clarifying the relationship between persons and substances, and after stating my proposal—and before returning to the difficulties raised by the divine rectification of memory—I want to ask why this is so.

The relationship between persons and substances troubled one of Locke's most prominent eighteenth-century commentators. Edmund Law, whose 'A Defence of Mr. Locke's Opinion concerning Personal Identity' was included in the standard editions of Locke's works, admitted that Locke's remarks in *Essay* II.xxvii were sometimes misleading.[8] But a coherent and defensible view of persons and their identity could, Law insisted, be extracted from them. Law took himself to be drawing out the implications of Locke's observation that 'person' is a forensic term. 'Used in the strict forensic sense', Law explained, the word denotes not a substance but a quality or modification—'such quality or modification in man as denominates him a moral agent, or an accountable creature; renders him the proper subject of laws, and a true object of rewards or punishments' (Law 1823*a*: 179–80). 'When we apply it to any man', Law continued, 'we do not

---

[8] Law's 'Defence' was published separately in Cambridge in 1769. It was then included in the 1777 edition of Locke's *Works* (an edition prepared by Law himself) and in editions appearing in 1794, 1801, and 1823. Law attributes the accompanying 'Appendix' to 'a friend' (Law 1823*b*: 199), but he endorses its contents and I will treat it as his own.

treat of him absolutely, and in gross; but under a particular relation or precision' (Law 1823a: 180). *Precision* was a common synonym for *abstraction*, and Law blamed the misunderstandings of Locke's critics on their failure to appreciate the importance of abstract ideas, a charge he illustrates by citing Berkeley. Law's own statements of Locke's position differ widely in their details; the following quotations illustrate their range:

Personality [is] solely a creature of society, an abstract consideration of man, necessary for the mutual benefit of him and his fellows; *i.e.*, a mere forensic term. (Law 1823a: 184)

And thus sameness of person stands to denote, not what constitutes the same rational agent, though it always is predicated of such; but we consider his rationality so far only, as it makes him capable of knowing what he does and suffers, and on what account, and thereby renders him amenable to justice for his behavior. (Law 1823a: 189)

Our inquiry . . . is not what enters into the natural constitution of a thing, but what renders it so far a moral one, and is the *sine qua non* of its being justly chargeable with any of its past actions, here or hereafter. . . . It is an artificial distinction, yet founded in the nature, but not the whole nature of man. (Law 1823a: 189–90)

The word person, then, . . . [stands for] a mixed mode, or relation, and not a substance (Law 1823b: 200)

The suggestion that a person is a mixed mode is not as far-fetched as it may seem, because there was a long tradition, rooted in the ancient understanding of *persona* as a mask or guise, according to which persons are constructions—often social constructions—somehow placed upon naturally occurring human beings. Law himself actually recalls the ancient precedent in words I omitted from the last quotation. The full text reads: 'The word person, then, according to the received sense in all classical authors, standing for a certain guise, character, quality *i.e.* being in fact a mixed mode, or relation, and not a substance'. After quoting Locke's definition of 'person' as 'a thinking intelligent being, that has reason and reflection', Law says the expression 'would have been more just, had he said that the word person stands for an attribute, or quality, or character of a thinking intelligent being' (Law 1823b: 199), which is, Law explains, the sense in which Cicero uses it. Law (Law 1823b: 199–200) quotes Cicero's *Pro Sulla* 3.8, which is translated here so as to bring out its affinities with the seventeenth-century passages I will turn to in just a moment: 'If on account of my actions you impose [*imponis*] this person [*personam*] on my whole life, Torquatus, you are badly mistaken. Nature wished me to be compassionate; my country wished me to be firm; neither my country nor nature wished me to be cruel; further, inclination and nature itself have now drawn off the violent and harsh person [*personam*] which occasion and the state then imposed [*imposuit*].' A role or guise, Cicero warns, is something imposed by human beings, acting individually or in concert, and it is not to be confused with the human being on whom it is imposed. That human being might be several persons at once—he might, that is, occupy several roles or guises at the same time—and he might shake off a person earlier imposed upon him.

Law's Ciceronian interpretation of Locke is, I think, mistaken, but it makes a good deal of sense when it is viewed in an early eighteenth-century setting. The Ciceronian understanding of persons had recently been extended by Samuel Pufendorf in his *De jure naturate et gentium (Of the Law of Nature and Nations)*, first published in 1672. Pufendorf divides the world into two kinds of entities, physical (*entia physica*) and moral (*entia moralia*). 'We may define our *Moral Entities*', he writes, 'to be *Certain Modes superadded to Natural Things and Motions, by Understanding Beings*' (Pufendorf 1703: I.i.3).[9] Physical entities are created, but moral entities, like Cicero's persons, are *imposed*: 'As the Original way of producing Natural Entities is *Creation*, so the Manner of Framing Moral Entities cannot be better express'd than by the Term of *Imposition* [*impositionis*]. For these do not proceed from Principles ingraffed in the Substance of Things [*non ex principiis intrinsecis substantiae rerum proveniunt*], but are added [*superaddita*], at the Pleasure of Intelligent Creatures, to Beings already perfect in a Natural Sense [*physice perfectis*]' (Pufendorf 1703: I.i.4). Moral entities 'fram'd with Analogy to Substances', Pufendorf writes, 'are call'd *Moral Persons*' (Pufendorf 1703: I.i.12). In the course of his discussion Pufendorf appeals to several passages from Cicero. Cicero is cited, for example, in support of Pufendorf's observation that 'one and the same Man . . . may sustain several *Persons* together', provided 'that the Duties attending those *Persons*' do not conflict (Pufendorf 1703: I.i.14).

Some of the passages Pufendorf quotes from Cicero (e.g. at Pufendorf 1703: I.i.7 and I.i.14) even speak of persons as being imposed. According to Pufendorf, such imposition is not the work of human beings alone. God too can impose moral entities on nature, and among the entities he imposes is what Pufendorf calls the state of being a man—the state of possessing the rights and duties that might be described as basic. A Lockean person is also the bearer of such basic rights and duties, and in one striking passage Pufendorf anticipates Locke's concern with identity and the beginning of existence: 'Since then the very being a Man is a *State*, obliging to

---

[9] For a brief account of Pufendorf's distinction between physical and moral entities, see Schneewind 1987: 124–8.

certain Duties, and giving a Title to certain Rights, it cannot be out of the way to consider the precise point of Time at which particular Persons may be said to enter on such a *State*. [And that is] the very first Moment, when any one may be truly call'd a Man, . . . that is, whensoever he begins to enjoy Life and Sense' (Pufendorf 1703: i.i.7).

I am claiming not that Pufendorf influenced Locke, but that his discussion of moral persons (of which 'men' are examples) makes Law's reading of Locke comprehensible.[10] Yet I do not think that Law's response to (1) and (2) can be accepted, because Lockean persons are not modes but substances.[11] There are at least four reasons for concluding this. First, 'finite intelligences' appear second in Locke's list of the three kinds of substance of which we have conceptions (E ii.xxvii.2: 329), and at E ii.xxvii.9: 335 Locke *defines* a person as a kind of intelligence. Second, anything satisfying Locke's definition of *person* also satisfies his very undemanding conception of substance, as articulated, for example, at E ii.xxiii.1: 295 and 14: 305. Third, there is as much reason to count oak trees and horses as modes as there is to count persons as modes, and Locke takes trees and horses to be clear cases of substance. It may seem as though a tree cannot be a substance because it cannot be identified with the atoms coursing through it in its lifetime (or with any collection of such atoms). But there is nothing to justify the assumption that, for Locke, a substance must be 'basic'—that is, either a material atom (a corpuscle which is, practically speaking, indivisible) or a simple immaterial substance. A Lockean substance can be something built up out of 'basic' substances: nothing in Locke's remarks about substance prevents it, and his scepticism regarding real constitutions suggests that he wants to leave room for it. In this respect Locke's conception of substance differs radically from the conception shared by Descartes and Spinoza. A Cartesian substance needs

---

[10] Locke read Pufendorf and recommended *Of the Law of Nature and Nations* as reading for young gentlemen. Pufendorf was, he thought, even better than Grotius (W iii: 296; W x: 176). Jean Barbeyrac, whose notes to the French translation of Pufendorf were included in English editions beginning in 1710, actually refers readers of Pufendorf on moral entities to Locke's discussion of mixed modes and moral relations at *Essay* ii.xxviii; see Pufendorf 1717: 3 n. 3. The 'Ciceronian' interpretation of 'person' played an important role in discussions of the Trinity. In his *Three Sermons concerning the Sacred Trinity*, John Wallis defines 'person' as '*the State, Quality or Condition of a Man, as he stands Related to other Men*' (Wallis 1691: 59). He then argues that it is neither contradictory nor absurd 'for the *same Man* to sustain *divers Persons*, (either successively, or at the same Time;) or *divers Persons* to meet in *the same Man*' (Wallis 1691: 60). Like Pufendorf (Pufendorf 1703: i.i.14), Wallis quotes Cicero's *De oratore* 2.24: 'I being One and the same Man, sustain Three Persons; that of my own, that of my Adversary, and that of the Judge.' 'What hinders', he then asks, 'but that *Three Divine Persons* . . . may be *One God?*' (Wallis 1691: 60–1). Richard Burthogge replied that 'it is not the same to say that one *sustains* Three persons, as to say that one *is* Three persons' (Burthogge 1694: 280).

[11] The same conclusion is defended by Margaret Atherton (Atherton 1983: esp. 286–7), and William P. Alston and Jonathan Bennett (Alston and Bennett 1988: esp. 38–40).

nothing but itself in order to exist. Locke imposes no such requirement, even though he does say (E II.xxiii.1: 295) that we accustom ourselves to believe in a substratum because we are unable to imagine how simple ideas can subsist by themselves. Finally, in a first-edition passage preserved in later editions and recalling Pufendorf's distinction between physical and moral entities, Locke makes it clear that what he calls 'the *moral Man*' is a substance:

As to Substances, when concerned in moral Discourses, their divers Natures are not so much enquir'd into, as supposed; *v.g.* when we say that *Man is subject to Law*: We mean nothing by *Man*, but a corporeal rational Creature: What the real Essence or other Qualities of that Creature are in this Case, is no way considered. And therefore, whether a Child or Changeling be a *Man* in a physical Sense, may amongst the Naturalists be as disputable as it will, it concerns not at all the *moral Man*, as I may call him, which is this immoveable unchangeable *Idea, a corporeal rational Being.* . . . The Names of Substances, if they be used in them, as they should, can no more disturb Moral, than they do Mathematical Discourses. (E III.xi.16: 516–17)

If a moral man is a substance there is no reason why a person should not be. It is true that the moral man as here described is corporeal, but the idea of this man reappears in E IV.iii.18: 549, shorn of all reference to body, as the idea of an understanding, rational being. There it seems no less able to figure as an idea of substance in Locke's projected science of morality.[12]

I have argued that Lockean persons can count as substances even if they supervene on what might be called 'basic' substances. The same point can be arrived at in another way. Suppose we allow that substance-stages—temporal slices of the enduring things Locke has in mind when he speaks of substances—can be the subjects of thoughts, feelings, and actions. Later substance-stages will represent the thoughts and actions of earlier ones, giving rise to relations of psychological continuity. These relations will generate *persons*, each of which will be a series of substance-stages bound together by relations of psychological continuity. An enduring plant or animal will *also* be a series of substance-stages, but one held together by different relations, some examples of which are catalogued by Locke in chapter xxvii. From an 'ontological' viewpoint, then, persons and living things are on the same level: entities of each kind are built up out of substance-stages. And in one and the same world we may find a person and a living body who share some but not all of their stages. As we trace persons and living bodies through time, in other words, we may find a given person and a given body coinciding—sharing a stage—and later diverging.[13]

[12] Ruth Mattern calls attention to these passages in Mattern 1980, reprinted as ch. XIV of this volume.

[13] For a proposal of roughly this sort, part of an account of personal identity claiming to be a descendant of Locke's, see Perry 1976: esp. 69–73.

My proposal cannot be attributed to Locke, if only because there is no hint in the *Essay* that substance-stages can (or should) be treated as building-blocks—as something more fundamental than the enduring substances which are, according to my proposal, constructed out of them. But my proposal is Lockean, I think, in its willingness to question the assumption that the notions of an enduring corpuscle, compound body, or simple immaterial substance are less problematic—more perspicuous, or known to be more firmly grounded in what there is—than the notion of person. According to my proposal, persons are not necessarily 'basic' substances, but they are not therefore something other than substances, and they are perhaps not even less fundamental than substances I have labelled 'basic': nothing I have said implies that building-blocks or substance-stages *dictate* principles for the identity and individuation of basic substances, or that such principles flow naturally from the stages in a way that the corresponding principles for persons do not. In each case we have to work to discover what the principles are, and the enduring things generated by relations of psychological continuity are no less natural or authentic than the enduring things generated by other relations. At several points in E II.xxvii Locke says that identity is not always determined by what he calls 'Unity of Substance' (E II.xxvii.7: 332) or 'Identity of Substance' (E II.xxvii.12: 337). But this is not because he thinks a person is not a substance. It is his way of saying that personal identity is not determined by the unity or identity of two kinds of substances in particular—immaterial souls and organized bodies.[14]

Locke, as I said above, does not worry very much about clarifying the relationship between persons and substances; and before returning to the problem of divine rectification I want to ask what this can tell us about his larger aims and concerns. I think Locke's immunity to worry here is characteristic of him. He is only mildly concerned with the way in which the category of person lines up with the categories of substance and mode that he inherited from the philosophical tradition. This is partly because he does not find the traditional categories all that clear in themselves—why should we fuss over adjusting the category of person to the category of substance when in talking of substance we are, as Locke says, 'like Children' (E II.xxiii.2: 296)?—and partly because he takes the categories that lend structure to our lives to be worthy subjects of philosophical investigation in their own right. *Essay* II.xxvii is only one of several passages in Locke's writings that reveal his impatience with traditional problems (or, more accurately, his impatience with too exclusive a fixation on traditional

---

[14] Other passages opposing identity of substance to personal identity include E II.xxvii.10, 16, 19, and 23: 335–6, 340–1, 342, and 344. All of them can be interpreted as I propose here.

problems) and his allegiance to certain features of the lived or common-sense world.

Locke's treatment of ideas is one example. The notion of an idea is arguably the central notion in the *Essay*. In its very first chapter Locke begs the reader's forgiveness for resorting to the term so often. He explains that he could not avoid using it frequently: 'it being that Term, which, I think, serves best to stand for whatsoever is the Object of the Understanding when a Man thinks, I have used it to express whatever is meant by *Phantasm, Notion, Species*, or whatever it is, which the Mind can be employ'd about in thinking' (E I.i.8: 47). This explanation troubled readers (John Sergeant, for example) who took phantasms and notions to be different things. But it is also unclear what place ideas are supposed to have in an even more basic vocabulary, the vocabulary of substance and mode. John Norris, in his *Cursory Reflections upon a Book call'd, an Essay concerning Human Understanding*, published soon after the *Essay* appeared, took Locke to task for exactly this. The nature of ideas, Norris says, is 'wholly omitted and passed over in deep silence' by the author of the *Essay*. Without doubt, Norris says later, ideas are 'Real Beings'. But 'are they Substances, or are they Modifications of Substances?' (Norris 1690: 3, 22, 23). Norris thinks there are problems for Locke on either alternative. Locke's reply (written in 1692 but first published after his death) is as follows:

Ideas may be real beings, though not substances; as motion is a real being, though not a substance; and it seems probable that, in us, ideas depend on, and are some way or other the effect of motion; since they are so fleeting. . . .

This therefore may be a sufficient excuse of the ignorance I have owned of what our ideas are, any farther than as they are perceptions we experiment in ourselves; and the dull unphilosophical way I have taken of examining their production, only so far as experience and observation lead me; wherein my dim light went not beyond sensation and reflection. (W x: 256)

These are tantalizing passages. In the first paragraph Locke stops just short of saying (and in any case strongly implies) that ideas are modifications. In the second paragraph that implication, though not exactly cancelled, is dampened or obscured: for clarification he looks not to traditional ontology, but to our own experience. We understand the notion of an idea well enough even if we cannot locate it in the classificatory scheme of the tradition. Norris was Malebranche's leading British follower, and in his *Examination of Malebranche* Locke turns the distinction between substance and mode against Malebranche himself. Malebranche, Locke reports, calls ideas 'beings, representative beings'. 'But whether these beings are substances, modes, or relations, I am not told; and so by being told they are spiritual beings, I know no more but that they are something, I know not what, and that I knew before' (W ix: 224). Real clarification is to be sought not in ontological inventories but in our own experience: 'supposing ideas real spiritual things ever so much, if they are neither substances nor modes, let them be what they will, I am no more instructed in their nature, than when I am told they are perceptions, such as I find them' (W ix: 220).[15]

Similar tendencies can be discerned in Locke's insouciant response to scepticism. Locke doesn't think that anyone can be sceptical enough to doubt the existence of the things he sees and feels. And if anyone can, he 'will never have any Controversie with me', Locke writes, 'since he can never be sure I say any thing contrary to his Opinion. As to my self, I think GOD has given me assurance enough of the Existence of Things without me: since by their different application, I can produce in my self both Pleasure and Pain, which is one great Concernment of my present state' (E iv.xi.3: 631). Throughout his discussion of our knowledge of the existence of physical things Locke blends the same serious point with the same kind of joking. The person who takes all that we see and feel to be a dream is reminded that 'if all be a Dream, then he doth but dream, that he makes the Question: and so it is not much matter, that a waking Man should answer him'. But he may want to dream that Locke ventures this answer: '*the certainty of* Things existing *in rerum Natura* when we have the *testimony of our Senses* for it, is not only *as great* as our frame can attain to, but *as our Condition needs.*' The evidence is as certain, he adds, as our happiness or misery, states which, as we have seen, play an important role in his discussion of personal identity, because beyond them 'we have no concernment, either of Knowledge or Being' (E iv.xi.8: 634–5).

These passages depict Locke as a practitioner of something like descriptive metaphysics, as a metaphysician of common life, or as an analyst of the lived world, a world bounded by our concern for happiness and misery. They seen right at home in a book that is said to be by 'John Locke, Gent.', a book described by its author as something undertaken '*for my own Information, and the Satisfaction of a few Friends*'. It is the work of '*some of my idle and heavy hours*', and the author is now too lazy or busy to make it shorter; it is an *Essay*—an attempt or venture—and not a definitive treatise (E Epis: 7 and 6).[16]

Locke's ambition is to carve out an area of philosophical investigation,

---

[15] See also W ix: 232–3, 234–5, and 247–8, as well as E i.i.2: 43, where Locke says he will not meddle with 'the Physical Consideration of the Mind'.

[16] James Lowde actually tempers his criticism by reminding himself that Locke's book is offered 'only by way of Essay' (Lowde 1699: 32).

one in which progress would only be impeded by too exclusive a fixation on certain inherited categories and concerns. His chapter on personal identity subserves this ambition: Locke delineates a notion which helps to lay down the structure of our lives, and he is less troubled than Norris or Butler would be by the task of accommodating the notion to the tradition. The *Essay* is written from a point of view which may not possess the objectivity or universality to which the notions of the tradition aspire, but Locke is convinced that what is seen from that viewpoint cannot be dismissed as illusory. Locke seeks a human philosophy, a philosophy adjusted to us, one free, to a greater extent than before, of a vocabulary that too easily suggests we can manage something grander.

But we have a way of getting beyond ourselves, and Locke cannot be read as if *this* world is all that interests him. This brings us back to the adjustments God will have to make when he resurrects us. Does the demand for rectification or adjustment run counter to the subjective constitution of the self?

Antony Flew believes it does: 'On Locke's view there could be no sense in his own fear that people might lose or escape their deserts because they remembered doing what they had not in fact done: if anyone can remember doing something then necessarily—according to Locke's account—he is in fact the same person as did that deed. By making this desperate appeal [to the goodness of God], Locke . . . tacitly confesses the inadequacy of his own account of personal identity' (Flew 1968: 164).

The task of adjustment or rectification calls for two things (though Flew in this passage mentions only the second): God has to make sure that the resurrected person acknowledges every thought or deed about to be punished or rewarded, and he has to guard against 'transference', the appropriation of thoughts or deeds that are not in fact one's own. But when God makes these adjustments, to what is he appealing?

Suppose there is an 'island' in what I might describe as my past—a time never recalled by me at any other time. Suppose I committed a crime then. What would be the difference between God's 'restoring' consciousness of the crime and his deluding me into thinking I had committed it? The memory can be restored, it seems, only by subverting the authority of the self: not only do I fail to acknowledge the act now, but no ancestor-self owns up to it either. Now it seems that God can pin the crime on me only by maintaining that it was committed by the substance with which I am (or in my earthly life was) associated. But if Locke's account of personal identity is correct, why should the deeds of the substance imply anything about *me?* Imagine someone on Judgment Day eager to avoid the imputation of a crime. Luckily he's read the *Essay*. He had been told that reading the *Essay* would be useful, but had no idea *how* useful. 'That's not *me* you're pointing to. It is a thinking substance which according to you bears some very intimate relation to me. I suppose I have to trust you when it comes to *that*; the substance is, I gather, the substance in which I am realized, the substance to which I am annexed. But it isn't *me*. The proof is that I might continue to exist even though the substance doesn't. All my survival would require is a transfer of my consciousness to a new home. Whether the substance you're pointing to matters to me depends on whether I acknowledge one of its acts (that is, on whether I acknowledge one of its acts, or one of my ancestor-selves acknowledges one of its acts) and *I don't*.'

Suppose, on the other hand, that upon resurrection I appropriate a criminal act which I did not in fact commit. God must see that I did not perform the act I now acknowledge, and it looks as if this has to mean something like the following: God recalls the substance in which my consciousness was realized (the substance to which I was annexed) and he sees that it did not perform the act. But why should the innocence of the substance entail *my* innocence? In view of Locke's account of personal identity I am guilty because I acknowledge the deed, and the innocence of the substance with which I am *otherwise* associated seems to be of no significance at all.

I think all that I have said about the challenge of rectification is in fact a bit hasty; we need to go over the same ground more carefully. The first part of the challenge involves islands in my past: if there are such islands, God must be able to build bridges to them. (The protest as I imagined it could not of course be made, but the underlying worry is genuine.) The obvious Lockean response (modelled on his way of dealing with the irremediable amnesia of § 20) is that what I have been calling islands in my past are not in *my* past at all. As far as the *restoration* of memory is concerned, God need not go beyond what I (that is, my various ancestor-selves) appropriated in the past.

But this way of meeting the first part of the challenge makes the difficulty of meeting the second part even starker. In thinking about the first I was assuming that God could legitimately restore a memory provided only that some ancestor-self was aware of the thought or action it represents. But suppose that I now remember a thought or action that no ancestor-self remembers. Why should my present self (my resurrection self, for example) play less a role than my past selves in determining which thoughts or actions are to count as mine now? The problem is that if we respond by saying that any thought or action appropriated by my present self is in fact mine, we lose (as Flew in effect insists) the possibility of divine criticism.

Flew complains that Locke can make no real sense of the worry that I might appropriate an act not my own, for, according to Locke's account, once I appropriate an act it *is* mine. If 'punishment is annexed to personality, and personality to consciousness', as Locke boldly proclaims at E II.xxvii.22: 344, then no one can object if I am punished for an act I remember as my own. We might respond on Locke's behalf by tightening the requirements for psychological continuity. We might say that it takes more than a single memory to make a substance-stage continuous with a person's later stages. Or we might say that a person can include no more than a single stage for every moment in his or her history. But the first modification does nothing to guard against elaborate delusions, and the second is unavailing in the absence of a way of determining which of the stages existing at a time should be incorporated into a person who lays claim to several.

At the very least, Flew's objection shows that the dominant themes in chapter xxvii—the subjective constitution of the self, and the possibility of objective criticism and adjustment—cannot easily be combined. Locke is uncertain about the nature of what it is in us that thinks, and he sets out to develop an account of personal identity that will not be disrupted by that uncertainty. The main difficulty with the account is that we are sometimes caused to remember what we did not in fact do. Although our spiritual bodies might be exempt from the imperfections that cause paramnesia in our earthly bodies, what grounds will God have for ignoring the false memories I may have had in this life, and for refusing to restore memories of every thought or deed performed by the person whose life (in small part) I falsely remember?

The difficulty can be sharpened if we return for a moment to my account of the accumulation of the self over time. I suggested that Locke can allow Reid's general to be the schoolboy, because in taking himself to be the young officer, the general commits himself to the actions the officer appropriated. But I passed over an important distinction: it is one thing for the general to identify himself with the young officer, and another thing for the general to commit himself to every one of the officer's acknowledged thoughts and deeds. The general is free to judge that some of those thoughts and deeds were wrongly appropriated. This shows that the authority of the self at any moment is even more precarious than I suggested. Later selves may want to criticize earlier selves, much the way God, when he resurrects us, may want to put some earlier memories aside.

Suppose that personal identity does not consist in consciousness, or in consciousness as we know it, but in something that underlies it. God may then see that I am not identical with x even though I have appropriated some of x's thoughts or deeds. Memory may still be necessary for personal identity (or necessary for the punishment which our identity with the criminal helps to justify), but it will not be sufficient. This proposal drives a wedge between the real self and the self I take myself to be, but the size and significance of the wedge depends on the relationship between consciousness (or consciousness as we know it) and whatever it is (at the moment known only to God) that underlies it. There is a *suggestion* of this kind of view in § 13, where Locke says that we do not know 'whether the consciousness of past Actions can be transferr'd from one thinking Substance to another' (E II.xxvii.13: 337), a claim that would be extremely odd if Locke thought that consciousness was something whose nature was transparent, and without a foundation that might be better known by God than by ourselves. The rest of § 13 strongly suggests that consciousness is *not* transparent—that it has (though this may be misleading) an unknown real essence.[17] If it does, it may well turn out that some of Locke's thought experiments do not represent real possibilities, but this accords with his general belief that there are necessary connections of which we may remain forever ignorant.

Locke leaves the suggestion undeveloped. It is entirely consistent with his repeated emphasis on our ignorance of the 'substance of Spirit' (at *Essay* II.xxiii.22: 308 and II.xxiii.28–30: 311–13 for example), but it subverts the subjective authority of the self. Criticism will no longer be based on the self's appropriations. As a result Locke will be under pressure to conclude that personal identity is constituted not by consciousness, but by its unknown foundation. It might be said on Locke's behalf that this foundation qualifies as the basis of identity only because it is *first* the basis of consciousness—the normal cause or basis of appropriation. But then the puzzle Locke does not address is why basis and consciousness should ever come into conflict, and why we should respect the basis when they do.

One final theme deserves emphasis. What is most striking in Locke's discussion is his 'forensic' or moral focus, and there is something undeniably attractive in the claim that consciousness of a crime is both necessary and sufficient for punishment and blame. But our views about punishment and blame depend not only on our views about identity but also on our views about the function of our retributive or corrective practices; in fact the very *relevance* of judgements of identity may depend on what we take to be the *point* of punishment and blame. If the justification of punishment is utilitarian, for example, identity will not be sufficient and perhaps not

---

[17] For the provocative development of a suggestion along these lines see Atherton 1983: 287–9.

even necessary, Now there are utilitarian elements in Locke's view of the function of *human* punishment (as in the *Second Treatise*, where punishment is undertaken even in the state of nature for the sake of restraint and reparation), but they seem to play no role at all in his view of divine punishment. Here the identity of the criminal and the proposed victim of punishment seems to be absolutely determinative, though Locke does not make clear exactly why. The justice of divine punishment may be the justice Leibniz describes as that which has for its basis 'neither improvement nor example, nor even redress of the evil', but 'the fitness of things, which demands a certain satisfaction for the expiation of an evil action' (Leibniz 1985: 161). But it could also be a kind of punishment in which repentance (or the opportunity for repentance) has an essential place.

APPENDIX

In *Essay* III.vi.4: 440 Locke writes that 'there is nothing I have, is essential to me'. Does this contradict what he says in chapter xxvii?

The claim comes in the midst of an argument that essence relates to sorts:

That *Essence*, in the ordinary use of the word, relates to *Sorts*, and that it is considered in particular Beings, no farther than as they are ranked into *Sorts*, appears from hence: That take but away the abstract *Ideas*, by which we sort individuals, and rank them under common Names, and then the thought of any thing *essential* to any of them, instantly vanishes: we have no notion of the one, without the other: which plainly shews their relation. 'Tis necessary for me to be as I am; GOD and nature has made me so: But there is nothing I have, is essential to me. An Accident, or Disease, may very much alter my Colour, or Shape; a Fever, or Fall, may take away my Reason, or Memory, or both; and an Apoplexy leave neither Sense, nor Understanding, no nor Life. . . . None of these are essential . . . to any Individual whatsoever, till the Mind refers it to some Sort or *Species* of things. (E III.vi.4: 440)

I think the clash between this passage and chapter xxvii is less dramatic than it seems. One of Locke's central claims in chapter xxvii can actually be used to defend the conclusions he reaches in the passage.

In chapter xxvii Locke endorses a mild version of the relativity of identity:

(1) '$y = x$' is proper and significant only if y and x are gathered under a sortal. (See e.g. E II.xxvii.7: 332, or E II.xxvii.20: 342, which I will discuss below.)[18]

---

[18] This is the version of the relativity thesis endorsed, for example, by Nelson Goodman, who

In Book III he seems to accept the following:

> (2) For any x, F is essential to x if and only if it is necessarily true that for any y, $y = x$ only if Fy.

(1) and (2) might then be used to argue for (3):

> 'F is essential to x' is proper and significant only if x has been placed beneath a sortal.

(1) and (2) do not *entail* (3). To arrive at (3) Locke needs a principle connecting the propriety or significance of a claim with the propriety or significance of the claims it presupposes (not to mention an account of presupposition). But it nevertheless seems to me that (1) and (2) afford some reason for accepting (3).

(3) does not tell us that nothing is essential to me, if that is understood to mean that every proposition assigning something to my essence is *false*; it tells us that it is improper to say that something is essential to me unless I am placed beneath a sortal, and E III.vi.4, in my view, tells us the same thing.[19] Chapter xxvii seems to reflect the same opinion. In § 20 Locke writes: 'Suppose I wholly lose the memory of some parts of my Life, beyond a possibility of retrieving them, so that perhaps I shall never be conscious of them again; yet am I not the same Person, that did those Actions, had those Thoughts, that I was once conscious of, though I have now forgot them? To which I answer, that we must here take notice what the Word *I* is applied to, which in this case is the Man only. And the same

writes that 'the response to the question "Same or not the same?" must always be "Same what?"' (Goodman 1978: 8). Locke's point in the passages cited is that this question must be respected (perhaps even anticipated) by the person making the identity claim. This version does not, as Goodman observes, call for any modification of Leibniz's Law. It is therefore exempt from the criticisms David Wiggins makes of more extreme versions of the thesis, and it is, in fact, close to Wiggins's own 'thesis of sortal dependency' (Wiggins 1980: 15). Thiel (Thiel 1983: 40–2) is the most recent in a long line of commentators who attribute a more extreme thesis to Locke: 'it is possible', he writes, 'that an individual preserves, over time, its identity as man, but not its identity as person, even though it is, at the different times, both man and person' [es ist möglich, daß ein Individuum seine Identität als Mensch über die Zeit hinweg erhält, nicht aber die als Person, obwohl es zu den verschiedenen Zeiten sowohl Mensch als auch Person ist] (Thiel 1983: 41). I do not think Locke accepts this, partly for the reasons given by Vere Chappell (Chappell 1989: 76–80). Thiel (Thiel 1983: 33 and 42) also attributes the milder thesis to Locke.

[19] Edwin McCann offers a somewhat similar reading of *Essay* III.vi.4 in McCann 1987. McCann writes that 'we can take Locke to be saying that if we judge his identity as a man, he does not survive the loss of life, but judged as a body, for example, he does remain the same thing, before and after death (at least for a time)' (McCann 1987: 66–7). My only quarrel is with McCann's suggestion that one and the same thing can be judged either as a man or as a body. Locke's view may instead be that we have *both* a man and a body on our hands. Our choice of a sortal would then be an indication of what it is in the environment that interests us. For a defence of such a reading, see Chappell 1989.

Man being presumed to be the same Person, *I* is easily here supposed to stand also for the same Person' (E ii.xxvii.20: 342). Here Locke confesses that 'I' is ambiguous; it is vital, he warns, that we attend to its referent. A claim of identity will depend for its truth on the kind of thing to which the 'I' refers. We can render chapter xxvii consistent with Book iii, chapter vi if we suppose that the 'I' of chapter xxvii is (for the most part) gathered, sometimes silently, under the sortal *person*.

There is one wrinkle. My emphasis on the subjective constitution of the self may suggest that the 'I' *carries a sortal along with it*. To employ the word—to be a self to oneself—is (at least typically) to take oneself to be a person. We can use the word to refer to a man, but that calls for some kind of warning, some indication that the usual force of the word is being cancelled. § 20 actually suggests that we owe our success in referring to the man to our assumption that the man is linked to the *person* to whom the 'I' (immediately and by default) refers. If this is correct, it is perhaps misleading of Locke to say that nothing is essential to me. Because I cannot think of my self without tacitly invoking the sortal *person*, the claim that something is essential to me can be perfectly appropriate as it stands.[20]

[20] An earlier version of this paper was delivered to the Locke Group at the 1988 NEH/ Council for Philosophical Studies Summer Institute on Early Modern Philosophy. I thank the members of the group for their comments. I am particularly grateful to Michael Ayers, who made a variety of helpful suggestions, and to Michael Seidler, whose presentation to the Institute's Moral Philosophy Group was my introduction to Pufendorf. I also thank Paul Hoffman for his written comments on a later draft.

IX

LOCKE ON LANGUAGE

E. J. ASHWORTH

INTRODUCTION

Locke's main semantic thesis is that words stand for, or signify, ideas. He says this over and over again, though the phraseology he employs varies. In Book III, chapter ii alone we find the following statements of the thesis: (1)'... *Words* ... come to be made use of by Men, as *the Signs* of their *Ideas*' (E III.ii.1: 405); (2)'The use then of Words, is to be sensible Marks of *Ideas*; and the *Ideas* they stand for, are their proper and immediate Signification' (ibid.); (3)'*Words in their primary or immediate Signification, stand for nothing, but the* Ideas *in the Mind of him that uses them* (E III.ii.2: 405); (4)'That then which Words are the Marks of, are the *Ideas* of the Speaker' (ibid.); (5)'... Words, as they are used by Men, can properly and immediately signify nothing but the *Ideas*, that are in the Mind of the Speaker' (E III.ii.4: 406). Locke offers no explanation of the terms he uses in these remarks, and I am going to take it that the phrases 'stand for', 'be a mark of', and 'be a sign of' are all roughly synonymous with the term 'signify'. The purpose of this paper is to explore what Locke intended to convey when he said that words signify ideas. I shall attempt to defend him against some, though not all, standard objections; and part of my defence will rest on the claim that Locke was using 'signify' in the same way that his scholastic predecessors used the Latin term '*significare*'. My paper falls into three parts. First, I shall give a general description of Locke's account of language; second, I shall look more closely at the scholastic theories of mental language and of signification, and their relation to Locke's theory; third, I shall return to Locke's text to examine what he has to say about the signification of general terms, and how it is that our ideas conform both to the ideas of other men and to external objects.

From *Canadian Journal of Philosophy*, 14: 1 (1984), 45–73.

I. LOCKE'S ACCOUNT OF LANGUAGE

In order to understand what Locke had to say about language, we must remind ourselves of his general epistemological position. Three points are particularly important: his use of the term 'idea'; his thesis that all complex ideas are made up of simple ideas; and his thesis that knowledge is the perception of the agreement and disagreement between ideas. Let us first consider his use of the term 'idea' (for further discussion, see McRae 1965 and Nathanson 1973). He wrote of it as follows: 'It being that Term, which, I think, serves best to stand for whatever is the Object of the Understanding when a Man thinks, I have used it to express whatever is meant by *Phantasm*, *Notion*, *Species*, or whatever it is, which the Mind can be employ'd about in thinking' (E I.i.8: 47). If we remember that a phantasm is an image, that 'notion' is the word Locke uses for such mixed modes as 'courage', 'drunkenness', 'sacrilege' and 'murder' (E II.xxii.2: 288); that 'species' includes both sensible species or particular sensings, and intelligible species, or whatever is abstracted from particular sensings, we can get some idea of the extraordinary flexibility with which Locke used the term 'idea'. It ranges over immediate sensings, sensations, memories, images, and concepts. As we shall see later, he often tends to emphasize the image aspect, but certainly not exclusively. When he says that courage is 'For a man to be undisturbed in Danger, sedately to consider what is fittest to be done, and to execute it steadily' (E II.xxx.4: 374), he surely does not suppose that his complex idea of courage is an image.

Second, we should note his thesis that all complex ideas are made up out of simple ideas, which goes together with the thesis that simple ideas all come to us from experience, whether sensation or reflection. It is tempting to argue that Locke was committed to a radical reductionism, whereby any legitimate statement I make using such complex terms as 'justice' must be equivalent without loss of meaning to a series of statements, perhaps infinitely many, about sense data, immediate sensings, or whatever the preferred locution. It may indeed be that this is the logically correct conclusion to be drawn from some of the things which Locke says, but it is essential to remember that philosophers do not always pursue the logical consequences of their remarks to the bitter end, and that they might be horrified if they did. Many of Locke's examples of simple ideas, and all of his examples of analysed complex ideas, suggest that he took a considerably more relaxed view of his general thesis than have some of his readers. For instance, he numbers such ideas as 'power', 'existence', and 'unity' among our simple ideas; and when he analyses 'murder' and 'sacrilege' he remarks: 'There be many of the parts of those complex *Ideas* which are not visible in the Action it self, the intention of the Mind, or the Relation of holy Things, which make a part of *Murther*, or *Sacrilege*, have no necessary connexion with the outward and visible Action of him that commits either' (E III.ix.7: 478–9). Other good examples are his analysis of 'Procession' (E III.v.13: 436), and 'Cassuary' (E III.vi.34: 461); and his remarks to Stillingfleet about our idea of substance, when he says that of course the mind can 'frame to itself ideas of relation' even when it lacks a clear idea of what the substratum is to which modes or accidents are related (W IV: 21; cf. E III.vi.21: 450).

Thirdly, there is his thesis that knowledge is 'nothing but *the perception of the connexion and agreement, or disagreement and repugnancy of any of our ideas*' (E IV.i.2: 525). I am going to take it that he meant this quite literally, and that under no circumstances did he allow that the mind or perceiving agent could be directly related to any object other than an idea or the mind itself.[1] He says so, more than once. For instance, he wrote that a man has 'no notion of any Thing without him, but by the *Idea* he has of it in his Mind' (E II.xxxii.25: 393); and that 'the Mind knows not Things immediately, but only by the intervention of the *Ideas* it has of them' (E IV.iv.3: 563). In his correspondence with Stillingfleet he explained how this applied even to ideas of real existence: 'Now the two ideas, that in this case are perceived to agree, and do thereby produce knowledge, are the idea of actual sensation (which is an action whereof I have a clear and distinct idea) and the idea of actual existence of something without me that causes that sensation' (W IV: 360). It must also be emphasized that Locke made it absolutely clear that he never intended to deny that we do, in many cases, have knowledge of the external world, and that we can be certain that we have such knowledge. Both his belief in the intermediary role of ideas, and his belief that we can know about external objects, are relevant to his thesis that words signify ideas, as we shall see below. It should also be noted that Locke's belief in the intermediary role of ideas is just as closely related to his scholastic sources[2] as is the thesis about words.

[1] For a discussion of the contrary view, see Woozley 1972.

[2] Such as, e.g., Martin Smiglecius:

I reply: Rather, indeed, knowledge is immediately of the object as it is in the mind, but of the thing outside the mind only as it is represented by that which is in the mind, as will appear more [clearly] in the following question. For to be known in the formal sense is to be known in the mind, and to be formed in the mind. Whence, whether things exist outside the mind or whether they do not exist, they are known under the guise of an object, because they exist formally in the mind, and as they are in the mind, so they are known. To be objectively, is to be in the mind, not outside the mind, for insofar as things are outside the mind, they are not known, except as represented by the mind. Whence the object of knowledge is the thing as it is in the mind, by virtue of which the thing outside the intellect is called the object. That is immediate, this ultimate; that intrinsic, this extrinsic; that essential, without which there can

Now let us consider the general tenor of his remarks about language. The temptation for modern readers is to take Locke as a paradigm case of the private-language philosopher, one who holds that our mental life consists of a succession of occult entities called 'ideas' to which reference is made whenever we utter words meaningfully.[3] On such a model it becomes totally mysterious how we could ever communicate with each other, and how we could ever come to believe that our utterances make references, at least some of the time, to such public objects as dogs, cats, trees, and birds. It has to be admitted that there are a number of passages in the *Essay* which lend support to such an interpretation of Locke. He took it that ideas are, historically at least, necessarily prior to words, and wrote: 'I confess, that in the beginning of Languages, it was necessary to have the *Idea* before one gave it the name' (E III.v.15: 437). He claimed that we have a mental language, made up of mental propositions which contain ideas, not words (E IV.v.3: 574; E IV.v.5: 575; cf. E II.xxxii.19: 391). In his remarks on how to avoid error and confusion he exhorted the reader to focus on ideas rather than on words. He twice praised mathematicians for doing that successfully (E IV.iii.30: 561; E IV.iv.9: 567), and he said 'the examining and judging of *Ideas* by themselves, their Names being quite laid aside' is 'the best and surest way to clear and distinct Knowledge' (E IV.vi.1: 579). Finally, in explaining why spoken language was necessary, he referred to the fact that our thoughts are 'invisible, and hidden from others' (E III.ii.1: 405) and said that we need words to convey thoughts from one mind to another (E III.i.2: 402), or to excite the same ideas in the hearer as the speaker has (E III.ii.8: 408). In the same context he said that we also need spoken language as an aide-mémoire for ourselves ' . . . for the recording of our own Thoughts' (E III.ix.1: 476), but that in this case any words would

be no knowledge, this non-essential and without whose actual existence there can be knowledge—for whether it exists or not, there is knowledge, by virtue of the mental object.

Respondeo. Imò verò scientiam esse immediatè de objecto ut est in mente, de re verò extra solùm est tanquam repraesentatâ per id quod est in mente, ut in sequenti quaestione magis patebit. Sciri enim formaliter, est in mente sciri, et in mente formari. Unde sive res extra mentem existant, sive non existant, scientur per modum objecti: quia formaliter existunt in mente, et ut sunt in mente sciuntur: et esse objectivè, est in mente esse non extra mentem, quatenus enim res sunt extra mentem, non sciuntur, nisi ut repraesentatae in mente. Quare objectum scientiae est res ut est in mente, ratione cujus res extra intellectum dicitur objectum: illud est immediatum, hoc ultimatum; illud intrinsecum, hoc extrinsecum; illud essentiale, sine quo non potest scientia, hoc non essentiale, et sine quo actu existente potest esse scientia, sive enim existat, sive non existat, est scientia ratione objecti mentalis. (Smiglecius 1638: 623)

[3] A.G.N. Flew wrote of Locke: '. . . he also provided what is perhaps the clearest statement in any classical philosopher of the view that, in another interpretation of the term "private," not just some, but all language is not merely contingently but essentially private' (Flew 1971: 6). Cf. O'Connor 1952: 132: 'Our languages are as private as our worlds. And once the representative theory of knowledge is taken seriously, it is difficult to see how it could be otherwise.'

do (E III.ix.2: 476). Seemingly Robinson Crusoe could get by with a language which was private in its use as well as its reference, at least until he met Man Friday.

However, the above remarks have to be balanced against other passages in which he emphasizes the social and public aspects of language. First of all, and most importantly, it is quite mistaken to suppose that our words, on Locke's view, never refer to or pick out things in the world.[4] He makes it quite plain that they do in several places. For instance, he summarized the ends of language as follows: '*First, to make known* one Man's Thoughts or *Ideas* to another. *Secondly*, To do it *with* as much ease and *quickness* as is possible; and *Thirdly*, thereby to *convey* the *Knowledge* of Things' (E III.x.23: 504). He wrote that 'Names of Substances' are 'not put barely for our *Ideas*, but' are 'made use of ultimately to represent Things' (E III.xi.24: 520) and he said that 'though our words signifie nothing but our *Ideas*' they are 'designed by them to signifie Things' (E IV.v.8: 577). Second, he emphasized the importance of increasing our knowledge of the world in order to make our words precise. If we want to speak correctly of things we must go beyond 'Grammar-rules' and study natural history (E III.xi.24: 521). This emphasis on the obvious fact that speech has to do with real things ties in well with his claim that knowledge must have to do with real things, even though the immediate objects of perception are always ideas.

Not only did Locke believe that some at least of our words do refer to physical objects; he also believed that talk about physical objects and processes is historically prior to talk about mental objects and processes. In an interesting passage at the beginning of Book III, he notes how many of our words for modes of thinking 'come from the Operations of sensible Things' (E III.i.5: 403) and he suggests that the 'first Beginners of Languages' (ibid.) were forced 'to borrow Words from ordinary known *Ideas* of sensation' when they wanted to make reference to the 'internal Operations of their own Minds' (ibid.).[5] These observations tie in with other remarks he made about the socially determined nature of ideas and hence of languages. Different countries have words for legal and religious notions which are peculiar to those countries (E III.v.8: 432–3) and even within the same linguistic group we find that smiths and chemists will each have their own specialized vocabulary for processes belonging to their trade (E. II.xviii.7: 225–6), a vocabulary which outsiders will neither

---

[4] Hanfling wrote: 'According to Locke words stand not, as is commonly supposed, for real things and real features of things, but for "the ideas in the mind of him that uses them"' (Hanfling 1973: 20).

[5] For the relation of this remark to the writings of the Dutch Cartesian Clauberg, see Aarsleff 1964: 186–7.

possess nor understand. It is true that his explanation of these phenomena has to do with the 'Thoughts, Notions and Ideas' of the members of these countries and groups (E III.ix.22: 489) but presumably the difference in ideas relates directly to the differences in practices and interests. As he remarked of kinship terms, 'Mankind have fitted their Notions and Words to the use of common Life' (E II.xxviii.2: 349). The interests are public interests, and there is no hint in these passages that language has mainly to do with the naming of occult entities.

To conclude this section, it must be emphasized that Locke never claimed that *all* words signified ideas.[6] He has rather a peculiar passage on words such as 'nothing' and 'ignorance' which he claims signify the absence of ideas (E III.i.4: 403) but, more importantly, he has a chapter devoted to syncategorematic terms, which he calls particles. He begins by saying 'Besides Words, which are names of *Ideas* in the Mind, there are a great many others that are made use of, to signify the *connexion* that the Mind gives to *Ideas or Propositions, one with another*' (E III.vii.1: 471). His account is admittedly rather cursory, despite his examination of five different senses of the word 'but' (E III.vii.5: 473). He makes passing references to the 'Postures of his Mind in discoursing' (E III.vii.3: 472) and the 'several Actions of our Minds in discoursing' (E III.vii.6: 473) which lead me to suspect that what we have here is a vague echo of scholastic discussions of linguistic acts such as affirmation, negation, and distribution, in terms of mental events of one sort and another. As we shall see below, the standard thesis was that mental propositions contained *notitie* or acts of knowing which corresponded to categorical or naming terms, and so-called syncategorematic acts, which corresponded to syncategorematic or logical terms. Locke does not say enough about the matter to make it worth pursuing here, but it is worth remarking that it is a mistake to argue that he really meant to say that particles signify ideas of reflection, as Bennett and others seem to suppose.[7] As Ockham had pointed out in the fourteenth

---

[6] Cf. Alston 1964: 24, where he asks in relation to Locke: 'Can you discern an idea of "when," "in," "course," "becomes," etc., swimming into your ken as each word is pronounced? . . . What are we supposed to look for by way of an idea of "When"? How can we tell whether we have it in mind or not?'

[7] Bennett 1971: 20: '. . . though he acknowledges the existence of "particles" such as "is" and "if," his very cursory treatment of them amounts to a depiction of them as classificatory after all—specifically, as words for classifying "the several postures of [the]mind in discoursing".' Cf. Clapp 1967: 496: 'Again a difficulty arises. If "is" and "is not" stand for the mind's act of affirming or denying, then either the mind directly apprehends its own actions in some way or we do have ideas of affirmation or denial. If we do have ideas of the mind's acts, then these words ought to signify the ideas of these acts; if we do not have ideas which these words signify, then either we do not apprehend them or something besides ideas is the object of the mind when it thinks.'

century, it is one thing to exercise an act of affirming or denying, and quite another thing to speak about that act (Ockham 1974: 194–5).[8] Particles indicate that a mental act is being exercised, they do not signify these acts as objects.

II. MEANING AND SIGNIFICATION

Having said this much about Locke's theories in general, it is time for me to turn back to his main semantic thesis, that words signify ideas, and to explore it in more detail. It is usually assumed that when Locke claimed that words signify ideas he was intending to present a theory of non-natural meaning (to use Grice's phrase). That is, he was not concerned with 'mean' in such contexts as 'Those clouds mean rain', 'I mean to visit Spain', and 'Philosophy means a lot to him'. Hence we must first consider what might be meant by the phrase 'theory of meaning'. It is surely obvious that Locke did not intend to offer a theory of meaning of the sort described by Dummett in the first of two papers entitled: 'What is a Theory of Meaning?', that is: 'a detailed specification of the meanings of all the words and sentence-forming operations of the language, yielding a specification of the meaning of every expression and sentence of the language (Dummett 1975: 97). I take it that the theory of meaning people such as Alston wish to attribute to Locke is much more modest, and that it could be summarized something like this: If we assume that (1) the verb 'means' in such sentences as 'The word "W" means x' is a relational term, and if we assume (2) that the phrase 'the meaning of "W"' is a referring phrase, then a theory of meaning is one which explains what type of entity it is that words are related to and which assigns a denotation to the referring phrases in question. Alston's claim about Locke then is that Locke took ideas to be the required entities, that they were literally the meanings of words.[9] Alston and others seem to credit Locke with two further claims,

---

[8] Ockham's logic was reprinted in Oxford in 1675, though there is no reason to believe that Locke read it.

[9] Alston 1964: 22: 'The classic statement of the ideational theory was given by the seventeenth-century British philosopher, John Locke . . .'. Bennett (1971: 27) remarked of the claim 'Words stand for ideas' that Locke 'seems to imply—implausibly—that a word stands for its meaning. Remember, though, that for Locke, "ideas" are also sense data . . . I further suggest that his acceptance of a statement which seems to imply "I use the word 'sugar' to stand for its own meaning" may be partly explained by his construing it so as to imply "I use the word 'sugar' to stand for sugar-as-I-experience-it, or for the sense-data I have when I see or taste or touch sugar".' Cf. O'Connor 1952: 131: 'When we reflect that "ideas" for Locke consist largely of sensory elements like sense data and images, it is not very difficult to see the defects of his view. It is, in fact, a particularly crude form of the "translation" theory of meaning . . .'.

namely that this analysis applies to all meaningful words, whether categorematic or syncategorematic; and that the ideas involved are all images. I shall have more to say about the latter claim in Part III; and the former has already been dealt with.

Before I go further I should make it quite clear that I agree with those critics of Locke who argue that ideas cannot be identified with meanings on the grounds that the presence of ideas as identifiable mental units is neither necessary nor sufficient for the meaningful use of language. I also agree that it is a mistake to suppose that there are meanings of any sort which can be identified; that is, I am convinced by those who argue that the verb 'means' is not a relational term, and that the phrase 'the meaning of "W"' is not a referring phrase (Stampe 1968). To give the meaning of a word is not to name some item, whether it be an idea, a physical object, or a set of behavioural responses. However, there are three separate issues here: (1) should one regard 'the meaning of "W"' as a referring phrase; (2) if it is a referring phrase, are ideas likely candidates for the items referred to; (3) do ideas have a role to play in language use, and if so, what is it? Locke clearly addressed himself to this third issue, but I do not think that Locke addressed himself to the first two issues at all. Indeed, I think that they would never have presented themselves *as* issues to Locke or any other seventeenth-century philosopher.[10]

Those who have studied the *Essay* carefully may at this point wish to object that my claims are simply false. After all, there are three passages in which Locke does seem to equate meanings with ideas. He speaks of the simple ideas 'that others have and mean, when they use the same Names' (E II.xxxii.9: 387); he writes that a definition is 'the explaining of one Word, by several others, so that the meaning, or *Idea*, it stands for, may be certainly known' (E III.iii.10: 413); and he says 'The meaning of Words, being only the *Ideas* they are made to stand for by him that uses them; the meaning of any Term is then shewed, or the Word is defined when by other Words, the *Idea* it is made the Sign of, and annexed to in the Mind of the Speaker, is as it were represented, or set before the view of another; and thus its Signification ascertained . . .' (E III.iv.6: 422). I noted seven other

---

[10] Ian Hacking makes this point when he argues 'Locke did not have a theory of meaning' and cites as evidence that priority was given to mental discourse and that 'signify' did not mean 'mean' (Hacking 1975: 52, 16, 20). As will be seen below, I am thoroughly in agreement with Hacking on these points. However, Hacking does not support his claim by considering any of the scholastic sources. Another author who realizes that 'signify' and 'mean' are not equivalent is D. M. Armstrong: 'So if a Lockean type of analysis is to go through it must be accepted that what a certain utterance *signifies* in the sense stipulated, and what it *means*, are two different things. (By the way, there are some indications that Locke saw, or half saw, this point although his language remains atrociously ambiguous.)' (Armstrong 1971: 430–1).

places where he uses the term 'meaning', and there are undoubtedly many others that I missed (E Epis: 10; E ɪ.iii.8: 78; E ɪɪɪ.ii.8: 408; E ɪɪɪ.iv.7: 422; E ɪɪɪ.iv.14: 427; E ɪɪɪ.vi.45: 468; E ɪɪɪ.xi.27: 524). However, it is doubtful whether much can be concluded from any of these passages about Locke's theory of meaning (if any). First, one of the standard uses of the word 'meaning' in Locke's day was as a synonym for 'signification' (*Oxford English Dictionary* 1888–1928: xɪ. 275); second, however inaccurate my count of the passages in which Locke uses the term, it is obvious that he uses it only infrequently and rather casually; third, the only place in which the word appears in the crucial second chapter of Book ɪɪɪ 'On the Signification of Words' is in the last paragraph, where he writes: 'But whatever be the consequence of any Man's using of Words differently, either from their general Meaning, or the particular Sense of the Person to whom he addresses them, this is certain, their signification, in his use of them, is limited to his *Ideas*, and they can be signs of nothing else' (E ɪɪɪ.ii.8: 408). This last quotation brings me back to a point I made at the beginning, that is, in so far as Locke has a technical semantic vocabulary, it centres on the words 'sign', 'signify', and 'signification'.

I have now arrived at the heart of my argument, for not only was 'signify' a quasi-technical term for Locke; it was a genuinely technical term in the Scholastic literature of the period, and indeed, in all medieval writings concerned with the theory of language. I wish to contend that Locke's use of the term 'signify' makes much more philosophical sense if one sees it against the Scholastic background than if one approaches it from the point of view of twentieth-century theories of meaning. It also makes a good deal more historical sense to suggest that Locke was influenced by his background, rather than being a complete innovator in every aspect of his thinking.

But before I examine the late and post-medieval doctrine of signification, I should explain my grounds for supposing that Locke was acquainted with it. Locke went to Oxford in 1652 at the age of 20, and he stayed there until 1665, first as an undergraduate at Christ Church, and then as a lecturer and tutor at the same college. The Oxford curriculum, as laid down by the Laudian statutes of 1636, covered a variety of subjects (see Ashworth 1988). The undergraduate was supposed to study grammar, rhetoric, logic, moral philosophy, political philosophy, geometry, and music; and at the MA level such subjects as metaphysics, natural philosophy, history, and Greek were added. In theory the main texts studied for logic and metaphysics (as for ethics, natural, and political philosophy) were those of Aristotle, but in practice secondary sources were used. The leading metaphysics texts included some by Catholics such as the Frenchman,

Eustace of St Paul, and some by Protestants, such as the German, Scheibler, and the Dutchman, Burgersdijck. They were all predominantly Scholastic in nature, by which I mean that they were highly organized, were heavily influenced by the renewed Aristotelianism of the sixteenth century, and were equally heavily influenced by such medieval authors as Thomas Aquinas (who was undoubtedly more popular in the seventeenth century than in the thirteenth) and Duns Scotus. Even the Protestant authors seem to have used mainly Catholic sources. The leading logic texts were also predominantly Aristotelian, with a few references to specifically medieval developments such as supposition theory. Two of the most popular at Oxford were by the Flemish Jesuit, Du Trieu, and the Polish Jesuit, Smiglecius, though Burgersdijck's logic text was used as well as his metaphysics text. Indigenous Oxford authors were represented by such men as the very popular Robert Sanderson whose logic text was repeatedly published up to 1841. Nothing that anyone would count as new philosophical work was being done at Oxford (except by Robert Boyle, who was not a member of the university) and hardly any attention was paid to such figures as Descartes. Locke himself may not have read Descartes until 1666 or 1667, after he had left Oxford.[11]

Locke's published writings contain few references to any of these figures. He spoke scornfully of the swarming Burgersdijcks and Scheiblers of his time in his work on Education (W IX: 86) and he mentions Robert Sanderson in his correspondence with Stillingfleet, as well as Burgersdijck, whom he classifies as a logician rather than as a metaphysician (W IV: 8, 449). However, there is some further evidence of his contact with the Scholastic authors I am concerned with.[12] He owned copies of Du Trieu and Sanderson, and his manuscripts include a set of notes from Du Trieu, though not in his own handwriting. Most interesting is a small book of accounts in which he entered the titles and authors of books purchased by his students in 1661 and 1662. Among the works mentioned are the metaphysics of Burgersdijck and the logic texts of Du Trieu, Sanderson, and Smiglecius. The latter appears twice. Since all these books were related to the Oxford curriculum on which Locke was tutoring his students, it is most implausible to suppose that he read none of them himself. I prefer to think that he knew them quite well and that unconsciously at least he was influenced by what Smiglecius and the others had to say about language.

---

[11] Various dates have been suggested including c.1656 and after 1671: see Schankula 1980: 461–3. I am following Cranston 1957: 99–100.

[12] For further details, see Ashworth 1981a. This paper pays much more attention to 17th-cent. Scholastics, and much less attention to Locke himself, than does the present paper. References to non-Scholastic authors whose theories may have influenced Locke will be found in Aaron 1971: 207 n. 1; Kretzmann 1968: 176; and Yolton 1956.

Scholastic theories of language could be said to have five important elements. First, there is the theory of terms, embracing divisions into abstract and concrete, categorematic and syncategorematic, and so on. Echoes of this theory are to be found in Locke's chapter on particles (E III.vii: 471–3) and his chapter on abstract and concrete terms (E III.viii: 474–5) but they are not important. Second, there is the theory of supposition which is partly a theory of reference and partly a theory of quantification. It is mentioned by Locke only once in passing (E III.x.20: 502). Third, there is the theory of definition which had at least a negative influence on Locke. According to the Scholastic texts, there were two kinds of definition: the *definitio quid nominis* or nominal definition, which explains the signification of a word; and the *definitio quid rei* which in Du Trieu's words is a 'definition which explains the nature of the thing signified by a name'.[13] He added that this type of definition was called 'essential' when it was given through those elements essential to the thing defined, such as animal and rational with respect to man. It applied only to substances. This is precisely the kind of definition which Locke spends so much time denying that we have a use for. The two crucial elements in Scholastic theories of language for our present purposes are the last two, the theory of mental language and the theory of signification.

The doctrine of mental language goes back to Aristotle's *De Interpretatione* 16a3 where he remarked that spoken words were signs of affections in the mind, but the real impetus for the development of a theory about mental language came from two sources, St Augustine's *De Trinitate* 15, and Boethius in his second commentary on Aristotle's *De Interpretatione*. After Boethius, philosophers all seem to have taken it for granted that there were three types of language, spoken, written, and mental. Spoken and written languages had conventional meaning and were in fact, though not necessarily so, different for different groups of people. Mental language, on the other hand, was thought to be necessarily common to all men because it had natural meaning; no choice or convention was involved, and mental terms were significative by virtue of their very nature. Mental language was taken to be logically prior to conventional language, and spoken sentences were said to be meaningful only if they were subordinated to mental sentences. Most late medieval logicians also recognized an intermediate level of mental language which was

---

[13] Du Trieu 1662: 85: 'Definitio quid rei est, quae rei per nomen significatae naturam explicat.' Cf. Smiglecius 1638: 729–39; Sanderson 1664: 61–2; Burgersdijck 1637: 153–4. Burgersdijck wrote: 'Definitio perfecta est, quae rei essentiam attributis essentialibus explicat perfectè.' 'A definition is perfect when it perfectly explains the essence of a thing by its essential attributes' (Burgersdijck 1637: 154).

conventionally meaningful. If a person 'speaks in his heart' by using the words of Latin or French without actually uttering them, then he is using mental language in an extended sense (cf. E IV.v.4: 574). From Ockham onwards there was a good deal of discussion of mental language. No question was raised about whether it ought to be postulated or what kind of criteria we could possibly employ when discussing its features. Instead, the focus was on two other issues, what kind of grammatical structure mental language exhibits (see Ashworth 1982) and how the unity of mental propositions is to be accounted for (see Ashworth 1981b). The discussion of these issues reveals that logicians did not, on the whole, hold the simplistic view that on the occasion of any utterance a sequence of ideas precisely corresponding to the spoken words passes through our minds. In the first place, the temporal connection between a spoken proposition and a mental proposition was obviously a loose one, since one can think of a mental proposition as being completed before all the words are uttered (see Ockham 1980: 193–7 and 251–3). In the second place, as mentioned earlier, spoken words were taken to be of two sorts. Categorematic terms, or ordinary lexical items, signified acts of knowing, or, if one prefers, concepts; but syncategorematic words, that is, logical connectives, quantifiers, adverbs, and so on, signified only 'in some way'. They corresponded not to concepts but to mental acts of affirmation, negation, distribution, or other ways of modifying the things thought about, and it was obvious to medieval and post-medieval logicians that there need be no straightforward correspondence between the number and position of syncategorematic words in a sentence and these mental acts. Nor did the linear ordering of the lexical items themselves have much to do with their role in the proposition. Of two categorematic terms one would typically be subject and one predicate but (especially in Latin) these roles are not simply a function of the way the words are placed in a sequence.

Intense and lengthy discussion of such issues seems to have ceased after the first three decades of the sixteenth century, when several people published entire books devoted to mental language; but even in seventeenth-century Oxford traces of the debate on mental language are to be found. For instance, in Robert Pinke's list of questions on logic, metaphysics, and ethics published in 1680 for the use of Oxford students, one of the logical questions to be considered was 'Is a mental proposition a simple quality?' (Pinke 1680: 12). More important for our purposes is the *Logica* of Martin Smiglecius, a book which was published in Oxford in 1634, 1638, and 1658 (the year Locke obtained his MA) and which was bought by two of Locke's students. A chapter of this work is devoted to the problem of the unity of mental propositions (Smiglecius 1638: 453–6). Smiglecius reproduces the arguments of the fourteenth-century philosopher, Gregory of Rimini, and says that Gregory was right when he argued that a mental proposition was not a mere aggregate of terms. Rather it is a complex unity. It results from a simple act of affirmation or negation which gives to the concepts involved their roles within the proposition.

Locke himself paid no particular attention to such problems, but it is reasonable to suppose that a belief in a mental language, distinct from and prior to spoken language, was just one of those philosophical commonplaces everyone, including Locke, took for granted.[14] He certainly makes references to mental propositions, as I have already mentioned; and he also remarks on the difficulty of discussing '*Truth* of Thought and *Truth* of Words distinctly one from another ... Because it is unavoidable, in treating of Mental Propositions, to make use of Words; and then the Instances given of *Mental Propositions*, cease immediately to be barely Mental, *and* become *Verbal*' (E IV.v.3: 574).

The theory of signification was a natural corollary to the doctrine of mental language. There were various developments of the theory during the earlier part of the Middle Ages which need not concern us here. By the early sixteenth century the standard definition of '*significare*' was 'to represent some thing or some things or in some way to the cognitive power', where 'in some way' was introduced in order to cover the case of such syncategorematic terms as 'all' and 'none'. In discussion of the definition, a distinction was first drawn between non-linguistic signs such as smoke or footprints, and linguistic signs.[15] Linguistic signs were further classified as natural or conventional. One kind of natural linguistic sign was an inarticulate utterance (i.e. one which could not be conveniently written) such as a laugh or a groan; but by extension concepts were also allowed to be naturally significative signs. Unlike laughs and groans, concepts were classified as formally significative, because their very nature was to represent; and it was assumed that they were the same for all men, or at least for all men with similar experiences.[16] Articulate linguistic signs with conventional signification were classified as instrumentally significative, because

[14] Hacking 1975: 16: 'If we are to make any sense at all out of theories of language of this period, we must acknowledge that at the time one accepted the priority of mental discourse to public speech.' Woolhouse suggests that Locke used the phrase 'mental proposition' to refer to 'that which is expressed by a sentence' (Woolhouse 1971: 5 n. 1). Landesman is also puzzled by Locke's references to mental propositions, and writes: 'By a mental proposition, Locke sometimes means the mental act by which the mind perceives a state of affairs; ideas as constituents of the mental act are signs of the constituents of the state of affairs. But sometimes he means by a mental proposition the state of affairs itself ...' (Landesman 1976: 26).

[15] For an easily accessible discussion, see John of St Thomas 1955: 30–3.

[16] Sanderson 1664: 73 wrote: '... *Conceptus* sunt à naturâ, & proinde ubique eadem.' 'Concepts are from nature, and hence everywhere the same.'

they represent only by virtue of an established link between the sign and whatever it is that is represented. This instrumental signification was spoken of as a causal and relational property. Any noun (to limit the scope of the discussion) was used significatively only if it had a causal effect upon the hearer's mind by virtue of the known relation between the word and its significates (given an attentive hearer speaking the same language) (cf. E III.ii.7: 408). The relation could be transitive: for instance, a written word may signify or make known in turn the same word as spoken, the appropriate concept, and the thing or things referred to, and all of these can be described as significates of the written word. As a result, the correct answer to the question 'What does this term signify?' could be given by a statement about the terms's total denotation, so that the word 'man' could correctly be said to signify Plato, Socrates, and Cicero. Moreover, it was perfectly correct to speak of proper names such as 'Peter' and 'Salamanca' (which John of St Thomas classified as a collective term) as having signification (John of St Thomas 1955: 35). Nor does this merely reveal a blunder on the part of medieval logicians, a failure to distinguish between proper names and general terms, for they made it quite clear that proper names are syntactically different from general terms in that they are not quantifiable; and that proper names are also different from general terms in that they do not have definitions. None of the claims I have made about instrumental signification can be made appropriately about meaning.

The matter is more complex than I have so far suggested, for it was usually felt that an order of priority ought to be established among the various significates of a particular word. Hence, from the late thirteenth century on we find philosophers addressing themselves to the question whether words primarily and immediately signify things or concepts (with the obvious proviso that the question concerned such words as 'dog' rather than such words as 'concept') (see Ashworth 1987). I should add that no one doubted that words are used to *refer* to public objects; the only question had to do with the description of the word-concept-thing relation. The very asking of this question strengthens my point that signification and meaning are not to be identified. If one takes the words 'Does a word signify concepts or things or perhaps both, but one less immediately than the other?' and replaces 'signify' by 'mean', one makes nonsense of the question; whereas replacing 'signify' by my preferred synonym, 'makes known', will preserve the sense.

One of several seventeenth-century accounts of this debate is found in the *Logica* of Martin Smiglecius. In good Scholastic fashion, he presented the standard arguments for and against the main thesis before reaching his own conclusion (Smiglecius 1638: 436–8).[17] Of particular interest to me are his four arguments for the view that concepts are immediately signified by words. The first argument, which is an appeal to Aristotle's authority, can be ignored. He then argues that words were given to man in order to make known his mind which is hidden and invisible; that a speaker who conceives nothing signifies nothing, as is the case with parrots; and fourthly, that words can only signify things by means of the concept [*ratio*] whereby the things are conceived. Smiglecius himself did not accept these arguments. He pointed out that to say that concepts are an essential element in the signifying process does not by itself establish that they are what is signified; and he also argued that we can only use words to find out about a speaker's thoughts if we first know the things to which his words refer. However, whether the arguments are acceptable or not, each one of them, apart from the appeal to Aristotle, is found in Locke's chapter on the signification of words. Locke first tells us that 'it was necessary, that Man should find out some external sensible Signs, whereby those invisible *Ideas*, which his thoughts are made up of, might be made known to others' (E iii.ii.1: 405); later on the same page, there is a passage whose main point is 'Words being voluntary Signs, they cannot be voluntary Signs imposed by him on Things he knows not' (E iii.ii.2: 405); and finally he mentions that to use words without a 'constant connexion between the Sound and the *Idea*, and a designation that the one stand for the other' (E iii.ii.7: 408; cf. E iv.viii.7: 614), is to speak like a Parrot. Locke does not tell us that these remarks constitute three of the standard arguments for the thesis that words signify ideas, but recent authors have identified these passages as being the only ones which could give support to Locke's thesis quite independently of any research into what seventeenth-century Scholastics took to be the standard arguments (Kretzmann 1968; Landesman 1976: 23–5; Odegard 1970).[18]

The conclusion drawn by Smiglecius was that words primarily signify things, and signify concepts only in an extended sense. However, many authors surveyed much the same package of arguments and came to a different conclusion. They all agreed both that concepts had a part to play in the signifying process, and that words are used to refer to things rather than concepts, but they preferred to describe the situation by saying that words signify concepts immediately whereas they signify things only mediately, by means of the intervening concept.[19] Du Trieu, Sanderson,

---

[17] For a more detailed discussion of his argument, see the paper cited in note 12.

[18] For a further discussion of Kretzmann and Landesman, see the paper cited in note 12, and see also Yolton 1970a: 208–14.

[19] Aaron obviously believed that Locke was being consciously innovative: 'Locke does not

and Burgersdijck all adopted this second position, though none of them offered any arguments for or against. Du Trieu and Sanderson both spoke of the concept as the immediate significate of a word, and individuals as the mediate significates (Du Trieu 1662: 93–4; Sanderson 1664: 81–2).[20] Burgersdijck wrote that: 'Articulate utterances signify the concepts of the mind, primarily that is, and immediately, for they also signify things, but by means of concepts.'[21] The parallel to Locke's remarks should be obvious. I assume that Locke adopted the second view of the order of priority between concepts and things because it fitted in so neatly with his own views on the place of ideas in knowledge, particularly knowledge of the external world. Ideas are immediate objects in language just as they are in knowledge, and things are mediate objects in language just as they are in knowledge.

So far I have offered reasons for supposing that when Locke said that words signified ideas he was not offering a theory of meaning of the kind attributed to him by Alston and others. However, he certainly did have a theory of meaning in one sense of that phrase: that is, he thought he could give criteria for the meaningful use of language. The *Essay* is full of practical hints on this matter, which are inevitably couched in terms of ideas. His main message is that we should avoid confused ideas, though it turns out that confusion in relation to ideas can only be defined in relation to language-use. For instance, I have a confused idea of a leopard if I annex the ideas 'beast with spots' to that name. The ideas are all right by themselves, but I won't be able to distinguish leopards from lynxes or other beasts with spots, and it is there that the confusion lies (E II.xxix.7: 365). The remedy for confusion is to make sure that our ideas are precise and determinate (E Epis: 13) by giving definitions (E IV.iii.20: 552), that is, by enumerating simple ideas (E III.iii.10: 413) where this is possible. If it is not possible to define, as in the case of colour words, we should be prepared to produce examples, as when we tell a Country-man that *Feuillemorte* is the 'Colour of wither'd Leaves falling in Autumn' (E III.xi.14: 515). He also emphasizes that we should use our words consistently, i.e. keep them

---

attempt to make a complete inventory of the kinds of signs in use. But he does face the more important question: What does the sign signify? To this question he puts forward an answer which he knew to be unusual, but to which none the less he consistently adheres. The word *table* is usually thought to be the sign of the physical object. Words it is usually supposed signify things, at least some words do. This Locke categorically denies' (Aaron 1971: 209).

[20] Cf. Sanderson 1664: 73: '*Conceptus* sunt signa sive notae rerum, *Voces* Conceptuum, *Literae* vocum.' 'Concepts are signs or marks of things, utterances of concepts, letters of utterances.'

[21] Burgersdijck 1637: 110: 'Voces articulatae significant animi conceptus, primò scilicet, atque immediatè: nam res etiam significant, sed mediantibus conceptibus.'

'steadily annex'd' to a determinate idea (E Epis: 13; E ii.xxix.9: 366; E iv.iii.20: 552; E iii.x.5: 492; E iv.xii.6: 642). Sometimes this is not possible, because there are more ideas than there are words to express them, but in this case one should either explain the shift in meaning or make the context do the job for one (E iii.xi.27: 523–4). His third main point is that we should make sure that our use of language is consistent with the use of others (E iii.vi.51: 471; E iii.xi.11: 514) since words are 'no Man's private possession, but the common measure of Commerce and Communication' (E iii.xi.11: 514). Of course, we sometimes have to refine on common use, since it is not sufficiently precise for philosophical purposes (E iii.ix.8: 479). Finally, if we don't understand how others are using their terms, we should simply ask them (E iii.vi.45: 468).

All these practical hints depend on Locke's account of the double conformity that the ideas signified by words ought to exhibit: on the one hand our ideas must conform to the ideas of other language users, and on the other hand our ideas must conform to the reality of things. Accordingly, the third and final section of this paper is devoted to an investigation of Locke's claims about the double conformity of concrete general terms, whether these are the names of simple ideas such as 'white', mixed modes such as 'justice' and 'triangle', or substances such as 'man' and 'gold'.

III. THE DOUBLE CONFORMITY OF IDEAS

I shall dispose of the names of mixed modes quite quickly, since the main problem here is not Locke's theory of language so much as the account he gives of mixed modes themselves. He claims that when we use such notions as 'justice' or 'triangle' we are dealing with 'Archetypes without Patterns' which have 'nothing to represent but themselves' (E ii.xxxi.3: 377). A simple way of putting this would be to say that what counts as an instance of 'justice' or 'triangle' is up to us; we have invented the notions, and insofar as there is any onus of match it is on the world to conform to our definitions rather than the reverse. Our ideas cannot avoid conformity to reality here, since the only reality is as determined by us. Even if we accept this part of Locke's theory, there are two problems which confront us. One is the function of the spoken term: Locke claims that since the way simple ideas are collected into a mixed mode is arbitrary, the collection of ideas is apt to disperse itself and ' 'Tis the Name which is, as it were the Knot, that ties them fast together' (E iii.v.10: 434). Thus it seems that the presence of a linguistic sign is a necessary condition for any retention of one type of complex idea, which seems to introduce an unexpected dependency of at least some parts of mental language on non-mental language. The other problem has to do with the conformity between the idea of one person with the ideas of other speakers of the language. Since there are no external archetypes, we have no external guide to help us ensure that we are using the names of mixed modes in the same sense that others do. Our only standard, he writes, is 'the *Ideas* of those, who are thought to use those Names in their most proper Significations; and so as our *Ideas* conform, or differ from them, they pass for true or false' (E ii.xxxii.12: 388). This leads to a great deal of uncertainty (E ii.xxxii.10: 387) and error (E ii.xxxi.4: 377). It is only by appealing to definitions, and making them perfectly explicit, that we can escape these difficulties (E iii.xi.17: 517; E iii.xi.18: 518). He thinks that if we could only get ourselves to do this, the whole process would be quite easy, especially where moral terms are concerned (E iii.xi.17: 517).

Names of simple ideas come next, but before we consider Locke's claims about our use of such terms as 'red', 'sweet', 'square', and so on, we must remind ourselves of the distinction between primary and secondary qualities which he took over from his friend Robert Boyle. The crucial claim for our purposes is this: 'That the *Ideas of primary Qualities* of Bodies *are Resemblances* of them, and their Patterns do really exist in the Bodies themselves; but the *Ideas produced* in us *by* these *Secondary Qualities, have no resemblance* of them at all' (E ii.viii.15: 137). Let us consider first the claim about resemblances. It will seem quite mysterious if we think of some supposed process whereby our idea of a square object is somehow put beside and compared with the square object itself; but a much less mysterious account can be given if we think of Locke as saying something like this: we can define such words as 'square' or 'circular' without any reference to our sensory states; and we can account for the contents of our sensory awareness by using terms of the same type for both the contents of our awareness and the objects we suppose to cause them. Thus I can say that I now seem to see something elliptical, and I can account for this in terms of there being a circular object within my visual field. Here the words 'elliptical' and 'circular' are both terms of the same sort, because they both pick out shapes, though not in this case the same shape. Now let us consider his claim that our ideas of secondary qualities do not resemble objects. Locke defines secondary qualities as powers objects have by virtue of their primary qualities to affect the perceiver in various ways; and he argues that just as when we see the sun melt wax we do not attribute softness to the sun, so when the sun causes us to have the experience of feeling warmth, we should not ascribe heat to the sun. The sun itself is to be described in terms of shape, surface texture, and so on; and our awareness of warmth is the result of a relation between our having the perceptual organs that we do have and the sun having the surface texture that it does have (given normal background conditions, of course) (E II.viii.24: 141).

Locke's account obviously rests on the assumption that we do have sensory states, and at least for the purposes of argument I propose to take it that sensory states are private to the perceiver; that talk about sensory states cannot be reduced to talk about brain states, behaviour, or other in–principle public phenomena; and that while talk about public objects may logically precede talk about private objects, we cannot use this as a reason to reject private objects. I also propose to take it that the hypothesis that a given individual could experience a reversed spectrum does make sense even if we could neither verify nor falsify such a hypothesis. That is, we can imagine that A sees violet where B sees red, A sees blue where B sees orange, and so on.

Let us now turn to Locke's account of our use of those words which pick out secondary qualities and which, in his terminology, signify simple ideas. The problems are obvious: first, in what sense does the word 'red' signify my idea; second, in what sense does my idea conform to the external object; and third, in what sense can my idea conform to the ideas of others. I shall take the second question first. Locke writes: 'Our *simple* Ideas *are all real*, all agree to the reality of things. Not that they are all of them the Images, or Representations of what does exist, the contrary whereof, in all but the Primary Qualities of Bodies, hath been already shewed' (E II.xxx.2: 372). Locke rather cavalierly dismisses such phenomena as sensory illusions, hallucinations, and after-images—to be accurate, he doesn't even mention them—and takes only the cases of veridical perception. In this case, he says, we know that there is an orderly correspondence between the properties of external objects and the contents of our sensory awareness (E II.xxx.2: 373). No further conformity can or need be looked for. In having simple ideas, what we have is an awareness of 'Marks of Distinction in Things, whereby we may be able to discern one Thing from another' (E II.xxxii.14: 388) and, Locke believes, under normal conditions the perceiver is always able to discriminate colours, tastes, and sounds in a way which is not only consistent but is also coherent with the discriminations made by other perceivers (E II.xxxii.9: 387). This seems to be just a basic fact about human experience. If we then raise the third question of how our ideas conform to the ideas of others, Locke has two answers. In the first place, if simple ideas are thought of as 'Marks of Distinction' and others make the same distinctions that we do, we can say that our ideas do conform to theirs simply on the basis of these public criteria. In the second place, if we ask whether our ideas are qualitatively similar to theirs, the answer is: 'Perhaps not, and in any case it doesn't matter.' There is a very interesting passage in which Locke suggests that the idea or sensory state produced in one man by a violet may be the same as the idea produced in another man by marigolds: Locke then observes that we could never know this to be the case, since we cannot enter into another man's mind, and so long as the correlation between object and idea is a regular one 'he would be able as regularly to distinguish Things for his Use by those Appearances, and understand, and signify those distinctions, marked by the Names *Blue* and *Yellow*, as if the Appearances, or *Ideas* in his Mind, received from those two Flowers, were exactly the same, with the *Ideas* in other Men's Minds' (E II.xxxii.15: 389). This passage, on my reading, conclusively disproves Bennett's claim that Locke 'genuinely does not distinguish' the two questions ' "Do you mean by 'violet' what I do?" and "Do violet things sensorily affect you as they do me?" ' (Bennett 1971: 7; cf. Hacking 1975: 47–50).

What now can be said in reply to the first question, that is, in what sense does the word 'red' signify *my* idea? I think only this, that when I identify objects as red, I do have a special kind of awareness, I am aware that I do, and I express to others that I do. However, I cannot put this awareness into words, for the names of simple ideas cannot be defined (E III.iv.4: 421) and if someone wants me to explain my idea of red all I can do is show him the things I distinguish as red (E III.iv.11: 425; E III.xi.14: 515). I can help him to understand the discriminations I am making, but I cannot ensure that his idea will be similar to mine in its sensory content. Once more I am rejecting a claim of Bennett's, namely that on Locke's account my idea is the meaning of the word and that therefore 'two people might use a word in the same way in the same circumstances and yet give it different meanings' (Bennett 1971: 6). Certainly two people can give the same word two different significations, insofar as it signifies sensory states which are as a matter of fact qualitatively dissimilar, but this has little to do with language meaning.

Finally, we must consider Locke's account of the names of substances. There are a number of important issues here which I shall ignore. I shall not investigate his interpretation of the Scholastic view of real essences, or his reasons for rejecting it; nor shall I investigate his own account of real essences as the 'true internal Constitution' of things from which all their properties flow (E III.vi.9: 444). I shall not enquire into the adequacy of his theory of abstraction (which of course applies to all general terms, not just the names of substances); and I shall not ask whether it is true that Locke anticipated Kripke (Mackie 1976; 93–100). What I am really interested in is Locke's account of how it is that our ideas of substances conform to external objects. We must first remind ourselves of Locke's two theses about types of things: on the one hand, nature really does present us with vast numbers of similarities and regularities (E iii.iii.13: 415; E iii.vi.37: 462) but, on the other hand, we can only pick out some of these regularities (E iii.vi.47: 469; E iii.ix.13: 482; E iii.ix.13: 483) with the result that the definitions we give of the terms we use are apt to be variable. We are certainly, in Locke's view at least, in no position to claim that our definitions capture real distinctions among things in such a way that we can make definitive classifications, nor that our definitions will capture real properties in such a way that they can be used to expand our knowledge by making deductions and necessary predictions based on this set of real properties. This is why Locke continually emphasizes that our definitions of substance terms give nominal essences and not real essences in either the Scholastic or the Lockean sense. To describe a nominal essence is simply to describe how we have chosen to use a word; to lay out those marks that we have decided shall be the marks of a man or of a piece of gold. In Scholastic terms our definitions are always *quid nominis* and never *quid rei.*

Hence if we demand that our ideas of substances conform to real essences, we are demanding a kind of conformity which is inappropriate and unobtainable (E ii.xxxii.5: 385). If we demand, as we should, that our ideas of substances conform to the ideas in other men's minds, we are on fairly safe ground because in most cases there are enough obvious distinctions between one sort of thing and another to preserve us from obvious discrepancies in classification (E ii.xxxii.10: 387; E iii.ix.15: 484). Difficulties only arise when we pass from 'confused or loose Notions' to 'more strict and close Enquiries' (E iii.ix.16: 484) and even here we have the usual remedy of discussing the matter, and getting our definitions out in the open.

To conclude, let us consider the conformity between our ideas of substances and external objects. In some places Locke speaks of our ideas of substances as if they were images or resemblances of things.[22] He says our ideas are 'as it were, the Pictures of Things' (E ii.xxix.8: 366) and of our ideas of substances he writes: 'Sometimes they are only design'd to be

---

[22] Bennett takes it that this was Locke's view: he writes 'Locke uses "agree with" to mean "resemble." I deny that an idea or mental image can resemble an extra-mental object . . .' and '. . . I have argued against only one of them, namely the theory that we classify extra-mental things on the basis of a prior ability to classify ideas and to spot resemblances. Clearly, if Locke is advancing a theory of this general sort it must be that one in particular' (Bennett 1971: 16, 18).'For a good criticism of Bennett's views on classification, see Minas 1979–80. However, Minas herself falls into one of Bennett's errors when she writes: 'A general word is applicable to a certain thing because that thing "agrees" with the idea which is that word's meaning; and since in his discussion of general terms Locke uses "agree" interchangeably with "resemble," he means that the thing resembles the word's meaning' (Minas 1979–80: 183).

Pictures and Representations in the Mind, of Things that do exist, by *Ideas* of those qualities that are discoverable in them' (E II.xxxi.6: 378). He uses the word 'likeness' (E II.xxxi.8: 381) as did his Scholastic sources,[23] and also the word 'copies' (E II.xxxii.18: 391). However, his most common claims use the words 'represent', 'agree', and 'conform'. He writes that our complex ideas of substances are intended to be 'Representations of Substances, as they really are' (E II.xxx.5: 374), that ideas are general 'when they are set up, as the Representatives of many particular Things' (E III.iii.11: 414; cf. E III.xi.24: 520; E II.xi.9: 159). He says repeatedly that a thing is correctly called by a general term when it conforms to or agrees with the 'idea to which the name is annexed' (E III.iii.12: 414; E III.iii.18: 419; E III.vi.31: 458; E III.vi.32: 460; E III.vi.36: 462; E III.vi.46: 468; E III.ix.11: 481). In none of these passages is there any hint that the word 'resemble' might have been used instead. Moreover, there are passages which I interpret as clearly ruling out a general reliance on resemblances. I say *'general* reliance' because Locke admits that often we identify sorts of things first by their shape, and he even proposes a dictionary with small pictures stamped in the margin to supplement inadequate verbal definitions (E III.xi.25: 522). Since shape is a primary quality we do here have a case in which Locke will want to say that our ideas do resemble things. However, resemblance drops out of the picture when we consider his other remarks about the identification of substance. First, our other common way of identifying things is by their colour (E III.vi.29: 456–7) and our ideas of colour do not resemble things. Second, the largest part of even moderately sophisticated ideas of types of things is made up of ideas of powers, and while we can show someone else the shape and colour of gold, we can only convey the notions of 'Ductility, Fusibility, Fixedness, and Solubility, *in Aqua Regia*' (E III.xi.22: 520) by giving verbal explanations. As Locke puts it *'Some part of the signification* [of gold] *will be better made known by enumerating those simple* Ideas *than in shewing the Substance it self'* (ibid.). What he says about substances here should be compared with what he says about modes. Presumably the ideas of at least some mathematical modes are images, given his claim that we can use 'Diagrams drawn on Paper' as

---

[23] Here too Locke may well be influenced by Scholastic writers. Smiglecius wrote: 'Illa enim similitudo quam intelligendo format intellectus, est similitudo realis realiter producta ab intellectu realiter repraesentans objectum, et non distincta ab ipsa intellectione, siquidem intellectio nihil aliud est, quàm formatio objecti, seu formatio similitudinis objecti in intellectu.' 'For that similitude which the intellect forms by understanding, is the similitude of something real really produced by the intellect really representing the object, and it is not distinct from that act of understanding, since indeed the act of understanding is nothing other than the formation of the object, or the formation of the similitude of the object, in the intellect' (Smiglecius 1638: 628).

He explicitly compared the mental similitude to an actual image (Smiglecius 1638: 631).

'Copies of the *Ideas* in the Mind' (E iv.iii.19: 550), but of moral ideas he writes: 'We have no sensible marks that resemble them, whereby we can set them down; we have nothing but Words to express them by . . .' (ibid.). It is a mistake to suppose that all Locke's ideas are images.[24]

What Locke really intends to convey by his talk of agreement and conformity is best illustrated by his example of the term 'palfrey'. If a Romance knight says that ' "Palfry" signifies these ideas: "*Body of a certain figure, four legg'd, with sense, motion, ambling, neighing, white, used to have a Woman on his back*" ' (E iv.viii.6: 613), then he intends to convey that 'the word *Palfry* in his, or Romance Language, stood for all these, and was not to be applied to any thing, where any of these was wanting' (E iv.viii.6: 614). If an idea of x contains n simple ideas, then a thing agrees with the idea just in case each of the n properties picked out by the simple ideas is found in the thing. Resemblance is not an issue.

O'Connor correctly points out that, strictly speaking, the agreement is not between thing and idea, but between idea and idea, that is, between the abstract general idea and the collection of experienced ideas or sensings, but even at this level he tries to introduce resemblances: 'The important notion here is that of "agreement" between things or (as Locke should say, to be consistent) ideas of things and the abstract general idea. And what can "agree" mean here but "resemble"?' (O'Connor 1952: 142). This view makes sense only if one supposes that ideas are invariably images, and that Locke thinks we classify by lining up two images and comparing them. I have already argued that the first point is wrong, and so far as the second is concerned, Locke gives us no detailed account of how he thinks we set about classifying. It seems that we just do. What makes the use of the term 'resemblance' even more implausible as a description of agreement among ideas is a consideration of the types of agreement that Locke describes: identity and diversity, relation, co-existence, and real existence (E iv.i.3: 525). My ideas of the square root of 16 and the whole number between 3 and 5 are identical, but one would hardly say that they resembled one another (but cf. Minas 1979–80: 188).

CONCLUSION

If Locke has been correctly absolved of the twin accusations that words mean ideas and that ideas are invariably images, his discussion of language

---

[24] Minas 1979–80: 190: 'I have assumed without argument that: (1) ideas, in the sense of images which can resemble experience in their content, can function successfully in the meaning of terms . . .'

can be viewed in a somewhat more sympathetic light than is usually the case. His emphasis on the place of ideas in the significative process can be interpreted as an emphasis on the importance of a speaker's concepts, beliefs, and experiences, in the process of communication; and he can be credited with a genuine awareness that there is also something public about language use. Not only must the things spoken of be publicly accessible (at least some of the time), but definitions too must be publicly ascertainable (and this all of the time). To this extent Hacking is wrong when he argues that Locke has no theory of meaning in the sense of a theory of public discourse (Hacking 1975: 52), but he is correct if we place the emphasis on the word 'theory'. Insofar as Locke had a fully fledged semantic theory, as opposed to a collection of observations, it was merely the theory of signification and mental language which he had taken over, albeit in a truncated form, from Scholastic philosophers.[25]

[25] I would like to thank my colleague, Anne C. Minas, for her helpful criticisms; the Department of Philosophy of the University of North Carolina at Chapel Hill for inviting me to read this paper to them; and the Social Sciences and Humanities Research Council of Canada for the generous grants which enabled me to do the research.

X

THE INESSENTIALITY OF LOCKEAN ESSENCES

MARGARET ATHERTON

LOCKE, in his discussion of essences, makes extensive use of a distinction he introduces between nominal and real essences. This distinction has always been found interesting and important, and in fact, R. I. Aaron said of it that 'there is no more important distinction in the *Essay'* (Aaron 1971: 194). Nevertheless, to say there has not been general agreement about what Locke was getting at is putting it mildly. Interpretations of Locke's point in making such a distinction have varied widely, depending upon whether the importance of the real or the nominal essence is stressed. Locke tells us we should distinguish the nominal essence, which is the abstract idea to which a general name is attached and for which it stands, from the real essence, which is the 'real internal, but generally in Substances, unknown Constitution of Things, whereon their discoverable Qualities depend' (E III.iii.15: 417; see also E III.vi.2: 439). When the nominal essence is taken to be more important, Locke's theory has been said to be the prime exemplar of a traditional, ideational theory of meaning: the nominal essence determines the extension of any term, while the real essence is dismissed as unknown.[1] More recent interpretations have attempted to do greater justice to what is seen as the scientific realism implicit in Locke's corpuscularianism: under such interpretations the real essence is thought to assume a wider role in determining the extension of a term (see e.g. Ayers 1977, Bolton 1976, repr. in this volume as Ch. VI). Locke is sometimes even held to have anticipated the contemporary rival to the traditional theory of meaning, the causal theory associated especially with Kripke and Putnam (see Troyer 1975).[2] Deciding between two such divergent views proves to be surprisingly difficult, for there seem to

From *Canadian Journal of Philosophy*, 14: 2 (1984), 277–93.

[1] Such an interpretation is very common in discussion of theories of meaning. See e.g. Alston 1964, or, for a recent example, see Schwartz 1977. Such a view is also common in commentaries on Locke. See e.g. Aaron 1971.

[2] J. L. Mackie points out resemblances between Locke's theory and Kripke's in Mackie 1976.

be passages supporting both interpretations.[3] What I want to propose is that neither one of these interpretations is correct, because Locke is not, in fact, in his discussion of essences, intending to tell us how the extension of a term is to be determined. He is not endorsing an essentialism of any kind, either with respect to meanings as derived from nominal essences, or of hidden structures of natural kinds, associable with real essences. Instead, I think Locke introduced the distinction to downplay the notion of an essence and to show how little mileage could be gained from its use.

I

When Locke is taken to be espousing the traditional theory of meaning, then what is considered to be important about his theory is the claim that our words can only stand for what we have ideas of and that our ideas are captured in the nominal essence. These essences are, as Locke says frequently, the 'Workmanship of the Understanding' (E III.iii.12: 415). We make an idea general by abstracting particularities from it and thus arrive at an abstract idea which provides the boundaries for a general sort or species. This abstract idea is the nominal essence of that sort or species. What Locke is taken to be saying is that our task in attaching general ideas to words is one that involves finding 'an unchangeable, immutable and permanent meaning' (Aaron 1971: 202). Thus, we will be able to use a general word meaningfully when we have grasped a set of necessary and sufficient conditions without which nothing can be an example of that particular sort. This set of necessary and sufficient conditions will be the nominal essence, the possession of which makes things like gold, water, or triangles be whatever it is they are.

There are several reasons, however, that suggest that it might be a mistake to identify Locke's nominal essence with a set of necessary and sufficient conditions for determining the reference of a term. The first is that Locke stresses that the ideas attached to a term must always be understood as relative to a speaker or user of a term. When I use a word, it is meaningful to me, not because it stands for something which can also be found in someone else's mind, nor for something that exists in reality, but only because it stands for my own ideas about what the word names (E III.ii.4–5: 406–7). In making this point, Locke says the ideas each person

---

[3] Among those that seem to recommend the former are: E III.vi.49: 469–70; E III.ii.5: 407; E III.x.17–21: 499–503. Support for the latter come from e.g. E III.iii.18: 418–19; E III.iii.15: 417; and E IV.iv.11–12: 568–9. Several of these passages are discussed in more detail below.

attaches to a word are different, that in using a word like 'gold', some people will have an idea which only includes some qualities, someone else will add others, while a child may even use it to stand for the colour alone (E III.ii.3: 406). It is this variability in our ideas, Locke says, that causes problems in our communicating with or understanding one another (E III.ii.8: 408). His point is not, however, that the different ideas people are discovered to have ought to be regarded as different approximations of a single essence that everyone's ideas should be trying to capture. It seems reasonable to suppose that by the nominal essence of gold, for example, Locke wants us to understand no more than those ideas or beliefs that a speaker has about gold. Such a nominal essence will not serve to sort the essential from the accidental properties of a thing. That Locke did not intend the nominal essence to function in this way is clear, for Locke says that each person's set of ideas is as entitled to be called the essence of gold as any other. He says:

Because these simple *Ideas* that co-exist, and are united in the same Subject, being very numerous, and having all an equal right to go into the complex specifick *Idea*, which the specifick Name is to stand for, Men, though they propose to themselves the very same Subject to consider, yet frame very different *Ideas* about it; and so the Name they use for it, unavoidably come to have, in several Men, very different significations. (E III.ix.13: 482; see also E III.ix.17: 485–6)

Thus it does not seem that Locke supposed the task of constructing abstract ideas to be one of selecting from among the properties of a thing those that are essential to it. Any property has an equal right to be included in an abstract idea as any other and so there can be no real distinction between essential and accidental properties and no sense in which one abstract idea rather than another is the 'right' one. While nominal essences are indeed eternal and immutable, this is only because a change in the set of ideas constitutes a new essence (E III.iii.14: 416). Locke does not seem to regard this as problematic or to suppose that understanding a word requires grasping an immutable meaning. Locke's repeated assertions that the nominal essence is just the abstract idea we attach to a term (E III.iii.12: 414–15; E III.iii.13: 415–16; E III.iii.16: 417) can be taken to convey that we do not grasp something essential about those things to which the term refers, since no property has a greater right to be called essential than any other. The meaningful use of terms requires no more than that each person can attach some appropriate set of ideas to the term.

A second reason for supposing that Locke is not, in fact, endorsing a traditional essentialist theory of meaning is that he himself carefully distinguishes between cases where such a view does not apply, cases where the ideas we attach to a term do not determine the reference of a term, and cases where they do determine the reference.[4] That is, he does seem to accept something like a traditional theory of meaning under some sorts of circumstances but he explicitly distinguishes those circumstances from others, and he uses the nominal/real essence distinction to do this. When a word can refer to all and only those things described by the ideas it stands for, Locke says the real and the nominal essence of the term coincide. The important examples of this sort of coinciding are simple ideas, like red, heat, or pain, and what Locke calls mixed modes, ideas which are formed by the mind without being intended to copy anything in nature (E II.xxii: 288–95). Examples of mixed modes are obligation, drunkenness, triangle, jealousy, and adultery. In all these cases, it is conformity to the ideas we attach to a word that makes it appropriate to apply that word to some thing, so it is the nominal essence alone that does the job of constituting the being of that thing and making it be what it is. Locke excludes from this account, however, the example of substances, cases where our terms are supposed to refer to something complex existing in nature, as gold, water, a horse, or a mandril.[5] In these sorts of cases, he says, the nominal and the real essence do not coincide. We do not suppose that our ideas are what makes things to be whatever they are, but instead take this to be the result of their inner consitution (E III.vi: 438–71). It is because we take our substance-terms to be referring to something that has an inner constitution that we can change our ideas about substances without changing the subject (E III.vi.43–8: 465–9). So it seems clear that Locke could not have distinguished between substance terms and terms for mixed modes and simple ideas as he did, and also have endorsed a traditional ideational theory of meaning. Since he argues in the case of substance terms that the nominal essence, the set of ideas each of us has about a thing, can diverge from its real essence, from the inner constitution on which its properties depend, it is impossible to suppose that he would have thought that a thing just is whatever our concept of the thing says it is. Locke's idea that we make general terms meaningful by grasping an abstract idea is not intended to be a claim that we have isolated a set of necessary and sufficient conditions defining the boundaries of some sort or kind. His point is that nominal essences can describe no more than a speaker's ideas about what is being talked about, and cannot capture anything essential to the being of kinds or species.

[4] For a discussion of Locke's use of the difference between mixed modes and substances to make this distinction, see Bolton 1976, repr. in this volume as Ch. VI.

[5] So Hilary Putnam is doing an injustice to Locke in claiming that he used the word 'gold' as an example and 'is not troubled by the idea that its meaning is a necessary and sufficient condition' (Putnam 1975: 271).

II

Our ideas of things which we put into nominal essences, can contain no more than those properties of things apparent to or discoverable by the user. But such a set of ideas, Locke frequently stresses, must be distinguished from whatever it is about the thing that is responsible for the ideas we have and on which they depend. The nominal essence can't be what constitutes the very being of a thing, because it is not the same as the real essence. Because Locke says this sort of thing, it makes it sound very much as though he thinks that the job of capturing what is essential about kinds of things is actually performed by the real essence. It is true that Locke thinks that when we use a substance-term, we intend it to apply to whatever thing the stuff in front of us turns out to be. For this reason, several have supposed (see Ayers 1977, Bolton 1976, Mackie 1976, Troyer 1975) that Locke would want to argue that whatever inner structure it is that determines the nature of that kind of thing will also be what determines the reference of the term. This would amount, as John Troyer has suggested, to the view that Locke thinks that the job of determining the reference is performed by the real essence, that is, the essential features of whatever kind of thing the term was originally applied to. But Locke's attitude towards real essences is more complicated and more equivocal than this interpretation would suggest. As John Mackie has emphasized, even though Locke apparently anticipated some of the insights of Saul Kripke and others, his theory cannot be said to be a version of the causal theory. This is because Locke regards the tendency to suppose our words to stand for real essences to be, in the case of substances, an abuse of language. Locke says:

For though the Word *Man* or *Gold*, signify nothing truly but a complex *Idea* of Properties, united together in one sort of Substance: Yet there is scarce any Body in the use of these Words, but often supposes each of those names to stand for a thing having the real Essence, on which those Properties depend. Which is so far from diminishing the Imperfection of our Words, that by a plain Abuse, it adds to it, when we would make them stand for something, which not being in our complex *Idea*, the name we use, can no ways be the sign of. (E III.x.18: 500)

Locke is apparently arguing, then, that, because real essences are unknown to us, it is a mistake to suppose our words can stand for these real essences.

It is, however, quite puzzling that Locke should have so unequivocally rejected the use of real essences to determine the reference of terms. His rejection depends upon a conviction that the inner constitutions of things as described by real essences remain beyond our grasp. Such an attitude is odd, for it seems to require considerable pessimism about the success of any scientific enquiry into inner constitutions. While a great deal of what Locke says about scientific progress is equivocal and controversial, there are many passages which are difficult to square with a wholesale rejection of the possibility of scientific discovery. He seems to be pretty heavily committed to adopting a realist position towards the inner structure of things on which our ideas depend. He offers at least qualified support for the corpuscularian theory (E iv.iii.16: 547) and he seems to have accepted without much doubt important aspects of the theory, such as the list of primary qualities making up the things of the world (E ii.viii: 132–43). So it is hard to see why Locke thinks that real essences should be so completely ignored, since he does not seem to think that the claims of contemporary science ought to be regarded as groundless. Surely, it would have been reasonable for Locke to recommend that we understand the reference of our terms to be determined by whatever the real essences of substance-terms turn out to be, and simultaneously recommend that people buckle down and discover what the real essences or hidden structures might be, using, if possible, the insights of corpuscularianism.

I think the solution to this problem lies in the fact that Locke did not intend the inner constitution or hidden structure of things, in whose existence he had no doubt at all, to be identified entirely with real essences, about which he was a good deal more sceptical. Perhaps a more accurate way of putting this would be to say that he did not suppose that everything thought to be true of real essences held of the inner constitution of things. In E iii.iii.17: 417–18, Locke distinguishes two opinions about the real essence of corporeal Objects:

The one is of those, who using the Word *Essence*, for they know not what, suppose a certain number of those Essences, according to which, all natural things are made, and wherein they do exactly every one of them partake, and so become of this or that *Species*. The other, and more rational Opinion, is of those, who look on all natural things to have a real, but unknown Constitution of their insensible Parts, from which flow those sensible Qualities, which serve us to distinguish them one from another, according as we have Occasion to rank them into sorts, under common Denominations. (See also E iii.x.21: 502–3)

Real essences, that is, are the inner constitutions of things, and as well, can be taken to be what divides things up into natural species or kinds. What this passage suggests is that Locke thinks that the fact that the constitutions of things are unknown should rule out absolutely our supposing them to come divided up into sorts or kinds, even though it is no bar to our taking them to be what is responsible for the qualities in things of which we are aware. He seems to be saying that it is irrational to suppose that there are inner structures essential to *kinds* of things. It might be possible to uncover the inner constitutions of things, but this will not amount to discovering the essential structure that makes something an example of a particular kind.

That this is Locke's view is made clearer by taking account of his claim about what is involved in holding a property to be essential. He says that the notion of something's being essential to a sort or kind of thing has relevance only with respect to the nominal essence or abstract idea we have about a thing. Insofar as we consider something as a particular existing thing, it is absurd to ask which of its properties are essential to it. Locke says:

> For I would ask anyone, What is sufficient to make an *essential* difference in Nature, between any two particular Beings, without any regard had to some abstract *Idea*, which is looked upon as the Essence and Standard of a *Species*? All such Patterns and Standards, being quite laid aside, particular Beings, considered barely in themselves, will be found to have all their Qualities equally *essential*; and every thing, in each Individual, will be essential to it, or, what is more true, nothing at all. (E III.vi.5: 441–2)

Things can only have an essence under a description, they can be essentially an-*x*-of-a-sort. But Locke has argued that no description or abstract idea we make to ourselves is privileged, that each abstract idea merely lists those properties the speaker takes to be important, and that no abstract idea or nominal essence can provide a definitive sorting into essential and accidental properties. It is only such nominal essences, however, that can provide the immutable standards by means of which we can announce that, unless some object meets the standard, it is not an example of that sort. Of itself, each parcel of matter has all of the qualities and powers it has and can lose any of them: 'But take away the consideration of its being ranked under the name of some abstract *Idea*, and then there is nothing necessary to it, nothing inseparable from it' (E III.vi.6: 442). Things certainly do have an inner structure, something on which their powers and sensible qualities depend, and, in that sense, the one Locke says is rational, they have real essences. But it is not by virtue of their inner structure that things belong to sorts or species, but only by conforming to some general abstract idea which we happen to have of them. Thus the essence or inner structure does not seem to have been thought of by Locke to be of any use in discriminating the essential properties of a thing from its accidental ones.[6]

Things can have inner constitutions on which their powers and sensible

---

[6] Note this claim will hold whether or not it should turn out that inner structures might in some cases resemble one another. A cold-in-the-head is whatever conforms to some general abstract idea of a cold, whether or not all colds have same or different internal structures. For more on this issue, see below.

qualities depend, and a knowledge of which would account for and explain their powers and sensible qualities. If this is the sense of real essence Locke approves of, then only particular things have real essences. The suggestion (made by Mackie, for example) that scientists since Locke's time have identified a lot of real essences is quite wrong, with respect to the kind of real essences Locke endorsed. If we think that scientific investigations typically uncover things like the atomic number of gold, then they are not directed to real essences in this sense. Locke does not give his approval to a sense of real essence that implies there are immutable species or natural kinds. The only sortings which do explicitly include some properties and exclude others do so in terms of speaker-relative abstract ideas and there is no reason to expect procedures of this sort to tell us anything about the hidden structure of the world. To understand the world as divided into essential kinds is a misapplication of something true of descriptions of the world. The things we actually encounter, Locke thinks, do not behave in the way our labelling processes encourage us to believe they must do. There are no immutable species, there are only individual things that can have or lose any of their properties. Locke repeatedly urges us to consider that the ideas we have even of the alleged species we are most familiar with, human beings, do not provide us with a classification scheme that we can count on fitting tight on to instances of the world (E iii.iii.17: 418; E iii.vi.22: 450–1; E iii.vi.26: 453–4).

It is true there are passages that seem to suggest that natural objects come in species, as E iii.iii.13: 415, where Locke says he is not intending to deny that 'Nature in the Production of Things, makes several of them alike.' Such passages are cited as evidence that Locke thought there were natural kinds (for example, by Mackie). But since Locke goes on in this section to emphasize that it is our abstract ideas that are to be used in classification, it is likely that he means here no more than that nature has produced things with observable similarities, which enter into our ideas, and not that things are alike because of similar hidden structures. Indeed, this possibility Locke seems to want to rule out. He names as a source of error, 'the supposition before mentioned, that Nature works regularly in the Production of Things, and set the Boundaries to each of those *Species*, by giving exactly the same real internal Constitution to each individual, which we rank under one general name' (E iii.x.20: 501). It seems clear that what he wants us to do to correct the error is to abandon the hypothesis that there are such similar internal mechanisms. We should instead recognize that the effects of things in us by means of which we sort them can be produced by Nature in many different ways. So presumably, Locke would not regard the discovery that some things which get called water have a different internal structure than others as a discovery that some things called water are not water. It is always a mistake, he thinks, to assume that, just because we rank things together, they have similar internal mechanisms.

III

My account of what Locke intends by his theory of real essences does not agree with several others which have recently been put forward, in particular that of John Mackie and Martha Brandt Bolton (Mackie 1976, Bolton 1976).[7] They each incline to the view that while Locke is concerned to show that our nominal essences do not coincide with the real essences of things, and hence that we don't know what the real essences of species are, still Locke does not intend to cast doubt on the claim that there are species having real essences. Both Mackie and Bolton think that Locke is in fact committed to such a view, because they think that his distinction between mixed modes and substances requires that substances are natural kinds, that is, are the sorts of things that can ultimately be distinguished from one another through their real essences. Locke says that the difference between mixed modes and substances is that, in the one case, the real and the nominal essences coincide, while in the second case they do not. What they take this to mean is that in the case of substances, our ideas are aimed at, but can miss, something real, existing in nature, while in the case of mixed modes, nothing natural is intended. Bolton's proposal is that in the case of mixed modes, what she calls the species-typical properties follow from a man-made definition, and hence represent conventional kinds, whereas, in the case of substances, the species-typical properties follow from the real constitutions and the laws of nature and hence represent natural kinds. Thus, the coincidence of real and nominal essences indicates something man-made or conventional, the divergence of real and nominal essences occurs when there is a natural kind or species in nature responsible for the properties the nominal essence attempts but fails to capture.

There are several occasions, however, where what Locke says fails to cohere neatly with this suggestion that the conventional can be equated with a convergence of essences, while the natural is to be identified with a

---

[7] There are others, e.g. Ayers, who share their views that real essences are natural kinds of substances, but whose arguments do not depend upon the use to which Locke puts the distinction between nominal and real essences. Ayers recognizes that Locke argues for the dependency of any classification on nominal essences, but still thinks that Locke recognizes natural kinds of broad sorts (see Ayers 1977).

divergence of essences. The first concerns artefacts and the second simple ideas. Bolton says that according to her account, artefacts like tables and postage stamps shouldn't count as substances, since they lack real essences, that is, are not natural kinds, although she does mention that Locke seems to think that some artefacts, like clocks, can be classified according to their causal powers and so be assimilable to substances. Locke nowhere specifically excludes artefacts as substances. What is more, he argues that we should see ourselves as doing the same sort of thing when we attach names to artifical and to real things. He says in E III.vi.39: 463–4 that whether a difference in the internal mechanisms of several watches will count as essential differences can depend only upon the complex idea that happens to be attached to the word 'watch', that different sorts of workings may cause the watchmaker, for example, to count each watch as of a different species, but will not do so for the ordinary watch user. And Locke goes on to say that exactly the same sorts of considerations will prevail for natural species, for differences in internal constitutions may be immaterial. He sums up by saying:

I must be excused here, if I think, *artifical Things are of distinct Species*, as well as natural: Since I find they are as plainly and orderly ranked into sorts, by different abstract *Ideas*, with general names attached to them, as distinct one from another as those of natural Substances. For why should we not think a Watch, and Pistol, as distinct Species one from another, as a Horse, and a Dog, they being expressed in our Minds by distinct *Ideas*, and to others, by distinct Appellations. (E III.vi.41: 465)

What is clear from this passage is that Locke does not think that the fact that horses or dogs are natural substances makes any interesting difference to the way we sort them into kinds. Locke does not want to distinguish the way we pick out natural things from the way we do artifical and this is because he thinks in both cases it is not some internal structure we are talking about, but only the ideas we attach to the term.

The example of simple ideas also proves troublesome for a straightforward classification into natural and conventional kinds. Locke says the names of simple ideas, like the names of mixed modes, stand for the real as well as the nominal essence (E III.iv.3: 421). But simple ideas are not man-made or conventional. An important characteristic of simple ideas is, of course, that we can't make them up, and Locke, moreover, in this context mentions that, unlike mixed modes, the names of simple ideas stand for something having real existence. As the outcome of a natural process, they are clearly governed by the laws of nature. So the case of simple ideas seems to provide serious problems for Bolton's proposal.

Mackie thinks that Locke is just wrong in what he says about simple ideas, that Locke thinks there is nothing more to an idea like whiteness than what is associated with the name, and has not taken proper account of the fact that whiteness has an external reference to whatever has the power to cause whiteness in me. For, Mackie says, surely this is enough to mark a divergence between a nominal and a real essence. Mackie is assuming that, for Locke, the real essence of a thing or property can be the same as its nominal essence only when it has no real or causal basis, and he is assuming that to say that a property has a causal basis in nature is the same as saying it has a real essence, in the sense, being of a natural kind. So he thinks Locke ought to have recognized that something can seem to me to be white, but not be white, if it fails to share the inner causal structure of other instances of white.

But what seems clear is that the dissimilarities between simple ideas and complex ideas of substances to which Locke wants to call our attention do not depend upon the presence or absence of a real causal basis. This emerges particularly clearly if we look at what Locke thinks makes these different kinds of ideas true. Simple ideas are all true, he says, whereas, if we used complex ideas to stand for 'the Representations of the unknown Essences of Things', then these ideas, Locke says, would be false (E II.xxxii.18: 390). But what makes the simple idea true is not that the thing it stands for is without a causal basis, but that any structure that causes yellow in me just *is* yellow, and hence it is the nominal essence, the idea in me, that makes anything really yellow. Thus he says all our simple ideas are true and would be true even 'if by the different Structure of our Organs, it were so ordered, that *the same Object should produce in several Men's Minds different Ideas* at the same time; v.g., if the *Idea*, that a *Violet* produced in one Man's Mind by his Eyes, were the same that a Marigold produced in another Man's, and *vice versa*' (E II.xxxii.15: 389). So, in the case of simple ideas, the nominal and the real essences coincide because when I identify things as yellow, I take myself to be indicating whatever particular aspects of the world have the power to cause ideas of this sort in me. So long as I am indeed having an idea of yellow, then it will be true that the piece of the world before me has the power to cause yellowness in me, no matter what its structure happens to be. It is the idea that I attach to the name yellow that determines whether something belongs to the kind yellow, even though we remain ignorant of those natural processes causally responsible for yellowness. If, on the other hand, we are saying something false when we use substance-terms to stand for real essences, it cannot be because substance-terms have a real external referent they do not copy, for this is true of simple ideas, nor can it be because the external referent is unknown, for this is true too. Rather, Locke must be supposing that the falsity lies in the specific equation between the causal basis of the ideas we happen to be having and an unknown essence of a complex idea of a substance.

Whatever differences can be found between simple ideas and ideas of substances presumably must be found in the complexity of the ideas of substances. Complex ideas of substances differ from simple ones only because in using a complex idea, we are indicating the presence of something on which, not just one idea depends, but that of a collection of co-existing ideas. If I point at something and call it 'gold', I am saying there is something out there on which the co-existence of all the ideas contained in my idea of gold depends. As in the case of simple ideas, I mean to indicate that thing out there, whatever it is, but unlike the case of simple ideas, I have no grounds for saying and no intention of saying that whatever it is before me has the capacity just to give rise to all and only what is contained in my complex idea. So, although I am prepared to say, when I single out only one simple property such as yellow, that whatever is causally responsible for what is contained in my simple idea of yellow just is yellow, I am not prepared to say the same sort of thing about complex ideas. I don't have any legitimate reason to expect that the next thing I indicate by the word 'gold' which also is a causal basis for the co-existence of some properties contained in my complex idea of gold will have the same properties and powers that this one has. Thus on several counts, the real essence which is responsible for the co-existence of all of the properties and powers of each particular thing fails to coincide with the nominal essence I have in mind when I call each thing 'gold'.

Locke repeatedly emphasizes that what is contained in a complex idea of a substance falls far short of being an exhaustive list of all the properties and powers belonging to that on which the complex idea depends (E II.xxxi.8: 381). Such a complex idea is intended to comprise only some sets of simple ideas I take to co-exist, to be reliably found in collections. The various difficulties and inadequacies we run into in framing ideas of substances all stem from uncertainties involved in putting together such collections. Since there are no or very few necessary connections perceivable among ideas, we cannot be sure that a particular set can be counted on to co-exist as a set, or that our set of co-existing properties does not have unfortunate or misleading omissions (E IV.iii.10–11: 544–5). But for the idea of a substance to be real, all that is necessary is for the ideas contained in it actually to have co-existed in nature. To expect anything more than this, as that the reality of the substance denoted requires that it pick out some specific essence, Locke says is a confusion: 'Whatever simple *Ideas* have been found to co-exist in any Substance, these we may with confidence join together again, and so make abstract *Ideas* of Substances. For whatever have once had a union in Nature, may be united again' (E IV.iv.12: 569). Thus, in the case of substances, the ideas we have about kinds of things are not intended to capture what it is about any particular instance that makes it what it is. While Locke did think that individual substances must have inner constitutions, he did not think that the reference of abstract terms picking out sorts of substances is determined by the structure of the inner constitution of substances. For an abstract substance-term is intended to capture only that a collection of simple ideas co-exist, whatever the mechanisms these ideas happen to depend upon.

IV

Thus, what Locke calls the nominal essence amounts to no more than whatever abstract ideas are attached by a speaker to a term. These ideas represent beliefs we have about properties that co-exist, but such beliefs, in the case of substances, are very far from being certain. Locke is not maintaining, therefore, that the abstract idea I attach to a term represents knowledge about properties essential to the being of whatever the terms stand for, nor is he saying that I will, for example, cease to call gold, 'gold', if I discover that yellowness does not co-exist with the rest of the properties making up my idea of gold. There is, therefore, nothing essential to any of the ideas that make up the nominal essence of gold. Locke is concerned to demonstrate that such a notion cannot be taken to be anything like a substantial form, since it represents no more than some things a speaker believes about what the word stands for.

Similarly, what Locke calls a real essence has nothing essential about it either. Real essences are in the interesting case, the case of substances, that inner constitution on which all the properties and powers of a particular thing depends. But when we sort into kinds of things, we are using our abstract ideas or nominal essences, and although, in the case of substances, each particular instance has an inner constitution, it would be entirely unwarranted to assume that all the inner constitutions of some set of things we point to using the same substance-term are alike. Real essences, in the sense of inner constitutions, will make a particular individual thing be the thing that is it, but they do not make a thing be the kind of thing that it is. Only particular things can be said to have real essences, but no property is more essential to the being of a particular thing than any other property.

Locke is not therefore arguing either that the nominal essence determines the reference of a term, as in the ideational theory of meaning, or that the real essence determines the reference. Insofar as any conclusions on this matter can be drawn from what Locke says, it would seem that his position is that nothing strictly determines the reference of terms. But this is not a particularly illuminating or accurate way of talking about Locke, for he was not actually concerned with issues that go into contemporary worries about reference. What is true is that Locke's use of the terms real and nominal essence is intended to be part of a refutation of the claim that our ways of sorting things in the world is a sorting into natural species having species-typical properties, and not a defence of such a claim. His effort has been to show that when we are talking about what determines the being of a thing or makes it be what it is, then we mean the inner constitution of a particular thing, whereas, if we ask about the means by which we sort things into kinds, we look to an abstract idea attached to a name of a set of co-existing properties. There is no reason to identify that which makes something be a particular thing with that which makes us call something a sort of a thing, to identify real with nominal essences. Whatever is natural about a thing, that is, what it is that by existing in nature makes something be what it is, is not the same as what makes it be a kind of thing for us. Thus, while we can certainly claim to be able to sort things into kinds, we cannot claim to have any insight into the essential nature of kinds of things. It would seem that Locke might at least be open to the charge of being misleading (since he has misled so many) in his usage of the word 'essence', were it not for the fact that he warns us that his usage is non-standard:

I have chose to explain this uncertainty of Propositions in this scholastick way, and have made use of the Terms of *Essences* and *Species*, on purpose to shew the absurdity and inconvenience there is to think of them, as of any other sort of Realities, than barely abstract *Ideas* with Names to them. To suppose, that the *Species* of Things are any thing, but the sorting of them under general Names, according as they agree to several abstract *Ideas*, of which we make those Names the signs, is to confound Truth, and introduce Uncertainty into all general Propositions, that can be made about them. Though therefore these Things might, to People not possessed with scholastick Learning, to be perhaps treated of, in a better and clearer way: yet those wrong Notions of *Essences* and *Species*, having got root in most Peoples Minds, who have received any tincture from the Learning, which has prevailed in this part of the World, are to be discovered and removed, to make way for that use of Words, which should convey certainty with it. (E iv.vi.4: 580–1)

If Locke's views about real and nominal essences are understood in this way as denying rather than asserting a theory of natural kinds, then his general attitude toward corpuscularianism can be made clearer. Locke can hold that it is an abuse of words to suppose that our words stand for unknown real essences and not for collections of our own ideas without in any way committing himself about the possibilities for progress in scientific enquiry. Locke can be a realist with respect to the corpuscles which probably constitute the inner constitutions of things (and therefore hold that substance-terms are always used to pick out things having a real existence) without being a realist about the kinds into which substance-terms sort things. He holds that it is a mistake to imagine that a term like 'gold' or 'water' stands for a species in nature with fixed boundaries, for such terms have as their function to sort ideas, whatever the inner constitutions giving rise to our ideas. It will not, therefore, be an appropriate goal of science to seek to discover such natural species. On the other hand, although Locke thinks there is a good deal we don't and may never know about the corpuscles that probably make up the inner constitutions of things, we have good grounds for putting forward the hypothesis that such corpuscles exist. Thus, while it is true that we don't and may never know about the actions of particles on one another, this is not the sort of thing we should regard as impossible to know. This way of reading Locke suggests, however, that the investigation into the nature of corpuscles is not going to be the dominant scientific enterprise, and this impression is supported by passages like this one where Locke says: 'In the Knowledge of Bodies, we must be content to glean, what we can, from particular Experiments: since we cannot, from a Discovery of their real Essences, grasp at a time whole Sheaves, and in bundles, comprehend the Nature and Properties of whole Species together' (E iv.xii.12: 647). An interesting problem for us to investigate will be what properties or powers of substances like gold or water reliably co-exist in our experience of them. We are not, however, going to be able to learn this by investigating the corpuscular state of instances of gold or water, but only by observing and experimenting on sets of co-existing ideas.[8]

[8] I am grateful to Robert Schwartz, Robert Cummins, Richard Feldman, and John Koethe for comments on earlier versions of this paper.

XI

THE RELEVANCE OF LOCKE'S THEORY OF IDEAS TO HIS DOCTRINE OF NOMINAL ESSENCE AND ANTI-ESSENTIALIST SEMANTIC THEORY

MARTHA BRANDT BOLTON

THE doctrine of real and nominal essence is important in Locke's *Essay*, because a number of his most provocative claims and theories are in large part derived from it. This is true of Locke's distinctive theory of what we can and cannot know in the various sciences. It is also true of Locke's account of the signification of general terms, his exposé of the abuses of language (which he claims have passed for erudition), and his aim to make a modest contribution to natural science by advocating observationally based definitions of classificatory terms. Much that is distinctive in these doctrines derives from the fact that the key account of nominal essence is opposed to the essentialist views of Locke's contemporaries. Versions of essentialism were advocated by many seventeenth-century philosophers, including Scholastics, less traditional Aristotelians, and Cartesians. The basic thesis they hold in common is that at least some of the kinds we use and for which we have names are determined by the natures or essences of things. In contrast, Locke's theory of nominal essence maintains that the boundaries of all the kinds we use are fixed by nothing but our own ideas.

In this paper, I want to consider the *basis* of Locke's theory of nominal essence. What reason does he have for opposing the traditional view that some kinds we use are determined by mind-independent, objective essences and urging instead that all the kinds we use are determined by nothing but our abstract ideas? One answer to this question is found in various versions in much of the secondary literature. According to this

From 'The Idea-Theoretic Basis of Locke's Anti-Essentialist Doctrine of Nominal Essence', in Phillip D. Cummins and Guenter Zoeller (eds.), *Mind, Ideas, and Objects* (Atascadero, Calif.: Ridgeview, 1992), 85–95. At the author's request, the title of this paper has been changed for its republication here.

familiar account, Locke opposes an essentialist view of the kinds we use, because he rejects the basic claim of essentialist metaphysics, that there *are* essences or natures of things. This metaphysical view, it is sometimes said, is implied by the progressive mechanist world-view which Locke advocated. If Locke did hold that there are no mind-independent essences, it seems a short step to his doctrine that all kinds we use are determined by nothing but our own ideas (nominal essences).[1] However, in this paper, I want to show that this is not the *only* basis for Locke's opposition to essentialist views. In the text of the *Essay*, we find an independent line of reasoning in support of the doctrine of nominal essence. This second argument involves only one controversial premiss. The premiss concerns the character of ideas, so I call the line of reasoning an 'idea-theoretic' argument. Here I do not want to dispute the familiar view that anti-essentialist metaphysics is *one* basis for Locke's doctrine of nominal essence, although I think there are difficulties for it. But I do want to argue that Locke's theory of ideas is *sufficient* to establish the anti-essentialist doctrine of nominal essence, regardless of what he may have thought about the *existence* of objective, mind-independent essences.

The controversial premiss in the idea-theoretic argument concerns the epistemic status of ideas. Locke is much more specific about the epistemic properties of ideas than about their metaphysical status (e.g. whether ideas are mental acts or objects existing in the mind). For, Locke makes it very clear that ideas involve objects of immediate perception whose identity is specified entirely in terms of what they are perceived to be (E iv.i.4: 526; E iv.ii.1: 531; E iv.iii.8: 544; E iv.vii.4: 592–4). There will not be time to examine in any detail the views of Locke's seventeenth-century predecessors on the epistemic properties of ideas. But I will try briefly to show that main essentialist thinkers of the period took a non-Lockean view on the question of what, in general, we know about our ideas.[2] I want to argue that the epistemic tenets of Locke's theory of ideas provide one basis for his key doctrine of nominal essence, and also to suggest that these tenets set Locke's theory of ideas apart from those of other main seventeenth-century philosophers.

To start, we need to consider what Locke's doctrine of nominal essence is and exactly how it is opposed to essentialist claims. Introducing the doctrine (in E iii.iii.15–18: 417–19), Locke maintains that kinds have essences of two types, nominal and real. What he calls the 'nominal essence' is an abstract or general idea, as he explains:

---

[1] This interpretation has been most fully developed in Woolhouse 1971: sects. 17–19; Ayers 1981*a*: 247–73; Jolley 1984: ch. 8; and Alexander 1985: 274–9.

[2] For more detail, see Bolton 1992.

But it being evident, that Things are ranked under Names into sorts or *Species*, only as they agree to certain abstract *Ideas*, to which we have annexed those Names, the *Essence* of each *Genus*, or Sort, comes to be nothing but that abstract *Idea*, which the General . . . Name stands for. (E iii.iii.15: 417)

Between the Nominal Essence, and the Name, there is so *near* a *Connexion*, that the Name of any sort of Things cannot be attributed to any particular Being, but what has this *Essence*, whereby it answers that abstract *Idea*, whereof that Name is the Sign. (E iii.iii.16: 417)

In other words, a nominal essence is an abstract idea that is basic and authoritative in fixing the boundaries of a kind for which we have a name.

In contrast, a *real* essence is that on which the observable or discoverable properties of a kind depend. In the case of substance kinds, real essences are the hidden constitutions of actual things.[3] Locke insists that we have no prospect of knowing the hidden structures that give rise to sensible qualities; but he favours the corpuscular hypothesis about the general character of inner constitutions of material things. In any case, inasmuch as a real essence is the causal basis of qualities, it exists in nature independently of our ideas. But Locke notes that there are two opinions about the real essences of substances (causal bases of qualities): one opinion is that real essences determine species and the other opinion is that real essences give rise to the qualities in terms of which a nominal essence determines the boundary of a kind (E iii.iii.17: 417–18). Locke attacks the former view and opts for the latter.[4] For Locke, the nominal essence specifies the kind-determining set of qualities and real essence is defined relative to those qualities as any structure that gives rise to them (see esp. E iii.vi.6: 442).

The anti-essentialist character of Locke's position is clear enough in the doctrine of dual essences as Locke introduces it (that is, as just described). Although Lockean real essences exist in nature, their status as *essences* in relation to kinds we name is derived from their connection with a nominal essence. And it is this *idea* that is basic and authoritative in determining the denominated kind. Moreover, the premisses of the idea-theoretic argument for the kind-determining function of ideas are already available in this initial account of nominal essence. But the anti-essentialist thrust, as well as the idea-theoretic argument, are more fully developed in later

---

[3] In the case of modal kinds, the real essence is the abstract idea that is the nominal essence (see E iii.iii.18: 418).

[4] The former alternative incorporates the traditional doctrine that species are associated with *propria*, i.e. features that are necessarily and *exclusively* attached to anything that has the real essence of a given kind. Further, the first alternative is not so much a view about the basis of species *tout court*, as it is about the species for which we have names. Both of these provisions are assumed in Locke's attacks on the first alternative (esp. E iii.iii.17: 418), but there is not time to discuss his argument here.

chapters on the signification of general names. Nominal essences are, after all, introduced as determining the kinds signified by names. So, I want to turn to Locke's defence of his theory of the semantics of kind terms and his arguments against what he takes to be its main competitor. In this context, we can most easily discern the idea-theoretic basis of Locke's anti-essentialism.

Advocates of essentialism in the seventeenth century tended to hold a rudimentary 'referential theory' of the semantics of natural kind terms. (The parallel with recent accounts that go by that name has been noted and discussed by several commentators; see Jolley 1984: ch. 8; Ayers 1981a; see also Atherton 1984, repr. in this volume as Ch. x) For our purposes, the salient claims of the standard theory are simply that we use (some) kind terms to signify things in naturally determined kinds and our doing so does not presuppose our knowing the essences of those kinds; nor does it presuppose our having a criterion that picks out all and only instances of the kinds. It is an interesting question what *does* establish the signification relation between general terms and natural kinds, according to seventeenth-century advocates of a 'referential' view. But there is not space to pursue that question here.[5]

Locke is well aware of the appeal of the standard, 'referential' view. He observes that most people take themselves to use general names to stand for things with the *real* essences of kinds. As he puts it: 'Who is there almost, who would not take it amiss, if it should be doubted, whether he call'd himself Man, with any other meaning, than as having the real Essence of a Man?' (E II.xxxi.6: 378). (Here Locke means a traditional real essence, not a relativized Lockean one.) But Locke nevertheless rejects the traditional semantic view and opts instead for a sort of 'descriptive' semantic theory. On his account, a general term immediately signifies an abstract idea; the idea sets conditions that anyone who understands the term must know and, further, these conditions definitively determine the things to which the term applies. Notice that this 'descriptive' semantic theory

---

[5] At least some 17th-cent. thinkers influenced by the Scholastic tradition subscribed to the view that the idea (or concept) of a kind involves the existence of the essence or form of the kind as a modification of the conceiving mind. The form existing as a modification of a mind was understood to be the means by which that mind's cognition is directed toward certain objects, rather than others. In particular, a mind modified by a certain form was said to perform an act of apprehending those things in which that 'same form' is materialized. The crucial notions were explicated in a variety of ways. Concepts were also often supposed to involve a conceptual content in some way accessible to the mind. The content was thought to be, at least in part, determined by the form that modifies the mind. But, as we will see, it was not supposed that, in general, these contents suffice to ground knowledge of the essence of the kind, or even knowledge of a universally correct criterion for members of the kind. On early 17th-cent. theories of concepts and their background, see esp. Nuchelmans 1983: ch. 1.

incorporates the doctrine of nominal essence, that abstract ideas are basic and authoritative in setting the boundaries of kinds named by general terms.

How does Locke argue for the 'descriptive' theory, which embeds the doctrine of nominal essence? He begins with a general semantic thesis: a word immediately signifies an idea in the mind of one who uses it and it stands for those existing things that are objects of that idea (E iii.ii.1–3: 404–6). (Certain words are later said to signify mental acts of combining ideas: these include the copula, its negation, and 'particles' or sentence connectives (E iii.vii: 471–3).) This initial account of (almost) all words is then adapted to the case of general terms: a *general* name immediately signifies an *abstract* idea in the minds of those who use it, and the name applies to just those things that are objects of the abstract idea (E iii.iii.6–11: 410–14).

Opposition to essentialism is hardly in evidence here. The semantic thesis that names signify ideas was well within the prevailing Aristotelian tradition. In seventeenth-century philosophy, language was often said to depend upon pre-linguistic mental discourse. It was thought that concepts are natural signs of their objects, whereas words are conventional signs. The signification of words that stand for things (categorematic terms) was said to presuppose concepts *of* those things. On this view, a word is an insignificant vocal sound until subordinated to a concept, whereby the sound becomes a word that signifies the things naturally signified by the concept (see Ashworth 1974: 35–46; Nuchelmans 1980: sects. 2.3, 2.5; Nuchelmans 1983: ch. 1). (The account of syncategorematic terms is slightly different. Locke's account of 'particles' roughly follows it.) This basic picture was shared by Descartes and his followers, as well as contemporary Aristotelians (Descartes 1985: II. 113; Descartes 1991: 185; Arnauld and Nicole 1965: I. i, ix). Further, it has been shown that Locke's doctrine that words *signify* ideas was not at all original with him. Locke's Scholastic predecessors debated whether it is correct say that words signify concepts, as well as things; and assuming that words do signify concepts, whether this is their primary and immediate signification. The opinion that words do immediately signify concepts did not always prevail, but it was held by some (Ashworth 1981*a*; Ashworth 1984: 60–4, repr. in this volume as ch. ix; Nuchelmans 1980: sect. 2.3.3).

However, despite the traditional nature of Locke's formula for the signification of general terms, he gives the theory a radical anti-essentialist turn. Immediately after stating it, he introduces relativist views clearly opposed to the traditional 'referential' account and he later argues at length for these claims (E iii.iii.12–14: 414–17; E iii.vi.7–39: 443–64). There are two of these relativist claims: (i) the kinds of substances we name are *not* determined by real essences—neither traditional 'supposed' real essences nor Lockean ones (see E III.iii.13: 415–16; E III.vi.8: 443–4; E III.vi.11–22: 445–51 *passim*); (ii) the abstract idea immediately signified by a general term determines the kind of things to which the term correctly applies; that is, the *idea* is basic and authoritative in determining membership conditions for the kind named (E III.iii.12: 414–15; E III.vi.7: 443). How does Locke transform the traditional formula often advocated by 'referential' theorists into a vehicle of his own anti-referentialist view, expressed in theses (i) and (ii)?

One of Locke's arguments for (i) is especially revealing of the light in which *he* understands the traditional semantic formula:

Nor indeed *can we* rank, and *sort Things*, and consequently (which is the end of sorting) denominate them *by their real Essences*, because we know them not . . . Therefore we in vain pretend to range Things into sorts, and dispose them into certain Classes, under Names, by their *real Essences*, that are so far from our discovery or comprehension. A blind Man may as soon sort Things by their Colours . . . as by those internal Constitutions which he knows not. (E III.vi.9: 444)

The reasoning is that we cannot classify by kinds determined by Lockean real essences (which exist) nor by traditional real essences (which perhaps do not exist), because we are ignorant of real essences in either case. The key to Locke's position is an epistemic requirement on possession of the idea of a kind: if we do not *know* what an (actual or purported) real essence is, then we cannot have an *idea of* the kind determined by it. Locke's traditional semantic formula conjoined with this epistemic requirement implies that we *cannot* have a name that signifies things in a kind determined by an *unknown* real essence. It follows at once that the 'referential theory' is false. It says we *can* have names for kinds whose boundary-determining essences we do not know.[6] In short, Locke begins with an uncontroversial formula for the semantics of kind terms accepted by advocates of the 'referential theory' and goes on to draw an anti-referential conclusion from it; he can do this, because his theory of ideas is different from that of the referentialists. He places an epistemic condition on possession of any idea that the 'referential' theorists do not require. The reasoning based on this epistemic requirement is the idea-theoretic argument to which I want to call attention.

---

[6] Although Cartesians claimed to know the essences of mental and corporeal substances, none of Locke's contemporaries could have sustained a claim to know the essences of kinds such as horse, water, or gold. The controversial point in Locke's position is not that we are ignorant of real essences, but that we cannot have an idea of a kind determined by a real essence unless we know what the essence is.

Locke's arguments for relativist thesis (ii) reveal a similar reliance on the distinctive Lockean view of the epistemic properties of ideas. Thesis (ii) is that the *idea* signified by a general term has authority to determine the kind of things named by the term. In the following passage, Locke draws this conclusion *immediately* from a statement of the traditional semantic formula:

... 'tis [an abstract idea] alone, that the name, which is the mark of the Sort, signifies. 'Tis impossible therefore, that any thing should determine the Sorts of Things, which we rank under general Names, but that *Idea*, which that Name is design'd as a mark for; ... How comes any particular thing to be of this or that *Sort*, but because it has that nominal essence, Or, which is all one, agrees to that abstract *Idea*, that name is annexed to? (E III.vi.7: 443; see also E III.iii.12: 414–15)

What entitles Locke to use the traditional formula to derive his non-traditional conclusion? As the formula was usually understood, the idea signified by a general name is an idea *of* a sort determined by something other than the idea, namely, an objective essence. But the formula is transformed by Locke's views about ideas: (a) that an abstract idea is what it is immediately perceived to be and (b) that the idea represents exactly those things that 'agree to it'. That is, the content of an abstract idea is just what it is immediately perceived to be and the content of the idea *determines* the basic necessary and sufficient condition for a thing's belonging to the sort the idea is of. Locke's contention that the kind named by a general term has a boundary set by one of our ideas *does* follow immediately from the traditional formula given his theory of ideas.

The crucial point for Locke is this: an idea of a kind determined by something extrinsic to the idea, and thus not fully known to the mind that has it, is *impossible*. It is a 'chimerical supposition', as Locke says in one attack on the 'referential' view (E II.xxxii.18: 390). Of course, this does not mean that we cannot have a general idea whose content is given by, say, 'an inner constitution like that of the matter in Locke's ring'. But that idea represents the kind defined by that content, not one defined by having a constitution like ABC (if that is the constitution of the stuff in question).[7] We could have an idea of the kind defined by 'a constitution like ABC', only if we had an idea whose content is 'constitution ABC'. The 'chimerical supposition' is that an idea can represent a kind whose boundary is determined by anything other than the exact content of the idea. In a

[7] Thus we cannot use the idea whose content is 'thing with an inner constitution like that of the matter in Locke's ring' to classify things, since we are unable to distinguish things that conform to that content from things that do not. If we tried to do so on the basis of some criterion other than this content (e.g. being yellow, malleable, and soluble in aqua regia), we would thereby *not* be classifying by the original idea, but rather by the idea whose content is 'thing that is yellow, malleable, and soluble in aqua regia'.

minute, we will look at the origin of this view in Locke's overall treatment of ideas and compare it to the theory of ideas held by some seventeenth-century adherents to the 'referential theory'.

My contention is that many, if not all, of the arguments we find in the *Essay* for relativist claims (i) and (ii) are to be understood as *presupposing* the Lockean account of ideas and their epistemic status. This is the controversial move in a recurring pattern of argumentation in which Locke cites some uncontroversial fact or doctrine (e.g. the traditional semantic formula); this is conjoined with his distinctive theory of ideas; and Locke derives his anti-referential conclusion. Consider another argument for relativist thesis (i), that the kind signified by a general term is *not* determined by a real essence. This argument cites the frustrations of practicing chemists. Locke reports that:

> ... Chymists ... sometimes in vain, seek for the same Qualities in one parcel of Sulphur, Antimony, or Vitriol, which they have found in others. For though they are Bodies of the same *Species*, having the same nominal *Essence*, under the same Name; yet they do often, upon severe ways of examination, betray Qualities so different one from another, as to frustrate the Expectation and Labour of very wary Chymists. But if Things were distinguished into *Species*, according to their real Essences, it would be as impossible to find different Properties in any two individual Substances of the same *Species*, as it is to find different Properties in two Circles, or two equilateral Triangles. (E III.vi.8: 443)

The argument is this: careful chemists apply the name 'sulphur' to samples that differ widely in the qualities that flow from their inner constitutions; things with the same real essence cannot have different properties (i.e. qualities that flow from the real essence) (see E III.iv.6: 422); thus, the diversity of qualities among samples of sulphur shows that they do not have the same real essence; therefore, the kind named 'sulphur' is not determined by a real essence. In reply to this, a proponent of a 'referential' theory will simply say that even 'very wary' chemists may have inaccurate tests for sulphur; they may just be wrong in thinking that the anomalous samples are sulphur, and so those samples provide no reason to deny that sulphur is determined by an (unknown) real essence. Locke's argument *assumes* that the chemists' tests (expressed in their abstract ideas) are definitive in determining samples of the kind. This controversial assumption is nothing other than Locke's theory that abstract ideas represent exactly those things that conform to the known content of the ideas. If this theory of ideas is granted, so is Locke's relativist claim.

There is one further argument for relativist claim (ii) that deserves mention, because it is liable to be misunderstood:

That then which general Words signify is a Sort of things; and each of them does that, by being a sign of an abstract *Idea* in the mind; to which *Idea*, as things existing are found to agree, so they come to be ranked under that name, or, which is all one, be of that sort. Whereby it is evident, that the *Essences* of the *sorts* . . . are nothing else but these abstract *Ideas*. For the having the Essence of any Species, being that which makes any thing to be of that Species, and the conformity to the *Idea*, to which the name is annexed, being that which gives a right to that name, the having the Essence, and the having that Conformity, must needs be the same thing: Since to be of any Species, and to have a right to the name of that Species, is all one. (E iii.iii.12: 414–15)

The difficulty is that Locke's conclusion may seem to imply that nothing is in a kind that has no name, and that there are no kinds apart from names. In other words, the passage may seem to suggest that a thing belongs to a kind if and only if there is a name for the kind and the name would be correctly applied to the thing. In fact, the argument requires only the innocuous claim that a thing belongs to a kind *for which there is a name* if and only if the name would be correctly applied to that thing.[8] That claim is one premiss of the argument (presumably an uncontroversial one). A second premiss is: a thing has a right to be called by a general term if and only if the thing 'conforms' to the idea immediately signified by the term. And the conclusion is the relativist claim that an *idea* determines the essence (basic membership conditions) of the kind named by a general term.

The second premiss is the controversial one. It says that an idea, not a mind-independent essence, determines what has a right to the name of a kind. At the start of the passage, we find a typical argument for that. Locke repeats the traditional formula that a general term is a sign of an abstract idea and then imports his theory of ideas, by declaring that the term applies to exactly those things that 'conform' to the *idea*. So, this passage, too, follows the pattern of argument whose only controversial premiss is Locke's distinctive theory of ideas.

Let's look more closely at the controversial aspects of the Lockean view of ideas. As we saw, there are two crucial provisions of his view: (a) an idea is (has) a content which is fully known by the mind that possesses the idea and (b) the idea represents exactly those things that conform to its content (i.e. conformity to the idea constitutes the boundary of the represented kind). The groundwork for (a) is laid in Books i and ii of the *Essay*, where Locke undertakes to show that every idea is either simple (and hence fully known) or a combination of simple ideas put together by the mind. One

---

[8] As the start of the passage makes clear, the discussion here is restricted to denominated kinds.

consequence is that a mind has full access to the composition and content of any of its ideas (see e.g. E II.xii.8: 166). Indeed, our ability to know what our ideas are is an axiom of the theory of knowledge in Book IV, where Locke says:

... [A] Man cannot conceive himself capable of a greater Certainty, than to know that any *Idea* in his Mind is such, as he perceives it to be; ... (E IV.ii.1: 531)

Again:

... [T]here can be no *Idea* in the Mind, which it does not presently, by an intuitive Knowledge, perceive to be what it is, and to be different from any other. (E IV.iii.8: 544; see also E IV.vi.4: 580)[9]

Point (b) is that the content of an abstract idea determines what it is to be an instance of the kind the idea is of. Brief statements of (b) were noted in passages quoted earlier, but the point is officially introduced in the following way:

... *Ideas* become general, by separating from them the circumstances of Time, and Place, and any other *Ideas*, that may determine them to this or that particular Existence. By this way of abstraction they are made capable of representing more Individuals than one; each of which, having in it a conformity to that abstract *Idea*, is (as we call it) of that sort. (E III.iii.6: 411)

For Locke, conformity to the content of the idea is the basic necessary and sufficient condition for membership in the kind represented by an abstract idea.

Many of Locke's predecessors in the seventeenth century did *not* subscribe to a theory of ideas (or concepts, taking these roughly to be the same) that incorporates both (a) and (b) (see above, n. 5). They supposed we have ideas of many kinds and yet are ignorant of the essences that determine their boundaries. It was common among Locke's contemporaries to classify ideas as clear vs. obscure on the basis of the sort of knowledge, or lack of knowledge, possession of an idea involves; an idea is clear to the extent that one who has it understands what fundamentally distinguishes the objects of the idea from other things. Among Renaissance Scholastics, a perfectly clear concept of a kind was associated with full knowledge of the essence of the kind; a concept was said to be obscure to

---

[9] Locke clearly maintains that *propositions* are the objects of knowledge and that propositions are formed by a mind's 'joining' or 'separating' of ideas. Merely having in mind an idea is not the affirmation of a proposition specifying what the idea is (or is not). So, strictly speaking, actual knowledge of what an idea is (or is not) cannot be inherent to the mere possession of an idea, according to Locke. He appears to think, however, that it is impossible for a mind to have an idea and lack the ability to have immediate and intuitive knowledge of what the idea is (is not).

the extent that it falls short of that ideal. Some thought that all human concepts (vs. ideas in the mind of God) are, to some extent, obscure in this way.[10]

As for Descartes, Leibniz, and other 'moderns', they indicate that we can have the idea of a kind without even knowing a distinguishing mark of its instances. Descartes wrote that an idea is *clear*, if it is 'present and apparent to an attentive mind'. I take this to mean that it represents something in such a way that it can easily be identified. In contrast, obscure ideas *lack* this degree of perspicuity (Descartes 1985: I. 207).[11] For Descartes, then, one can have the idea of a thing although ignorant of its essence; indeed, one can have the idea, even though uncertain of anything that distinguishes its object from other things. Leibniz, also, has a minimal cognitive requirement for having the concept of a thing:

A concept is obscure if it does not suffice for recognizing the thing represented, as when I only remember some flower or animal which I have once seen but not well enough to recognize it when placed before me and to distinguish it from similar ones.

Leibniz goes on to say that when one has a clear, but confused, concept, one can identify an instance when it is placed before one. But although instances of the concept are distinguished by a mark that can be explicated, the person with a clear, but confused, concept does not know what the distinguishing characteristic is (Leibniz 1969: 291).[12]

This brief survey of some of Locke's referentialist opponents should suffice to show that he is unlike other important early modern philosophers in holding that possession of the idea of a kind ensures knowledge of what determines the boundary of the kind. The implications of this distinctively Lockean view extend to many of the theories and claims in the *Essay*. But the point I want to stress is that the doctrine is intrinsic to the theory of ideas on which the *Essay* is built.

Let me review the idea-theoretic basis of Locke's anti-essentialist doctrine of nominal essence. That doctrine says that the kind represented by an abstract idea is determined by nothing but that idea (in particular, it is

---

[10] Ashworth quotes two passages that express this sort of view of confused ideas in the context of issues in semantic theory: Ashworth 1981a: 318.

[11] The passage goes on to say that in order to be clear and distinct, an idea must 'contain within itself nothing but what is clear'. Apparently this means that whereas a clear and confused idea contains elements that are not clearly articulated (although the combination of elements is easily identified), a clear and distinct idea has no elements that are not individually clear. However, there are difficulties about the interpretation of the difference between clear and distinct ideas, which we do not need to discuss here.

[12] For another account of confused ideas by 17th-cent. essentialist philosophers, see Arnauld and Nicole 1965: I.viii.

not determined by an objective, mind-independent essence). The idea-theoretic argument for this doctrine depends on Locke's view of what an abstract idea is. The basis on which an idea represents certain things, rather than others, is that the idea has a content defined by what is immediately perceived and intuitively known, and the idea represents exactly those things that conform to its content. So, as Locke sometimes says, it is *impossible* to have an idea that represents a kind whose boundary consists of something other than conformity to the known content of the idea. A referentialist theory of the signification of kind terms is precluded by the way Lockean ideas function.

As I mentioned at the outset, commentators often say that Locke's anti-essentialist doctrine of nominal essence is based on his denial of the metaphysical claim that there *are* objective essences. I have urged that the text offers an idea-theoretic argument for the doctrine of nominal essence. I want now briefly to bring out that Locke is free to use that argument whatever he may think on the metaphysical question. The issue of essentialist metaphysics is irrelevant to the idea-theoretic argument.

As we saw, Locke sometimes argues that we are ignorant of real essences and thus have no ideas of kinds determined by them. This point clearly is unaffected by the issue of the existence of objective essences. We are ignorant of them, whether or not there are such things. But as I interpret the idea-theoretic argument, its key premiss is not that we are ignorant of objective essences. The key premiss is that conformity to the immediately known content of an abstract idea is the basis on which the idea represents the kind it does. Abstract ideas would function in this way, even if it should turn out that there are objective essences *and* we came to know them. In that case, we should have abstract ideas that express idea-independent essences and those ideas would represent kinds that exactly coincide with naturally determined kinds. But the ideas would not cede their authority to determine the boundaries of the kinds the ideas represent. To be sure, many of the provocative consequences of Locke's doctrine of nominal essence depend on the point that our ideas do not express objective essences (we are ignorant of them). What I want to stress is that without making any assumption about Locke's stand on the existence of objective essences, we can trace the anti-essentialist doctrine of nominal essence to his theory of ideas.[13]

[13] I want to thank my commentator, Don Garrett, whose presentation was very helpful to me in making some revisions in my original paper. For supporting my work on this paper, I want to express my appreciation to the Institute for Advanced Study and a gift to the Institute from Mr. and Mrs. J. Richardson Dilworth.

XII

LOCKE: 'OUR KNOWLEDGE, WHICH ALL CONSISTS IN PROPOSITIONS'

RUTH MATTERN

LOCKE often writes that our knowledge is the perception of the agreement or disagreement of ideas. For example, he refers to 'our Knowledge consisting in the perception of the Agreement, or Disagreement of any two Ideas' in the second chapter of the *Essay's* book on knowledge (E IV.ii.15: 538). Similarly, at the beginning of this book he characterizes knowledge as 'the perception of the connexion and agreement, or disagreement and repugnancy of any of our Ideas' (E IV.i.2: 525). Since commentators remark on this formula so frequently, one would expect that major questions about its interpretation would have been settled long ago. But not so. Controversy still prevails about Locke's intent, and especially about his assumption that the knowledge of the existence of real things counts as an instance of the perception of the agreement or disagreement of ideas (E IV.i.3,7: 525, 527).

Scholars have put forward two sorts of problems about the attempted assimilation of knowledge of real existence in Locke's formula. One objection alleges that no conceivable knowledge of real existence could fall within the scope of this characterization of knowledge, because there is a *logical* conflict between the requirements for being a case of knowledge of real existence and those requisite for being an instance of the formula. In particular, how can knowledge of the existence of some real being count as perception of the agreement or disagreement of *ideas*? The other type of objection is that *some* sorts of knowledge of real existence as we humans have such knowledge cannot be subsumed under the formula. Knowledge of physical objects through sensation is particularly susceptible, in the eyes of many interpreters, to the charge of falling outside the scope of the description of knowledge as the 'perception of the agreement or disagreement of ideas'.

From *Canadian Journal of Philosophy*, 8: 4 (1978), 677–95.

The first sort of problem, the apparent logical conflict that excludes all possible knowledge of real existence from the scope of the formula, is my concern in this essay. In section 1, I cite some formulations of this objection, and show that it survives Yolton's attempt to explain away the problem as a simple misreading of the phrase 'the agreement or disagreement of ideas'. Then I turn to another attempt to assimilate knowledge of real existence to Locke's stated conception of knowledge, an attempt which interprets the problematic reference to the agreement or disagreement of ideas as deriving from his account of knowledge as propositional in nature. This rendition of Locke's formula has been unjustifiably neglected, I think; so far as I know, it has not been discussed in the last forty years by any commentaries in English. I cite additional evidence which adds to the credibility of this approach, but then I indicate that an attempt to fill in the details of the interpretation of the 'agreement or disagreement of ideas' on the basis of Locke's account of true propositions may raise again the initial difficulty, for it still seems to leave knowledge of real existence outside the scope of the formula. In section 2, I try to defend the interpretation against this possible difficulty by further analysis of Locke's use of the phrase 'agreement or disagreement'. The net result is that Locke is guilty only of unclear formulation of his views, not of logical contradiction or extreme incoherence.

1. PROPOSALS AND PROBLEMS

The main ground for the accusation of logical conflict in Locke's treatment of knowledge of real existence is that in this sort of knowledge the object of cognition is some entity distinct from ideas, or the agreement of an idea with such an entity; the object is not the agreement or disagreement of *ideas* with each other. T.H. Green, for example, wrote that in including real existence as a type of agreement, Locke

departs at once and openly from his definition, making it an agreement, not of idea with idea, but of an idea with 'actual real existence'. (Green 1874–5: I 20)

Gibson characterizes the 'logical contradiction' as follows:

The recognition of a knowledge of real existence stands in formal contradiction to his general definition of knowledge. . . . However much we may insist upon the objective character of Locke's ideas, the existential judgment which declares that the content of my idea characterizes something actually existing, cannot be represented as merely setting forth a connection of ideas. . . .
It is . . . clear that he never fully realised the difficulty of bringing a knowledge of real existence into line with his general conception of knowledge. Even the formal

contradiction, between the admission of a knowledge which transcends ideas and a definition which restricts knowledge to a perception of agreements or disagreements among ideas, receives no recognition.... (Gibson 1917: 166–7, 176)

Others have made a similar objection to Locke.[1]

Yolton's Interpretation

John Yolton argues that even the appearance of a logical conflict concerning knowledge of real existence rests on a misreading of the phrase 'the agreement or disagreement of ideas'. Locke is saying that an idea has a relation of agreement or disagreement with something else, but according to Yolton he is not saying that knowledge is always the perception of the agreement or disagreement of ideas *with each other*. So by this interpretation, Locke's characterization of knowledge can include the case in which an idea agrees with a real existent (Yolton 1970a: 110–11).

This interpretation, however, is rendered implausible by the fact that Locke's recapitulations of the 'perception of agreement or disagreement of ideas' formula do refer to the agreement or disagreement between two ideas. Yolton himself, and his critic A. D. Woozley (Woozley 1972: 13), acknowledge some of these passages; for example, in the *Conduct of the Understanding* Locke states that real knowledge consists 'in the perception of the habitudes and respects our ideas have one to another' (W III: 236). Woozley also quotes *Essay* E iv.ii.15: 538): 'our knowledge consisting in the perception of the agreement or disagreement of any two ideas ...' Additional passages not cited by these authors make Yolton's interpretation even more suspect. In Book II of the *Essay*, Locke distinguishes three sorts of perception and describes one type that is obviously what he refers to as 'knowledge' in Book IV: 'The Perception of the Connexion or

---

[1] For example, J. L. Mackie (Mackie 1976: 4) writes that Locke's 'definition of knowledge ... is hard to reconcile with the reality of discoveries about the physical world'. J. D. Mabbott (Mabbott 1973: 90) writes that there is a 'logical difficulty' which 'comes out when [Locke] says that this belief [in the existence of real objects] concerns the agreement of two ideas (and not the relation between an idea and a real world).' This statement expresses concern about the apparent logical conflict between saying that knowledge of real existence involves the agreement between ideas and that it involves agreement between ideas and the world; elsewhere on this page, however, Mabbott appears concerned with a different problem, that of *justifying* knowledge of real existence. D. J. O'Connor. (O'Connor 1952: 163) states that knowledge of real existence is quite different from the other three sorts of knowledge, since 'a statement affirming that something exists does not assert a relation or the lack of a relation between two ideas'. Richard Aaron (Aaron 1971: 238) also expresses concern with the problem of conflict between saying that knowledge is perception of the agreement or disagreement of ideas, and saying that 'we can know that things (which are neither ideas nor relations between ideas) exist''. Like some of the other commentators, Aaron tends not to distinguish sharply between this logical problem about the *nature* of knowledge and the problem of *justifying* claims about real existence.

Repugnancy, Agreement or Disagreement, that there is *between any of our Ideas*' (E II.xxi.5: 236: emphasis added). Another striking piece of evidence is found in the 'Abstract of the Essay', a summary of the *Essay* published by Locke a couple of years before the first edition appeared. Here Locke writes of Book IV, chapter i: 'The first chapter shows that knowledge is nothing but the perception of the agreement or disagreement of *any two ideas*' (King 1830: II. 275; emphasis added).

This evidence shows that we must read Locke's characterization of knowledge as a statement about the relation of ideas to each other. Woozley draws this conclusion, too; but his own account is disappointing in its failure to carry through the search for an alternative solution to the problem of logical conflict. He never provides an answer to his own question whether Locke had any good reason for treating knowledge of real existence 'as a perception of a relation *between ideas*' (Woozley 1972: 15).

The Propositional Interpretation

At least two commentators have tried to explain why Locke refers to the agreement or disagreement *between ideas* while applying his characterization of knowledge to the cognition of things existing outside the mind. A 1935 dissertation by Albert Hofstadter and a recent German commentary by Lorenz Krüger advance the view that the reference to ideas in Locke's formula derives from his belief that ideas are the components of *propositions*. Hofstadter writes that knowledge is 'the perception of the truth of the proposition' (Hofstadter 1935: 61). Krüger states that since knowledge is knowledge of truth, and truth is a feature of propositions, Locke makes propositions the object of knowledge; and propositions consist of connected ideas (Krüger 1973: 146–7).

This propositional interpretation appears to obviate the need for supposing that Locke contradicted himself when he labelled knowledge of real existence an instance of 'the perception of the agreement or disagreement of ideas'. One could, at least, dismiss the version of the objection assuming that perception of the agreement or disagreement between ideas cannot also be cognition of states of affairs distinct from ideas. O'Connor, for example, criticizes Locke because 'a statement affirming that something exists does not assert a relation or the lack of a relation between two ideas' (O'Connor 1952: 163). But if the 'perception of agreement or disagreement of ideas' formula affirms the propositional nature of knowledge, it need not commit Locke to the claim that all knowledge is merely about ideas. To say that knowledge is propositional leaves quite open the question of the contents of the propositions.

Locke does express elsewhere a belief in the propositional nature of knowledge. He writes in his correspondence with Stillingfleet that 'Every thing which we either know or believe, is some proposition' (W IV: 357) and he refers in Book II of the *Essay* to 'our Knowledge, which all consists in Propositions' (E II.xxxiii.19: 401; Hofstadter 1935: 53 also cites this passage). Also, this approach to Locke's characterization of knowledge is made more attractive by the fact that in a later work, the *Elements of Natural Philosophy*, he writes that knowledge 'consists in the perception of the truth of affirmative or negative propositions' (W III: 329).

Locke acknowledges the application of this propositional conception of knowledge to knowledge of real existence; one piece of evidence for this is the continuation of the passage cited earlier from the correspondence with Stillingfleet:

Every thing which we either know or believe, is some proposition: now no proposition can be framed as the object of our knowledge or assent, wherein two ideas are not joined to, or separated from one another. As for example, when I affirm that 'something exists in the world, whereof I have no idea', existence is affirmed of something, some being. . . . (W IV: 357)

There is much merit, then, in the attempt to interpret Locke's famous characterization of knowledge as the 'perception of the agreement or disagreement of ideas' in light of his less famous statements about knowledge as propositional.

A Problem

What has been said so far shows that it is desirable to interpret 'the perception of the agreement or disagreement of ideas' as equivalent to the statement in the *Elements of Natural Philosophy* that knowledge 'consists in the perception of the truth of affirmative or negative propositions' (W III: 329). This interpretation will succeed if we can equate 'the agreement or disagreement of ideas' with 'the truth of affirmative or negative propositions'. To show that this can be done, we need to determine the function of the terms 'agreement' and 'disagreement' in Locke's formula. Does Locke think that 'agreement' expresses that relation between two ideas in a proposition which makes the proposition affirmative, and that 'disagreement' expresses that relation which makes the proposition negative? In that case, the phrase 'perception of agreement or disagreement of ideas' would leave out the crucial requirement that the *truth* of the propositions be perceived; the two formulae would not be equivalent.

What motivates Locke's conception of knowledge as propositional is his belief that knowledge implies truth, and that truth is a feature of propositions; as he writes in *Essay*, Book III, knowledge 'being conversant about Truth, had constantly to do with Propositions' (E III.ix.21: 488). He states that truth implies propositions in passages like the following:

Truth, or Falshood, being never without some Affirmation, or Negation, Express, or Tacit, it is not to be found, but where signs are joined or separated, according to the agreement, or disagreement, of the Things they stand for. (E II.xxxii.19: 391)

As this passage suggests, Locke's notion of truth may lead to a second hypothesis about the function of the terms 'agreement' and 'disagreement'. For it seems that 'agree' and 'disagree' designate relations of the things in the state of affairs that renders a proposition true.

Both Hofstadter (Hofstadter 1935: 60) and Krüger (Krüger 1973: 143–4)[2] assume that when Locke characterized knowledge as the perception of the agreement or disagreement of ideas, he was thinking of *mental* propositions, those 'wherein the Ideas in our Understandings are without the use of Words put together' (E IV.v.5: 575). Locke defines *truth* for such propositions in the following way:

When Ideas are so put together, or separated in the Mind, as they, or the Things they stand for do agree, or not, that is, as I may call it, mental Truth. (E IV.v.6: 576)

In an earlier chapter of his book, Krüger claims that Locke really has two models of truth here (Krüger 1973: ch. 12). One is a 'correspondence' model: 'when Ideas are so put together, or separated, . . . as the *Things they stand for* do agree, or not . . .' The other is an 'idea-theoretic' model of truth: 'When Ideas are so put together, or separated in the Mind, as *they* . . . do agree, or not . . .' Fortunately, it is not necessary for our purposes to decide whether idea-theoretic truth is completely distinct from the correspondence model, or whether it is a special case of this model as is suggested by Locke's assertions that all truth involves correspondence:

Truth, or Falshood . . . is not to be found, but where signs are joined or separated, according to the agreement, or disagreement, of the Things they stand for. (E II.xxxii.19: 391)

---

[2] Though it is true that the concept of propositions relevant here is the concept of affirmations and negations composed of *ideas*, these propositions need not be 'mental propositions' in Locke's technical sense of propositions without words altogether. He remarks 'that there is so close a connexion between Ideas and Words . . . that it is impossible to speak clearly and distinctly of our Knowledge, which all consists in Propositions, without considering, first, the Nature, Use, and Signification of Language' (E II.xxxiii.19: 401; also see E III.ix.21: 488–9 and E IV.vi.3: 579–80). However, one should not construct an interpretation of Locke's characterization of knowledge which *requires* that known propositions have attached verbal propositions, since knowledge does not necessarily involve words at all. Locke sometimes even recommends considering ideas without words: 'the examining and judging of Ideas by themselves, their Names being quite laid aside, [is] the best and surest way to clear and distinct Knowledge . . . (E IV.vi.1: 579).

Truth . . . seems to me, in the proper import of the Word, to signify nothing but the joining or separating of Signs, as the Things signified by them, do agree or disagree with one another. The joining or separating of signs here meant is what by another name, we call Proposition. (E IV.v.2: 574)

In these statements, the references to 'joined' and 'separated' signs indicate the relations between signs that make propositions affirmative and negative. Locke writes that the mind forms mental propositions when it puts ideas

into a kind of Proposition affirmative or negative, which I have endeavoured to express by the terms Putting together and Separating. But this Action of the Mind, which is so familiar to every thinking and reasoning Man, is easier to be conceived by reflecting on what passes in us, when we affirm or deny. . . . (E IV.v.6: 576)

Here, it is reasonable to suppose, Locke follows Arnauld in the Port-Royal *Logic*; Arnauld states that we form propositions when we take ideas and

unite or separate them. This is called *affirming* or *denying*, and in general *judging*. (Arnauld and Nicole 1996: 82)

By Locke's account of truth, then, *agreement* between two things renders true an affirmative mental proposition (a proposition consisting of two 'joined' ideas); *disagreement* between two things renders true a negative mental proposition (consisting of two 'separated' ideas). In what Krüger terms the 'idea-theoretic' cases, such agreement or disagreement will hold between two *ideas*; for in these cases it is the agreement or disagreement of the ideas themselves with each other that renders true various propositions. Let us look more carefully now at the sorts of cases that fall into this category.

Locke's conceptualism leads him to interpret most general truths as claims about ideas.[3] For example, he treats the assertion that white is not black as a claim about the disagreement of two ideas, the idea of white and the idea of black (see e.g. E IV.i.2: 525). Propositions about the identity or diversity of two general qualities become, on Locke's conceptualist interpretation, assertions of the 'identity or diversity of ideas'. This sort of agreement or disagreement of ideas, he holds, is apprehended by the mind 'by Intuition, or the immediate comparing [of] any two Ideas' (E IV.iii.2: 539):

As to Identity and Diversity, in this way of the Agreement, or Disagreement of our Ideas, our intuitive Knowledge is as far extended as our Ideas themselves. . . . (E IV.iii.8: 543–4)

---

[3] Claims about co-existence are a partial exception to this generalization; I believe that he vacillates between treating these as general claims about ideas and as universally quantified claims about particulars, but a case for this interpretation would take me very far beyond the confines of this paper.

The mind is immediately aware, for example, of the state of affairs rendering true the proposition that white is not black.

Demonstrative knowledge of general truths does not have such immediacy, but Locke also interprets the truth of these propositions in terms of the agreement and disagreement of ideas. As his conceptualism would lead us to expect, he treats general claims about the relations of geometrical angles and figures as claims about relations of ideas. Geometrical demonstrations reveal to the mind these relations of ideas:

> when the Mind cannot so bring its Ideas together, as by their immediate Comparison . . . to perceive their Agreement or Disagreement, it is fain, by the Intervention of other Ideas . . . to discover the Agreement or Disagreement, which it searches; and this is that which we call *Reasoning*. Thus the Mind being willing to know the Agreement or Disagreement in bigness, between the three Angles of a Triangle, and two right ones, cannot by an immediate view and comparing them, do it. . . . In this Case the Mind is fain to find out some other Angles, to which the three Angles of a Triangle have an Equality; and finding those equal to two right ones, comes to know their Equality to two right ones. . . . (E iv.ii.2–3: 531–2)

In contexts where the idea-theoretic account of truth applies, Locke in effect treats agreement as a variable ranging over several sorts of relations between ideas. 'Agreement' can designate identity of concepts, or equality in some respect (for example, equality of size, as in the expression 'the Agreement or Disagreement in bigness, between the three Angles of a Triangle' (E iv.ii.2: 532)).[4] Here, of course, it is the contents of the ideas that is important; in Cartesian terminology, the agreement or disagreement holds between ideas taken *objectively* rather than formally. For what is at issue in Locke's discussion of the agreement or disagreement of geometrical ideas, for example, is not the size of the ideas themselves. It is not the ideas *qua* mental states that 'agree or disagree in bigness'; rather, it is ideas as representative, as bearers of content, that can be compared with respect to size.

This discussion gives some idea of Locke's usage of 'agreement or disagreement' for the case of idea-theoretic truth. Since truths of this type are for Locke propositions about ideas, they are rendered true by the agreements or disagreements of *ideas*. But as it has been explicated so far, the 'agreement or disagreement of ideas' is intelligible *only* in reference to these idea-theoretic cases, and so it is not clear how any knowledge except knowledge of such truths can be described as the 'perception of the agreement or disagreement of ideas'. We may pose the question, then, whether knowledge of real existence will not be left outside the scope of this description of knowledge even on this interpretation. Truths about the real

---

[4] The compatibility or incompatibility of concepts is another sort of agreement and disagreement relevant to idea-theoretic truth. See E iv.v.8: 577–8 and n. 6 below.

existence of things are not truths about ideas; Locke's general correspondence model of truth, rather than the idea-theoretic account, will apply
here. We can still understand 'agreement' or 'disagreement' for truths of
real existence as applying to the state of affairs rendering a mental proposition true; but this state of affairs will not be a relation *between ideas*. So
the concept of agreement and disagreement in Locke's account of truth
has not given us an interpretation that permits us to equate 'the perception
of the agreement or disagreement of ideas' with 'the perception of the
truth of affirmative or negative propositions'.

2. TRUE PROPOSITIONS AND THE AGREEMENT OR DISAGREEMENT OF IDEAS

So far we have not explained Locke's application of the phrase 'the agreement or disagreement of *ideas*' to knowledge of the existence of things
outside the mind. However, I hope to show that there are independent
grounds for positing a usage of this phrase other than the one discussed in
the last section, and that this other usage fills out the propositional interpretation of Locke's characterization of knowledge.

Some precedent for a broader usage of 'agreement or disagreement of
ideas' is found in Arnauld's logic textbook, a work which was famous in the
seventeenth century and which was found in Locke's library (Harrison
and Laslett 1965). Arnauld used the term 'convenir' when writing of the
way that ideas are related in all affirmations. There is plausibility in supposing the French term 'convenir' to express the same concept which was
expressed by the seventeenth-century English term 'agree'. For example,
when Pierre Coste translated the *Essay* into French during Locke's lifetime, he used the term 'convenance' where Locke had written of the
'agreement' of ideas in his characterization of knowledge (Locke 1700). So
it is appropriate that Arnauld's terms 'conviennent' and 'ne conviennent
pas' are translated 'agree' and 'do not agree' in one rendition of his
statement that propositions are formed when we take ideas

and, finding that *some agree* together, and that others *do not agree*, we unite or
separate them, which is called affirming or denying. . . . (Arnauld 1851: 111)[5]

This translation helps make clear the similarity between Arnauld's and
Locke's views of affirmation and denial. For Locke, in a passage quoted in
part earlier, describes affirmation and denial as follows:

---

[5] The French text is found in Arnauld and Nicole 1965. In Jill Buroker's translation (Arnauld
and Nicole 1996), 'conviennent' is translated 'belong together'.

The Mind, either by perceiving or supposing the Agreement or Disagreement of any of its Ideas, does tacitly within it self put them into a kind of Proposition affirmative or negative, which I have endeavoured to express by the terms Putting together and Separating. (E IV.v.6: 576)

Arnauld does not say that what makes two ideas agree or not must be intrinsic to the ideas themselves. He is talking about every sort of proposition in this section, contingent propositions such as 'Louis XIII took Rochelle' as well as necessary truths. So presumably Arnauld intends to say that our finding *agreement* between two ideas does not require that they are themselves related in any special way. Our discovery that Louis XIII did take Rochelle would count as our finding that the idea of Louis XIII agrees with the idea of taking Rochelle. Only by construing *agreement* between ideas in this broad way can one make sense of Arnauld's statement as a general account of affirmation and denial.

In this sense of *agreement*, to say that two ideas forming a proposition *agree* is in effect to say only that the proposition *is true*. That Locke also has such a concept of agreement is suggested by the similarity between his account and Arnauld's, but it is also confirmed by the *Essay's* description of merely probable judgement, i.e. the sort of judgement which involves assent without the certainty necessary to knowledge. In judgement without knowledge, he writes,

the Mind takes its Ideas to agree, or disagree; or which is the same, any Proposition to be true, or false, without perceiving a demonstrative evidence in the Proofs. ... (E IV.xiv.3: 653)

Similarly, in the 'Abstract of the Essay' Locke refers to judgement as that 'whereby the mind takes ideas to agree or not to agree, i.e. any proposition to be true or false, without perceiving a demonstrative evidence in the proofs' (King 1830: II. 289).

The usage of 'agreement or disagreement of ideas' in these passages is different from the usage of this expression discussed in the last section, where the phrase described the state of affairs rendering a mental proposition true. For if the two usages were the same, then it would be unintelligible why Locke implies here that the *disagreement* of ideas is equivalent to the *falsity* of a proposition. The disagreement of ideas in the sense discussed earlier can make a proposition turn, namely a negative proposition. So it is preferable to interpret Locke as employing a second usage of 'disagreement of ideas', one which is tantamout to saying that a proposition is false. Also, taking Locke at his word here when he equates the agreement or disagreement of ideas with the truth or falsity of propositions would explain why he describes all merely probable judgements in terms of this relation of ideas. Surely Locke intends probable judgements to include contingent judgements about real existence. It would be unintelligible how he could include such judgements within his description here unless he were using a sense of 'agreement or disagreement of ideas' different from the one discussed earlier, for we have already seen the difficulty in applying that sense to truths of real existence. But there is no problem in including judgements of real existence within the scope of a description of judgement as the mind's taking propositions as true or false without demonstrative proof.

The supposition that Locke has this second usage of 'agreement or disagreement of ideas' receives additional confirmation from the light it sheds on his account of the truth of verbal propositions. Locke distinguishes between mental propositions, which are made up of ideas, and verbal propositions, which are composed of words standing for ideas (E IV.v.5: 576). He defines the truth of verbal propositions in accord with his general definition of truth as 'the joining or separating of Signs, as the Things signified by them, do agree or disagree one with another' (E IV.v.2: 574). Since words signify ideas by Locke's account of meaning, this formula applies to verbal propositions as follows:

Truth of Words . . . is the affirming or denying of Words one of another, as the Ideas they stand for agree or disagree. (E IV.v.6: 576)

How will this formula apply to verbal proposition asserting the existence of external objects? Clearly the 'agreement or disagreement of ideas' in this context must be interpreted as applying only to true propositions. For a verbal proposition cannot be true simply by matching a proposition composed of ideas; it must represent correctly a *true* proposition. And the proposition it stands for will be true in accord with Locke's general rules for the truth of propositions composed of ideas; its truth may be 'idea-theoretic', internal to the ideas themselves, or it may result from correspondence with some state of affairs involving an external object. In the latter case, which is the one relevant to claims about real existence, 'the agreement or disagreement of ideas' will not designate the state which renders the mental proposition true; rather, it can only indicate that the proposition is true. So Locke's definition of truth of words will apply correctly to true verbal propositions about real existence if 'the agreement or disagreement of ideas' is used in the sense explicated in this section, but not in the sense discussed in the last section.[6]

---

[6] Locke does not discuss explicitly the case of verbal propositions asserting the existence of external things here; he alludes only to the truth of two other sorts of verbal propositions: (i) trifling verbal propositions, which have only what he terms 'verbal truth'; verbal truth, he writes

I have tried to give evidence here for a second sense of 'the agreement or disagreement of ideas', a broader sense that makes intelligible Arnauld's account of affirmation and denial, Locke's description of probable judgements, and the Lockean definition of truth of words as applied to assertions of real existence. Positing a second sense of the expression 'the agreement or disagreement of ideas' is a small price to pay for avoiding incoherence in these contexts, especially when Locke does say quite explicitly in his account of probable judgements what this other sense is: the truth or falsity of propositions.

Fortunately, this is precisely the sense of the expression 'the agreement or disagreement of ideas' that is necessary in order to carry out the propositional interpretation of Locke's characterization of knowledge sketched earlier in the paper. For this sense of the expression allows us to interpret the formula of *Essay* Book IV, 'the perception of the agreement or disagreement of ideas', as equivalent to the characterization of knowledge in the *Elements of Natural Philosophy*: 'the perception of the truth of affirmative or negative propositions'. To endorse this interpretation it is only necessary to make the plausible assumption that the perception of *the truth or falsehood of propositions* is equivalent to the perception of *the truth of affirmative or negative propositions*.

Locke's account of knowledge is parallel to his account of judgement; the difference is only that in knowledge the mind has certain perception of the agreement of disagreement of ideas, while in merely probable judgement the agreement or disagreement is not perceived but 'presumed' or 'supposed' (E IV.xiv.4: 653). Locke frequently speaks of the two sorts of cognition together, as when he characterizes affirmation and denial in general as arising when the mind 'either by perceiving or supposing the Agreement or Disagreement of any of its Ideas, does tacitly within itself

---

is that 'wherein Terms are joined according to the agreement or disagreement of the Ideas they stand for without regarding whether our Ideas are such, as really have, or are capable of having, an Existence in Nature' (E IV.v.8: 577–8). The 'agreement or disagreement of ideas' to which Locke refers here must be a sort of idea-theoretic truth, namely the compatibility or incompatibility of two ideas. Locke also refers here to (ii) one type of real truth, namely that which arises when 'these signs are joined, as our Ideas agree; and when our Ideas are such, as we know are capable of having an Existence in Nature' (E IV.v.8: 578). This comment immediately follows the other one and is plausibly assumed to employ the same sense of 'agreement or disagreement of ideas', namely that involving mere compatibility or incompatibility of ideas. Locke claims here that real truth implies this relation of ideas *plus* the possible existence of real things to which these ideas apply. Clearly he is talking here about the sort of real truth that pertains to mathematics and ethics, for he thinks that such truth requires only possible and not actual application. Truths asserting real existence cannot be subsumed under either category because such truth does require the actual existence of an external thing. My claim concerns the interpretation of 'agreement of disagreement of ideas' which Locke must assume in order that his account of verbal truth can apply correctly to such cases.

put them into a kind of Proposition affirmative or negative. . . .' (E iv.v.6: 576). So there is good reason for interpreting the 'agreement or disagreement of ideas' as it relates to knowledge in light of Locke's usage of this phrase in his account of merely probable judgement, where he equates it with 'the truth or falsity of propositions'.

At this point it will be helpful to return to Chapter i of *Essay* Book iv, since the text here presents a problem for any interpretation that cannot be ignored. After his opening characterization of knowledge in terms of the agreement or disagreement of ideas, Locke goes on to explain 'wherein this agreement or disagreement consists' (E iv.i.2: 525); he gives a list of four sorts of agreement or disagreement, one of which is 'real existence'. However, in his expanded discussion of this fourth type of agreement and disagreement, he talks not about the agreement between ideas but about the agreement of ideas with real existence (E iv.i.7: 527). Granting that Locke's initial reference to agreement or disagreement designates a relation *between* ideas, as was shown above in the discussion of Yolton's interpretation, Locke's move from one type of agreement or disagreement to the other seems peculiar. In particular, it is odd that he gives the four sorts of agreement or disagreement as an answer to the question 'wherein this agreement or disagreement *consists*', since this refers back to his initial characterization of knowledge and suggests an impossible identity of the agreement or disagreement between ideas and the four sorts of agreement or disagreement. On the view that Locke's characterization of knowledge contradicts his application of it to knowledge of real existence, this transition is symptomatic of that underlying conflict. The identification of the two types of agreement and disagreement is, on that account, only a thinly disguised attempt to stretch a characterization of knowledge beyond its initially stated bounds.

However, this transition is subject to a more charitable interpretation. Though Locke's term 'consists' *suggests* identity, he sometimes uses the term with other connotations. For example, Locke is referring to the causal *basis* of qualities when he writes in Book ii of the *Essay* that 'we are no more able to discover, wherein the Ideas belonging to Body *consist*, than those belonging to Spirit' (E ii.xxiii.29: 312). Locke does not have in mind a *causal* basis in his discussion in Book iv, but he may plausibly be read as concerned with a basis of another sort, namely with the basis of the truth of propositions. By the interpretation of Locke's characterization of knowledge defended in this paper, at least one of the things he has in mind when he writes of the agreement or disagreement between ideas is simply the relation between ideas which obtains when propositions are true or false; it is by virtue of this broad usage of 'agreement or disagreement of ideas' that his characterization of knowledge is applicable to knowledge of real existence. I believe that his transition to a discussion of the four types of agreement and disagreement is a move to enumerate the types of propositions there are in terms of the various subject matters of propositions. This, in effect, is an enumeration of the types of states of affairs that render propositions true and false; it is a discussion of what Locke later in the chapter terms the 'grounds of Affirmation and Negation' (E iv.i.7: 527).

It is understandable, I think, why Locke does not separate more sharply his discussion of the agreement and disagreement within propositions, and the agreement and disagreement that render propositions true. Though he counts knowledge of real existence as a type of knowledge, knowledge of idea-theoretic truths is probably for him the paradigm case of knowledge, the preferred sort of example that is at the centre of his attention.[7] This would make it natural for him to pass from one sort of agreement or disagreement to the other without calling attention to the difference, and to use the vague term 'consists' which can designate the nature of something in two senses: what it is, and what its basis is. In the case of idea-theoretic truth, the two sorts of agreement coincide; the relation *between* ideas is both the state rendering the proposition true and the state of the proposition expressing this truth. So though Locke may be accused of unclarity, he need not be convicted of logical contradiction; and even his unclarity may be understood if not forgiven.

CONCLUSION

I have argued here for the plausibility of interpreting Locke's reference to the 'perception of the agreement or disagreement of ideas' in terms of his characterization of knowledge as the 'perception of the truth of affirmative or negative propositions'. Since the term 'perception' occurred in both formulae, my discussion focused not on the explication of this term but on the task of showing the equivalence of 'the truth of affirmative or negative propositions' and one Lockean usage of 'the agreement or disagreement of ideas'. This equivalence makes intelligible the reference to the agreement or disagreement of ideas in a characterization of knowledge that applies even to knowledge of real existence; it removes the apparent logical conflict engendered by his reference to ideas in that formula.

---

[7] For example, one may note the fact that both of the examples of knowledge that Locke gives at E iv.i.2: 525 are cases of idea-theoretic knowledge, for he mentions here only knowledge of the identity and diversity of ideas and mathematical knowledge.

However, the term 'perception' in Locke's formula is significant too, for according to him the distinction between knowledge and mere probable judgement is marked by the boundary between *perception* and *supposition* of the agreement or disagreement of ideas. Commentators rather frequently remark that cognition of real existence cannot, even on his own terms, have the *certainty* that distinguishes this perception from mere supposition; no cognition of the existence of something real is sufficiently justified to count as knowledge (see e.g. Mackie 1976: 4; Aaron 1971: 238). They sometimes cite Locke's own weakly stated contention that knowledge through sensation merely 'passes under the name of knowledge' (E IV.ii.14: 537) as his acknowledgement of the borderline status of knowledge of real existence (e.g. Woozley 1972: 15) However, even if Locke is not sure whether all cognition of objects through sensation is sufficiently certain to count as knowledge,[8] he never questions the certainty of two other sorts of knowledge of real existence: intuitive knowledge of the existence of the self, and demonstrative knowledge of the existence of God. These are types of knowledge which he thinks of as more certain than sensitive knowledge; this factor may have influenced his use of the example 'God is' to illustrate knowledge of real existence in his opening chapter on knowledge (E IV.i.7: 527). Whether or not one has sympathy for Locke's confidence in these types of knowledge of real existence, the possibility of at least one sort of certain cognition of existing objects shows that there is not a logical obstacle barring subsumption of all knowledge of real existence under his formula. The problem of certainty does not necessarily infect all conceivable sorts of knowledge of real existence, but is rather a difficulty of the second sort mentioned at the beginning of the paper: a possible problem with the attempt to show that *all* knowledge of real existence falls within the scope of Locke's formula.

The question what certainty is for Locke and how far it extends is, then, an issue that remains for further investigation. It is a question that would need to be answered to give a full account of the concept of perception that is relevant to 'the perception of the agreement or disagreement of ideas'. But this concept of perception is so closely related to his concept of knowledge that one must question the common assumption that the formula 'the perception of the agreement or disagreement of ideas' gives a *definition* of knowledge. Rather than construing the formula as a definition

---

[8] I believe that Locke may not intend to call into question all sensitive knowledge of physical objects in passages like E IV.ii.14: 537–38; but the complex question of the epistemic status of sensitive knowledge in Locke raises many issues outside the bounds of this paper.

that is circular, it may be more fruitful to look on it as a generalization about knowledge that already presupposes a distinction between knowledge and belief; it is a statement about the sort of object that knowledge has, namely true propositions.[9]

[9] For helpful comments on previous versions of this paper I am grateful to Harvey Lape, Lorenz Krüger, Martha Bolton, Margaret Wilson, Fabrizio Mondadori, and John Immerwahr.

XIII

LOCKEAN MECHANISM

EDWIN McCANN

LOCKE subscribed to the Mechanical Philosophy, in Gassendi's and Boyle's version of it. On this view, all of the powers and qualities of bodies, and all the changes in these powers and qualities which result from the actions of these bodies one upon the other, issue entirely from the 'two grand principles of bodies, matter and motion' (Boyle 1979: 20). The main points of the view, more particularly, were these: (a) all bodies are made up of matter, and only of matter; (b) the essence of matter consists in the qualities of extension and solidity; (c) bodies large enough to be perceived are compounded out of physically indivisible bits of matter too small to be perceived (the so-called *minima naturalia*) and have no other constituents (in particular, no immaterial constituents); (d) in consequence of being extended and finite, each body has a determinate bulk or size and figure; and finally, (e) any change in the qualities of a body is the result of the alteration of the bulk, figure, relative situation and/or motion of the solid parts of the body, the latter alteration being due to the action upon that body, perhaps through a material medium, of the mechanical affections of the solid parts of some other body or bodies.[1] A very strong case can be

From A. J. Holland (ed.), *Philosophy, Its History and Historiography* (Dordrecht: Reidel, 1985), 209–31. As originally published, this paper included an Appendix entitled 'Was Boyle an Occasionalist?', which is here omitted. [Editor's note]

[1] Boyle gives a nice summary statement of this view in a passage in the *Origin of Forms and Qualities* (1666) where he is stating his aims in that work: 'That, then, which I chiefly aim at is to make it probable to you by experiments (which I think hath not yet been done) that almost all sorts of qualities, most of which have been by the Schools either left unexplicated, or generally referred to I know not what incomprehensible substantial forms, *may* be produced mechanically—I mean by such corporeal agents as do not appear either to work otherwise than by virtue of the motion, size, figure, and contrivance of their own parts (which attributes I call the mechanical affections of matter, because to them men willingly refer the various operations of mechanical engines); or to produce the new qualities, exhibited by those bodies their action changes, by any other way than by changing the *texture*, or *motion*, or some other *mechanical affection*, of the body wrought upon' (Boyle 1979: 17). Notice that these characterizations of mechanism are at variance with that given by Michael Ayers in Ayers 1981*b*. He says that

made for the ascription of these doctrines to Locke; I will not go into this here as Locke's commitment to mechanism is so widely acknowledged. Nevertheless, I will quote at the outset a sentence (the last sentence, in fact) from Locke's late, posthumously published, *Elements of Natural Philosophy*; it is a nice succinct statement of the view:

By the figure, bulk, texture, and motion of these small and insensible corpuscles, all the phenomena of bodies may be explained. (W III: 33)[2]

This is the view I will call 'mechanism'.

Margaret Wilson has recently argued that Locke is not a consistent mechanist; she maintains that other doctrines of his conflict with his Boylean 'official position', on which the qualities and powers of a body 'flow from' the real essence of that body (Wilson 1979). She instances his view that matter might have the power of thought superadded directly to it by God; his insistence that we cannot conceive there to be any connection between the primary qualities of (the constituent solid parts of) bodies and the sensations they cause in us, and hence between those primary qualities and the sensible secondary qualities of bodies; his pessimism about the prospects for an adequate account of the cohesion of bodies; and his concession that gravity cannot be understood as a mechanical phenomenon, that is, that gravitational attraction does not seem to involve the transfer of motion through impulse.

In this paper I will argue that Locke is in fact a consistent mechanist. He does hold all of the doctrines Wilson mentions, but these doctrines are not inconsistent with mechanism of the sort set out in the quote above, when this is properly understood.

1.

I want first of all to identify more precisely the obstacle to a straightforward reading of Locke as a mechanist. This is important, as there are a number of issues here that can get tangled up together.

mechanism 'was the view that the laws of physics can be explained, in principle if not by us, by being deduced from the attributes possessed essentially by all bodies *qua* bodies; i.e., from the nature or essence of the uniform substance, matter, of which all bodies are composed' (Ayers 1981*b*: 210). In the first place, as Ayers himself recognizes, mechanists make use of motion in their explanations, but motion is not part of the essence or nature of matter. In the second place, neither Gassendi nor Boyle (nor Locke) speaks of deriving or deducing the laws of physics; instead, for them the goal of mechanism is to resolve particular phenomena in mechanistic terms.

[2] Note that in this work explicit notice has been taken of Newton's account of gravity.

We should note first that the lacunae in the mechanist account of the world to which Wilson draws our attention are of quite different sorts. Locke's worry about cohesion, for example, is simply that there are objections to all the extant proposals for a mechanical resolution of the phenomenon; he does not suggest that cohesion is inherently non-mechanical, or that it cannot be explained mechanistically, but only that we do not now know how to do so. In this case, as well as in the more problematic case of gravity, Locke does not cite any particular reasons for thinking the phenomenon to be insusceptible of mechanical explanation.[3] In the case of the possibility that certain systems of matter may have the power of thought, the situation is different. Thought and matter as we conceive them are of such different natures that we cannot see how they could possibly be

---

[3] On cohesion, see E II.xxiii.23–7: 308–11. Interestingly, these remarks on the problematic character of cohesion are located in the chapter on solidity in the 1685 draft of the *Essay* known as Draft C, which is in the Pierpont Morgan Library in New York. Locke does not mention the problem of gravity in the *Essay*; the passages cited by Wilson and Ayers are these, from *Some Thoughts concerning Education* (1693) and from the third of his replies to Stillingfleet (1699):

... it is evident, that by mere matter and motion, none of the great phaenomena of nature can be resolved: to instance but in that common one of gravity, which I think impossible to be explained by any natural operation of matter, or any other law of motion, but the positive will of a superiour Being so ordering it. (W IX: 184)

(Note by the way Locke's denial here that it is by any 'natural operation' of matter that it attracts other matter.)

'Tis true, I say, 'That Bodies operate by impulse, and nothing else'. [E II.viii.11, which Locke altered in the fourth edition to accord with the concession in this passage] And so I thought when I writ it and yet can conceive no other way of their operation. But I am since convinced by the Judicious Mr. Newton's incomparable Book, that it is too bold a Presumption to limit God's Power, in this point, by my narrow Conceptions. The gravitation of Matter towards Matter, by ways inconceivable to me, is not only a Demonstration that God can, if he pleases, put into Bodies, Powers and ways of Operation, above what can be derived from our Idea of Body, or can be explained by what we know of Matter, but also an unquestionable and every where visible Instance, that he has done so. (W IV: 467–8)

A couple of pages earlier on in the *Answer to Second Letter* (W IV: 464–5) Locke had pointed out that to explain gravity in terms of self-motion in matter, or as action at a distance, involves us in difficulties, as we cannot conceive matter to be able to move itself, nor can we conceive action at a distance. He nowhere criticizes attempts to explain gravity mechanistically, as for example Boyle's invocation of an aether composed of 'peculiar sorts of corpuscles' (see Boyle 1772: III. 309, 316), nor could he have taken from Newton the suggestion that gravity is definitely a non-mechanical phenomenon. Newton certainly did not claim in his incomparable book (*Principia*, 1st edition) that it is, but only that we are not in a position to decide among various mechanical and non-mechanical hypotheses as to the physical basis of gravitational attraction, i.e. as to what feature or features of bodies makes them able to influence each other's motion without apparent contact between them. So in the Stillingfleet passage Locke must be speaking about what we are now in a position to derive from our idea of body or what we know of matter, and, in the *Education* one, about what we are now in a position to explain. Note that the *Education* passage, with its reference to 'the positive will of a superiour being so ordering it' as an *explanation* of gravity, gives encouragement to the reading of E IV.iii.29 that I have proposed.

connected; we might put this by saying that thought, sensation, the power of moving the parts of one's body by willing, etc. seem to us to be inherently non-mechanical phenomena. This deep explanatory gap extends to the connections between the primary qualities of bodies and their secondary ones, in view of the fact that these connections depend on the connections between the primary qualities of bodies and the sensations these bodies cause in us. This last problem is especially troubling since, as Locke notes in the chapter on our ideas of substances, most of the powers and qualities we recognize in bodies are secondary qualities, or else powers defined in relation to the sensations they produce in us (see E ii.xxiii.8, 9, 10, 37: 300, 300–1, 301, 316–17).[4]

Although the recalcitrant phenomena resist mechanistic explanations for different reasons, Locke puts them in one basket in the following passage:

> But the coherence and continuity of the parts of Matter; the production of Sensation in us of Colours and Sounds, *etc.* by impulse and motion; nay, the original Rules and Communication of Motion being such wherein we can discover no natural connexion with any Ideas we have, we cannot but ascribe them to the arbitrary Will and good Pleasure of the Wise Architect. (E iv.iii.29: 559–60)[5]

The problem, at bottom, for those who wish to read Locke as a consistent mechanist lies in the ascription of the recalcitrant phenomena to God's arbitrary will and good pleasure. Bodies would have the powers and qualities in question not simply in virtue of their mechanical constitutions (what Locke calls their real essences), but instead they would have these

---

[4] That it is the difference in nature between thought or sensation and matter that makes for the problem of conceiving primary/secondary quality relations is made plain in a number of passages:

> These mechanical affections of Bodies, having no affinity at all with those *Ideas*, they produce in us, (there being no conceivable connexion between any impulse of any sort of Body, and any perception of a Colour, or Smell, which we find in our Minds) we can have no distinct knowledge of such Operations beyond our Experience; and can reason no otherwise about them, than as effects produced by the appointment of an infinitely Wise Agent, which perfectly surpass our Comprehensions. As the *Ideas* of sensible secondary Qualities, which we have in our Minds, can, by us, be no way deduced from bodily Causes, nor any correspondence or connexion be found between them and those primary Qualities which (Experience shews us) produce them in us; so on the other side, the Operation of our Minds upon our Bodies is as unconceivable. How any thought should produce a motion in Body is as remote from the nature of our *Ideas*, as how any Body should produce any Thought in the Mind. (E iv.iii.28: 558–9; see also E iv.iii.6, 12–13, 29: 539–43, 545, 559–60)

[5] Locke's inclusion of 'the original Rules and Communication of Motion' among the problematic phenomena is not remarked by Wilson. Locke might be thinking of the difficulty we have of conceiving how motion is transferred by impulse, a difficulty noted at E ii.xxiii.28: 311; but the word 'original' suggests that the problem he has in mind has instead to do with God's institution of laws of motion and his originally setting some bodies in motion. We are in the dark concerning exactly what he did in this regard, as well as about how he did it.

powers and qualities in virtue of God's arbitrary action. Thus, Margaret Wilson, discussing the problem of primary/secondary quality connections, writes:

> ... at first thought it might seem that Locke could consistently hold that a body's powers to produce ideas flow naturally from its real essence, while also maintaining that the ideas themselves are arbitrarily annexed to whatever motions of matter habitually cause them. But of course this is not really the case. For it follows from Locke's account that a body has its powers to produce ideas only *because of* the divine acts of annexation. Therefore, ... we find conflict with the official position that there is in reality an *a priori* conceptual connection between a body's real essence and its secondary qualities. (Wilson 1979: 147; see also Wilson 1982: 251)

We have to be careful how we take Wilson's claim. She might seem to be attributing a sort of occasionalism to Locke, in light of the emphasis on God's action and the consequent arbitrariness of the annexation.[6] Wilson does not suggest, however, that Locke thinks that bodies or their powers and qualities have no causal efficacy; indeed, she suggests that Locke's view is that these powers and qualities do produce the effects in question, but are able to do so only by virtue of God's having ordained the requisite general laws connecting the primary qualities of bodies with these effects. But this means that there are no suitable explanatory connections between the mechanical affections of a body and its secondary qualities.

The connections that are lacking, on this reading, are connections in *rerum natura*, and not merely connections perceived or apprehended by us. It would be a short way with the problem to read the passages we have been discussing as having only an epistemological import. Then, Locke is saying only that we do not know the explanatory connections that are in fact there, connections apprehended by God and the angels. Ayers takes this approach, drawing attention for example to the fact that in the passage I have quoted from E IV.iii.29 Locke talks of the ideas *we* have, wherein *we*

---

[6] Ayers (Ayers 1981*b*: 219) takes Wilson to be urging, on the basis of passages such as E IV.iii.28, that Locke was inclined to favour Malebranchean occasionalism, an imputation Wilson rejects (Wilson 1982: 249). There is a widespread misapprehension about the status of laws of nature according to occasionalism, so although Wilson and Ayers are free of it, it will still be worthwhile to point out here that Malebranchean occasionalism does not deny that there are laws of nature governing phenomena. On the contrary, Malebranche insists as much as anyone ever did that there are such laws, understanding them to be the general intentions with which God created the natural order. The key tenet of occasionalism is instead its denial of second causes, God being the only genuine causal agent (with perhaps an exception made for the wills of created spirits). The chief argument for occasionalism rests on the doctrine of continuous re-creation; the motion of a body, for example, consists in its being re-created from moment to moment in a succession of contiguous positions, and the laws of motion governing the body are simply general rules God follows in placing bodies from one moment to the next. (See Malebranche 1980: esp. 153–63.) In seeing this as the main argument for occasionalism I am in agreement with T. M. Lennon (Lennon 1980: 816–18), and in disagreement with L. Loeb (Loeb 1981: 200–5).

can discover no natural connexions, so that *we cannot but ascribe* them to the arbitrary determination of God's will. There are two reasons why we should resist the suggestion that Locke's point is merely an epistemological one. In the first place, on the face of it the appeal to God's will is more than an epistemological place-holder. If it were only this, it would have been much more appropriate for us to simply admit that while we suspect there are connections here, we do not know what they are or even what they are like; why appeal to God's will, if all we mean to mark is our ignorance of the connections? To ascribe the connections to God's arbitrary will and good pleasure must be to issue an hypothesis, however tentative and unsupported it may be, concerning the causal ancestry of the connections. Ayers himself notes that in some cases Locke's appeal to God's will is meant to carry ontological weight (Ayers 1981*b*: 225–6); I do not see any clear basis for reading E iv.iii.29 and kindred passages in a different way. Second, and most important, Locke would seem to have no good reason to suppose that there are mechanistically intelligible connections here, of which we are simply ignorant. He does go on to say, in E iv.iii.29, that

The Things that, as far as our Observation reaches, we constantly find to proceed regularly, we may conclude, do act by a Law set them; but yet by a Law, that we know not: whereby, though Causes work steadily, and Effects constantly flow from them, yet their *Connexions* and *Dependancies* being not discoverable in our *Ideas*, we can have but an experimental Knowledge of them. (E iv.iii.29: 560)

We conclude that there are lawlike connections of some sort because of the regularities we observe in the powers and qualities of bodies. There is no licence given here to suppose that these connections must be mechanistically explicable, however, and Locke's talk of a law *set them* certainly has in it the suggestion of divine action. It would sort better with Locke's general agnosticism about the ultimate explanation of the qualities and operations of bodies to see him as issuing the least specific hypothesis available as to the source of the connections, rather than dogmatically insisting that they derive from matter and motion in some as yet unknown manner.[7]

The problem for a mechanistic reading of Locke is therefore this: because of our inability to conceive a mechanistic explanation of such phenomena as the cohesion of bodies, their mutual gravitational attraction, their power to cause sensations in perceivers in a regular manner and thus their possession of secondary qualities and other powers defined in reference to sensation, we are forced to ascribe these phenomena to God's

---

[7] I have in mind the agnosticism expressed in passages such as E iv.iii.11, 16: 544–5, 547–8, and E iv.xii.10: 645; as well as the more specific difficulties concerning cohesion, and so on, that are discussed in the chapter on ideas of substances (E ii.xiii).

action as determined by his arbitrary will. Since this ascription is not merely an epistemological place-holder but is instead an hypothesis about the causal ancestry of the phenomena, it is inconsistent with the mechanist's claim that all the phenomena of bodies can be explained in terms of the bulk, figure, texture, and motion of their solid parts.

2.

At this point I want to consider what might be involved in God's superadding powers or qualities to bodies, for by doing so we shall see how we can square Locke's commitment to mechanism with his concession that God's action is required if bodies are to have the powers and qualities in question. When he first comes to speak, in E IV.iii.6, of the possibility that God might superadd the power of thought directly to matter, thus making matter capable of thinking, he puts this possibility in the following way:

We have the *Ideas of Matter* and *Thinking*, but possibly shall never be able to know, whether any mere material Being thinks, or no; it being impossible for us, by the contemplation of our own *Ideas*, without revelation, to discover, whether Omnipotency has not given to some Systems of Matter fitly disposed, a power to perceive and think, or else joined and fixed to Matter so disposed, a thinking immaterial Substance ... (E IV.iii.6: 540–1)

His reason for thinking this is given as follows:

For I see no contradiction in it, that the first eternal thinking Being should, if he pleased, give to certain Systems of created senseless matter, put together as he thinks fit, some degrees of sense, perception, and thought. (E IV.iii.6: 541)

Looked at in the context of our present problem, certain phrases in these passages which might easily be overlooked or treated as throwaways take on importance. It is not simply matter, but certain systems of matter fitly disposed, or put together as God thinks fit, to which God is supposed to have superadded the power of thought. These phrases recur often in Locke's extended defence of his claim that God may endow matter with the power of thought against the objections of Stillingfleet, talking there of God's superaddition of thought to matter 'ordered as he sees fit', or 'so disposed as he thinks fit', and the like (see e.g. W IV: 466, 468, 471, 474). Perhaps the most interesting passage along these lines is this one, in which Locke is answering Stillingfleet's charge that he will be unable to explain why we are capable of abstract thought, whereas brutes are not, if we and the brutes are, equally, merely material things:

... if Omnipotency can give Thought to any solid Substance, it is not hard to conceive, that God may give that Faculty in an higher or lower Degree, as it pleases him, who knows what Disposition of the Subject is suited to such a particular way or degree of Thinking. (W IV: 465)

These passages suggest a picture of superaddition on which God superadds a power or quality to body by somehow connecting that power or quality with a certain type or types of material constitution, i.e. with a certain disposition of parts.

There is an alternative interpretation of these passages, on which the connections between the primary-quality constitutions of bodies and the powers or qualities that are to be superadded are somehow already there, laid out in the nature of things.[8] God would then be seen as superadding powers or qualities to particular bodies by contriving them so that they satisfy the structural descriptions implicit in the antecedently existing connections. This interpretation, it seems to me, involves the attribution to Locke of an unreasonable commitment to the correctness and adequacy of the corpuscularian hypothesis; it sorts ill with those passages in which Locke agnostically stresses the tentativeness of his espousal of the hypothesis (see e.g. E IV.iii.11, 16: 544–5, 547–8; E IV.xii.9–13: 644–8). It also fails to fit with those central passages in which Locke insists that even if we knew the real essences of bodies we would be unable to tell what their consequent powers and qualities might be; for this we need to know the connections between primary and secondary qualities as well (see e.g. E IV.iii.12–13: 545; E IV.vi.7: 582). It is hard to see what this 'other and more incurable part of our ignorance', over and above our ignorance of the real essences, would consist in, if the relevant connections were a matter of mechanical necessity laid out in the nature of things. For given access to the real essences of the bodies involved, what would stand in the way of our simply working out the powers and qualities that flow from the real essence, given that the connections themselves are a matter of mechanical necessity?

We do better to interpret these passages as implying that God actually forges the connections between types of material constitution and the superadded powers and qualities. Taking this route enables us to avoid the difficulties of the alternative interpretation, and further it chimes in well with those passages in which Locke stresses the arbitrariness of the connections and their dependence on God's will. We have already looked at E IV.iii.29, in which Locke talks of bodies acting according to a law set them;

---

[8] I take Ayers's view to be something like this; See Ayers 1981b: 213–15, 222–31, 244–6.

in the section just preceding that one, Locke has set up this claim by arguing that ordinary experience convinces us that thoughts (acts of will) can produce motion in bodies and that bodies can produce thoughts (sensations) in the mind, although we cannot conceive how this should be so:

These, and the like, though they have a constant and regular connexion, in the ordinary course of Things: yet that connexion being not discoverable in the *Ideas* themselves, which appearing to have no necessary dependance one on another, we can attribute their connexion to nothing else, but the arbitrary Determination of that All-wise Agent, who has made them to be, and to operate as they do, in a way wholly above our weak Understandings to conceive. (E iv.iii.28: 559)

In E iv.iii.6, the passage on superaddition, Locke says something similar, and he also suggests that God superadds the power to produce sensations of a certain sort by annexing the sensations to motion of a certain kind:

... Body as far as we can conceive being able only to strike and affect body: and Motion, according to the utmost reach of our *Ideas*, being able to produce nothing but Motion, so that when we allow it to produce pleasure and pain, or the *Idea* of a Colour, or Sound, we are fain to quit our Reason, go beyond our *Ideas*, and attribute it wholly to the good Pleasure of our Maker. For since we must allow he has annexed Effects to Motion, which we can no way conceive Motion able to produce, what reason have we to conclude, that he could not order them as well to be produced in a Subject we cannot conceive capable of them [i.e. 'in some Bodies themselves, after a certain manner modified and moved'], as well as in a Subject we cannot conceive the Motion of Matter can any way operate upon? (E iv.iii.6: 541)

And finally, in E iv.vi.14 he says that to establish truths about substances that are universal and certain (and non-trifling), we would have to know

... what Changes the *primary Qualities* of one Body, do regularly produce in the *primary Qualities* of another, and how. Secondly, we must know what *primary Qualities* of any Body, produce certain Sensations or *Ideas* in us. This is in truth, no less than to know all the Effects of Matter, under its divers modifications of Bulk, Figure, Cohesion of Parts, Motion, and Rest. (E iv.vi.14: 589)

And this, he goes on to say, we can know only by revelation.

All this points to the following as Locke's position: God superadds a power or quality to body by ordaining that a law holds connecting a certain type or types of material constitution (i.e. a certain arrangement of the mechanical affections or primary qualities of the constituent parts of bodies) with the power or quality. The law is arbitrary in that it is only one of a number of possible but mutually exclusive connections that might hold between types of constitution and resultant qualities, and that it is the one that does obtain is due only to the undetermined action of God. Nevertheless, the connection thus forged between the primary qualities of the body and the secondary qualities and other of its powers is a necessary connection, in Locke's sense, since God is thought of here as decreeing a *law* connecting the qualities. This will guarantee that every time a body has the appropriate inner constitution it will have the associated powers and qualities, and it will make true many counterfactuals of the form, 'if a body were to have such-and-such a constitution it would have such-and-such a quality, and would do so-and-so in such-and-such circumstances'.

In keeping with Locke's injunction not to limit God's omnipotence by our narrow conceptions,[9] and his insistence on our ignorance with regard to these matters, we should take this picture of superaddition to be nothing more than our best conjecture (or rather, the only even provisionally satisfying one we can construct) as to how bodies might have powers and qualities which we cannot see how to connect with their mechanical affections. Even so, the position we have arrived at for Locke is, I will argue in the next section of the paper, compatible with mechanism and can even serve to bolster it.

Before I leave the topic of superaddition I should comment on a passage from Locke's third letter to Stillingfleet which has come into prominence in the recent discussions of mechanism and superaddition. It runs as follows:

The Idea of Matter is an extended solid Substance; wherever there is such a Substance, there is Matter, and the Essence of Matter, whatever other Qualities not contained in that Essence, it shall please God to superadd to it. For example, God creates an extended solid Substance, without the superadding anything else to it, and so we may consider it at rest: To some parts of it he superadds motion but it still has the Essence of Matter: Other parts of it he frames into Plants, with all the excellencies of Vegetation, Life, and Beauty, which is to be found in a Rose or a Peachtree, &c. above the Essence of Matter in general, but it is still but Matter: To other parts he adds Sense and Spontaneous Motion, and those other Properties that are to be found in an Elephant. Hitherto it is not doubted but the Power of God may go, and that the Properties of a Rose, a Peach, or an Elephant, superadded to Matter, change not the Properties of Matter; but Matter is in these things Matter still. But if one venture to go one step further and say, God may give to Matter, Thought, Reason, and Volition, as well as Sense and Spontaneous Motion, there are Men ready presently to limit the Power of the Omnipotent Creator, and tell us, he cannot do it; because it destroys the Essence, *changes the essential Properties* of Matter. To make good which Assertion they have no more to say, but that Thought and Reason are not included in the Essence of Matter. I grant it; but whatever Excellency, not contained in its Essence, be superadded to Matter, it does not destroy the Essence of Matter, if it leaves it an extended solid Substance ... (W IV: 460–1)

---

[9] We have encountered hints of this stance in the quotation from E IV.iii.28: 558–9 given above, and it is also to be found in E IV.iii.6: 539–43; it is a major theme of the discussion of the issue of thinking matter in *Answer to Second Letter* (W IV: 459–74).

This passage has become the focus of a controversy between Ayers and Wilson over the propriety of the phrase 'superadded property'. The dispute has, it seems to me, been resolved (see Wilson 1982: 251–2); in fact, I doubt there was ever any deep disagreement on this point. The real issue between them lies elsewhere. It concerns the sense in which superadded qualities are not natural to the bodies that have them. Ayers and Wilson agree that in this passage Locke distinguishes between the properties a body has by virtue of being an extended solid thing and those it has by virtue of being a body of this or that particular sort (peach-tree, elephant, etc.), these latter qualities having to be superadded to the body; they can thus be said to fall outside the 'natural powers' of matter.

Ayers takes the passage to show how limited this claim is; in saying that the superadded powers or qualities are not natural to matter Locke is recording only that they are not contained in, or entailed by, the essence or nature of matter, viz. extension and solidity (Ayers 1981b: 226–31 (esp. 229), 238–9).[10] This would leave it open to Locke to say that the qualities do flow naturally from the body's mechanical constitution, in the sense that it would be a matter of mechanical necessity that a body constituted in a certain way would have these qualities. Wilson, on the other hand, takes the distinction between the properties of matter or body as such and the properties a body has as a member of a particular species of body to be inconsistent with a 'thorough mechanism about real essences', presumably since she thinks that the 'hidden constitution' from which the latter qualities flow is not material (Wilson 1982: 250–1).[11] On her view, then, it would seem that the superadded powers and qualities do not flow naturally even from the determinate real essence of the body, if this is taken to consist only in the bulk, figure, texture, and motion of the body's solid parts, which are only modifications of matter.

[10] For arguments that one or another quality is not essential to body if not every body has the quality, see E IV.x.10, 14: 623–4, 626. There is a very interesting application of this argument in the wind-up of the passage we are now looking at:

> In all such Cases, the superinducement of greater Perfections and nobler Qualities, destroys nothing of the Essence of Perfections that were there before; unless there can be shewed a manifest Repugnancy between them; but all the Proof offered for that, is only, That we cannot conceive how Matter, without such superadded Perfections, can produce such Effects; which is, in Truth, no more than to say, Matter in general, or every part of Matter, as Matter, has them not; though we cannot conceive how Matter is invested with them, or how it operates by Vertue of those new Endowments. Nor is it to be wonder'd that we cannot, whilst we limit all its Operations to those Qualities it had before, and would explain them, by the known Properties of Matter in general, without any such superinduced Perfections. (W IV: 462)

[11] Wilson indicates that the view expressed here is somewhat altered from the one she held in her earlier paper.

Our previous discussion indicates that both of these construals of the passage are slightly off the mark. In this passage Locke is trying to flatten out the notion of superaddition, so that God's act of superadding the power of thought to matter is seen to be of a piece with the superaddition of motion to matter or that of any of the qualities going into the nominal essence of a species of bodies. To this end he focuses on the strong sense in which a quality might be said not to flow naturally from a body, viz. that it does not follow from the attributes of extension and solidity. But this cannot be the only sense in which qualities such as the power of thought or the power to produce certain sensations are not natural to body. We have already encountered passages in the *Essay* in which Locke denies that there are any conceivable connections between the mechanical affections of a body and its secondary qualities, so that we must attribute the existing connections to God's action (see the passages cited in n. 4 above, particularly E IV.iii.28 and 29: 558–60). This affords a perfectly good sense in which these powers or qualities are not natural to matter: they do not flow from the body's inner nature, or real essence, alone; left to itself, with no action on God's part, the body would not have those secondary qualities or other of the powers that it does in fact have. This, we have seen, is what we commit ourselves to when we put the connections down to God's arbitrary will. It is not just a matter of what is or is not entailed by extension and solidity, but also of what can and what cannot be supposed to flow with mechanical necessity from the determinate real essence or mechanical affections of a body, taken by itself.

On the other hand, there is no basis in the passage for taking it as Locke's view that in superadding powers or qualities to bodies God is adding any immaterial or non-mechanical constituent to them, as Wilson seems to do. Indeed, the context of the passage points to quite the opposite view, for Locke goes on to argue that one cannot come up with a reason why a merely material thing cannot have the power of thought if one grants that merely material creatures can have sense and spontaneous motion, as Stillingfleet, no Cartesian on this score, does, while still maintaining that brutes have no immaterial souls, as Stillingfleet, quite orthodox on this score, also does. On the understanding of superaddition that we have come to, in superadding powers and qualities to bodies God does not add anything to them at all, at least in terms of real constituents. By instituting the relevant laws, God gives the mechanical affections of a body—its determinate real essence—dispositions to cause the appropriate effects. Nothing has changed in the body itself, nor have any new constituents of any kind been added to it; the body, or more particularly its mechanical affections, is simply able to produce more, and different sorts of, effects than it was able to do before.[12] Thus, if there is a sense in which superadded powers or qualities are not natural to the bodies endowed with them, there is another sense in which they are natural to them: in the course of nature, as God has created it (in part by ordaining the appropriate connections), the powers or qualities flow naturally from, in the sense of being necessarily connected with, the determinate real essence or mechanical constitution of the body. We see, then, that the passage we have been considering poses no problem for the interpretation I have given, and indeed accords quite well with it.

3.

We have arrived at a consistent view for Locke, but is it mechanism? The outstanding reason for doubting that it is stems from the fact that God's action is required for the appropriate connections to hold, and thus cannot be eliminated from any complete explanation of 'all the phenomena of bodies'. This problem is highlighted in both of Wilson's papers; we have encountered it in the quotation given above (p. 246), and in her later paper she says that Locke's doctrines about superadded qualities entail that '... mechanistic principles, or primary qualities, have limited explanatory power in Locke's considered view: the purposive action of an eternal thinking being is also required to account for phenomena' (Wilson 1982: 251). Although Wilson is right in thinking that Locke denies that we can explain how a body has the secondary qualities and other of the powers it in fact has without adverting to God's action, this is no bar to his being a thoroughgoing mechanist.

First of all, we should note that God's actions are required only to set the general background for any particular causal interactions among bodies, and thus for a particular body's having a certain set of causal powers; he does not directly work any of the effects which proceed from the superadded powers or qualities, nor need he superadd the qualities to particular bodies on a case-by-case basis. If we have to appeal to the actions of God only in such a general way, we needn't see these actions as interventions in the natural order; far from interfering with or supplement-

---

[12] Note that this model gives us a straightforward solution to another, related problem raised by Wilson (Wilson 1979: 146; see also Ayers 1981b: 218), viz. what it means to say that a superadded power or quality *belongs* to a body, given that it does not derive from the body's real essence alone. Against the background of the laws God has ordained, the power or quality does derive from the real essence alone; it is that that is the sole basis in actuality for the power, and it is that that is the proper causal agent responsible for bringing about the relevant effects.

ing the natural workings of matter-in-motion, these actions establish (in part) what are these natural workings.[13]

At this point we need to remind ourselves of the going alternatives to the mechanical philosophy, as these presented themselves to Locke (and Boyle).[14] First and foremost, and most familiar to us, there was the Aristotelian or Scholastic view (in a number of variants). Roughly speaking, on this view natural phenomena are explained by appealing to substantial forms and real qualities as the causal agents in natural change; these causal agents, if not explicitly immaterial, always operate in the light of final causality, hence non-mechanically. Less well known to us, but of great concern to Boyle, was what he called spagyritic chemistry and what we know as iatrochemistry, the 'philosophers by fire', among whom the most prominent were Paracelsus and, closer to Locke's and Boyle's time, J. B. van Helmont. Their three basic principles (salt, sulfur, and mercury) were held to be essentially active forces, and hence living or vital forces. Finally, and perhaps of more concern to Locke than to Boyle, were the Cambridge Platonists. Henry More and Ralph Cudworth both argued for the need to recognize immaterial, animate causal agents—'plastic natures' or 'plastic principles'—which determine all natural change, matter being essentially passive. Cudworth even argued for an *anima mundi* to accomplish the aims with which God created the world.[15]

Although I have given only very sketchy descriptions of these competing views, it can be seen that they are quite different. They have one thing in common, however, which sets them off from the mechanical philosophy: they all assert the existence in bodies of non-mechanical (and usually immaterial) causal agents which are ultimately responsible for some if not all of a body's natural operations. Seen in this light, it is clear that the distinctive feature of mechanism is its refusal to postulate any causal agents in bodies except for the bulk, figure, texture, and motion of their solid parts. Locke's position, as we have come to understand it, is thoroughly mechanistic. God ordains certain general laws and gives matter its initial disposition and motion; against this general background or 'frame' of the world the mechanical affections of bodies come to have certain causal powers which they otherwise would not have had. But it is the mechanical affections which have these powers; it is the mechanical

---

[13] See Boyle's interesting discussion of the universal and particular notions of nature, in *A Free Inquiry into the Vulgarly Received Notion of Nature* (published probably in 1685 or 1686, but started in 1666) (Boyle 1979: 187–8).

[14] For discussion of this background, see Dijksterhuis 1961: 433–6; Boas 1952; Kuhn 1952; Heilbron 1979: 19–46; and for the best short introduction, see Westfall 1971: esp. chs. 2 and 4.

[15] For plastic natures in Cudworth, see the selections from *The True Intellectual System of the Universe* in Patrides 1969: 288–325.

affections of body which are the only causally efficacious agents in any natural change.

Even if Locke is a mechanist in this sense, it might still be thought that his views on scientific explanation are not consistent with the views we have been discussing. In the characterization of the problem given by Wilson (quoted above), she gives as Locke's (and presumably Boyle's) 'official position' that there is an a priori conceptual connection between the real essence of a body and its secondary qualities. She apparently bases this attribution on the strict analogy she finds in Locke between explanation in natural philosophy and geometrical demonstration. She says in her original paper that 'Many passages show that Locke conceives the relation of real essence to derivative properties as analogous to that between the definition of a geometrical figure and the properties deducible from the definition' (Wilson 1979: 143), and in her later paper she glosses the problem she raises for a consistent mechanism in Locke in this way:

My claim, however, was just that Locke thought these qualities [secondary qualities, and superadded qualities generally] cannot 'arise naturally' from Boylean primary qualities, in the sense that the former cannot be 'explained' (through something like geometrical demonstration) in terms of the latter. (Wilson 1982: 249)

Although there is no doubt that Locke did compare explanations in natural philosophy with geometrical demonstrations, it is important to see that the similarity between them to which Locke points is limited to this, that in each we have (or would have, if we could achieve the relevant explanations) non-experimental knowledge of the properties of the object in question. The knowledge we would have from explanations in natural philosophy, if we were in a position to give them, would thus be a priori; but this does not mean that the connections figuring in such explanations would be conceptual, or just like the ones involved in geometrical demonstrations.

Let us consider the passages which are supposed to show that Locke thinks of the relation between the real essence of a body and its derivative powers and qualities as analogous to that between the definition of a triangle (which, triangles being modes, is both its real and its nominal essence) and its derivative properties. Wilson cites four such passages, of which two are the ones most commonly cited as support for the attribution to Locke of a 'rationalist' or 'deductivist' conception of natural science. These are from E II.xxxi.6 and E IV.iii.25, respectively:

The complex *Ideas* we have of Substances, are, as it has been shewn, certain Collections of simple *Ideas*, that have been observed or supposed constantly to exist together. But such a complex *Idea* cannot be the real Essence of any Substance; for then the Properties we discover in that Body, would depend on that complex *Idea*, and be deducible from it, and their necessary connexion with it be known; as all Properties of a Triangle depend on, and as far as they are discoverable, are deducible from the complex *Idea* of three Lines, including a Space. (E II.xxxi.6: 379)

I doubt not but if we could discover the Figure, Size, Texture, and Motion of the minute Constituent parts of any two Bodies, we should know without Trial several of their Operations one upon the other, as we do now the Properties of a Square, or a Triangle. (E IV.iii.25: 556)

The first of these passages is concerned not with the relation between the corpuscularian real essence of the body and its qualities, however, but instead with the relation of the nominal essence to those qualities. Locke is giving a *reductio* argument against the Scholastic doctrine of substantial forms, which he interprets as holding, in effect, that the real essence of a body is its nominal essence. If this were so, Locke is arguing, then we would have demonstrative knowledge of the properties of substances, just as we have of those of modes; but in fact we have no such knowledge. The reason for this, Locke goes on to say, is precisely that the real essence of a substance is not its nominal essence: '. . . it being nothing but Body, its real Essence, or internal Constitution, on which these Qualities depend, can be nothing but the Figure, Size, and Connexion of its solid Parts' (E II.xxxi.6: 379).

The other passage, from E IV.iii.25, does not say that if we knew the real essences of bodies we could give demonstrations in natural philosophy strictly analogous to those we give in geometry; it only says that we could know 'without trial' not all, but 'several', of the operations of bodies, just as we know without trial or experiment the properties of triangles, in their case on the basis of geometrical demonstration. It is instructive to consider the examples Locke gives of the knowledge we might have if we had ideas of the real essences of substances; if we knew, he says, 'the Mechanical affections of the Particles' of rhubarb, hemlock, opium, and a man,

. . . as a Watchmaker does those of a Watch, whereby it performs its Operations, and of a File which by rubbing on them will alter the Figure of any of the Wheels, we should be able to tell before Hand, that Rhubarb will purge, Hemlock kill, and Opium make a Man sleep; as well as a Watch-maker can, that a little piece of Paper, laid on the Balance, will keep the watch from going, till it be removed; or that some small part of it, being rubb'd by a File, the Machin would quite lose its Motion, and the Watch go no more. (E IV.iii.25: 556)

What the watchmaker and the geometer have in common is their ability to know, without trial or experiment, what properties the objects of their respective areas of concern have, or what they might be expected to do in certain circumstances. The natural philosopher would have this ability, too, with respect to those operations of bodies that lend themselves to the simplest kind of mechanical understanding. We could imagine discovering, for example, that the constituent particles of opium are so shaped as to plug up pores through which normally pass some of our animal spirits, thus reducing our activity and making us drowsy; we could then know in advance of trying it that this particular sample of opium will put Philip Marlowe out of commission, just as Marlowe's locksmith friend could fashion from memory a key which he knows will a fit a certain lock. There is nothing in this of demonstration, or conceptual connections.

As regards the other passages Wilson cites, E IV.vi.11 just makes the same point as E IV.iii.25: if we had ideas of the real essences of substances, *and* knew 'how those Qualities flowed from hence', we would no more need to make experiments to find out the properties of gold than we do to find out the properties of a triangle. And in E III.xi.23, the passage Wilson quotes, Locke says that we cannot conceive 'the manner' in which angels know what properties and operations flow from the real essence of a substance; this speaks against the idea that they come to this knowledge by geometrical demonstration, or something very much like it, drawn exclusively from the real essence of the substance.

Even more telling, I think, is the fact that Locke explicitly contrasts the connections that figure in geometrical demonstrations with those that figure in natural philosophy, and this in one of the passages that is central to the topic of mechanism and superaddition. At the start of E IV.iii.29 Locke says that in geometry, for example, '. . . there are certain Relations, Habitudes, and Connexions, so visibly included in the Nature of the *Ideas* themselves, that we cannot conceive them separable from them, by any Power whatsoever . . . Nor can we conceive this Relation, this connexion of these two *Ideas*, to be possibly mutable, or to depend on any arbitrary Power, which of choice made it thus, or could make it otherwise' (E IV.iii.29: 559). The next sentence is the one I quoted on p. 245 above; the connections that figure in natural philosophy are not like the ones in geometry, but instead depend on the arbitrary power of God: in other words, they are not conceptual connections. That Locke should see a contrast of this kind between the connections involved in geometrical demonstrations and those involved in explanations in natural philosophy is prefigured not only in his general distinction between modes (where the real essence and the nominal essence, or defining idea, are identical) and substances (where they are distinct), but also in the distinction he draws at the beginning of Book IV between knowledge of relations of ideas and knowledge of co-existence or necessary connexions of ideas (see E IV.i.3, 5–6: 525, 526–7; E IV.iii.538–62 *passim*). A careful consideration of Book IV, chapters iii and vi, where Locke discusses the reasons why we cannot obtain knowledge of the necessary connection or co-existence of qualities in substances will make it clear that what is required for such knowledge is (a) knowledge of the real essences or internal constitutions of the substances, and (b) the connections between these real essences and the powers or qualities of the substances. These latter connections are not conceptual ones, depending as they do on God's arbitrary choice; but they are such that, if we could come to know them (say through revelation) we would be able to know in advance, and with certainty, what bodies would do in various circumstances (supposing we knew their real essences as well), and this is just to have proper scientific knowledge of the powers and qualities of bodies.

Even given the high standards Locke set for explanation in natural philosophy, then, there is no inconsistency between his commitment to mechanism and his treatment of secondary qualities, or of superadded qualities in general. I think we have arrived at a picture of Locke as not only a consistent mechanist, but a sophisticated one as well. Or rather, a relatively sophisticated one. For this picture of Locke does not leave him looking so very modern. In this respect I am quite in agreement with Wilson (Wilson 1979: 143–4, 147 n. 15), who remarks with disapproval the tendency among recent commentators to see Locke as basing his arguments on a scientific theory that is in essentials the correct one. This underestimates both the very large differences between Boylean corpuscularianism and modern-day physics and physical chemistry and the nature and extent of the gaps in arguments for Locke's and Boyle's views based on the scientific adequacy or superiority of corpuscularianism. (I think that Locke rarely, if ever, argues from the scientific adequacy of corpuscularianism, even in the case of the distinction between primary and secondary qualities. But that is another story, to be reserved for another occasion.)

On the other hand, if this picture of Locke does not make him look very much at home in modern science, it does situate him squarely in the tradition of late seventeenth-century English natural philosophy, and particularly in the tradition of natural religion. Starting with the work of Walter Charleton, and particularly prominent in Boyle, and later, in Newton and his acolytes Samuel Clarke and Richard Bentley (both of whom were Boyle lecturers), there was a concerted effort to rid the mechanical philosophy of its taint of atheism, and even to show that the being and attributes of God could be established by rational arguments drawn from natural philosophy.[16] Central to these arguments was the need to call

---

[16] See Charleton's *Physiologia Epicuro-Gassendo-Charletoniana, or a Fabric of Philosophy*

upon the providence and omnipotence of God in order to understand natural phenomena, and this of course is a feature of Locke's mechanism.

Seeing this is crucial to the understanding of Locke's views; otherwise they will look to be inconsistent, or at least subject to internal tensions. Many contemporary commentators would prefer to do away with, or failing this, overlook Locke's need to appeal to God's providence in squaring his commitment to mechanism with his views about the limited extent of our knowledge. Behind some of this, at any rate, is the view that any appeal to God's providence or omnipotence must be bad philosophy, in that any invocation of a *Deus* in philosophy must be an invocation of a *Deus ex machina*. There is nothing wrong with this view, as long as it does not blind us to the fact that, given the constraints on seventeenth-century theology, appeal to God's providence and omnipotence are not a case of 'anything goes'. Such disputes as those between Leibniz and Clarke show that the resolution of such issues involves recognizably philosophical arguments, and a high level of philosophy at that. One of the things I hope my discussion of Locke has shown is that a proper appreciation of the ways in which God, his attributes, and/or his actions figure in the philosophical positions of some of the philosophers of the seventeenth and eighteenth centuries will not only enable us better to understand their views, but to see them to be (relatively speaking, at least) more philosophically defensible than they otherwise might seem to be.[17]

Naturall founded upon the Hypothesis of Atomes (1654), a work based very much on Gassendi's *Syntagma*. For general discussions of these issues, see Kargon 1966: esp. chs. 8–9; Redwood 1976: chs. 2 and 4; and Westfall 1966: ch. 5, esp. 108–10.

[17] Earlier versions of this paper were given at the Conference on Locke's Philosophy at Rutgers University, June 1983, and at the Royal Institute of Philosophy Conference on the History of Philosophy at the University of Lancaster, Sept. 1983. My thanks to participants at those conferences for their remarks, and special thanks to the organizers of those conferences, James Buickerood and John Yolton for the Rutgers conference and Alan Holland for the Lancaster conference, both for their invitations and the splendid arrangements. I want to thank colleagues and friends whose comments and criticisms helped so much: Michael Ayers, Joshua Cohen, Paul Hoffman, Jeremy Hyman, Thomas Kuhn, Thomas Lennon, John Milton, G. A. J. Rogers, Margaret Wilson, and Kenneth Winkler.

XIV

MORAL SCIENCE AND THE CONCEPT OF PERSONS IN LOCKE

RUTH MATTERN

LOCKE'S concept of persons in his discussion of personal identity has received a great deal of critical attention. But the chapter on identity was added to the *Essay* in the Second Edition; it appears to be a digression and an afterthought.[1] Locke scholars have generally thought it futile to attempt to make any interesting connections between his concept of persons and the broader epistemological themes of the *Essay*. Eric Matthews, for example, explicitly denies such connections with his statement that Locke's

scattered remarks in the *Essay* on the concept of a person . . . are clearly incidental to a discussion of the *Essay*'s main theme, 'the original, certainty, and extent of human knowledge'. (Matthews 1977: 9)

I aim to show in this paper that this view about Locke's concept of persons is mistaken. The mistake arises, I believe, from the assumption that the only philosophical function which the concept has for Locke is its role in his famous treatment of personal identity, his account of the reidentification of the moral agent. I want to show here that Locke believed it to have another function as well; he thought that the systematic moral science which he envisioned required a concept of this sort.

In the first section of the paper, I will indicate how Locke's early confidence that ethical truths could be drawn from the concept of human nature was undermined by his doubts about the possibility of any universal, certain, non-trivial knowledge. Locke later attempted to develop an answer to the problem of a priori knowledge in mathematics, and he believed that this answer suggested the possibility of a demonstrative science of ethics; I will indicate the relevance of his concept of *moral man* to this

From *Philosophical Review*, 89: 1 (1980), 24–45. Copyright 1980 Cornell University. Reprinted by permission of the publisher and the author.

[1] There is a brief discussion of personal identity in the First Edition of the *Essay* (E II.i.11: 109–10); but the main discussion of the topic was added in the Second Edition (E II.xxvii: 328–48).

proposed system of ethics in the second section. The third section will trace the development of Locke's concept of persons after that precursor to the concept. This section will argue that Locke thought of his concept of rational selves, introduced in his discussion of the possible science of ethics, as identical with his concept of persons in the chapter on identity. Finally, I will comment briefly on the significance of this development of the concept of persons in the context of ethical knowledge.

I. THE CONCEPT OF HUMAN AND THE PROBLEM OF UNIVERSAL KNOWLEDGE

In Locke's early writings on ethics, the concept of the being subsumed under moral law is the concept of *human*; it is this idea which he assumes in the early 1660s to have systematic connections with other moral concepts. General moral truths about our obligations rest, Locke thinks, on recognized universal truths about *human nature*. He writes that the law of nature

> is a fixed and permanent rule of morals, which reason itself pronounces, and which persists, being a fact so firmly rooted in the soil of human nature. Hence human nature must needs be changed before this law can be either altered or annulled . . . all those who are endowed with a rational nature, i.e. all men in the world, are morally bound by this law. . . . In fact it seems to me to follow just as necessarily from the nature of man that, if he is a man, he is bound to love and worship God and also to fulful other things appropriate to the rational nature, i.e. to observe the law of nature, as it follows from the nature of a triangle that, if it is a triangle, its three angles are equal to two right angles. (EL vii: 199)

At this stage of his thinking, Locke takes quite literally the interpretation of *human* as *rational animal*. But when he wrote the first draft of the *Essay concerning Human Understanding* a decade later, he was deeply troubled about the status of universal claims such as 'all men are rational'. He denied that such truths can be both instructive and certain as he once assumed, claiming instead that they fall into the following dilemma (D I: 55):

> [A]ll universal propositions that are certain are only verball or words applyd to our owne Ideas and not instructive: and vice-versa all universal propositions that are instructive (i.e. informe us any thing about the nature qualitys and operations of things existing without us) are all uncertain, i.e. we cannot certainly know them to be true . . . (D I: 50)

Locke explicitly says that this difficulty applies to the claim that all men are rational. Interpreted as a claim whose predicate is contained in the definition of the subject, it is a proposition which is 'only verbal'; interpreted as a truth which is more than verbal, it is not certain:

[W]hen I affirme that simple Idea of any name which simple Idea I conteine in the very diffinition of that name, . . . then the proposition is always true but also only verbal, as a man is rational, for I have noe certain knowledge that things doe soe exist. . . . Or else when I have observd this simple Idea to belong to all the individuals of that species that my senses have met with and then predicate it of but doe not include it in the definition of the name of that species and then the predication is real but not certainly true nor have I a certaine knowledg of it. (D I: 27)

Part of the basis of Locke's denial of the certainty of the claim that *all humans are rational* is his contention that this generalization fails to fit all known instances:

it being evident that children for some time and some men all their live times are not soe rational as a horse or dog at which time I cannot see how the Idea rational doth belong to them or can be affirmed of them. Soe that by frameing such Ideas within us we cannot make universal propositions which shall be true of things without us of which we have or can have a certain knowledg that they doe soe exist . . . (D I: 27–8)

But the first draft of the *Essay* also elaborates a more general reason for doubting the certainty of universal real propositions. Locke asserts that in order to be certain of a universal proposition not true by definition, we would need to have one of two sorts of evidence which we cannot usually obtain: either direct experience of all the members of a kind (which is possible only if the kind is very restricted), or experience which assures us about things beyond our experience.

[W]hen I proceed to universall propositions . . . I have noe certain knowledg that things doe soe exist. Unlesse it be when I certainly know the specific essentiall Ideas that belong to every particular individual of any species (which can be had only by the testimony of my owne senses and observation and soe seldom happens) and then I have a certain knowledg that such an universal proposition is true of things soe existing extra without me. (D I: 27)

[A]lthough I have constantly observd such a particular set of simple Ideas to be constantly united in a great number of sensible objects which I therefor ranke into one kinde or species, yet I cannot be sure or certainly know (though it be highly probable) but only by my owne senses that the same number of simple Ideas are in the same manner united in other subjects that I have not seen nor imployd my senses about. Because such a connection of such a number of simple Ideas (though it be ordinary) yet is not in its owne nature necessary, and it is noe contradiction that it should be otherwise. (D I: 50)

As I interpret Locke's problem, what precludes our certainty about universal instructive propositions is the inaccessibility of the states which render these propositions true. Though a trifling, 'merely verbal' proposition is true by virtue of the containment of predicate idea in subject idea, a proposition giving information about real things is true by virtue of the states of those things. But in the ordinary case in which we only experience a limited few of the members of a kind, we have incomplete experience of the states of things which make the universal propositions true.[2]

Another condition for certainty about universal instructive propositions is mentioned in the published version of the *Essay*:

[B]ecause we cannot be certain of the Truth of any general Proposition, unless we know the precise bounds and extent of the Species its Terms stand for, it is necessary we should know the Essence of each Species, which is that which constitutes and bounds it. (E iv.vi.4: 580)

This condition provides another reason for denying the certainty of some universal propositions.

Concepts of natural kinds are particularly susceptible to this difficulty, on the basis of Locke's claim that these are inadequate ideas: 'all our complex Ideas of Substances are imperfect and inadequate' (E ii.xxxi.11: 382). The reason is that we lack, on Locke's view, a complex idea of all of the properties specific to a natural kind, and we also lack knowledge of the inner constitution which gives rise to all of the species-specific properties (see e.g. E ii.xxxi.8: 381; E ii.xxxi.13: 383). Though we know particular external instances of many natural kinds, the ideas formed by observing those instances are not perfect and complete copies of these external 'patterns' or 'archetypes' (see e.g. E ii.xxxi.8: 381). And Locke thinks that we are not only ignorant in fact of the inner constitutions of things, but also 'destitute of Faculties' to attain knowledge 'of the internal Constitution, and true Nature of things' (E ii.xxiii.32: 313).

Locke is quite aware that the idea of human falls within the scope of his general claim that ideas of substances are inadequate. We are doomed to ignorance of the inner constitution of our own species, Locke thought; though we know some of the typical powers of humans and include these in our complex Ideas of the species,

The foundation of all those Qualities which are the Ingredients of our complex Idea is something quite different; And had we such a Knowledge of that Constitution of Man, from which his Faculties of Moving, Sensation, and Reasoning, and other Powers flow; and on which his so regular shape depends, as 'tis possible Angels have, and 'tis certain his Maker has, we should have a quite other Idea of his Essence, than what now is contained in our Definition of that Species, be it what it will ... (E iii.vi.3: 440)

---

[2] These remarks are intended as an interpretation rather than mere exposition. A more detailed discussion would require an analysis of Locke's views about truth and certainty in the early draft.

Because we lack knowledge of the inner constitution of humans, the key to the species-specific properties of the kind, we cannot remedy our uncertainty about 'the precise bounds and extent of the Species'. Locke describes this uncertainty as follows:

> [I]f several Men were to be asked, concerning some odly-shaped Foetus, as soon as born, whether it were a Man, or no, 'tis past doubt, one should meet with different Answers. . . . So uncertain are the boundaries of Species of Animals to us, who have no other Measures, than the complex Ideas of our own collecting: And so far are we from certainly knowing what a Man is; though, perhaps, it will be judged great Ignorance to make any doubt about it. And yet, I think, I may say, that the certain Boundaries of that Species, are so far from being determined, and the precise number of simple Ideas, which make the nominal Essence, so far from being setled, and perfectly known, that very material doubts may still arise about it . . . (E III.vi.27: 454–5)

II. THE CONCEPT OF 'MORAL MAN' AND DEMONSTRATIVE SCIENCE

In spite of the considerations discussed in the last section, Locke does assert in the published *Essay* that mathematics is a demonstrative science, and that certain, universal, instructive propositions in ethics are possible in principle. Defending the possibility of a demonstrative science of ethics, Locke claims that uncertainty about the boundaries of natural kinds (ideas of substances) does not affect the status of moral propositions:

> Nor let anyone object that the names of Substances are often to be made use of in Morality . . . from which will arise obscurity. For as to substances, when concerned in moral Discourses, their diverse Natures are not so much enquired into, as supposed: e.g. when we say that *Man is subject to Law*, we mean nothing by *man* but a corporeal rational creature; what the real essence or other qualities of that creature are in this case is no way considered. And therefore, whether a child or changeling be a man in a physical sense may amongst the naturalists be as disputable as it will, it concerns not at all the *moral man*, as I may call him, which is this immovable unchangeable idea, a corporeal rational being . . . (E III.xi.16: 516–17)

The definition of 'moral man' looks much like the definition of 'human' as 'rational animal'. But Locke is not defining 'human' in this context. He is trying to clarify an atypical usage of this word, a term which is ordinarily used as a name of a natural kind. This attempt at clarification results in a new concept, the idea *moral man*.

What exactly is the status of this concept, and why does Locke think that it promises a solution to his earlier doubts about certainty in ethics? After sketching Locke's answer to the problem of the possibility of mathematical knowledge, I will discuss the basis and limitations of his attempt to extend this account to ethics.

Mathematical Knowledge

I indicated earlier that Locke formulates in a general way his initial 'dilemma' concerning universal propositions in the first draft of the *Essay*. He was particularly concerned about the implications of this dilemma for mathematical truth, and from the first draft to the published version of the *Essay* he laboured over a theory designed to accommodate the possibility of certainty about universal, instructive propositions in mathematics. I will not dwell on the details of his rather complicated and problematic theory here,[3] since the following summary should suffice for our present purposes.

As we saw earlier, Locke thought that one condition for our certainty about general propositions is that 'we know the precise bounds and extent of the Species its Terms stand for' (E IV.vi.4: 580). He does not think that this condition poses a problem for mathematical kinds such as *circle* and *triangle*. The reason is that he believes in the adequacy of our ideas of mathematical kinds; there is no further condition for membership in these kinds beyond the essential features explicit in our general ideas of the kinds. Unlike the Platonist who believes that externally existing mathematical objects are the patterns for membership in these kinds, Locke holds the conceptualist view that our own ideas are the 'archetypes and essences' of the mathematical sorts.[4] He thinks that this position gives us certainty of the 'precise bounds and extent of the Species' for all conventional kinds (which he terms *mode* kinds), in spite of the inadequacy of natural kinds concepts (*substance* kinds).[5] Locke writes that in the case of modes, it is not difficult to 'know the precise bounds and extent of the Species',

For in these, the real and nominal Essence being the same; or which is all one, the abstract Idea, which the general Term stands for, being the sole Essence and boundary, that is or can be supposed, of the Species, there can be no doubt, how far the Species extends, or what Things are comprehended under each Term: which, 'tis evident, are all, that have an exact conformity with the Idea it stands for, and no other. (E IV.vi.4: 580)

---

[3] So far the best discussion of the development of Locke's views about mathematics is contained in Krüger 1973: see esp. sect. 15.

[4] For substance ideas, Locke modifies his conceptualism to say that external particulars are 'archetypes' of ideas of the kinds (cf. E III.vi.47: 469; E II.xxxi.6: 378–80).

[5] Locke's distinction between substances and modes is interpreted as a distinction between conventional and natural kinds in Bolton 1976: 488, repr. in this volume as Ch. VI. While issues about the interpretation of the substance/mode distinction are relevant to the present topic, it would complicate this essay unnecessarily to discuss these issues here.

Locke's denial of the certainty of universal instructive propositions in the first draft of the *Essay* was motivated, we saw earlier, by a problem about the inaccessibility of the truth-conditions of such propositions. How could we be *certain* of universal truths, Locke asked, if we are acquainted with only a limited set of individual things of a kind, and if there is no necessary connection between the states of the things we know and the states of the things beyond our immediate apprehension? Locke's answer to this problem for mathematical knowledge is to reinterpret the truth-conditions of universal mathematical claims. Instead of construing statements about external particulars as the basis of mathematical generalizations, the *Essay* interprets propositions about mathematical *ideas* as the basic mathematical claims. Mathematical knowledge, he writes,

is only of our own Ideas. The Mathematician considers the Truth and Properties belonging to a Rectangle, or Circle, only as they are in Idea in his own Mind. (E IV.iv.6: 565)

On this interpretation of the basis of mathematical truth, certain knowledge of relations of mathematical ideas suffices for certainty that a mathematical proposition is true. By apprehending these relations of ideas, the mathematician avoids the need to wait for acquaintance with indefinitely many particular instances of a mathematical kind. In effect, Locke's later view of mathematics denies that universal propositions of this sort are true by correspondence with states of external particulars; they are true by virtue of relations of ideas, and particular mathematical propositions are true as instances of these general claims.[6]

On this view of mathematical knowledge, mathematical propositions are *universal* because they are composed of general ideas, and we are *certain* of the propositions because we are capable of apprehending relations of ideas with certainty. But why are mathematical propositions *instructive* rather than 'merely verbal'? Locke accounts for this only by introducing a further claim about mathematical essences. In addition to specifying completely the necessary and sufficient conditions for membership in mathematical kinds, Lockean real essences in mathematics function as foundations of species-specific properties. For example, he writes that

a Figure including a Space between three Lines, is . . . the very Essentia, or Being, of the thing it self, that Foundation from which all its Properties flow, and to which they are all inseparably annexed. (E III.iii.18: 418)

---

[6] This claim is also to be read as an interpretation, the full justification of which would require a much longer discussion. One useful reference on Locke's views about truth is Krüger 1973: ch. 12.

Locke's descriptions of this function of mathematical real essences are largely metaphorical, and he does not explain the status of the claim that these essences are *both* defining properties of the kinds and the logical foundations of other properties.[7] But the fact that mathematical real essences perform both functions is the basis of Locke's claim that mathematical theorems such as 'the external angle of all triangles is bigger than either of the opposite internal angles' are instructive propositions: we can know, he writes,

the Truth of two sorts of Propositions, with perfect *certainty*; the one is, of those trifling Propositions, which have a certainty in them, but 'tis but a verbal Certainty, but not instructive. And, secondly, we can know the Truth, and so may be *certain* in Propositions, which affirm something of another, which is a necessary consequence of its precise complex *Idea*, but not contained in it. As that *the external Angle of all Triangles, is bigger than either of the opposite internal Angles*; which relation of the outward Angle, to either of the opposite internal Angles, making no part of the complex *Idea*, signified by the name Triangle, this is a real Truth, and conveys with it instructive *real Knowledge*. (E IV.viii.8: 614)

Such mathematical theorems count as instructive rather than trifling claims because their predicate ideas are not contained in their subject ideas. They also count as 'real' propositions in the sense introduced in the first draft of the *Essay*, for they are propositions containing information about real particulars.[8] Since the mathematical ideas are essences which define membership in the mathematical kinds, whatever follows from the essential features will be true of any instance of the kind. Mathematical propositions are, then, informative about real particulars as well as certain:

---

[7] Locke's explanation of the distinction between real and nominal essences at E III.iii.15–18: 417–19 makes it sound as though it is a matter of definition that real essences serve as the foundation of discoverable properties. But at E IV.vi.4: 580, it sounds as though Locke might have in mind a conception of essence which only implies that the essence constitutes membership in the kind. He writes that for simple ideas and modes, 'the real and nominal Essence being the same; or which is all one, the abstract Idea, which the general Term stands for, being the sole Essence and Boundary, that is or can be supposed, of the Species, there can be no doubt, how far the Species extends . . .'

[8] Locke's distinction between *real* propositions and *merely verbal* propositions is closely allied with his distinction between *trifling* and *instructive* propositions. He writes as though he is referring to a single distinction when he says that the truth of propositions involving words 'is twofold, Either purely Verbal, and trifling . . . or Real and instructive' (E IV.v.6: 576). In the first draft of the *Essay*, he treats instructiveness as implying informativeness about real particulars: 'all universal propositions that are instructive (i.e. informe us any thing about the nature qualitys and operations of things existing without us) are all uncertain' (D I: 50). Similarly, 'real' propositions give 'knowledg of things existing in rerum natura' (D I: 27). In the *Essay* chapter on trifling propositions, the distinction between instructive and trifling is explicated as a contrast between propositions whose predicate ideas are or are not contained in the subject ideas (E IV.viii: 609–17), suggesting that the two sorts of propositions have different bases of truth. A full interpretation of these distinctions would require much more discussion than the present essay allows.

The Mathematician considers the Truth and Properties belonging to a Rectangle, or Circle, only as they are in Idea in his own Mind. . . . But yet the knowledge he has of any Truths or Properties belonging to a Circle, or any other mathematical Figure, are nevertheless true and certain, even of real Things existing: because real Things are no farther concerned, nor intended to be meant by any such Propositions, than as Things really agree to those Archetypes in his Mind. Is it true of the Idea of a Triangle, that its three Angles are equal to two right ones? It is true also of a Triangle, where-ever it really exists. Whatever other Figure exists, that is not exactly answerable to that Idea of a Triangle in his Mind, is not at all concerned in that Proposition. (E iv.iv.6: 565)

The Possible Demonstrative Science of Ethics

Locke's account of a priori knowledge in mathematics raises a host of questions,[9] but what concerns us now is the fact that he believes in the possibility of an a priori science of ethics analogous to deductive systems of mathematics. Even in his very early writings, Locke had suggested an analogy between mathematics and moral knowledge. We saw earlier that in his *Essays on the Law of Nature*, he wrote that there is a 'fixed and permanent rule of morals' grounded in human nature, just as geometrical truths are grounded in the nature of geometrical figures (EL vii: 199).[10] Instead of dropping the analogy as he developed his later theory of mathematics, Locke retained and developed it. In 1681, he wrote the following remark in his journal after discussing the way in which mathematical truth is based on knowledge of ideas:

[T]he first and great step . . . to knowledg is to get the minde furnishd with true Ideas which the minde being capeable of haveing of morall things as well as figure I cannot but thinke morality as well as mathematiques capeable of demonstration if men would imploy their understanding to thinke more about it and not give themselves up to the lazy traditional way of talkeing one after another . . . (Locke 1936: 116–17)

The published *Essay* asserts at several points that a demonstrative science of ethics is possible. For example, Locke writes:

---

[9] One question, for example, is why Locke assumes that mathematical real essences do have necessary connections with ideas not immediately contained in them; some commentators, such as David Perry, charge that Locke 'does not establish the existence of necessary synthetic connections between ideas', and 'leaves unexplained the supposed possibility of arriving at certain, yet instructive propositions' (Perry 1967: 235). Another question is whether Locke has not significantly weakened the sense of 'real' in his later interpretation of mathematical propositions.

[10] At this early stage of his thought, Locke had not yet acknowledged the a priori status of mathematics. He held that the basic presuppositions of mathematics are derived from sense experience (EL iv: 149), and he interpreted the 'light of nature' as including both sensory and rational faculties (EL iv: 147–57).

[I] am bold to think, that Morality is capable of Demonstration, as well as
Mathematicks: Since the precise real Essence of the Things moral Words stand for,
may be perfectly known; and so the Congruity, or Incongruity of the Things themselves, be certainly discovered, in which consists perfect Knowledge. (E iii.xi.16:
516)

Locke's optimism about the possibility of a demonstrative science of
ethics rests on three assumptions, in addition to the claims necessary to
secure the status of universal, certain, instructive mathematical propositions. First, Locke must assert that the ethical ideas are adequate. He
commits himself to this claim by saying that the moral ideas are 'archetypes themselves' (E iv.iv.7: 565), and that we know the 'precise real
Essence of the Things moral Words stand for' (E iii.xi.16: 516), as well as
by explicitly stating that our moral ideas are adequate (E iv.iv.7: 565).
Locke thinks that moral ideas give the essential qualities of moral kinds, so
that ethics is not subject to uncertainty due to vagueness of the boundaries
of the sorts, and so that abstract ethical propositions are true of the
concrete cases falling within these sorts.

Second, it is necessary for Locke's proposed moral science that the real
essences represented by our moral ideas serve as 'foundations' from which
other moral properties 'flow', that is, that the moral real essences have
necessary connections with other moral features so that there is a systematic logical structure of real essences. Third, it is necessary that it be
humanly possible to discover these necessary connections, given a knowledge of the real essences.

Locke's expressions of optimism about systematic ethics stress the claim
that the moral ideas are adequate. However, he gives some evidence of
recognizing that the second and third assumptions are distinct from the
first, since he lists the existence of discoverable connections between moral
real essences as a separate condition in the following passage:

Morality is capable of Demonstration, as well as Mathematicks. For the Ideas that
Ethicks are conversant about, being all real Essences, *and such as, I imagine, have
a discoverable connexion and agreement one with another*; so far as we can find their
Habitudes and Relations, so far we shall be possessed of certain, real, and general
Truths . . . (E iv.xii.8: 643; emphasis added).[11]

---

[11] Here Locke does not treat it as a matter of definition that the real essences function as the
foundation of properties (cf. n. 7 above). He states it as an additional claim that they perform
this function, and he seems to be less certain that they have this function than he is that they are
real essences. If he were treating it as a matter of definition that real essences generate properties in the way he describes at E iii.iii.18: 418, then he would not be entitled to assert that ethical
ideas are real essences without already knowing that there are necessary connections between
real essences.

Locke does not say why he assumes that these connections are discoverable, but his admission that the projected demonstrative science of ethics is not an actual one points up the importance of the additional assumptions.

Locke sounds less confident about the possibility of a science of ethics after the publication of the *Essay*; the fact that he could neither fill in the details of such an ethical system nor prove that moral real essences have 'discoverable connections' may account for his shift of attitude. In the *Reasonableness of Christianity*, written five years after the appearance of the *Essay*, Locke conceded that 'it is too hard a task for unassisted reason to establish morality in all its parts upon its true foundation with a clear and convincing light' (W vii: 139). Admitting that the demonstrative science of ethics may be unattainable after all, Locke says that revelation of ethical truths from God is a better guide to conduct:

[S]ome parts of that truth lie too deep for our natural powers easily to reach and make plain and visible to mankind without some light from above to direct them. (W vii: 144)

Philosophy seemed to have spent its strength and done its utmost. Or, if it had gone farther (as we see it did not) and from undeniable principles given us ethics in a science like mathematics, in every part demonstrable, yet this would not have been so effectual to man in this imperfect state nor proper for the cure. (W vii: 145–6)

In his correspondence with William Molyneux, who had urged him to develop the demonstrative science of ethics, Locke not only modestly refrains from announcing himself as the Euclid of ethics but also reveals again his dampened enthusiasm for the project:

Did the world want a rule, I confess there could be no work so necessary, nor so commendable. But the gospel contains so perfect a body of ethics, that reason may be excused from that inquiry, since she may find man's duty clearer and easier in revelation, than in herself. (C v: 595)

These considerations should help to put Locke's optimism about a demonstrative science of ethics, and the claim about the adequacy of moral ideas which underlies this optimism, in perspective. The assumption of the adequacy of moral ideas is not itself sufficient for the demonstrative science, and Locke came to realize this. But the fact that Locke did at one time have considerable confidence about the possibility of demonstrative ethics helps in understanding the significance of his introduction of the concept 'moral man' during that phase of his thought. There is good reason to interpret Locke's distinction between the biological and ethical concepts of human as intended to serve his analogy between mathematics and ethics. In stipulating that the term 'man' in the context of ethics stands for the unchangeable idea of 'corporeal rational being', Locke is trying to set aside the inadequacy of the natural kinds concept of man; and he is doing this in order to remove an obstacle to the proposed a priori ethics. Locke must be able to say that we do know the real essence of *man*, in order to be able to say that he is confident of the possibility of a moral science *because* he thinks that 'the precise real essence of the things moral words stand for may be perfectly known' (E III.xi.16: 516).

Even on his own terms, this response to his problem is not completely satisfactory. Locke's suggestion makes the term 'man' ambiguous, since that word would function as a natural kinds term in some contexts and as a mode term in other contexts. This means that Locke's practice falls short of the *Essay*'s preachings about clear use of language. One of the cardinal points of Locke's preceding chapter is that words should not be applied 'very unsteadily, making them stand now for one, and by and by for another Idea' (E III.x.23: 505).

Locke is also violating his rule that one should not 'apply the common received names of any Language to Ideas, to which the common use of that Language does not apply them' (E III.x.23: 504). For the usage of the term 'man' as 'moral man' is really quite different from the ordinary usage as Locke explicates it. Also, as Locke says in that passage, being a human is not logically necessary for falling within the scope of the term 'moral man':

For were there a Monkey, or any other Creature to be found, that had the use of Reason, to such a degree, as to be able to understand general Signs, and to deduce Consequences about general Ideas, he would no doubt be subject to Law, and, in that Sense, be a Man, how much soever he differ'd in Shape from others of that Name. (E III.xi.16: 517)

'Moral man' is a misleading term for the concept of the moral agent, because it suggests that being human is a necessary condition for falling within the scope of the moral law.

In his passage on the concept of moral man, Locke does not go so far as to say explicitly that the concept of human is completely distinct from the concept of the moral agent. But that is the direction in which he is heading here, and his doubts about the universal claim 'all men are rational'[12] give impetus to this move. We will see in a moment that later in the *Essay*, the natural kinds term 'man' disappears altogether from Locke's discussion of ethical propositions.

[12] See above, sect. I. That Locke still questions the certainty of the claim 'All men are rational' in the published edition of the *Essay* is clear from his remark that a faculty of reasoning 'appears not at first, and in some never' (E III.xi.20: 519).

III. THE CONCEPTS OF RATIONAL SELVES AND PERSONS

The Concept of Rational Selves

In the fourth book of the *Essay*, Locke writes:

> The Idea of the supreme Being, infinite in Power, Goodness, and Wisdom, whose Workmanship we are, and on whom we depend; and the Idea of our selves as understanding, rational Beings, being such as are clear in us, would I suppose, if duly considered, and pursued, afford such Foundations of our Duty and Rules of Action, as might place Morality amongst the Sciences capable of Demonstration: wherein I doubt not, but from self-evident Propositions, by necessary Consequences, as incontestable as those in Mathematicks, the measures of right and wrong might be made out, to any one that will apply himself with the same Indifferency and Attention to the one, as he does to the other of these Sciences. The Relation of other Modes may certainly be perceived, as well as those of Number and Extension: and I cannot see, why they should not also be capable of Demonstration, if due Methods were thought on to examine, or pursue their Agreement or Disagreement. (E iv.iii.18: 549)

This passage offers another concept of moral agent for use in the propositions of the proposed demonstrative science of ethics: the concept of 'our selves, as understanding, rational Beings'. Obviously, Locke does not think that this idea is obscure; on the contrary, he cites the clearness of the idea as the basis of his optimism about the possibility of a systematic moral science. There is reason to interpret 'clear' in this context as 'adequate' in Locke's technical sense implying representation of the real essence of a mode kind.[13] Notice that later in the passage, Locke reaffirms his point about the possibility of a demonstrative science of ethics by saying that 'the relation of other Modes may certainly be perceived as well as those of Number and Extension'. In short, this passage's answer to the problem of the inadequacy of the idea of human is to interpret the relevant concept of moral agents as the concept of rational selves, and to interpret that concept as a mode idea.[14]

---

[13] Locke writes that 'inadequate ideas are such which are but a partial or incomplete representation of those archetypes to which they are referred', where 'archetypes' designates those things which the ideas are supposed to represent (E ii.xxxi.1: 375). The archetype of a mode idea is the real essence. While Locke uses the term 'clear' in the passage at E iv.iii.18: 549, at E iv.iv.7: 565 he uses the term 'adequate' to express the same point.

[14] One difference between the concept *moral man* and the concept *rational selves* is that the former, as Locke explicates it, implies corporeality while the latter does not. This difference allows Locke to include incorporeal rational beings within the scope of the concept of moral agents. Since he believes that there are actually incorporeal agents, namely angels, this difference is probably an advantage from his point of view. While one might view Locke's inclusion of corporeality in the definition of *moral man* as evidence of a Strawsonian insight about the nature of persons, it seems more likely that it is a vestige of his incomplete departure at that stage from the identification of *human being* as the concept of the moral agent.

The Concept of Persons

There is reason to suppose that Locke thought of the idea of rational selves as the same as the idea of persons appearing in his famous chapter on identity. We have seen that in the discussion of the demonstrative science of ethics, selves are interpreted as 'understanding, rational Beings' (E iv.iii.18: 549); similarly, he says that 'person' stands for 'a thinking intelligent Being' (E ii.xxvii.9: 335). In both contexts, the idea is intended as the idea of the sort of being which is subject to moral law. When Locke writes in his chapter on personal identity that persons are 'intelligent agents, capable of a law' (E ii.xxvii.26: 346), he intends to identify the person as the moral agent, the being whose actions are subject to law and who merits praise or blame for those actions. 'Person', he writes, 'is a Forensick Term appropriating Actions and their Merit . . .' (E ii.xxvii.26: 346); 'in this *personal identity* is founded all the Right and Justice of Reward and Punishment' (E ii.xxvii.18: 341).

There is a difference of emphasis in Locke's discussion of the concept of selves or persons in the two contexts. In his treatment of the possibility of the demonstrative science of ethics, Locke stresses the capacity for abstract thought, the ability to apprehend general laws, as necessary for being a moral agent. This capacity is what 'rationality' designates in the passage on the concept of 'man' as *moral man*; Locke asserts that a monkey could qualify as a moral man if it 'had the use of Reason, to such a degree, as to be able to understand general Signs, and to deduce Consequences about general Ideas' (E iii.xi.16: 517). But the chapter on personal identity emphasizes 'consciousness', the capacity to 'reflect'.

Sometimes Locke refers to reflection as a mental capacity distinct from rationality itself, as though it were an additional condition for being a person. He writes that 'person' designates a being 'that has reason *and reflection, and can consider it self as it self, the same thinking thing in different times and places*' (E ii.xxvii.9: 335; emphasis added). On Locke's view, though, consciousness is not really a separate condition but a necessary concomitant of rationality; he writes that consciousness 'is inseparable from thinking, and as it seems to me essential to it' (E ii.xxvii.9: 335).[15] And

---

[15] It is not clear, of course, that this necessary connection would suffice to justify the claim that the *concept* of rational selves is the same as the *concept* of persons. But Locke is committed to this claim, since he holds that continuity of consciousness may be used to reidentify the person, and he says that the idea for which the word stands determines the conditions for identity (E ii.xxvii.7: 332). Though Locke emphasizes the capacity for abstract thought in his discussion of the concept of moral agent relevant to the demonstrative science of ethics, it is quite possible that he would say that the capacity to reflect is also relevant to subsumption under the moral law; in order to be a moral being, one must be able to recognize that one falls under the moral law. Locke does include the claim that 'there is a harmony between this law and the rational

so Locke uses consciousness as the basis of his account of the identity of the person or self:[16]

Any Substance vitally untied to the present thinking Being, is a part of that very same self which now is: Any thing united to it by a consciousness of former Actions makes also a part of the same self, which is the same both then and now. *Person*, I take it, is the name for this *self*. (E II.xxvii.25–6: 346)

[E]very one finds, that whilst comprehended under that consciousness, the little Finger is as much a part of it *self*, as what is most so. Upon separation of this little Finger, should this consciousness go along with the little Finger, and leave the rest of the Body, 'tis evident the little Finger would be the *Person*, the same *Person*. . . . That with which the *consciousness* of this present thinking thing can join it self, makes the same *Person*, and is one *self* with it . . . (E II.xxvii.17: 341)

CONCLUSION

The fact that Locke's concept of persons has relevance to moral matters is familiar to students of his chapter on personal identity. But if my interpretation is correct, then this concept relates to ethical concerns in an additional, less obvious way; it is relevant to Locke's views about the scope of possible *knowledge* of ethics. Ethics, Locke thinks, is a centrally important kind of knowledge. He describes it as one of the three branches of learning (E IV.xxi.3: 720), and some of his remarks suggest that an interest in moral epistemology may be one of the main motives for his enquiry into the nature and limits of knowledge. He writes, for example, that

Our Business here is not to know all things, but those which concern our Conduct. If we can find out those Measures, whereby a rational Creature put in that State, which Man is in, in this World, may, and ought to govern his Opinions, and Actions depending thereon, we need not be troubled, that some other things escape our Knowledge. (E I.i.6: 46)

I have suggested here that the development of Locke's concept of persons is part of the epistemological enterprise which is the *Essay*'s central focus.

In spite of Locke's later admission that his confidence in the possibility of a priori ethics was naïve, his view about the role of the concept of persons in ethical theorizing has both philosophical and historical interest.

---

nature, and this harmony can be known by the light of nature' as justification for the claim that 'all those who are endowed with a rational nature . . . are morally bound by this law', in the *Essays on the Law of Nature* (EL vii: 199).

[16] Obviously, a fuller analysis of Locke's conception of 'reflection' or 'consciousness' would be needed for a complete interpretation of his views about the relation of this capacity to reason. His remarks about consciousness are very difficult and complex, so a discussion of this topic must be saved for another occasion.

Locke claims that rationality rather than some specific inner constitution is the property relevant to systematic ethics, while the inner constitution rather than the derivative properties would be relevant to systematic natural science.[17] This insight need not be discarded with the rejection of his overly narrow Euclidean model of systematic ethics. The idea that a concept of persons is relevant to ethics, that this concept is distinct from the natural kinds concept of humans, and that the extension of this concept does not rest on issues about the inner structure of the individuals, is central to some of the contemporary literature on ethics.[18]

Considering the relevance of the concept of persons to Locke's proposal for a demonstrative science of ethics also promises to illuminate some aspects of his own philosophy. Thought Locke's doubts about the possibility of this science probably started as early as the Second Edition of the *Essay*,[19] his early concern with the analogy between ethical and mathematical concepts may have paved the way for the famous chapter on personal identity. A crucial feature of Locke's views about mathematical kinds was that membership in these kinds does not depend on the stuff of which the entities are made; in the second draft of the *Essay*, Locke wrote concerning a geometrical figure that

[17] Thus, one cannot hope to establish the foundations of a systematic natural science simply by stipulating a definition for each natural kind, even though this move would remove the problem about the uncertainty of the boundaries of the natural kind. There might be a few discoverable necessary connections at the level of the discoverable properties, but discovery of the real essence would be a necessary condition of establishing a whole systematic science: '[T]he Names of Substances, when made use of as they should be, for the Ideas Men have in their Minds, though they carry a clear and determinate signification with them, will not yet serve us to make many universal Propositions, of whose Truth we can be certain. Not because in this use of them we are uncertain what Things are signified by them, but because the complex Ideas they stand for, are such Combinations of simple ones, as carry not with them any discoverable connexion or repugnancy, but with a very few other Ideas' (E iv.vi.6: 582).

[18] The extension of the concept of person is taken by some writers to be important to the abortion, infanticide, and euthanasia issues. For example, see Tooley 1973; Tooley 1979; Warren 1973; and Warner 1980. More general issues about the concept of person are discussed by Harry Frankfurt in Frankfurt 1971. The view that being a person does not depend logically on having some particular sort of inner constitution has been discussed by many; Hilary Putnam treats some of the issues in Putnam 1964.

[19] That there was at least some erosion of Locke's confidence in the possibility of demonstrating ethical claims between the First and Second Editions of the *Essay* is suggested by a change in the wording of his discussion of the demonstrative science of ethics at one point. In the First Edition, he wrote at E iv.ii.9: 534 n. that 'It is not only Mathematicks, or the Ideas alone of Number, Extension, and Figure, that are capable of Demonstration . . .' In the Second Edition, Locke formulated this passage as follows: 'It has been generally taken for granted, that Mathematicks alone are capable of demonstrative certainty; But to have such an agreement or disagreement, as may intuitively be perceived, being, as I imagine, not the privilege of the Ideas of Number, Extension, and Figure alone, it may possibly be the want of due method, and application in us; and not of sufficient evidence in things, that Demonstration has been thought to have so little to do in other parts of Knowledge . . .' (E iv.ii.9: 534).

wherever that figure exists, it will always have all the same properties it had when I contemplated it in my own understanding; there being no difference in the properties of the same angle or figure, whether it be drawn upon paper, carved in marble, or only fancied in my understanding. (D I: 152)

In the *Essay*'s passage on the concept of moral man, Locke wrote that

The Names of Substances, if they be used in them, as they should, can no more disturb Moral, than they do Mathematical Discourses; Where, if the Mathematicians speak of a Cube or Globe of Gold, or any other Body, he has his clear setled Idea, which varies not . . . (E III.xi.16: 517)

In the mathematical assertion about a cube or globe of gold, the occurrence of 'gold' is entirely irrelevant; it simply does not matter what kind of stuff the cube or globe is made out of, since the geometer is only concerned about the shape. The analogous move in the chapter on personal identity is to set aside as irrelevant the substance constituting a person:

Self is that conscious thinking thing, (whatever Substance, made up of whether Spiritual, or Material, Simple, or Compounded, it matters not) which is sensible . . . and so is concern'd for it *self*, as far as that consciousness extends. (E II.xxvii.17: 341)

And of course the distinction between the concepts *human* and *person*, whose development we have traced in connection with the possible science of ethics, is crucial to the analysis of personal and human identity in Locke's famous chapter on identity:

[T]o conceive, and judge of it aright, we must consider what Idea the Word it is applied to stands for: It being one thing to be the same *Substance*, another the same *Man*, and a third the same *Person*, if *Person*, *Man*, and *Substance*, are three Names standing for three different Ideas . . . (E II.xxvii.7: 332)

Examining the connection between Locke's concept of persons and his proposal for a systematic ethics also shows that here, as in many contexts, Roger Woolhouse's emphasis on the 'real essence' model of a priori truth in Locke is fundamentally correct. Though Woolhouse does not discuss the demonstrative science of ethics, my interpretation confirms his claim that for Locke, 'the possibility of a *priori* knowledge of instructive truths rests on the knowledge of real essences' (Woolhouse 1972: 422).[20] The

---

[20] Woolhouse also expands considerably his discussion of the relevance of real essences and mode ideas to Lockean demonstrative knowledge in Woolhouse 1971. I would add one qualification to Woolhouse's claim that for Locke, 'the possibility of a *priori* knowledge of instructive truths rests on the knowledge of real essences'. This claim makes it sound as though there are absolutely no instructive, universal, certain propositions except through knowledge of the real essence; but Locke does leave open the possibility that there are *a few* instructive a priori propositions for substance concepts even though we are ignorant, on his view, of the real essences of substances (cf. E IV.vi.6: 582).

applicability of this model of a priori knowledge to Locke's views about moral knowledge has not always been recognized. John Yolton, for example, *denies* that Locke thought essences to be relevant to the proposed moral science:

Locke had a set of beliefs about man's nature—that he is frail, made by God, dependent upon God, rational, etc.—which was quite adequate for his subsequent account of morality. The demonstrative morality was not, in other words, to be a deduction from essence. (Yolton 1970*a*: 170)

That interpretation, though, goes counter to Locke's explicit statement that he believes in the possibility of a demonstrative science of ethics *because* he takes moral ideas to represent real essences (see E iii.xi.16: 516).[21] Attention to his remarks about the demonstrative ethics can free one from an overly narrow interpretation of his conception of real essences. Locke thought of his concept of moral agents as a tool which promised ethics an escape, by way of his general model of demonstrative science, from his earlier scepticism about certain, instructive, universal knowledge.[22]

---

[21] Space does not permit attention to Locke's conception of 'adequacy', though more discussion of this topic would be useful here. It is not clear that Locke commits himself to saying that each token of a mode idea is adequate, but at most only that the type is adequate. What exactly adequacy amounts to for mode ideas, and what relevance this has to the nature of a priori truth in Locke, are topics needing more investigation.

[22] For helpful written comments on a previous version of this essay, I am grateful to Roger S. Woolhouse and to Martha Brandt Bolton. I am also grateful to Martha Bolton, Margaret Wilson, Robert Sleigh, Willis Doney, and Vere Chappell for discussion of this paper in June 1979 at the Institute for Advanced Study. I also wish to thank Donna Catudal for comments on an earlier version, in the seminar on A Priori Truth at the University of Pennsylvania in Dec. 1977. Finally, I want to thank Elinor Anne Mattern, whose birth in Ecuador on June 23, 1979 made typing the last draft less boring.

XV

LOCKE AND THE ETHICS OF BELIEF

J. A. PASSMORE

I PROPOSE to look critically at Locke's answer to three closely related questions:

(1) Are there any circumstances whatsoever in which we can properly be described as 'choosing', or 'deciding', whether or not to believe *p*?

(2) If there are such circumstances, does our decision to believe *p* rather than to disbelieve it ever make us liable to moral censure?

(3) If there are no such circumstances, are there any other circumstances in which we can properly be praised or blamed for believing *p*?

If I have chosen to subject Locke, in particular, to such a triune inquisition this is for three reasons. First, because his discussion of these questions is lengthy, detailed, and honest; secondly, because it has been very little explored by Locke scholars; thirdly, because on the face of it Locke falls into puzzling inconsistencies, which need some sort of explanation.

To begin from the last point. A passage in Locke's *A Letter on Toleration* lays it down quite explicitly that 'to believe this or that to be true is not within the scope of our will' (Locke 1968: 121).[1] And, as we shall see, this is by no means the only occasion on which he so definitely denies that men can ever choose what they shall believe. Yet no less explicitly, this time in his *Essay concerning Human Understanding*, he distinguishes a class of cases in which 'Assent, Suspense, or Dissent, are often voluntary Actions' (E IV.xx.15: 716). ('Belief', one should note, he identifies with assent.) Throughout his account of belief, furthermore, Locke relies upon that doctrine which he sums up in one of his running heads: 'Our Assent ought

The British Academy 1980. Reproduced by permission from *Proceedings of the British Academy*, Vol. LXIV (1978), 185–208.

[1] The original latin reads: 'Ut hoc vel illud verum esse credamus, in nostra voluntate situm non est.'

to be regulated by the grounds of Probability' (E iv.xvi.1: 657). Assuming only that 'ought' implies 'can', that 'ought' means something stronger than 'it would be nice if', the Utopian sense of 'ought' in which we might tell someone that he ought to be President of the United States, this appears to entail that we are free thus to regulate, or not to regulate, our assent. Indeed, Locke's main contribution to philosophy, so Gilbert Ryle has somewhat narrowly but not absurdly argued, consists in his having shown us that 'the tenacity with which people hold their opinions is not always, but ought always, to be proportioned to the quantity and quality of the reasons which can be adduced for them' (Ryle 1971: I. 156). And 'ought always to be proportioned' seems to commit Locke to something like W. K. Clifford's main thesis in 'The Ethics of Belief': 'It is wrong always, everywhere, and for anyone, to believe anything upon insufficient evidence' (Clifford 1947: 77). (Although Ryle, we note with interest, ascribes to Locke not 'an ethics of belief' but an 'ethics of thinking'.)

I said that Locke's views had been neglected. Although it presents us with such striking problems in interpretation, the penultimate segment of the *Essay* (iv.xix–xx: 697–719) in which Locke presents his theory, or his theories, on belief, has never been, so far as I know, closely studied. Aaron takes the view that Locke was tiring of his task when he came near to its end, and offers in evidence the fact that he did not revise these chapters as closely as he did their predecessors (Aaron 1971: 248). Admittedly, they contain an exceptional degree of repetition, a common sign of fatigue. Yet they are quite fundamental for Locke. There were two projects particularly dear to his heart: the first, to advocate, if only within limits, religious toleration; the second, to undermine one particular sort of religion, 'enthusiasm', fanaticism, yet without weakening religious faith. The epistemological foundations of his argument are, in both cases, expounded in these chapters. He did not revise them, one might plausibly suggest, not because he was tired but because the ideas they contain were so fundamental to his thinking, not revisable; the repetitions arise from his determination to hammer home the crucial points. (He added to the fourth edition, indeed, a new chapter 'Of Enthusiasm', still further to insist upon them.)

To turn now to the detail and the honesty of Locke's argument, let us look first at the definition of belief which he offers us: 'the admitting or receiving any Proposition for true, upon Arguments or Proofs that are found to persuade us to receive it as true, without certain Knowledge that it is so' (E iv.xv.3: 655). Believing, it will be plain, is on this view an imperfect surrogate for knowing, made necessary, Locke tells us, by the fact that true knowledge is 'very short and scanty' (E iv.xiv.1: 652). When immediate intuition does not suffice, demonstration can give us knowledge; we *see* that the conclusion of the demonstration must be true. But where such demonstrations are lacking, as they mostly are, we have no option but to fall back upon probable reasoning. Notice that on Locke's definition there is no such thing as an entirely groundless belief; we are persuaded by 'Arguments or Proofs' to accept as true those propositions we believe to be true. This is so, even although the 'proofs' do not amount to demonstrations. Locke defines belief, then, as a purely intellectual operation, in a way which emphasizes at once its likeness, and its inferiority, to knowledge.

It is not at all surprising, in the light of this definition, that Locke generally prefers to speak in terms of 'assent' rather than of 'belief', even although, as we said, he takes them to be synonymous. The mere having of an idea as the result of experience does not for Locke, as it does for Hume, count as believing (cf. Passmore 1977). We 'believe' only when a proposition is before us for our consideration and there are 'inducements' for us to accept it as true—grounds, that is, which make it seem probable, likely to be true. These 'inducements' may be of either of two sorts, the conformity of the proposition with 'our own Knowledge, Observation and Experience' or 'the Testimony of others, vouching their Observation and Experience'.

The two grounds of probability will, in favourable circumstances, reinforce one another. '[A]s the conformity of our Knowledge, as the certainty of Observations, as the frequency and constancy of Experience, and the number and credibility of Testimonies, do more or less agree, or disagree with it, so is any Proposition in it self, more or less probable' (E IV.xv.6: 657). Many people, Locke confesses, give assent to propositions on much weaker grounds than this; they assent to propositions, indeed, merely because someone tells them that they are true. But this is a 'wrong ground of Assent'; those who have recourse to it are not proceeding rationally.

The Mind if it will proceed rationally, ought to examine all the grounds of Probability, and see how they make more or less, *for or against* any probable Proposition, before it assents to or dissents from it, and upon a due balancing the whole, reject, or receive it, with a more or less firm assent, proportionably to the preponderancy of the greater grounds of Probability on the one side or the other. (E IV.xv.5: 656)

On the assumption that for Locke belief is involuntary, his choice of language in this analysis of belief and probability may somewhat surprise us. When we believe, he has said, we 'admit' propositions as true, we 'receive' them as such. As the *Oxford English Dictionary* explicitly points out, the primary use of the word 'admit' is voluntary. We can admit, or we can refuse to admit, a person to our house; we can admit, or we can refuse to admit, to a fault, to a responsibility, or that something is the case. The word 'receive' is more often involuntary in its connotations. But when, as here, it is linked with 'admit', it is natural to read it as having that sense in which a person 'receives callers' or 'receives guests' or 'receives stolen goods'—in each case a voluntary act. A 'received opinion', we might add in favour of this interpretation, is surely an opinion which is generally *accepted*. And 'accepting' is, in most contexts, something we choose to do.

Coupling Locke's analysis of the way in which the beliefs of a rational man are founded on the probabilities with his use of such words as 'admitting' and 'receiving' to describe our coming to believe, we should very naturally interpret his analysis of rational belief in something like the following manner: a proposition is put before us, or we put it before ourselves, for our consideration; we estimate its probability in the light of the arguments for and against its being true; we give our assent to it with a degree of assurance proportionate to its relative probability. But this analysis is precisely parallel to the analysis we should offer if we were asked to give an account of what we mean by a rational *decision*. A proposed course of action, we might then say, is put before us, or we put it before ourselves, for our consideration; we estimate its desirability in the light of the considerations for and against it; we agree to it if the considerations *pro* are stronger than the considerations *contra*. So on this interpretation belief would simply be one form of decision-making, that form in which the considerations *pro* and *contra* are considerations of probability. And if such decision-making is not voluntary, then what *is* voluntary? The only question which could remain is whether irrational belief is also voluntary. Yet Locke, as we saw, asserts all belief to be involuntary, whether it be rational or irrational.

Faced with so absolute a contradiction between what seems to be entailed—viz. that belief is one form of voluntary decision—by the interpretation we have so far favoured and the doctrine to which Locke so firmly commits himself, that belief is *not* a voluntary decision, we have no option but to look again at our interpretation. Then we notice that even although Locke certainly tells us that a man must *if he will proceed rationally* assent to a proposition with a degree of assurance proportional to its probability, where the phrase 'if he will proceed rationally' would suggest that irrational people do not thus regulate their assent, he also tells us that no one, rational or irrational, can help giving his assent to the more probable proposition. The probability, for Locke as not for Hume, is one thing, the degree of assurance another, but the first necessarily engenders the second. '[T]hat a Man should afford his Assent to that side, on which the less Probability appears to him, seems to me utterly impracticable, and as impossible, as it is to believe the same thing probable and improbable at the same time' (E IV.xx.15: 717). If we take this to be Locke's considered opinion, two conclusions seem to follow. The first, that where we went wrong in our previous analysis of Locke's argument was in supposing that after considering the *pro* and *contra* probabilities a person, on Locke's view, *decides* to believe or not to believe. No such decision, it would now appear, enters into the situation. Finding the probabilities *pro* a proposition to be more powerful than the consideration *contra* that proposition, a person cannot but believe the proposition with a degree of assurance proportional to the degree to which it seems to him to be more probable. There is no choice in the matter. The second conclusion is that when Locke tells us that 'our Assent ought to be regulated by the grounds of Probability', i.e. the actual or real grounds of probability, he must after all be using 'ought' in its Utopian sense, must be saying that the world would be a better place if people so regulated their assent, rather than that they are under a moral obligation to do so. And Ryle, too, must be using 'ought' in this Utopian sense when he sums up Locke's conclusion in the maxim that 'the tenacity with which people hold their opinions is not always, but ought always, to be proportioned to the quantity and quality of the reasons which can be adduced for them'. No doubt, in an ideal world assent would be governed by *the* grounds of probability, by the reasons which *can* be adduced. But in any actual world human beings will believe not in accordance with the grounds which *can* be adduced but in accordance with the grounds they actually have before them, however feeble they may be; they will automatically give their assent to what seems to them, at that moment, the most probable view. To tell them that they ought to believe in accordance with the *real* probabilities, the grounds that *can* be adduced, as distinct from the immediately obvious probabilities, is to tell them they ought to do what they cannot possibly do. 'Admit' and 'receive' have, on this showing, their passive sense, that passive sense in which wax admits, or receives, impressions. Does not Locke tell us that the mind is like a piece of wax? A 'received opinion' is not, it would seem, an opinion we have accepted—for the concept of 'acceptance' is irremediably voluntary—but rather an opinion which has impressed itself upon us.

But setting out to avoid an interpretation of Locke which led inevitably to the conclusion that belief was a voluntary decision we have now substituted an analysis which Locke would find quite as unpalatable, with its consequence that no one can ever be blamed for believing as he does, since we believe as we must. As a defender of toleration, to be sure, Locke might find this conclusion palatable but not as a critic of enthusiasm. He wants to be able to blame the enthusiast, as indeed the atheist, for believing as he does.

Perhaps there is a way out. We distinguished two senses of the phrase 'grounds of Assent'—the sense in which it means the *real* grounds as they would be known to an ideal human observer, the Utopian grounds, and the sense in which it means the grounds as an agent immediately perceives them. But when Locke talks about 'the grounds of Assent' or 'the real grounds' or, in Ryle's phrase, 'the reasons which can be adduced', he usually means something which falls between these two extremes. He means the grounds, the reasons, which would be available to us if we chose to enquire, the reasons which somebody—not an ideal observer, but someone who has investigated further than we have done—would be in a position to put before us, or which we ourselves could discover, if we enquired further. It is *these* grounds, we might now suggest, which ought, on Locke's view, to regulate our assent. We can be blamed for not regulating the degree of our assent by reference to them, just because we can be blamed for not carrying our enquiries as far as we should have done.

Such an interpretation, one might continue by arguing, would square with Locke's attempt, towards the very end of his *Essay* (E IV.xx.16: 717–18), to draw a parallel, in respect to the character and limits of their involuntariness, between belief, perception, and knowledge. To see the point of this parallel, we shall have to revert to an earlier chapter (xiii) in which Locke attempts to establish the involuntariness of perception and knowledge while yet leaving open a very restricted sense in which they are voluntary. It in no way depends on a perceiver's will, Locke there says, whether he sees something as black or yellow, whether he feels it as cold or as scalding hot. 'The Earth will not appear painted with Flowers, nor the Fields covered with Verdure, whenever he has a Mind to it: in the cold Winter, he cannot help seeing it white and hoary, if he will look abroad' (E IV.xiii.2: 650). We are free, in respect to perception, only this far; we are free to decide whether to inspect such a landscape more closely 'and with an intent application, endeavour to observe accurately all that is visible in it' or, on the contrary, simply to take it in at a glance and pass on to other matters.

Similarly with knowledge. In respect to its voluntariness as in so many other respects, 'knowledge', Locke argues, 'has a great Conformity with our Sight'. Like perception, it is *neither wholly necessary nor wholly voluntary*. Just as, if only we open our eyes, we cannot help seeing the winter landscape as white, so too, if we choose to compare our ideas, we cannot but see that they are related in particular ways, and thus arrive at knowledge. Given only that we have the concepts of one, two, three, and six we see at once, if we take the trouble to compare them, that, taken together, one, two, and three make six. Given, too, that we compare the concepts of frail dependent man and omnipotent God we cannot but see that 'Man is to honour, fear, and obey GOD'. But if we do not choose to compare our ideas, this knowledge, mathematical or moral, will never come our way.

> [A]ll that is *voluntary* in our Knowledge [so Locke sums up], is the *employing*, or with-holding any of *our Faculties* from this or that sort of Objects, and a more, or less accurate survey of them: But they being employed, *our Will hath no Power to determine the Knowledge of the Mind* one way or other; that is done only by the Objects themselves, as far as they are clearly discovered. (E ɪv.xiii.2: 650–1)

What we have before our minds, that is, determines what we know. Our knowledge is voluntary only in so far as we can decide what we *do* have before our minds.

Now for the comparison with belief.

> As Knowledge, is no more arbitrary than Perception [Locke writes], so, I think, Assent is no more in our Power than Knowledge. When the Agreement of any two *Ideas* appears to our Minds, whether immediately, or by the Assistance of Reason, I can no more refuse to perceive, no more avoid knowing it, than I can avoid seeing those Objects, which I turn my Eyes to, and look on in day-light: And what upon full Examination I find the most probable, I cannot deny my Assent to. . . . Yet *we can hinder both Knowledge and Assent, by stopping our Enquiry*, and not imploying our Faculties in the search of any Truth. If it were not so, Ignorance, Error, or Infidelity could not in any Case be a Fault. Thus in some Cases, we can prevent or suspend our Assent: But can a Man, versed in modern or ancient History, doubt whether there be such a Place as *Rome*, or whether there was such a Man as *Julius Caesar*? (E ɪv.xx.16: 717)

Notice the progress of Locke's argument, which is consistent with our initial assumptions about his intentions. He is far from denying that ignorance, error, and infidelity can in some circumstances be a fault. ('Infidelity', of course, in that sense which links it with 'being an infidel', with disbelieving.) The enthusiast and the atheist can be condemned on moral grounds, for believing what they should not believe. The only problem, as he sees it, is to reconcile this undoubted truth with his other, no less firm, conviction that belief is never, in the full sense, voluntary.

He tries to reconcile his two basic convictions by applying to the case of belief what he had previously said about perception and knowledge. In the same sense in which we cannot help perceiving that the landscape before our eyes is white, or knowing that two and two make four, we cannot help believing that there is such a city as Rome and that there was such a person as Julius Caesar. But just as it lies within our power to decide whether merely to glance at the snow or to look at it closely, to study or not to study arithmetic, so too, he argues, it lies in our power to decide whether to scrutinize a proposition carefully before we assent to it. Only so far is belief voluntary.

It would seem, then, that Locke gives a clear and definite answer to each of our original three questions. There are *no* circumstances in which we decide to believe *p*; the question whether we can be blamed for thus deciding does not, therefore, ever arise. Nevertheless, there are circumstances in which we can be blamed for believing *p*. This is when we believe *p* without having sufficiently explored the possibility that it is false and if we had done so would have disbelieved it.

Not, Locke now hastens to add, that it is always our duty to enquire before we believe. We are not called upon to submit *all* our beliefs to critical investigation. Precepts so rigorous as this would place an intolerable burden on us. In a great many cases it is a matter of no consequence, whether to ourselves or to other people, what we believe—'whether our King *Richard* the Third was crook-back'd, or no; or whether *Roger Bacon* was a Mathematician, or a Magician'. In such instances ' 'tis not strange, that the Mind should give it self up to the common Opinion, or render it self to the first Comer'—not strange, and perfectly forgiveable. We do not decide to believe such propositions; we simply acquiesce in them without enquiry. He suggests, even, that in respect to such opinions we are free; 'the Mind lets them float at liberty'. This is not merely a loose metaphor. For he continues thus: 'where the Mind judges that the Proposition has concernment in it . . . and the Mind sets it self seriously to enquire, and examine the Probability: there, I think, it is not in our Choice, to take which side we please, if manifest odds appear on either. The greater Probability, I think, in that Case, will determine the Assent' (E iv.xx.16: 717–18). So Locke is drawing a contrast. He is arguing that it is only when we enquire closely that we are not free to choose—'*there*, it is not in our Choice, to take which side we please'; 'the greater probability will *in that Case* determine the Assent'. He is leaving open the possibility, which he had previously rejected, of our 'taking what side we please'—if only in respect to unimportant beliefs into the grounds of which we have not deeply enquired.

We can, however, save Locke's central doctrine that belief is involuntary, even if at the cost of this contrast, by withdrawing his concession that in the case of the floating opinion we are free to choose what to believe. Such an opinion, he might have said, simply enters our mind and lodges there. He himself compares it, indeed, with a mote entering our eye. But in that case he will have to modify his earlier definition of belief. For these will then be *groundless* beliefs. Perhaps we should rather suggest, as being Locke's central view, that such beliefs are accepted by us on the ground that they are commonly asserted. What Locke is really telling us, on this view, is that only if we enquire will our beliefs be regulated by real probabilities, as distinct from such 'wrong grounds of Assent' as popular opinion.

One now begins to understand why Ryle ascribed to Locke an 'ethics of thinking' rather than an 'ethics of belief'. For where we go wrong, on this interpretation, is in failing to investigate rather than in believing or failing to believe. Our investigations, Locke freely admits, may in some cases lead us astray. As a result of investigating, we may arrive at a false belief which, had we not investigated, would never have occurred to us. But that does not mean that we were then wrong to investigate. 'He that examines, and upon a fair examination embraces an error for a truth', he writes in a *Commonplace Book* entry, 'has done his duty', the 'duty to search after truth' (King 1830: II. 75–6).

If we accept this interpretation, then we could put Locke's argument thus: 'Just as what we know depends on what ideas we have before us, so what we believe depends on what *evidence* we have before us. But it is often the case that we would have had different evidence before us had we investigated further. When the question at issue is one of great importance we ought therefore to investigate it further. So to say that our beliefs *ought* to be regulated by the grounds of probability—that these grounds are not only "the Foundations on which our *Assent* is built" but also "the measure whereby its several degrees are, or ought to be, *regulated*" (E IV.xvi.1: 657)—means that although the evidence we at any time have before us will *in fact* determine the degree of our assent, yet our degree of assent *ought* to be regulated by the evidence we *would* have had before us had we chosen to enquire'.

Clearly, however, something has now gone seriously wrong, at least on the assumption that 'ought' implies 'can'. If our degree of assurance is inevitably determined by the evidence we have before us, if belief is simply something we passively have in the presence of such evidence, just as the perception of a snowy landscape is something we passively have, on Locke's view, in the presence of such a landscape, what is the point of telling us that we ought not to believe until we enquire further? It would certainly be quite ridiculous to say that we ought not to perceive the landscape until we have examined it more closely. Remember Locke's definition of rational procedure: '*the Mind . . . ought to examine all the grounds of Probability*, and see how they make more or less, *for or against* any probable Proposition, before it assents to or dissents from it' (E IV.xv.5: 657). This *simply isn't possible*, if we automatically respond with the appropriate degree of assurance to any proposition as soon as we have it before us.

Once more, our attempt to interpret Locke seems to have reached an impasse. Perhaps we had better look again at the alleged parallelism between belief and knowledge in case that is what has been misleading us. In the course of drawing this parallel, Locke tells us that we can 'suspend or prevent' our belief. And this is exactly what he must be urging us to do, when he lays it down that our beliefs ought to be regulated by the evidence we *could* have had before us had we investigated rather than by the evidence we have before us prior to investigation. For this implies that we can stop ourselves from believing until we have conducted these investigations. What corresponds to such suspension or prevention in the case of knowledge? Locke's answer is clear enough: *'we can hinder both Knowledge and Assent by stopping our Enquiry.'* We can prevent ourselves from knowing any geometry by not studying it, we can suspend our knowledge of geometry by ceasing to study it. Similarly, then, we can prevent ourselves from believing that Caesar was assassinated by not studying ancient history and suspend any further beliefs about his assassination by ceasing to read as soon as we discover that he was assassinated. But that is not at all what Locke has in mind when he grants that we can sometimes suspend our belief. Neither is it what we ordinarily have in mind when we use that phrase. (Incidentally, we never speak of ourselves as 'suspending our knowledge'.)

Suppose, for example, I go to see a play about the assassination of Julius Caesar. I may wonder whether it gives an accurate account of the assassination. I describe myself as 'suspending' my belief that it does, or does not, until I can enquire further, perhaps by reading a history textbook when I return home. (This is not at all the same thing, I should perhaps add, as the Coleridgian 'willing suspension of disbelief'.) 'Suspending my belief' is by no means equivalent, then, to ceasing to enquire. Rather, I suspend my belief until I *can* enquire, perhaps because I previously knew nothing about Julius Caesar but know that plays are not always historically accurate, perhaps because the playwright depicts an incident which conflicts with what I had previously believed about the assassination of Julius Caesar. My suspension of belief has grounds, then, but that does not stop it from being voluntary. My decisions normally have grounds. 'Voluntary' is not a synonym for 'arbitrary'.

We can blame someone for not knowing something or for not having perceived something: 'You ought to know that', 'you ought to have seen that'. This is certainly equivalent to 'If you had looked carefully, or if you had reflected for a moment, you would have known that'. In a parallel way, one might be blamed for believing as a result of inadequate enquiry—'You wouldn't have believed that, if you had looked into the matter more closely.' One can be blamed, too, for claiming to know when one does not know, claiming to have perceived when one has not looked, claiming to have good grounds for a belief when one has no such grounds. But one cannot be blamed for knowing *prior* to comparing or for perceiving without looking; this is impossible. One can in contrast be blamed for believing before investigating—and it is then for *believing*, not merely for not investigating, that one is blamed.

So the attempt to assimilate the voluntariness of belief to the voluntariness of knowledge breaks down. It is not just that we can decide not to enquire; we can decide, it would seem, not to believe until we have enquired. Locke's dictum 'What upon full Examination I find the most probable, I cannot deny my Assent to' now assumes a fresh significance. What is the phrase 'upon full examination' doing in this dictum? If the analogy with perception and knowledge were a perfect one, then Locke should simply have written: 'What I find the most probable, I cannot deny my Assent to'. Instead, he adds the phrase 'after full examination' with the suggestion that I *can* deny my assent to what looks to be probable after a *less than full* examination. The parallel at this point is not, indeed, between Locke's theory of belief and his theory of knowledge but between his theory of belief and his theory of desire.

Our will, he suggested in the first edition of the *Essay*, is determined by what we immediately perceive to be the greater good; that is parallel to saying that our belief is determined by what we immediately perceive to be the greater probability. If we sometimes choose wrongly, Locke went on to add, this is because we do not always fully investigate the remote consequences of our actions. That is parallel to saying that if we sometimes believe wrongly this is because we do not always fully explore the probability of what we believe. As Locke's theory of the will stands in the first edition, however, 'choose wrongly' cannot mean 'choose in a manner in which the agent morally should not have chosen'. An outside observer may be in a position to remark: 'had he considered remoter consequences he would have chosen differently'. From the outsider's point of view the choice is then a wrong one. But the agent himself, and of necessity, has chosen what seemed to him the greater good; he cannot be blamed for doing so. It would have been *better* had he chosen otherwise. So in the Utopian sense of 'ought', he ought to have chosen differently. But in the moral sense of 'ought', no such judgement can be passed upon him. For how can the mind wait to explore before choosing, if it is always automatically determined by the greater good as it perceives it?

In the second edition of the *Essay*, Locke therefore introduced a fundamental change into his discussion of voluntary action. The mind, he now says, has a power to suspend its desires. '[D]uring this *suspension* of any desire', he writes, 'before the *will* be determined to action, and the action (which follows that determination) done, we have opportunity to examine, view, and judge of the good or evil of what we are going to do; and when, upon due *Examination*, we have judg'd, we have done our duty . . . ; and 'tis not a fault, but a perfection of our nature to desire, will, and act according to the last result of a fair *Examination*' (E II.xxi.47: 263–4).

We are no longer allowed to excuse ourselves, then, by explaining that we responded to what we perceived to be the greater good, that the remoter consequences we did not perceive. For we would have inhibited our impulse to act until we had explored further; the mere perception of a course of action as being to our greater good does not immediately and irresistibly compel us to choose it.

The parallel between Locke on desire and Locke on belief should by now be obvious. From the point of view of an outside observer an agent believes wrongly if he believes as he would not have believed had he explored further. But the agent might reply: 'I believed as I had to believe on the evidence before me. If I had had your information, my belief would have been different. But it was not in fact before me. My belief may be *incorrect*, wrong in that sense, but nonetheless it was not wrong of me to hold it.' Locke's counter-argument, or so I am suggesting, could run something like this:

'During the suspension of any belief, we have an opportunity to examine, view and judge the probability of what we are being asked to believe; and when, upon due examination, we have judged, we have done our duty . . . ; it is not a fault but a perfection of our nature, to believe according to the last result of a fair examination.'

Our duty, then, is to hold ourselves back from choosing, or from believing, until we have considered the situation fully; people who do not do this can properly be blamed. But after such an examination, we cannot but choose what then seems to us the greater good, cannot but believe what seems to us most probable. And this is not as a result of some defect, some limitation on our freedom. On the contrary, it is 'a perfection of our nature' thus to believe. At this level, the truth of freedom is necessity.

One might argue, of course, that Locke was mistaken in supposing that we can voluntarily suspend our beliefs. Perhaps the true situation, as Professor Curley has suggested, is this: the arguments *pro* and *contra* are sometimes so balanced that our belief is suspended, as a balance is suspended by equal weights on either side (Curley 1975: 175). So suspension of belief is no more voluntary than is believing or disbelieving, it is equally determined by the perceived probabilities.

But Locke cannot take this way out. We ought, on his view, to suspend our beliefs whenever we discover that they rest on unexamined grounds. This does not at all imply that the case against them is as strong as the case for them. That we do not yet know. The analogy is with suspending a policeman from his duties, pending enquiries. We have some ground for suspicion: that is all. Unless it is possible for human beings to suspend their belief in this sense, it is quite pointless to tell them that they ought not to accept beliefs on inadequate evidence. They will automatically believe whatever at that moment seems to them probable, with no choice in the matter. To those who reply that it is indeed pointless thus to rebuke them, that we *cannot* suspend our beliefs, Locke would have replied, I think, as he does to those who doubt whether we can suspend our desires: experience shows us that we can (E II.xxi.47: 263).

Such an appeal to introspection might dissatisfy us; we may suspect Locke, both in relation to belief and desire, of employing, in the concept of suspension, an *ad hoc* device for reconciling his moral conviction that we ought to hold certain beliefs, make certain choices, with his theoretical conviction that our belief is always determined by our perception of probabilities, our choice by our perception of the greater good. But to describe him as proceeding in an *ad hoc* manner would be unfair; that we can suspend our belief is certainly a common presumption. It might turn out to be mistaken, but it is certainly not the merely factitious product of a theoretician's dilemma. So, for example, in his *The Scientific Imagination*, Gerald Holton has argued that the scientist must learn both to suspend his belief and to suspend his disbelief, neither believing as soon as a plausible hypothesis presents itself nor disbelieving as soon as some accepted view is apparently overthrown by new evidence (Holton 1978: 71). He does not take this view as a way out of problems in the theory of belief, but rather as a result of reflection on what actually happens within the institutions of science.

Locke would not be satisfied with the suggestion, made explicit by Bernard Williams, that we wrongly suppose ourselves to have some degree of control over our believing only because belief naturally passes over into public assertion and we do have a degree of control over what we publicly assert. As Locke emphasizes, there are many societies in which people cannot, without making a martyr of themselves, publicly assert their beliefs; they learn to be careful about what they say. If we live in such a society, it is still our duty, as Locke sees the situation, not to *believe* without examination. And insofar as to ascribe such a duty is to assume that belief can be voluntarily suspended, Locke is committed to the conclusion that belief lies under our control.

But our story is still not complete. Locke is more than a little perturbed by the fact that people's beliefs are so often not in accordance with the real probabilities, even if we take this to mean the probabilities as they would be estimated by someone who had scrupulously examined the available information, as distinct from the probabilities as an ideal human observer would estimate them. '[I]f', he writes, 'Assent be grounded on Likelihood, if the proper Object and Motive of our Assent be Probability [notice the transition from "grounded on" to "*proper* Object"] . . . it will be demanded, how Men come to give their Assents contrary to Probability' (E IV:xx.1: 706). Locke is convinced that he can satisfactorily reply to this objection. He attempts to do so, indeed, *before* he formulates his final view that belief is voluntary only in the sense in which knowledge is voluntary.

There are two distinct sets of cases to be considered, the first in which men do not have the relevant information before them, the second in which they have the relevant information before them but use, Locke says, 'wrong measures of probability'. In the first set of cases, Locke sees no theoretical difficulty. If people are so exhausted by hard labour or so politically restricted or so lacking in intelligence or so lazy that they are unable or unwilling to enquire, then it is only to be expected that the opinions they hold will be at variance with the real probabilities. For theological reasons, Locke has to maintain that these obstacles are never so formidable as to render a person incapable of discovering the fundamental truths of religion. But he can freely grant that such intellectually handicapped persons may, in respect to a wide range of their beliefs, hold beliefs which further enquiry would show them to be highly improbable—and, except where they are lazy, cannot be blamed for so believing.

The second class of cases Locke finds much more troublesome. There are men, he has to confess, who, 'even where the real Probabilities appear, and are plainly laid before them, do not admit of the conviction, nor yield unto manifest Reasons, but do either *epechein*, suspend their Assent, or give it to the less probable Opinion' (E IV.xx.7: 711). How can this be so if belief is an automatic response to the greater probability? Where such men go wrong, Locke tries to persuade us, is in *their estimates of probability*. They do not 'yield unto manifest reasons' because they assign probabilities wrongly. Note once again the close connection with Locke's theory of the will. He himself brings out the parallel. '[T]he Foundation of Errour', he writes, 'will lie in wrong Measures of Probability; as the Foundation of Vice in wrong Measures of Good' (E IV.xx.16: 718).

But how, in turn, does *this* mistake arise, this false belief that *p* has a greater probability that it really has? First, according to Locke, human beings tend to give too great a weight to general principles, principles which were instilled into them when they were children and which they therefore wrongly take to be innate and unquestionable. Indeed, they 'will disbelieve their own Eyes, renounce the Evidence of their Senses, and give their own Experience the lye, rather than admit of anything disagreeing with these sacred Tenets' (E IV.xx.10: 713). Locke roundly condemns those who act thus; at this point his theory of belief links with his rejection of innate principles. But this is not because they have *deliberately decided* to give a higher probability to these principles than they ought to give them; the principles were not deliberately adopted but were 'riveted there by long Custom and Education' (E IV.xx.9: 712). When Locke condemns such dogmatists—although with a measure of tolerance—it is in his usual fashion for *not enquiring*, not testing, not examining, their fundamental beliefs. This, he thinks, they could have done, had they so chosen.

Now, it is relatively easy to understand how a person educated all his life to hold a certain belief should ascribe to it so high a probability that nothing can outweigh it. But Locke includes the 'enthusiast' in this same category. 'Let an Enthusiast be principled, that he or his Teacher is inspired, and acted upon by an immediate Communication of the Divine Spirit, and you in vain bring the evidence of clear Reasons against his Doctrines' (E IV.xx.10: 713). In this instance, a person has *come to* assign a high probability to a quite preposterous proposition, a proposition which, furthermore, may be quite at variance with those principles to which, from childhood, he had been accustomed to assign a high probability. We cannot explain how *he* comes to make his mistakes by assimilating him to the person who was brought up to hold a particular belief.

Perhaps Locke has his classifications wrong. Perhaps he should have brought the enthusiast within the ambit of a third case he has described, when the objective grounds of probability do not accord with men's passions and appetites. 'Tell a Man, passionately in Love, that he is jilted; bring a score of Witnesses of the Falsehood of his Mistress, 'tis ten to one but three kind Words of hers shall invalidate all the Testimonies. *Quod volumus, facilè credimus; what suits our Wishes, is forwardly believed*' (E IV.xx.12: 715).

This, however, is more than a little startling. For we had been encouraged to assimilate belief to knowledge and to perception where, on Locke's view, passion has no such power. In the present instance, men do not deny the probabilities; at the same time they refuse to accept the conclusions which follow from them. Is this not a clear case of choosing to believe the less probable? The lover's friends would certainly describe the situation in these terms: 'he chose to believe his mistress rather than us'.

Locke tries to offer an alternative analysis of the situation, consistent with the general course of his argument as we have so far presented it: 'Not but that it is the Nature of the Understanding constantly to close with the more probable side, but yet a Man hath a Power to suspend and restrain its Enquiries, and not permit a full and satisfactory Examination, as far as the matter in Question is capable, and will bear it to be made.' But in the present instance this now-familiar tactic will not work. The evidence is *already* before the lover; he needs no more evidence. Neither does he suspend his belief: he believes his mistress and does not believe the witnesses, witnesses in whom, on other matters, the would have implicit faith.

So Locke tries a different tack, still working with his intellectualist conception of belief. In such cases, Locke argues, the person who faces the evidence squarely and yet says 'Although I cannot answer, I shall not yield', is still relying on grounds which seem to him probable. Fresh evidence, he will tell himself and his critics, may emerge, a hidden fallacy may be revealed, a witness may turn out to be unreliable, a conspiracy to be afoot. Locke is not suggesting that this is *always* a possible rejoinder. '[S]ome Proofs in Matter of Reason, being suppositions upon universal Experience, are so cogent and clear; and some Testimonies in Matter of Fact so universal, that [a man] cannot refuse his Assent' (E IV.xx.15: 716). But few philosophers, at least in their cooler moments, have ever supposed that it is *always* possible to choose what to believe. The only question is whether this is *ever* possible. And now Locke makes the concession we began by quoting: 'in Propositions, where though the Proofs in view are of most Moment, yet there are sufficient grounds, to suspect that there is either Fallacy in Words, or certain Proofs, as considerable, to be produced on the contrary side, there Assent, Suspense, or Dissent are often voluntary Actions'. The arguments we have before us in such instances we admit to be extremely powerful, and yet, as we say, we 'refuse to believe' the conclusion which would follow from them, we 'do not choose to believe' that it is true.

The fact that in such situations we so unselfconsciously use such expressions as 'refuse to believe', 'choose to believe' does not, of course, finally settle the matter. These expressions might rest on intellectual confusions, myths about our own capacities; or they might be idiomatic ways of talking, misleading only if we (wrongly) take them literally. Perhaps Locke need not have made his concession. Very strong evidence has been produced, let us say, that a political leader we have been accustomed to admire has betrayed us. We say that we 'do not choose to believe' or 'prefer not to believe' that he is guilty. But all this may mean is that out of loyalty we are not prepared to *admit* that he is guilty.

Such an interpretation would link very neatly with the set of observations with which Locke ends this section of his *Essay*. After all his explanations, he is still worried about the fact that men have so many false beliefs, beliefs contrary to probabilities of which they are well aware, even although, in his view, their beliefs are naturally determined by the evidence before them. What men call their 'beliefs', he therefore suggests, are very often not beliefs at all but expressions of party loyalty. 'They are resolved to stick to a Party, that Education or Interest has engaged them in; and there, like the common Soldiers of an Army, shew their Courage and Warmth, as their Leaders direct, without ever examining, or so much as knowing the Cause they contend for' (E iv.xx.18: 719).

It is not just that such 'common soldiers' have acquiesced without reflection in some current opinion, like the man who acquiesces in the view that Richard III was a hunch-back. For he at least understands what he is acquiescing in; he gives the proposition enough attention to be confident that it is not utterly ridiculous, even if he does not closely examine its truth. In contrast, Locke is suggesting, the majority of the members of a party or a Church do not even *understand* the views to which their membership commits them. Their so-called 'beliefs' are, on their lips, mere catch-cries, expressing their resolution to stick by their party. So their apparent capacity to believe what cuts clean across the evidence is improperly so described. It is a capacity, only, to utter certain phrases when their party or Church calls upon them to do so. And if 'I believe *p*', can sometimes thus be equated with 'I stand by the party which asserts *p*', then equally 'I refuse to believe that *p*', 'I like to believe that *p*', 'you ought to believe that *p*', can be expressions of, or exhortations to, loyalty, whether to a person or a party.

Locke puts forward a very similar argument in his *Commonplace Book* (King 1830: ii. 76–7). He then asks us to consider the case of a man who adheres, without critical reflection, to what Locke calls 'a collection of certain professions'—let us say the Thirty-nine Articles or the Westminster Confession. Such an adherence, Locke tells us, 'is not in truth believing but a profession to believe'.

Yet, one naturally objects, if we ask the loyal adherent: 'Do you believe *p*?', he will certainly, and sincerely, reply 'Yes'. Furthermore, if the belief is of the kind that carries actions as a consequence, he will engage in those actions; he will not merely tell us that God is present in the consecrated wafer, to take Locke's own example of transubstantiation, he will approach Communion reverently. If we ask him to explain to us in detail in what the doctrine of the Real Presence consists, he will no doubt rapidly become confused, should we not be satisfied with the stock-catechism answers. But does this imply that he does not actually believe in the Real Presence? One is reluctant either on the one side to identify a merely habitual response—in which utterances 'are made, actions performed, but without any understanding whatsoever'—with a genuine belief or on the other side to permit oneself to speak of 'beliefs' only in those instances where the situation has been fully comprehended. Some degree of under- standing, some capacity to answer relevant questions, seems to be required for a genuine belief. But *what* degree of understanding is quite another matter. Unless we put the criteria high, we shall not find it possible to avoid the conclusion, which Locke wants to avoid, that a great many people hold quite absurd beliefs. Yet if we do set them high, we make it impossible for anybody to believe, as distinct from merely parroting phrases, unless he has considerable intellectual gifts, a conclusion which seems quite monstrous.

So far, I have had nothing to say about the chapter on 'Enthusiasm' which Locke introduced into the fourth edition of the *Essay* immediately prior to that chapter on 'Wrong Assent, or Errour' to which our attention has latterly been directed. One is indeed tempted to pass it over as of merely historical interest. But in fact it entirely disrupts the argument he has so far developed and continues to develop in the chapter which now succeeds it. In discussing the enthusiasts we might expect him to experi- ence his greatest difficulties in defending his intellectualist account of belief. And this is precisely what we do find. We find, too, confirmation of our suggestion that the enthusiast should be classified with the lover who believes against the evidence. Locke now begins to describe rational belief not in terms of a purely intellectual weighing-up but rather in terms of the operations of a certain form of passion—the love of truth.

No doubt, he links his new emphasis on passion with the course of his previous argument. There is, he says, one unerring mark of the lover of truth: 'The not entertaining any Proposition with greater assurance than the Proofs it is built upon will warrant' (E IV.xix.1: 697). But whereas we had once been given to understand that human beings were so constituted as inevitably thus to adjust their degree of assurance to the evidence, we are now told that 'there are very few lovers of Truth for Truths sake, even amongst those, who perswade themselves that they are so'. What happens, then, when men believe a proposition with greater assurance than the evidence for it warrants? In such instances, Locke now informs us, ''tis plain all that surplusage of assurance is owing to some other Affection, and not to the Love of Truth'. Or again, 'Whatsoever Credit or Authority we give to any Proposition more than it receives from the Principles or Proofs it supports it self upon, is owing to our Inclinations that way, and is so far a Derogation from the Love of Truth as such.' That dictum which in earlier versions of the *Essay* was little more than a passing remark—'what suits our wishes is forwardly believed'—comes to occupy the centre of the stage. It is no longer surprising that believing, as Locke's argument proceeded, came to be parallel to desiring rather than to knowing. In rational men, men inspired by the love of truth, belief is no doubt founded on the evidence and nothing but the evidence. If belief is in their case ever voluntary, it is only so in those very special instances in which they continue to believe, with the probabilities against them, in the expectation that fresh information will turn up. But such lovers of truth, Locke now thinks, are rare. What he is now prepared explicitly to call 'groundless fancies' play a much greater part in human life than he had at first been prepared to admit. Indeed, whereas a belief had at first been *defined* as a proposition received as true *upon arguments and proofs*, this definition, it would now appear, applies only to rational, or relatively rational, beliefs; men can believe from inclination, or at the very least they can believe from inclination with much greater assurance than they should believe. (And in the case of the enthusiast, with his 'groundless fancies', the degree of assurance should be zero.)

Can they be blamed for believing? Locke seems to take it for granted that our inclinations lie in some measure under our control. 'He that would seriously set upon the search of Truth', he writes, 'ought in the first Place to prepare his Mind with a Love of it' (E iv.xix.1: 697)—as if this 'preparation of the mind', with the subduing of inclinations which it entails, lies within our power. 'He that hath not a mastery over his inclinations', he tell us in *Some Thoughts Concerning Education*, '... for the sake of what reason tells him is fit to be done, wants the true principle of virtue and industry' (W ix: 36)

Finally, a word or two about 'faith', in the narrow sense of the word, the acceptance of a belief because it is taken to be divinely revealed. Historically speaking, this has occupied the very centre of the debate about whether men can decide to believe. Many Christian theologians, from Clement of Alexandria to Newman, have thought it a central assumption of Christianity that assent lies in a man's power, that men can choose to believe what God teaches them, even when it is contrary to experience, perhaps even to reason. For they have wanted to blame 'men of little faith', the Doubting Thomases of this world.[2] And they were conscious of what Jesus is reported as saying in Mark: that men are to be saved for believing,

---

[2] That assent, or belief, is an act of the will has continued to be a very widely held doctrine amongst Roman Catholic philosophers. So Lonergan tells us that 'it is a free and responsible decision of the will to believe a given proposition as probably or certainly true or false' (Lonergan 1958: 709). The extent of conflict on this point is brought out in Needham 1972: 81–6.

damned for not believing (16: 15–16). How could this be, if men are not free to believe? Not all theologians, of course, have taken this view. Faith, many of them have argued, is a grace of God; men can believe only when God enables, or perhaps compels, them to do so. If Jesus condemned them for not believing, this is only to express God's mysterious judgement upon them. Or like Aquinas they have sought to compromise. Faith he describes as 'an act of the intellect assenting to Divine truth at the command of the will moved by the grace of God' (*Summa theologiae*, ii-ii.ii.9), an act of free choice, even although a choice men can make only when God permits them to do so. But when philosophers and theologians have asserted man's freedom to believe, this has most often been in order to leave room, as Locke also wants to do, for condemning infidelity. Or else, as in Clifford's case, for condemning credulity as the wrongful making of a decision.

Locke, however, and without calling on divine grace, does not make of faith an exception to his view that the rational man will believe only with a degree of assurance proportional to the evidence. Once again he begins from the case of knowledge. '[*N*]*o Proposition*', he says, '*can be received for Divine Revelation*, or obtain the Assent due to all such, *if it be contradictory to our clear intuitive Knowledge*' (E iv.xviii.5: 692). It is only reason that can tell us a particular book is divinely inspired; and no evidence that it is so inspired can be as clear and certain as the principles of reason itself. '*Nothing that is contrary to, and inconsistent with the clear and self-evident Dictates of Reason, has a Right to be urged, or assented to, as a Matter of Faith*' (E iv.xviii.10: 696). We are to have faith in what revelation tells us, only if all we can set against it are '*probable Conjectures*' (E iv.xviii.8: 694).

Here, very obviously, Locke is writing in moralistic terms. 'Nothing that is contrary to the Dictates of Reason has a *right* to be assented to.' It is not at all being suggested that we *cannot* believe what is contrary to reason. '*I believe, because it is impossible*, might', he says, 'pass for a Sally of Zeal', but it 'would prove a very ill Rule for Men to chuse their Opinions, or Religion by' (E iv.xviii.11: 696). A 'very ill rule' no doubt, but on the view from which he originally set out, it would be not only 'ill' but *impossible* to adopt such a rule. In short, the existence of the enthusiast constantly undermines Locke's hopeful view of man, as a being who naturally, and inevitably, responds to the most probable hypothesis—much as the very existence of twentieth-century enthusiasts has undermined the similar confidence we partly inherited from Locke himself, but without paying adequate attention to his vacillations and reservations.

There can be no doubt, I think, that Locke would have liked consistently to maintain two theses, the first that rational human beings will regulate their degree of assurance in a proposition so that it accords with the evidence—the ideal of an objective science, the Enlightenment ideal. The second, that human beings are so constituted as naturally to do this, were created rational, that they go wrong only when some of the evidence is not before them. But he finds it impossible to reconcile this second thesis with his experience of the actual irrationality of human beings, brought home to him with peculiar sharpness by the Civil War and, more particularly, by the 'enthusiasm' of the Puritan sectaries. At first, he does what he can to reconcile his theories with his experience by suggesting that what, from the point of view of better-informed observers, are irrational beliefs have a rational foundation, that they rest upon errors of fact rather than errors of judgement—errors of fact arising either out of ignorance or the assignment of wrong measures of probability. If only men could bring themselves to enquire, he argues in this spirit, they would cease to hold irrational beliefs. But then he still has on his hands a residue of cases, in which men have all the evidence before them which they could possibly need, and yet still believe irrationally. Perhaps, he is at one point led to suggest, they do not under these circumstances *believe*, in the proper sense, at all; they merely mouth phrases. But it is very hard to take this view about an ardent enthusiast, convinced that he is personally inspired by God. And so in the end Locke is led to conclude that men can believe falsely, not as the result of having inadequate evidence, but as a result of being dominated by powerful inclinations. And so he is gradually driven into a new picture of belief, in which it is no longer a weaker form of knowledge, but rather, like desire in Locke's second-edition account of desire, an attempt to remove uneasiness, to satisfy our inclinations. The rational man is then the man who is dominated by a passion for truth, as distinct from party passions. Conscious of the fact that his beliefs are often based upon evidence which from the point of view of an ideal observer is inadequate, such a rational man will be tolerant, as the enthusiast, confusing his beliefs with knowledge, will not be tolerant. But at the same time the rational man will *blame* the enthusiast, whether on Locke's first view, for not properly enquiring or, on Locke's second view, for not properly controlling his inclination to believe beyond the evidence.

NOTES ON THE CONTRIBUTORS

E. J. ASHWORTH is Professor of Philosophy at the University of Waterloo. She is the author of *Language and Logic in the Post-Medieval Period* (Reidel, 1974) and *Studies in Post-Medieval Semantics* (Variorum, 1985) and of many articles in journals. She edited and translated *Paul of Venice: Logica Magna, Part II Fascicule 8, Tractatus de obligationibus* for the British Academy (Oxford, 1988), and is subject editor for the Renaissance section of the *Routledge Encyclopedia of Philosophy* (forthcoming).

MARGARET ATHERTON is Professor of Philosophy at the University of Wisconsin–Milwaukee. She is the author of *Berkeley's Revolution in Vision* (Cornell, 1990) and of several articles on early modern philosophers and in other fields of philosophy. She also edited *Women Philosophers of the Early Modern Period* (Hackett, 1994).

MICHAEL R. AYERS is Fellow of Wadham College and Professor of Philosophy at Oxford University. He is the author of *Locke: Epistemology and Ontology*, 2 vols. (Routledge, 1991) and of many articles on Locke and other early modern philosophers. He is also co-editor, with Daniel Garber, of the *Cambridge History of Seventeenth-Century Philosophy* and subject editor of the seventeenth-century section of the *Routledge Encyclopedia of Philosophy* (forthcoming).

JONATHAN BENNETT is Professor of Philosophy at Syracuse University, Fellow of the American Academy of Arts and Sciences, and Corresponding Fellow of the British Academy. He is the author of *Locke, Berkeley, Hume* (Oxford, 1971), as well as of books on Spinoza (Hackett, 1984) and Kant (Cambridge, 1966 and 1974) and on several non-historical topics, the most recent of which is *The Act Itself* (Oxford, 1995). He has also published many articles, on a wide variety of subjects, in collections and journals.

MARTHA BRANDT BOLTON is Professor of Philosophy at Rutgers University. She is author of articles on a range of topics and figures in early modern philosophy. Her current work focuses on Locke's *Essay* and Leibniz's *New Essays*.

JOHN CAMPBELL is Fellow and Tutor in Philosophy at New College, Oxford. He is the author of *Past, Space and Self* (MIT, 1994) and of articles, *inter alia*, on the self and on colour.

VERE CHAPPELL is Professor of Philosophy at the University of Massachusetts. He is the co-author, with Willis Doney, of *Twenty-Five Years of Descartes Scholarship* (Garland, 1987), and editor of the *Cambridge Companion to Locke* (1994). He has also edited *Essays on Early Modern Philosophers*, 12 vols. (Garland, 1992) and *Descartes's Meditations* (Rowman and Littlefield, 1997). His other publications include articles on Descartes and other early modern philosophers, as well as several on Locke.

J. L. MACKIE was Fellow of University College and Reader in Philosophy at Oxford University and Fellow of the British Academy at the time of his death in 1981. He is the author of *Problems from Locke* (Oxford, 1976) and of many books and articles on other subjects, including *Truth, Probability, and Paradox* (Oxford, 1973), *The*

Cement of the Universe (Oxford, 1974), *Ethics: Inventing Right and Wrong* (Penguin, 1977), *Hume's Moral Theory* (Routledge, 1980), and *The Miracle of Theism* (Oxford, 1982). Two collections of Mackie's articles have been published as well, *Logic and Knowledge* and *Persons and Values* (both Oxford, 1985).

RUTH MATTERN is currently a physician working for the Indian Health Service on the Navaho Indian Reservation of north-east Arizona; she is Chief of Ophthalmology at the Tuba City Indian Medical Center. Before obtaining a medical degree, she taught philosophy at Rice University and at the University of Pennsylvania. Mattern's publications include articles on Locke, Descartes, and Spinoza; she also edited a set of excerpts from Locke's 1685 Draft ('Draft C') of the *Essay* (*Philosophy Research Archives*, 1981).

EDWIN MCCANN is Associate Professor and Director of the School of Philosophy at the University of Southern California. He is the author of the chapter on the history of philosophy of mind in the seventeenth and eighteenth centuries in the *Blackwell Companion to the Philosophy of Mind* (Blackwell, 1995) and of several articles on Locke and other early modern philosophers.

JOHN PASSMORE is Emeritus Professor of Philosophy in The Institute for Advanced Studies and Visiting Fellow in the Research School of Social Studies, Historical Studies Program at the Australian National University. He is the author of many books and articles in several different fields of philosophy, including *Ralph Cudworth* (Cambridge, 1951), *Hume's Intentions* (Cambridge, 1952), *A Hundred Years of Philosophy* (Duckworth, 1957), *Philosophical Reasoning* (Duckworth, 1961), *The Perfectibility of Man* (Duckworth, 1970), *Man's Responsibility for Nature* (Duckworth, 1974), *The Philosophy of Teaching* (Harvard, 1980), *Recent Philosophers* (Duckworth, 1985), and *Serious Art* (Open Court, 1991).

KENNETH P. WINKLER is Class of 1919 Professor of Philosophy at Wellesley College. He is the author of *Berkeley: An Interpretation* (Oxford, 1989) and of many articles on early modern philosophers, including Descartes and Hume as well as Berkeley and Locke. He has also done an edition of Berkeley's *Principles* (Hackett, 1982) and an abridged version of Locke's *Essay* (Hackett, 1996), besides editing the *Cambridge Companion to Berkeley* (forthcoming).

SELECTED BIBLIOGRAPHY

This bibliography is divided into two parts. The first lists Locke's own works, both as published during his lifetime and in later collections and editions. The second contains works about Locke and his thought.

Both lists are highly selective. Three considerations have guided the selection of works for the second list: (1) that they be of decent quality, (2) that they be intelligible to non-specialists, and (3) that they be recent, that is, published in the last twenty years or so, since the appearance of Tipton's *Locke on Human Understanding* (1977). (A few older or more specialized works have, however, been included because of their unusual significance.)

The 'Specific Topics' listed correspond to those treated by the essays included in this volume, in the same order; this is also the order in which these topics are treated by Locke in the *Essay*. Note that many of the works included in this section bear on topics other that those under which they are listed. In only a few cases, however, is the same work listed under more than one topic.

Fuller bibliographies, some covering primary as well as secondary sources, are provided in the works listed under 'Research Tools' by Hall and Woolhouse (1983), Attig (1985), and Yolton and Yolton (1985), and by the 'Recent Publications' section in Roland Hall's annual *Locke Newsletter* (1970 ff.).

LOCKE'S OWN WORKS

Individual Works Published during Locke's Lifetime

Epistola de tolerantia (Gouda, 1689); tr. as *Letter on Toleration*, by William Popple (London, 1689); 2nd edn. (1690).

Two Treatises of Government (London, 1690); 2nd edn. (1694); 3rd edn. (1698).

An Essay concerning Human Understanding (London, 1690); 2nd edn. (1694); 3rd edn. (1695); 4th edn. (1700); tr. as *Essai philosophique concernant l'entendement humain*, by Pierre Coste (Amsterdam, 1700); tr. as *De intellectu humano*, by Ezekiel Burridge (London, 1701); 5th edn. (London, 1706).

Some Thoughts concerning Education (London, 1693); 2nd edn. (1693); 3rd edn. (1695); 4th edn. (1699); 5th edn. (1705).

The Reasonableness of Christianity, As Delivered in the Scriptures (London, 1695); 2nd edn. (1696).

A Letter to the Right Reverend Edward, Lord Bishop of Worcester, Concerning some Passages relating to Mr. Locke's Essay of humane Understanding: In a late Discourse of his Lordship's, in Vindication of the Trinity (London, 1697).

Mr. Locke's Reply to the Right Reverend the Lord Bishop of Worcester's Answer to his Letter, concerning Some Passages Relating to Mr. Locke's Essay of Humane Understanding: in a Late Discourse of his Lordships, in Vindication of the Trinity (London, 1697).

Mr. Locke's Reply to the Right Reverend the Lord Bishop of Worcester's Answer to his Second Letter: Wherein, besides other incident Matters, what his Lordship has said concerning Certainty by Reason, Certainty by Ideas, and Certainty by Faith. The Resurrection of the Same Body. The Immateriality of the Soul. The Inconsistency of Mr. Locke's Notions with the Articles of the Christian Faith, and their Tendancy to Scepticism, is Examined (London, 1699).

Collections and Later Editions

The Works of John Locke, new edn., corrected, 10 vols. (London, 1823); repr. (Aalen: Scientia, 1963).

The Clarendon Edition of the Works of John Locke, ed. Peter H. Nidditch, John W. Yolton, et al., *c.*30 vols. (Oxford: Clarendon Press, 1975–).

The Correspondence of John Locke, ed. E. S. de Beer, Clarendon Edition, 9 vols. (Oxford: Clarendon Press, 1976–).

Drafts for the Essay concerning Human Understanding *and Other Philosophical Writings*, ed. Peter H. Nidditch and G. A. J. Rogers, Clarendon Edition, 3 vols. (Oxford: Clarendon Press, 1990–).

An Essay concerning Human Understanding, ed. Peter H. Nidditch, Clarendon Edition (Oxford: Clarendon Press, 1975); repr. (1979).

An Essay concerning Human Understanding, abridged and ed. Kenneth P. Winkler (Indianapolis: Hackett, 1996).

Essays on the Law of Nature, ed. W. von Leyden (Oxford: Clarendon Press, 1954).

Locke on Money, ed. Patrick Hyde Kelly, Clarendon Edition, 2 vols. (Oxford: Clarendon Press, 1991).

A Paraphrase and Notes on the Epistles of St Paul, ed. Arthur W. Wainwright, Clarendon Edition, 2 vols. (Oxford: Clarendon Press, 1987).

Some Thoughts concerning Education, ed. John W. Yolton and Jean S. Yolton, Clarendon Edition (Oxford: Clarendon Press, 1989).

WORKS ABOUT LOCKE

Research Tools

ATTIG, JOHN C., *The Works of John Locke: A Comprehensive Bibliography from the Seventeenth Century to the Present* (Westport, Conn.: Greenwood Press, 1985).

HALL, ROLAND, 'Recent Publications' *Locke Newsletter*, 1– (1970–).

——and WOOLHOUSE, ROGER, *80 Years of Locke Scholarship: A Bibliographical Guide* (Edinburgh: Edinburgh University Press, 1983).

YOLTON, JEAN S., and YOLTON, JOHN W., *John Locke: A Reference Guide* (Boston: Hall, 1985).

YOLTON, JOHN W., *A Locke Dictionary* (Oxford: Blackwell, 1993).

Locke's Life and Times

CRANSTON, MAURICE, *John Locke: A Biography* (London: Longman, 1957); repr. (Oxford: Oxford University Press, 1985).

MARSHALL, JOHN, *John Locke: Resistance, Religion and Responsibility* (Cambridge: Cambridge University Press, 1994).

MILTON, J. R., 'The Scholastic Background to Locke's Thought', *Locke Newsletter*, 15 (1984), 25–34.

——'Locke at Oxford', in G. A. J. Rogers (ed.), *Locke's Philosophy: Content and Context* (Oxford: Clarendon Press, 1994), 29–47.

——'Locke's Life and Times', in Vere Chappell (ed.), *The Cambridge Companion to Locke* (Cambridge: Cambridge University Press, 1994), 5–25.

YOLTON, JOHN W., *John Locke and the Way of Ideas* (Oxford: Oxford University Press, 1956).

Locke's Philosophy in General

AARON, RICHARD I., *John Locke* (Oxford: Clarendon Press, 1937); 3rd edn. (1971).

AYERS, MICHAEL R., *Locke: Epistemology and Ontology*, 2 vols. (London: Routledge, 1991).

BENNETT, JONATHAN, *Locke, Berkeley, Hume: Central Themes* (Oxford: Clarendon Press, 1971).

JENKINS, JOHN J., *Understanding Locke* (Edinburgh: Edinburgh University Press, 1983).

JOLLEY, NICHOLAS, *Leibniz and Locke: A Study of the* New Essays on Human Understanding (Oxford: Clarendon Press, 1984).

LEIBNIZ, G. W., *Nouveaux essais* (Amsterdam, 1765); ed. Andre Robinet and Heinrich Schepers (Berlin, 1962); tr. as *New Essays on Human Understanding*, by Peter Remnant and Jonathan Bennett (Cambridge: Cambridge University Press, 1981).

LOWE, E. J., *Locke on Human Understanding* (London: Routledge, 1995).

MACKIE, J. L., *Problems from Locke* (Oxford: Clarendon Press, 1976).

WOOLHOUSE, R. S., *Locke's Philosophy of Science and Knowledge* (Oxford: Blackwell, 1971).

——*Locke* (Brighton: Harvester, 1983).

YOLTON, JOHN W., *Locke and the Compass of Human Understanding: A Selective Commentary on the* Essay (Cambridge: Cambridge University Press, 1970).

——*Locke: An Introduction* (Oxford: Blackwell, 1985).

Collections of Articles

ASHCRAFT, RICHARD (ed.), *John Locke: Critical Assessments*, 4 vols. (London: Routledge, 1991).

BRANDT, REINHARD (ed.), *John Locke: Symposium Wolfenbüttel 1979* (Berlin: de Gruyter, 1981).

CHAPPELL, VERE (ed.), *The Cambridge Companion to Locke* (Cambridge: Cambridge University Press, 1994).

HALL, ROLAND (ed.), Locke *Newsletter*, 1– (1970–).

MARTIN, C. B., and ARMSTRONG, D. M. (eds.), *Locke and Berkeley: A Collection of Critical Essays* (Garden City, NY: Doubleday, 1968).

ROGERS, G. A. J. (ed.), *Locke's Philosophy: Content and Context* (Oxford: Clarendon Press, 1994).

TIPTON, I. C. (ed.), *Locke on Human Understanding* (Oxford: Oxford University Press, 1977).

YOLTON, JEAN S. (ed.), *A Locke Miscellany: Locke Biography and Criticism for All* (Bristol: Thoemmes, 1990).

YOLTON, JOHN W. (ed.), *John Locke: Problems and Perspectives* (Cambridge: Cambridge University Press, 1969).

Specific Topics

Innate Knowledge

ADAMS, ROBERT M., 'The Locke–Leibniz Debate', in Stephen P. Stich, (ed.) *Innate Ideas* (Berkeley: University of California Press, 1975), 37–67.
—— 'Where Do Our Ideas Come From?—Descartes vs. Locke', in Stephen P. Stich (ed.), *Innate Ideas* (Berkeley: University of California Press, 1975), 71–87.
HARRIS, JOHN, 'Leibniz and Locke on Innate Ideas', *Ratio*, 16 (1974), 226–42; repr. in I. C. Tipton (ed.), *Locke on Human Understanding* (Oxford: Oxford University Press, 1977), 25–40.
ROGERS, G. A. J., 'Locke, Newton, and the Cambridge Platonists on Innate Ideas', *Journal of the History of Ideas*, 40 (1979), 191–205.
WALL, G., 'Locke's Attack on Innate Knowledge', *Philosophy*, 49 (1974), 414–19; repr. in I. C. Tipton (ed.), *Locke on Human Understanding* (Oxford: Oxford University Press, 1977), 1–18.

Ideas and Perception

AYERS, MICHAEL R., 'Locke's Doctrine of Abstraction: Some Aspects of its Historical and Philosophical Significance', in Reinhard Brandt (ed.), *John Locke: Symposium Wolfenbüttel 1979* (Berlin: de Gruyter, 1981), 5–24.
—— 'Locke's Logical Atomism', *British Academy Proceedings*, 67 (1981), 209–25.
—— 'Are Locke's "Ideas" Images, Intentional Objects or Natural Signs?', *Locke Newsletter*, 17 (1986), 3–36.
BOLTON, MARTHA BRANDT, 'A Defense of Locke and the Representative Theory of Perception', *Canadian Journal of Philosophy*, Supp. 4 (1978), 101–20.
—— 'The Epistemological Status of Ideas: Locke Compared to Arnauld', *History of Philosophy Quarterly*, 9 (1992), 409–24.
—— 'The Real Molyneux Question and the Basis of Locke's Answer', in G. A. J. Rogers (ed.), *Locke's Philosophy: Content and Context* (Oxford: Clarendon Press, 1994), 75–99.
CHAPPELL, VERE, 'Locke's Theory of Ideas', in Vere Chappell (ed.), *The Cambridge Companion to Locke* (Cambridge: Cambridge University Press, 1994), 26–55.
HALL, ROLAND, 'Locke and Sensory Experience', *Locke Newsletter*, 18 (1987), 11–31.
—— ' "Idea" in Locke's Works', *Locke Newsletter*, 21 (1990), 9–26.
KULSTAD, MARK A., 'Locke on Consciousness and Reflection', *Studia Leibnitiana*, 16 (1984), 143–67.
OWENS, DAVID, 'A Lockean Theory of Memory Experience', *Philosophy and Phenomenological Research*, 56 (1996), 319–32.
STEWART, M. A., 'Locke's Mental Atomism and the Classification of Ideas', *Locke Newsletter*, 10 (1979), 53–82; 11 (1980), 25–62.
VINCI, THOMAS, 'A Functionalist Interpretation of Locke's Theory of Simple Ideas', *History of Philosophy Quarterly*, 2 (1985), 179–94.

Qualities

ALEXANDER, PETER, *Ideas, Qualities and Corpuscles: Locke and Boyle on the External World* (Cambridge: Cambridge University Press, 1985).
BENNETT, JONATHAN, 'Ideas and Qualities in Locke's *Essay*', History *of Philosophy Quarterly*, 13 (1996), 73–88.

BOLTON, MARTHA BRANDT, 'The Origins of Locke's Doctrine of Primary and Secondary Qualities', *Philosophical Quarterly*, 26 (1976), 305–16.

——'Locke and Pyrrhonism: The Doctrine of Primary and Secondary Qualities', in Myles Burnyeat (ed.), *The Skeptical Tradition* (Berkeley: University of California Press, 1983), 353–75.

CUMMINS, ROBERT, 'Two Troublesome Claims about Qualities in Locke's *Essay*', *Philosophical Review*, 84 (1975), 401–18.

McCANN, Edwin, 'Locke's Philosophy of Body', in Vere Chappell (ed.), *The Cambridge Companion to Locke* (Cambridge: Cambridge University Press, 1994), 56–88.

Power and Freedom

BENNETT, JONATHAN, 'Locke's Philosophy of Mind', in Vere Chappell (ed.), *The Cambridge Companion to Locke* (Cambridge: Cambridge University Press, 1994), 89–114.

CHAPPELL, VERE, 'Locke on the Intellectual Basis of Sin', *Journal of the History of Philosophy*, 32 (1994), 197–207.

LOWE, E. J., 'Necessity and Will in Locke's Theory of Action', *History of Philosophy Quarterly*, 3 (1986), 149–63.

MATTERN, RUTH, 'Locke on Active Power and the Obscure Idea of Active Power from Bodies', *Studies in History and Philosophy of Science*, 11 (1980), 39–77.

Substance

ALEXANDER, PETER, 'Locke on Substance-in-General', *Ratio*, 22 (1980), 91–105; 23 (1981), 1–19.

AYERS, MICHAEL R., 'The Ideas of Power and Substance in Locke's Philosophy', *Philosophical Quarterly*, 25 (1975), 1–27; repr. in I. C. Tipton (ed.), *Locke on Human Understanding* (Oxford: Oxford University Press, 1977), 77–104.

BERMÚDEZ, JOSÉ LUIS, 'Locke, Metaphysical Dualism and Property Dualism', *British Journal for the History of Philosophy*, 4 (1996), 223–45.

McCANN, EDWIN, 'Locke's Philosophy of Body', in Vere Chappell (ed.), in *The Cambridge Companion to Locke* (Cambridge: Cambridge University Press, 1994), 56–88.

PELLETIER, F. J., 'Locke's Doctrine of Substance', *Canadian Journal of Philosophy*, Supp. 4 (1978), 121–40.

Identity and Persons

ALSTON, WILLIAM P., and BENNETT, JONATHAN, 'Locke on People and Substances', *Philosophical Review*, 97 (1988), 25–46.

ATHERTON, MARGARET, 'Locke's Theory of Personal Identity', *Midwest Studies in Philosophy*, 8 (1983), 273–93.

BENNETT, JONATHAN, 'Locke's Philosophy of Mind', in Vere Chappell (ed.), *The Cambridge Companion to Locke* (Cambridge: Cambridge University Press, 1994), 89–114.

BOLTON, MARTHA BRANDT, 'Locke on Identity: The Scheme of Simple and Compounded Things', in K. F. Barber and J. J. E. Gracia (eds.), *Individuation and Identity in Early Modern Philosophy: Descartes to Kant* (Albany, NY: SUNY Press, 1994), 103–31.

CHAPPELL, VERE, 'Locke on the Ontology of Matter, Living Things, and Persons', *Philosophical Studies*, 60 (1990), 19–32.

HELM, PAUL, 'Locke's Theory of Personal Identity', *Philosophy*, 54 (1979), 173–85.

McCANN, EDWIN, 'Cartesian Selves and Lockean Substances', *Monist*, 69 (1986), 458–82.

—— 'Locke on Identity: Matter, Life, and Consciousness', *Archiv für Geschichte der Philosophie*, 69 (1987), 54–77.

MATTHEWS, H. E., 'Descartes and Locke on the Concept of a Person', *Locke Newsletter*, 8 (1977), 9–34.

MENDUS, SUSAN, 'Personal Identity and Moral Responsibility', *Locke Newsletter*, 9 (1978), 75–86.

THIEL, UDO, 'Locke's Concept of a Person', in Reinhard Brandt (ed.), *John Locke: Symposium Wolfenbüttel 1979* (Berlin: de Gruyter, 1981), 181–92.

WIGGINS, DAVID, 'Locke, Butler and the Stream of Consciousness: and Men as a Natural Kind', *Philosophy*, 51 (1976), 131–58.

Language

ASHWORTH, E. J., ' "Do Words Signify Ideas or Things?" The Scholastic Sources of Locke's Theory of Language', *Journal of the History of Philosophy*, 19 (1981), 299–326.

GUYER, PAUL, 'Locke's Philosophy of Language', in Vere Chappell (ed.), *The Cambridge Companion to Locke* (Cambridge: Cambridge University Press, 1994), 115–45.

KRETZMANN, NORMAN, 'The Main Thesis of Locke's Semantic Theory', *Philosophical Review*, 77 (1968), 175–96; repr. in I. C. Tipton (ed.), *Locke on Human Understanding* (Oxford: Oxford University Press, 1977), 123–40.

LANDESMAN, CHARLES, 'Locke's Theory of Meaning', *Journal of the History of Philosophy*, 14 (1976), 23–35.

LAPORTE, JOSEPH, 'Locke's Semantics and the New Theory of Reference to Natural Kinds', *Locke Newsletter*, 27 (1996), 41–64.

LOSONSKY, MICHAEL, 'Locke on Meaning and Signification', in G. A. J. Rogers (ed.), *Locke's Philosophy: Content and Context* (Oxford: Clarendon Press, 1994), 123–41.

TROYER, JOHN, 'Locke on the Names of Substances', *Locke Newsletter*, 6 (1975), 27–39.

Essences

AYERS, MICHAEL R., 'Locke versus Aristotle on Natural Kinds', *Journal of Philosophy*, 78 (1981), 247–71; repr. in *Philosopher's Annual*, 5 (1982), 41–66.

BOLTON, MARTHA BRANDT, 'Locke on Substance Ideas and the Determination of Kinds: A Reply to Mattern', *Locke Newsletter*, 19 (1988), 17–45.

LAW, STEPHEN, 'Locke and Two Notions of Natural Kind', *Locke Newsletter*, 26 (1995), 69–94.

MATTERN, RUTH, 'Locke on Natural Kinds as the "Workmanship of the Understanding" ', *Locke Newsletter*, 17 (1986), 45–92.

OWEN, DAVID, 'Locke on Real Essence', *History of Philosophy Quarterly*, 8 (1991), 105–18.

PHEMISTER, PAULINE, 'Real Essences in Particular', *Locke Newsletter*, 21 (1990), 27–55.

Knowledge

ATHERTON, MARGARET, 'Knowledge of Substance and Knowledge of Essence in Locke's *Essay*', *History of Philosophy Quarterly*, 1 (1984), 413–28.

AYERS, MICHAEL R., 'Mechanism, Superaddition and the Proof of God's Existence in Locke's *Essay*', *Philosophical Review*, 90 (1981), 210–51.

DOWNING, LISA, 'Are Corpuscles Unobservable in Principle for Locke?', *Journal of the History of Philosophy*, 30 (1992), 33–52.

FERREIRA, M. JAMIE, 'Locke's "Constructive Skepticism"—A Reappraisal', *Journal of the History of Philosophy*, 24 (1986), 211–22.

McCANN, EDWIN, 'Locke's Philosophy of Body', in Vere Chappell (ed.), *The Cambridge Companion to Locke* (Cambridge: Cambridge University Press, 1994), 56–88.

ROGERS, G. A. J., 'Locke and the Sceptical Challenge', in G. A. J. Rogers and Sylvana Tomaselli (eds.), *The Philosophical Canon in the 17th and 18th Centuries: Essays in Honor of John W. Yolton* (Rochester, NY: University of Rochester Press, 1996), 49–66.

SCHANKULA, H. A. S., 'Locke, Descartes, and the Science of Nature', *Journal of the History of Ideas*, 41 (1980), 459–77; repr. in Reinhard Brandt (ed.), *John Locke: Symposium Wolfenbüttel 1979* (Berlin: de Gruyter, 1981), 163–80.

SCHOULS, PETER A., 'Locke and the Dogma of Infallible Reason', *Revue Internationale de Philosophie*, 42 (1988), 115–32.

SOLES, DAVID E., 'Locke's Empiricism and the Postulation of Unobservables', *Journal of the History of Philosophy*, 23 (1985), 339–69.

WILSON, MARGARET D., 'Superadded Properties: The Limits of Mechanism in Locke', *American Philosophical Quarterly*, 16 (1979), 143–50.

——'Superadded Properties: A Reply to M. R. Ayers', *Philosophical Review*, 91 (1982), 247–52.

WOOLHOUSE, R. S., 'Locke's Theory of Knowledge', in Vere Chappell (ed.), *The Cambridge Companion to Locke* (Cambridge: Cambridge University Press, 1994), 146–71.

Probability and Belief

ASHCRAFT, RICHARD, 'Faith and Knowledge in Locke's Philosophy', in John W. Yolton (ed.), *John Locke: Problems and Perspectives* (Cambridge: Cambridge University Press, 1969), 194–223.

HELM, PAUL, 'Locke on Faith and Knowledge', *Philosophical Quarterly*, 23 (1973), 52–66.

LOSONSKY, MICHAEL, 'John Locke on Passion, Will and Belief', *British Journal for the History of Philosophy*, 4 (1996), 267–83.

OWEN, DAVID, 'Locke on Reason, Probable Reasoning, and Opinion', *Locke Newsletter*, 24 (1993), 35–79.

SNYDER, DAVID C., 'Faith and Reason in Locke's *Essay*', *Journal of the History of Ideas*, 47 (1986), 197–213.

WILLIAMS, STEPHEN N., 'John Locke on the Status of Faith', *Scottish Journal of Theology*, 40 (1987), 591–606.

WOLTERSTORFF, NICHOLAS, *John Locke and the Ethics of Belief* (Cambridge: Cambridge University Press, 1996).

Others

LENNON, THOMAS M., 'Locke's Atomism', *Philosophy Research Archives*, 9 (1983), 1–28.

ROGERS, G. A. J., 'Locke's *Essay* and Newton's *Principia*', *Journal of the History of Ideas*, 39 (1978), 217–32.

——'Locke, Law and the Laws of Nature', in Reinhard Brandt (ed.), *John Locke:*

Symposium Wolfenbüttel 1979 (Berlin: de Gruyter, 1981), 146–62.

SPELLMAN, W. M., 'The Christian Estimate of Man in Locke's *Essay*', *Journal of Religion*, 67 (1987), 474–92.

TULLY, JAMES, 'Governing Conduct', in Edmund Leites (ed.), *Conscience and Casuistry in Early Modern Thought* (Cambridge: Cambridge University Press, 1988), 12–71.

REFERENCES

AARON, RICHARD I. (1971), *John Locke* (London, 1937); 3rd edn. (Oxford: Clarendon Press).

AARSLEFF, HANS (1964), 'Leibniz on Locke on Language', *American Philosophical Quarterly*, 1: 165–88.

ADAMS, ROBERT MERRIHEW (1975), 'Where Do Our Ideas Come From?', in Stephen P. Stich (cd.), *Innate Ideas* (Berkeley: University of California Press), 71–87.

ALEXANDER, PETER (1974), 'Boyle and Locke on Primary and Secondary Qualities', *Ratio*, 16: 51–67.

——(1985), *Ideas, Qualities and Corpuscles* (Cambridge: Cambridge University Press).

ALGER, WILLIAM ROUNSEVILLE (1864), *Critical History of the Doctrine of a Future Life* (Philadelphia).

ALSTON, WILLIAM P. (1954–5), 'Particulars—Bare and Qualified', *Philosophy and Phenomenological Research*, 15: 253–8.

——(1964), *Philosophy of Language* (Englewood Cliffs, NJ: Prentice Hall).

——and BENNETT, JONATHAN (1988), 'Locke on People and Substances', *Philosophical Review*, 97: 25–46.

ANSCOMBE, G. E. M. (1981), 'Substance', in G. E. M. Anscombe, *Metaphysics and the Philosophy of Mind* (Minneapolis: University of Minnesota Press), 37–43.

AQUINAS, *Summa theologiae*.

ARISTOTLE, *Metaphysics*.

——*Posterior Analytics*.

ARMSTRONG, D. M. (1971), 'Meaning and Communication', *Philosophical Review*, 80: 427–47.

ARNAULD, ANTOINE (1851), *The Port-Royal Logic*, tr. Thomas Spencer Baynes (London).

——and NICOLE, PIERRE (1965), *La Logique, ou l'art de penser* (Paris, 1662); ed. Pierre Clair and François Girbal (Paris: Vrin).

————(1996), *La Logique, ou l'art de penser*, tr. Jill Vance Buroker (Cambridge: Cambridge University Press).

ARONSON, C., and LEWIS, DOUGLAS (1970), 'Locke on Mixed Modes, Knowledge and Substances', *Journal of the History of Philosophy*, 8: 193–9.

ASHWORTH, E. J. (1974), *Language and Logic in the Post-Medieval Period* (Dordrecht: Reidel).

——(1981a), ' "Do Words Signify Ideas or Things?" The Scholastic Sources of Locke's Theory of Language', *Journal of the History of Philosophy*, 19: 299–326.

——(1981b), 'Mental Language and the Unity of Propositions: A Semantic Problem Discussed by Early Sixteenth-Century Logicians', *Franciscan Studies*, 41: 61–96.

——(1982), 'The Structure of Mental Language: Some Problems Discussed by Early Sixteenth-Century Logicians', *Vivarium*, 20: 59–83.

——(1984), 'Locke on Language', *Canadian Journal of Philosophy*, 14: 45–73; repr. in this volume as Ch. IX.

——(1987), 'Jacobus Naveros on the Question: "Do Spoken Words Signify Concepts or Things?"', in L. M. de Rijk and H. A. G. Braakhuis (eds.), *Logos and Pragma: Essays on the Philosophy of Language in Honour of Professor Gabriel Nuchelmans* (Nijmegen: Ingenium), 189–214.

——(1988), 'Oxford', in Jean-Pierre Schobinger (ed.), *Die Philosophie des 17. Jahrhunderts*, Band 3. *England* (Basel: Schwabe), 6–9, 26–7.

ATHERTON, MARGARET (1983), 'Locke's Theory of Personal Identity', *Midwest Studies in Philosophy*, 8: 273–93.

——(1984), 'The Inessentiality of Lockean Essences', *Canadian Journal of Philosophy*, 14: 277–93; repr. in this volume as Ch. X.

AYERS, MICHAEL R. (1977), 'The Ideas of Power and Substance in Locke's Philosophy, *Philosophical Quarterly*, 25 (1975), 1–27; repr. in I. C. Tipton (ed.), *Locke on Human Understanding* (Oxford: Oxford University Press), 77–104.

——(1981a), 'Locke versus Aristotle on Natural Kinds', *Journal of Philosophy*, 78: 247–71.

——(1981b), 'Mechanism, Superaddition and the Proof of God's Existence in Locke's *Essay*', *Philosophical Review*, 90: 210–51.

——(1991), *Locke*, 2 vols. (London: Routledge).

BARNES, JONATHAN (1972), 'Mr. Locke's Darling Notion', *Philosophical Quarterly*, 22: 193–214.

BEHAN, DAVID P. (1979), 'Locke on Persons and Personal Identity', *Canadian Journal of Philosophy*, 9: 53–75.

BENNETT, JONATHAN (1971), *Locke, Berkeley, Hume: Central Themes* (Oxford: Clarendon Press).

——(1987), 'Substratum', *History of Philosophy Quarterly*, 4: 197–215; repr. in this volume as Ch. VII.

——(1988), 'Response to Garber and Rée', in Peter H. Hare (ed.), *Doing Philosophy Historically* (Buffalo, NY: Prometheus), 62–9.

BERKELEY, GEORGE (1948–57), *The Works of George Berkeley*, ed. A. A. Luce and T. E. Jessop, 8 vols. (London: Nelson).

BOAS, MARIE (1952), 'The Establishment of the Mechanical Philosophy', *Osiris*, 10: 412–541.

BOLTON, MARTHA BRANDT (1976), 'Substances, Substrata and Names of Substances in Locke's *Essay*', *Philosophical Review*, 85: 488–513; repr. in this volume as Ch. VI.

——(1988), 'Locke on Substance Ideas and the Determination of Kinds: A Reply to Mattern', *Locke Newsletter*, 19: 17–45.

——(1992), 'The Epistemological Status of Ideas: Locke Compared to Arnauld', *History of Philosophy Quarterly*, 9: 409–24.

BOYLE, ROBERT (1772), *The Works of the Honourable Robert Boyle*, ed. Thomas Birch (London, 1744); new edn., 6 vols. (London).

——(1979), *Selected Philosophical Papers of Robert Boyle*, ed. M. A. Stewart (Manchester: Manchester University Press).

BRACKEN, H. M. (1967), 'Innate Ideas—Then and Now', *Dialogue* 6: 334–46.

BRAMHALL, JOHN (1655), *A Defence of True Liberty* (London).

——(1842), *The Works of John Bramhall, D.D.*, 4 vols. (Oxford).

BURGERSDIJCK, FRANCO (1637), *Institutionum logicarum libri duo* (Cambridge).

BURTHOGGE, RICHARD (1694), *An Essay upon Reason, and the Nature of Spirits* (London).

BUTLER, JOSEPH (1813), *The Works of Joseph Butler, LL.D.* (Edinburgh).

CHAPPELL, VERE (1989), 'Locke and Relative Identity', *History of Philosophy Quarterly*, 6: 69–83.

CHOMSKY, NOAM (1965), *Aspects of the Theory of Syntax* (Cambridge, Mass.: MIT Press).

——(1966), *Cartesian Linguistics* (New York: Harper & Row).

——(1968), *Language and Mind* (New York: Harcourt Brace).

——(1975), *Reflections on Language* (New York: Pantheon).

——(1980), *Rules and Representations* (New York: Columbia University Press).

——and Katz, Jerrold J. (1975), 'On Innateness: A Reply to Cooper', *Philosophical Review*, 84: 70–87.

CLAPP, JAMES GORDON (1967), 'Locke', in Paul Edwards (ed.), *Encyclopedia of Philosophy* (New York: Macmillan), IV. 487–503.

CLIFFORD, W. K. (1947), 'The Ethics of Belief', *Contemporary Review* (1877); repr. in Leslie Stephen and Sir Frederick Pollock (eds.), *The Ethics of Belief and Other Essays* (London: Watts).

COLLINS, ANTHONY (1717), *A Philosophical Inquiry concerning Human Liberty* (London).

CRANSTON, MAURICE (1957), *John Locke: A Biography* (London: Longmans).

CUMMINS, ROBERT (1975), 'Two Troublesome Claims about Qualities in Locke's *Essay*', *Philosophical Review*, 84: 401–18.

CURLEY, E. M. (1969), *Spinoza's Metaphysics* (Cambridge, Mass.: Harvard University Press).

——(1975), 'Descartes, Spinoza and the Ethics of Belief', in Eugene Freeman and Maurice Mandelbaum (eds.), *Spinoza: Essays in Interpretation* (LaSalle, Ill: Open Court), 159–89.

DESCARTES, RENÉ (1964–74), *Oeuvres de Descartes*, ed. Charles Adam and Paul Tannery, 11 vols. (Paris 1897–1909); new edn. (Paris: Vrin).

——(1976), *Descartes' Conversation with Burman*, tr. John Cottingham (Oxford: Clarendon Press).

——(1985), *The Philosophical Writings of Descartes*, tr. John Cottingham, Robert Stoothoff, and Dugald Murdoch, 2 vols. (Cambridge: Cambridge University Press).

——(1991), *The Philosophical Writings of Descartes*, III. *The Correspondence*, tr. John Cottingham, Robert Stoothoff, Dugald Murdoch, and Anthony Kenny (Cambridge: Cambridge University Press).

DIGBY, KENELM. (1644), *Two Treatises* (Paris).

DIJKSTERHUIS, E. J. (1961), *The Mechanization of the World Picture*, tr. C. Dikshoorn (Oxford: Oxford University Press).

DU TRIEU, PHILIP (1662), *Manuductio ad logicam* (Oxford).

DUMMETT, M. A. E. (1975), 'What is a Theory of Meaning?', in Samuel Guttenplan (ed.), *Mind and Language* (Oxford: Clarendon Press).

DUNCAN, WILLIAM (1748), *Elements of Logic* (London).

EDGLEY, ROY (1970), 'Innate Ideas', in G. N. A. Vesey (ed.), *Knowledge and Necessity* (London: Macmillan), 1–33.

EDWARDS, JONATHAN (1957), *A Careful and Strict Enquiry into . . . Freedom of the Will* (Boston, 1754); ed. Paul Ramsey (New Haven: Yale University Press).

FLEW, ANTONY (1968), 'Locke and the Problem of Personal Identity', *Philosophy*, 26 (1951); repr. in C. B. Martin and D. M. Armstrong (eds.), *Locke and Berkeley* (Garden City, NY: Doubleday), 155–78.

——(1971), 'Foreword', in O. R. Jones (ed.), *The Private Language Argument*

(London: Macmillan), 5–6.

FODOR, JERRY (1981), *Representations* (Cambridge, Mass.: MIT Press).

FOX, CHRISTOPHER (1988), *Locke and the Scriblerians: Identity and Consciousness in Early Eighteenth-Century Britain* (Berkeley: University of California Press).

FRANKFURT, HARRY G. (1971), 'Freedom of the Will and the Concept of a Person', *Journal of Philosophy*, 68: 5–20.

——(1988), *The Importance of What We Care About* (Cambridge: Cambridge University Press).

GASSENDI, PIERRE (1658), *Opera omnia*, 6 vols. (Lyons).

——(1981), *Institutio logica* (Lyons, 1658); tr. Howard Jones (Assen: Van Gorcum).

GIBSON, JAMES (1917), *Locke's Theory of Knowledge and its Historical Relations* (Cambridge: Cambridge University Press).

GOODMAN, NELSON (1967), 'The Epistemological Argument', *Synthese*, 17: 23–8.

——(1978), *Ways of Worldmaking* (Indianapolis: Hackett).

GREEN, T. H. (1874–5), 'Introductions to Hume's *Treatise of Human Nature*', in *The Philosophical Works of David Hume*, ed. T. H. Green and T. H. Grose, 4 vols. (London: Longmans), I. 1–371.

HACKING, IAN (1975), *Why Does Language Matter to Philosophy?* (Cambridge: Cambridge University Press).

HANFLING, OSWALD (1973), *Philosophy of Language*, I (Milton Keynes: Open University Press).

HARRISON, JOHN, and LASLETT, PETER (1965), *The Library of John Locke* (Oxford: Oxford University Press).

HEILBRON, J. I. (1979), *Electricity in the Seventeenth and Eighteenth Centuries* (Berkeley: University of California Press).

HOBBES, THOMAS (1651), *Leviathan* (London).

——(1655), *De corpore* (London).

——(1840), 'Of Liberty and Necessity', in *The English Works of Thomas Hobbes*, ed. Sir William Molesworth (London), IV. 239–78.

HOFSTADTER, ALBERT (1935), *Locke and Skepticism* (New York: Albee).

HOLTON, GERALD (1978), *The Scientific Imagination* (Cambridge: Cambridge University Press).

HUME, DAVID (1739–40), *Treatise of Human Nature* (London).

——(1748), *Enquiry concerning Human Understanding* (London).

JAMES, SUSAN (1987), 'Certain and Less Certain Knowledge', *Aristotelian Society Proceedings*, 87: 227–42.

JOHN OF ST THOMAS (1955), *Outlines of Formal Logic*, tr. F. C. Wade (Milwaukee: Marquette University Press).

JOLLEY, NICHOLAS (1984), *Leibniz and Locke* (Oxford: Clarendon Press).

KANT, IMMANUEL (1783), *Prolegomena zu einer jeden künftigen Metaphysik* (Riga).

KARGON, R. H. (1966), *Atomism in England from Hariot to Newton* (Oxford: Clarendon Press).

KATZ, JERROLD J. (1966), *Philosophy of Language* (New York: Harper & Row).

KING, PETER, LORD (1830), *The Life of John Locke* (London, 1829); new edn., 2 vols.

KRETZMANN, NORMAN (1968), 'The Main Thesis of Locke's Semantic Theory', *Philosophical Review*, 77: 175–96.

KRÜGER, LORENZ (1973), *Der Begriff des Empirismus: Erkenntnistheoretische Studien am Beispiel John Lockes* (Berlin: de Gruyter).

KUHN, THOMAS (1952), 'Robert Boyle and Structural Chemistry in the Seventeenth Century', *Isis*, 43: 12–36.

LANDESMAN, CHARLES (1976), 'Locke's Theory of Meaning', *Journal of the History of Philosophy*, 14: 23–35.

LAW, EDMUND (1781), 'Notes', in William King, *De origine mali* (London, 1702), tr. Edmund Law (London, 1731); 5th edn. (London), *passim*.

——(1823*a*), *A Defence of Mr. Locke's Opinion concerning Personal Identity* (Cambridge, 1769); repr. in *The Works of John Locke*, ed. Edmund Law, 8th edn., 4 vols. (London, 1777); new edn., 10 vols. (London), III. 177–99.

——(1823*b*), 'Appendix', in *The Works of John Locke*, ed. Edmund Law, 8th edn., 4 vols. (London, 1777); new edn., 10 vols. (London), III. 199–201.

LEIBNIZ, G. W. (1969), *Leibniz: Philosophical Papers and Letters*, tr. and ed. Leroy E. Loemker (Chicago: University of Chicago Press, 1956); 2nd edn. (Dordrecht: Reidel).

——(1981), *Nouveaux essais* (Amsterdam, 1765); tr. Peter Remnant and Jonathan Bennett (Cambridge: Cambridge University Press).

——(1985), *Essais de Theodicée* (Amsterdam, 1710); tr. E. M. Huggard (London: Routledge & Kegan Paul, 1951); repr. (LaSalle III: Open Court).

LENNON, THOMAS M. (1980), 'Philosophical Commentary', in Nicolas Malebranche, *The Search after Truth*, tr. Thomas M. Lennon and Paul J. Olscamp (Columbus: Ohio State University Press), 755–848.

LIMBORCH, PHILIPPUS VAN (1982), Letters, in *The Correspondence of John Locke*, ed. E. S. de Beer (Oxford: Clarendon Press), VII. *passim*.

LOCKE, DON (1975), 'Three Concepts of Free Action', *Aristotelian Society*, Supp. 49: 95–112.

LOEB, LOUIS E. (1981), *From Descartes to Hume* (Ithaca, NY: Cornell University Press).

LONERGAN, B. J. F. (1958), *Insight*, rev. edn. (London: Longmans).

LONG, A. A., and SEDLEY, D. N. (1987) (eds.), *The Hellenistic Philosophers*, 2 vols. (Cambridge: Cambridge University Press).

LOWDE, JAMES (1699), *Moral Essays* (York).

MABBOTT, J. D. (1973), *John Locke* (London: Macmillan).

McCANN, EDWIN (1987), 'Locke on Identity: Matter, Life, and Consciousness', *Archiv für die Geschichte der Philosophie*, 69: 73–90.

MACINTOSH, J. J. (1976), 'Primary and Secondary Qualities', *Studia Leibnitiana*, 8: 88–104.

MACKIE, J. L. (1976), *Problems from Locke* (Oxford: Clarendon Press).

McRAE, ROBERT (1965), '"Idea" as a Philosophical Term in the Seventeenth Century', *Journal of the History of Ideas*, 26: 175–90.

MALEBRANCHE, NICOLAS (1980), *De la recherche de la vérité* (Paris, 1674–5); tr. Thomas M. Lennon and Paul Olscamp (Columbus: Ohio State University Press).

——(1980), *Entretiens sur la métaphysique et sur la religion* (Rotterdam, 1688); tr. Willis Doney (New York: Abaris).

MATTERN, RUTH (1980), 'Moral Science and the Concept of a Person', *Philosophical Review*, 89: 24–45; repr. in this volume as Ch. XIV.

MATTHEWS, H. E. (1977), 'Descartes and Locke on the Concept of a Person', *Locke Newsletter*, 8: 9–34.

MERSENNE, MARIN (1652), *La Verité des sciences contre les sceptiques ou Pyrrhoniens* (Paris).

MINAS, ANNE C. (1979–80), '*Locke on Generality*', *Philosophical Forum*, 11: 182–92.

NAGEL, THOMAS (1979), *Mortal Questions* (Cambridge: Cambridge University Press).

NATHANSON, STEPHEN L. (1973), 'Locke's Theory of Ideas', *Journal of the History of Philosophy*, 11: 29–42.

NEEDHAM, RODNEY (1972), *Belief, Language, and Experience* (Oxford: Blackwell).

NORRIS, JOHN (1690), *Cursory Reflections upon a Book call'd, an Essay concerning Human Understanding* (London).

NUCHELMANS, GABRIEL (1980), *Late Scholastic Theories and Humanist Theories of the Proposition* (Amsterdam: Koninklijke Nederlandse Akademie van Wetenschappen).

——(1983), *Judgment and Proposition: From Descartes to Kant* (Amsterdam: North Holland).

OCKHAM, WILLIAM (1974), *Ockham's Theory of Terms: Part I of the Summa Logicae*, tr. M. J. Loux (Notre Dame, Ind.: University of Notre Dame Press).

——(1980), *Quodlibita Septem*, ed. Joseph C. Wey (St Bonaventure, NY: St Bonaventure University Press).

O'CONNOR, D. J. (1952), *John Locke* (Harmondsworth: Penguin).

——(1967), 'Substance and Attribute', in Paul Edwards (ed.), *Encyclopedia of Philosophy* (New York: Macmillan), VIII. 36–40.

ODEGARD, DOUGLAS (1970), 'Locke and the Significance of Words', *Locke Newsletter*, 1: 11–17.

O'HIGGINS, J. (1976), 'Introduction' and 'Notes', in *Determinism and Freewill: Anthony Collins' A Philosophical Inquiry concerning Human Liberty* (London, 1717), ed. J. O'Higgins (The Hague: Nijhoff), 1–45 and 115–24.

OWEN, DAVID (1993), 'Locke on Reason, Probable Reasoning, and Opinion', *Locke Newsletter*, 24: 35–79.

Oxford English Dictionary (1888–1928), 20 vols. (Oxford: Clarendon Press).

PASSMORE, J. A. (1977), 'Hume and the Ethics of Belief', in G. P. Morice (ed.), *David Hume: Bicentenary Papers* (Edinburgh: Edinburgh University Press), 77–92.

PATRIDES, C. A. (1969) (ed.), *The Cambridge Platonists* (London: Arnold).

PERRY, DAVID L. (1967), 'Locke on Mixed Modes, Relations, and Knowledge', *Journal of the History of Philosophy*, 5: 219–35.

PERRY, JOHN (1976), 'The Importance of Being Identical', in Amélie Oksenberg Rorty (ed.), *The Identities of Persons* (Berkeley: University of California Press), 67–90.

PINKE, ROBERT (1680), *Quaestiones selectiones in logica, ethica, physica et metaphysica inter authores celebriores repertae* (Oxford).

PUFENDORF, SAMUEL (1703), *De jure naturae et gentium* (Lund, 1672); tr. Basil Kennett and William Percivale (Oxford).

——(1717), *De jure naturae et gentium* (Lund, 1672); tr. Basil Kennett and William Percivale (Oxford); 3rd edn. (London).

PUTNAM, HILARY (1964), 'Robots: Machines or Artificially Created Life?', *Journal of Philosophy*, 61: 668–91.

——(1975), 'The Meaning of "Meaning"', in Keith Gunderson (ed.), *Language, Mind and Knowledge* (Minneapolis: University of Minnesota Press); repr. in Hilary Putnam, *Mind, Language and Reality* (Cambridge: Cambridge University Press), 215–71.

REDWOOD, J. (1976), *Reason, Ridicule, and Religion* (Cambridge, Mass.: Harvard University Press).

REID, THOMAS (1872), *The Works of Thomas Reid, D.D.*, ed. Sir William Hamilton (Edinburgh, 1846); 7th edn., 2 vols.

RYLE, GILBERT (1933), 'John Locke on the Human Understanding', in J L. Stocks (ed.), *John Locke: Tercentenary Addresses* (Oxford: Oxford University Press), 15–38.

—— (1971), 'John Locke', *Critica*, 1; repr. in Gilbert Ryle, *Collected Papers*, 2 vols. (London: Hutchinson), I. 147–57.

SANDERSON, ROBERT (1664), *Logicae artis compendium* (Oxford).

SCHANKULA, H. A. S. (1980), 'Locke, Descartes and the Science of Nature', *Journal of the History of Ideas*, 41: 459–77.

SCHNEEWIND, J. B. (1987), 'Pufendorf's Place in the History of Ethics', *Synthese*, 72: 123–55.

SCHWARTZ, STEPHEN P. (1977), 'Introduction', in Stephen P. Schwartz (ed.), *Naming, Necessity, and Natural Kinds* (Ithaca, NY: Cornell University Press), 13–41.

SEARLE, JOHN (1973), 'Chomsky's Linguistics', *New York Review of Books*, 22 Feb.

SHOEMAKER, SYDNEY (1963), *Self-Knowledge and Self-Identity* (Ithaca, NY: Cornell University Press).

SMIGLECIUS, MARTIN (1638), *Logica* (Oxford).

SPELLMAN, W. M. (1988), *John Locke and the Problem of Depravity* (Oxford: Clarendon Press).

STAMPE, DENNIS W. (1968), 'Toward a Grammar of Meaning', *Philosophical Review*, 77: 137–74.

STICH, STEPHEN P., (1975) (ed.), *Innate Ideas* (Berkeley: University of California Press).

STUMP, ELEONORE (1988), 'Sanctification, Hardening of the Heart, and Frankfurt's Concept of Free Will', *Journal of Philosophy*, 85: 395–420.

THIEL, UDO (1983), *Lockes Theorie der personalen Identität* (Bonn: Bouvier).

TOOLEY, MICHAEL (1973), 'A Defense of Abortion and Infanticide', in Joel Feinberg (ed.), *The Problem of Abortion* (Belmont, Calif.: Wadsworth), 51–91.

—— (1979), 'Decisions to Terminate Life and the Concept of a Person', in John Ladd (ed.), *Ethical Issues Relating to Life and Death* (New York: Oxford University Press), 62–93.

TROYER, JOHN (1975), 'Locke on the Names of Substances', *Locke Newsletter*, 6: 27–39.

WAINWRIGHT, ARTHUR W. (1987), 'Introduction', in John Locke, *A Paraphrase and Notes on the Epistles of St. Paul*, ed. Arthur W. Wainwright, 2 vols. (Oxford: Clarendon Press).

WALKER, D. P. (1964), *The Decline of Hell: Seventeenth-Century Discussions of Eternal Torment* (Chicago: University of Chicago Press).

WALLIS, JOHN. (1691), *Three Sermons concerning the Sacred Trinity* (London).

WARNER, RICHARD (1980), *Morality in Medicine* (Sherman Oaks, Calif.: Alfred).

WARREN, MARY ANNE (1973), 'On the Moral and Legal Status of Abortion', *Monist*, 57: 43–61.

WEBB, THOMAS (1857), *The Intellectualism of Locke* (Dublin).

WESTFALL, RICHARD S. (1966), *Science and Religion in Seventeenth-Century England* (Ann Arbor: University of Michigan Press).

—— (1971), *The Construction of Modern Science* (New York: Wiley).

WIGGINS, DAVID (1980), *Sameness and Substance* (Oxford: Blackwell).

WILSON, MARGARET D. (1978), *Descartes* (London: Routledge & Kegan Paul).

—— (1979), 'Superadded Properties: The Limits of Mechanism in Locke', *American Philosophical Quarterly*, 16: 143–50.

—— (1982), 'Superadded Properties: A Reply to M. R. Ayers', *Philosophical Review*, 91: 247–52.

WOLF, SUSAN (1981), 'The Importance of Free Will', *Mind*, 90: 386–405.

WOLTERSTORFF, NICHOLAS (1996), *John Locke and the Ethics of Belief* (Cambridge: Cambridge University Press).

WOOLHOUSE, R. S. (1971), *Locke's Philosophy of Science and Knowledge* (Oxford: Blackwell).

——(1972), 'Locke on Modes, Substances, and Knowledge', *Journal of the History of Philosophy*, 10: 417–24.

WOOZLEY, A. D. (1972), 'Some Remarks on Locke's Account of Knowledge', *Locke Newsletter*, 3: 7–17.

YOLTON, JOHN W. (1956), *John Locke and the Way of Ideas* (Oxford: Oxford University Press).

——(1961), 'Introduction', in John Locke, *An Essay concerning Human Understanding*, ed. John W. Yolton, 2 vols. (London: Dent), i. ix–xxii.

——(1970a), *Locke and the Compass of Human Understanding* (Cambridge: Cambridge University Press).

——(1970b), 'Locke on Knowledge of Body', in *Jowett Papers* 1968–1969 (Oxford: Blackwell), 69–94.

INDEX OF NAMES

INDEX LOCORUM

Note: boldface numerals indicate particular editions of the *Essay*.